D0154045

THE LINE OF DUTY _____

Recent Titles in
Contributions in American History

Series Editor: Jon L. Wakelyn

Voting in Revolutionary America: A Study of Elections in the Original Thirteen States, 1776–1789
Robert J. Dinkin

Good and Faithful Labor: From Slavery to Sharecropping in the Natchez District, 1860–1890
Ronald L. F. Davis

Reform and Reformers in the Progressive Era
David R. Colburn and George E. Pozzetta, editors

History of Black Americans: From the Emergence of the Cotton Kingdom to the Eve of the Compromise of 1850
Philip S. Foner

History of Black Americans: From the Compromise of 1850 to the End of the Civil War
Philip S. Foner

The Southern Enigma: Essays on Race, Class, and Folk Culture
Walter J. Fraser, Jr., and Winfred B. Moore, Jr., editors

Crusaders and Compromisers: Essays on the Relationship of the Antislavery Struggle to the Antebellum Party System
Alan M. Kraut, editor

Boston 1700–1980: The Evolution of Urban Politics
Ronald P. Formisano and Constance K. Burns, editors

The Great "Red Menace": United States Prosecution of American Communists, 1947–1952
Peter L. Steinberg

At Home on the Range: Essays on the History of Western Social and Domestic Life
John R. Wunder, editor

The Whiskey Rebellion: Past and Present Perspectives
Steven R. Boyd, editor

Law, Alcohol, and Order: Perspectives on National Prohibition
David E. Kyvig, editor

THE LINE OF DUTY

Maverick Congressmen and the Development of American Political Culture, 1836–1860

JOHANNA NICOL SHIELDS

CONTRIBUTIONS IN AMERICAN STUDIES, NUMBER 80

Greenwood Press
WESTPORT, CONNECTICUT • LONDON, ENGLAND

Library of Congress Cataloging in Publication Data
Shields, Johanna Nicol.
    The line of duty.

    (Contributions in American studies, ISSN 0084–9227 ;
no. 80)
    Bibliography: p.
    Includes index.
    1. United States—Politics and government—1815–1861.
2. Legislators—United States—History—19th century.
3. United States. Congress—History—19th century.
4. Dissenters—United States—History—19th century.
I. Title. II. Title: Maverick congressmen and the
development of American political culture, 1836–1860.
III. Series.
E338.S535   1985   328.73′09   84–25205
ISBN 0–313–24470–7 (lib. bdg.)

Library of Congress Catalog Card Number: 85–25205
ISBN: 0–313–24470–7
ISSN: 0084–9227

First published in 1985

Greenwood Press
A division of Congressional Information Service, Inc.
88 Post Road West, Westport, Connecticut 06881

Printed in the United States of America

10 9 8 7 6 5 4 3 2 1

FOR MY GRANDMOTHERS:

Anna Marshall Clapp
(1894–1983)

Johanna Monnish Nicol
(1887–1982)

Contents

List of Illustrations   ix

List of Tables   xi

Acknowledgements   xiii

Introduction   xv

Part I. The Maverick Presence

1. An Introduction to Mavericks and Conformists   3

2. The Cultural Dimensions   11

**Part II. The Congressional Leadership of Mavericks
and Conformists**

3. Conformists and the Regularization of the House   29

4. Mavericks and the Elevated Stage of Politics   45

**Part III. Patterns of Conviction: The Political Ideas
of Mavericks and Conformists**

5. The Democratic Conformists   61

6. The Democratic Mavericks   77

7. The Whig and Republican Conformists   99

8. The Whig and Republican Mavericks   113

Part IV. The Maverick Mentality

 9. The Maverick Intellect   153

10. The Maverick Ego   177

11. The American Congressional Maverick, 1836–1860:
    Causes and Consequences   193

Appendixes

    Appendix I. Method of Selecting Mavericks and Conformists   221

    Appendix II. Scale Positions for Mavericks   225

    Bibliography   235

    Index   291

List of Illustrations

(Illustrations follow page 140.)

John Armor Bingham of Ohio, 1815–1900.

Francis Preston Blair, Jr., of Missouri, 1821–1875.

Caleb Cushing of Massachusetts, 1800–1879.

Muscoe Russell Hunter Garnett of Virginia, 1821–1864.

Charles Jared Ingersoll of Pennsylvania, 1782–1862.

Preston King of New York, 1806–1865.

James Lawrence Orr of South Carolina, 1822–1873.

Joseph Rogers Underwood of Kentucky, 1791–1876.

John Wentworth of Illinois, 1815–1888.

Henry Alexander Wise of Virginia, 1806–1876.

List of Tables

1. Mavericks in the 24th through the 36th Congresses, as a Raw Value and Percent of All Congressmen by Region and Party   8

2. Mean Terms of Service for All Mavericks and Conformists in the 24th through the 36th Congresses   9

3. Rank Ordered Mean Terms of Service for All Mavericks and Conformists in the 24th through the 36th Congresses, by Region and Party   9

4. Rank Ordered Mean Terms of Service for All Mavericks and Conformists in the 24th through the 36th Congresses by Region   9

5. Mavericks and Conformists Who Served as Speakers of the House or Chairmen of Standing Committees, 24th through the 36th Congresses, by Committee and Congress   34

6. Mean Terms Served in the House of Representatives Prior to their Service as Chairmen of the Standing Committees or Speakers of the House, for Mavericks and Conformists, by Committee   36

7. An Example of Scale Positions Containing Mavericks and Conformists, Taken from *Sectional Stress and Party Strength*   223

Acknowledgments

This study has slowly evolved into a book, and the debts I have accumulated in over a decade of work are too extensive to describe in detail. The one scholar who has attended to my progress from the beginning is Thomas B. Alexander, whom I would thank not only for his critical evaluation of the work in its various stages but for his constant encouragement and support. The character of this work differs fundamentally from his manner of analysis, and I hope that the present study contributes to a general understanding that quantification and other methods of historical study are complementary rather than competitive.

My colleagues and friends at the University of Alabama in Huntsville have provided invaluable criticism, insights, and editorial commentary through several revisions; and I am grateful for their patient contributions. I hope that the numerous students who have been the testing ground for my ideas benefitted as much from our conversations as I did. The American Association of University Women provided a fellowship that enabled me to spend a year at the Library of Congress in the early stages of the research; further financial support was granted by the University of Alabama in Huntsville Research Committee. This book could never have been completed without my family's unflagging enthusiasm for my project despite its demands on time they might have shared with me. Nicholas, Anna, and Katherine know, in any case, how central is their place in whatever I accomplish.

Despite all that I have gained from others, the shortcomings of this work are my own.

Introduction

Whether American culture has favored the development of a nation of individualists or of conforming masses has been a point of debate among analysts of American society from the colonial period forward. The framers of the Constitution, who admired independence from the relatively comfortable perspective of a homogeneous political elite, would probably have neither predicted nor appreciated the fact that the Congress they created would become an institution perennially characterized by political conformity. Those who have followed independent courses in the legislature have constituted a decided minority, whatever the incidence of individualism in the society at large.

Members of this maverick minority have been variously regarded as visionary heroes, determined defenders of moral right, or eccentric crackpots—what nineteenth-century political conformists called "one-ideaed enthusiasts." In part, this diversity in the reputations of mavericks results from a fundamental ambiguity in American political theory about the nature and meaning of representation. On the one hand, maverick nonconformity seems to run counter to mainstream notions that the representative should mirror his constituents' interests and that political parties will expedite this process. On the other hand, respect for the independent judgments of those leaders whom the founding fathers called men of wisdom and virtue has persisted. Perhaps as importantly, the maverick politician seems to evoke sympathy from a voting public that conspicuously reveres individualism, if it does not display it.[1]

Developing patterns of legislative conformity in antebellum Congresses were created in large part by political parties, institutions that were unanticipated by those who designed the constitutional structure and that stimulated important changes in legislative behavior and ideology. Although the long-range result of these changes may have been greater political stability, the growth of new organizations within a constitutional arrangement that was by no means universally regarded as permanent aggravated misunderstanding about the character of the American political system. As contemporaries commonly observed, the Civil War represented a near failure of the new constitutional system, although the conflict grew from significant economic and cultural divisions within the country. Clearly, the political machinery had rumbled slowly toward its near demise, and those institutional flaws that had clogged the gears throughout the antebellum period and had compounded serious national problems were not repaired by the War and Reconstruction. The exact nature of the relationship between institutional weaknesses, inadequate statesmanship, and the constitutional crisis has yet to be determined; and it is a problem beyond the object of this analysis. It is certain, in any case, that much remains to be understood about the legislative body and its members in the several decades before the Civil War.

Understanding any facet of legislative history involves two rather contrary kinds of knowledge which do not mesh easily.[2] Metaphorically speaking, it is necessary to distinguish the legislature's *machineness* from the particular characteristics of the machine and its parts at a given time. Historians have typically been more interested in aspects of specific Congresses, leaving to political scientists the task of abstracting machineness from the whole. This study attempts to integrate the concrete detail usually associated with classical historical studies and the functional abstractions about legislative behavior resulting from political science research. Furthermore, the effort is couched within a method of analysis which combines certain aspects of social and behavioral psychology. Rather than employing rigid models for legislative or human behavior, an attempt has been made to extract those features of social science theory most relevant to the particular historical problems treated here.

The major personae of this historical drama are a large group of maverick congressmen in the late antebellum period; their words and actions are set against those of the more numerous conformist congressmen who served with them. Because mavericks' nonconforming behavior was extensive, their group biography becomes a kaleidoscope of individual pecularities; moreover, the institutional setting, changing over the quarter century of this study, provides an unstable stage, not nearly as amenable to abstraction as would be desirable. When the diverse characters and shifting stage scenery are placed in the proper perspective of nineteenth-century society, making valid generalizations is at best a tenuous matter.

The sweeping changes of the mid-century decades stimulated an acute public self-consciousness about American culture. This concern was reflected in the pages of the relatively new mass medium of the press as well as in the more elevated journals which catered to the interests of the educated classes. Maverick congressmen spoke to this cultural sensitivity, but not all congressmen were equally alive to cultural change. Even though the major political decisions made by the Congress in the decades before Fort Sumter were fraught with consequences outside of the political arena, there is little evidence that many congressmen considered the nonpolitical effects of their decisions. Indeed, the great majority of congressmen, however privately aware they may have been of the complexity of the political issues of the day, behaved as if partisan positions, sometimes modified by sectional interests, sufficiently guided them to political decisions. On the other hand, for a small minority of congressmen, this pattern of partisan behavior was not a consistent characteristic. Patently, their voting behavior cannot be explained in terms of party affiliation, even when sectional differences are taken into account.

The study that follows analyzes the political character of the mavericks in the United States House of Representatives between 1836 and 1860, assessing the explanations they offered for their independent roles and, through their ideas, exploring some larger dimensions of American political culture. Part I, ''The Maveri:k Presence,'' introduces basic definitions and assumptions that shaped the study, then describes aspects of social and political change essential to understanding the mavericks. Part II, ''The Congressional Leadership of Mavericks and Conformists,'' outlines the ways in which mavericks were distinguished from conformists in their exercise of leadership in the House, speculating upon the significance of the alternative styles. Part III, ''Patterns of Conviction,'' presents the political ideas of mavericks and conformists, contrasting the ideological creativity of the former with the close adherence to partisan ideologies of the latter. Part IV, ''The Maverick Mentality,'' treats intellectual patterns and personality traits typical of mavericks; finally, a consideration of mavericks in the larger context of the cultural change of their century explains more about how changing political culture affected the conduct of the legislators and how they in turn altered the institutions within which they worked.

For the most part, this analysis of political culture rests upon the words in which mavericks and conformists presented themselves and with which their contemporaries described them.[3] The public character of most speeches and writings by antebellum congressmen makes them an excellent source for information about the relationship between politics and other aspects of American culture. All of the men described in this study were to some degree successful politicians; their efforts at communication with the general public or with special constituent groups rested upon the cultural ideas and assumptions they shared with these potential supporters. Whether the public expressions of mavericks and conformists were deliberately constructed for effective persuasion, artificially ornamented to impress the audience with the speaker's intelligence and education, or casually delivered to a familiar and friendly crowd, the ideas reflected the author's understanding of the common ground between himself and his audience. Analysis of the ideas used by congressmen in addressing the public should, therefore, provide insight into the manner in which these mavericks and conformists perceived their cultural environment.

Cultural perceptions of antebellum congressmen were of considerable weight in shaping their impact upon politics. The economic and social changes of the dynamic mid-century culture had direct political consequences, and political decisions often carried significant meaning for social and cultural developments. If the politicians of the day were to be able to preserve order and give direction to change, it was critically important that they understand the nature of the society they were chosen to govern. Yet cultural alertness alone was insufficient to render a congressman competent to suggest direction; it was also necessary that the man perceive himself as being in a position from which he could provide guidance to the flow of events. How a congressman perceived politics, what he thought his duties and opportunities were—these considerations would of necessity vitally affect his inclination and ability to act. Thus, as far as congressional action relating to the cultural stresses of the mid–nineteenth century is concerned, effective decision making had to rest on two grounds: on accurate assessment of the threatening or creative possibilities inherent in the economic, social, and cultural changes and on a theory of politics which assigned to the individual legislator partial power and responsibility for bringing order to the nation.

Ralph Waldo Emerson, in "The American Scholar," his famous summons to action for thinking Americans, prescribed the proper course of behavior for those who would bring order and direction to the developing society:

If the single man plant himself indomitably on his instincts, and there abide, the huge world will come round to him. Patience—patience; with the shades of all the good and great for company; and for solace the perspective of your own infinite life; and for work and study and communication of principles, the making those instincts prevalent, the conversion of the world.[4]

"Conversion of the world" on the basis of self-reliance and adherence to principles—Emerson's formula for achieving the American dream—may seem like an impossible standard for political behavior; yet the extent to which this advice was followed by mavericks and conformists is partial index to their involvement in the cultural life of the nation. The opposite possibility—"not to be reckoned one character; not to yield that peculiar fruit which each man was created to bear, but to be reckoned in the gross, in the hundred, or the thousand, of the party, the section, to which we belong; and our opinion predicted geographically, as the north, or the south"[5]—may more accurately describe the realities of political life for the majority of congressmen in the turbulent decades of the middle of the nineteenth century.

NOTES

1. The popular reception of John F. Kennedy's *Profiles in Courage* (New York: Harper & Bros., 1956) is an excellent illustration of public interest in nonconforming politicians. At the same time, Kennedy's authorship indicated the persistence of respect for political independence within the central tradition in American politics.

2. David M. Potter has commented trenchantly on this problem and others relating to the study of antebellum political history in "Roy F. Nichols and the Rehabilitation of American Political History." While the essay is primarily a tribute to Nichols' scholarly contributions, Potter's reflections upon Nichols' pioneering work provide an excellent framework for appreciation of the conceptual and practical difficulties involved in writing

legislative history; and the essay succeeds in communication without bearing the obscurities of language and style that often discourage nonpractitioners from reading about theories of social science history. The essay is reprinted in a collection of some of Potter's finest articles, *History and American Society*, ed. by Don E. Fehrenbacher (New York: Oxford University Press, 1963).

3. All congressmen have brief biographies in U. S. Congress, *Biographical Directory of the American Congresses, 1774–1961* (Washington, D. C.: U. S. Government Printing Office, 1961); hereafter cited as *BDAC*. For a minority there were also scholarly biographies, all of which are listed in the bibliography under the congressman's name.

4. Ralph Waldo Emerson, "The American Scholar," in *The Selected Writings of Ralph Waldo Emerson*, ed. by Brooks Atkinson (New York: Random House, Modern Library College Editions, 1940), p. 63.

5. Ibid.

Part I

THE MAVERICK PRESENCE

CHAPTER 1

An Introduction to Mavericks and Conformists

On entering the House of Representatives in Washington, one is struck by the vulgar demeanor of that great assembly. Often there is not a distinguished man in the whole number. Its members are almost all obscure individuals, whose names bring no associations to mind.

Alexis de Tocqueville, *Democracy in America*

I maintain that the House of Representatives is, under our constitution of government, the greatest deliberative body, the greatest assemblage of men on earth, which did ever exist, of which we have any knowledge.

John Reynolds, *Congressional Globe*

Between 1836 and 1860, more than a thousand men sat in the United States House of Representatives, and most of them were not distinguished men—even if Tocqueville's aristocratic bias exaggerated their obscurity. Congressman Reynolds' proud assertion was equally prejudiced, confirming Tocqueville's opinion that American orators "not infrequently abandon the great in order to reach the gigantic."[1] But of course there were outstanding men in the House; Reynolds himself was addressing an ex-President, a future President, a future Associate Justice of the Supreme Court, and several prospective senators and cabinet members. Nonetheless, a quick glance at the complete list of mavericks and conformists in this study (see Appendix II) will suffice to convince any reader that these subjects were selected without regard for the magnitude of their reputations. They were selected, instead, with the aid of systematic analysis and quantitative methods. Indeed, they were initially known by identification numbers on computer printouts, not by names at all.

The Line of Duty rests primarily upon traditional methods of historical research, but it began by drawing upon the work of a pioneer in the "new political history," Thomas B. Alexander. Although some familiar connotations of the words maverick and conformist became appropriate as the study progressed, they originally had carefully restricted definitions rooted in the voting-behavior patterns he analyzed. The conditions attached to those original definitions affect the scope of generalizations that can be drawn from what follows, so it is important to begin by introducing the reader to the process used to select these congressmen from among their colleagues. Readers wary of social science methods and quantification may be assured that this essential introduction is quite brief.[2]

In 1967, historians' knowledge of antebellum politics was augmented by the publication of two important books: Thomas B. Alexander's *Sectional Stress and Party Strength: A Study of Roll-Call Voting Patterns in the United States House of Representatives, 1836-1860* and Joel Silbey's *The Shrine of Party: Congressional Voting Behavior, 1841-1852*. Both demonstrated the primacy of party in forming the voting patterns of antebellum Congresses, while Alexander's work also emphasized the crosscurrents of sectional loyalties.[3] As Emerson's lament suggests, most congressmen "reckoned in the gross," voting with others from their home region and party.

The works of Alexander and Silbey reflected a resourceful application of social science methods to American historical materials. Unlike political scientists who scrutinize contemporary Congresses, historians are handicapped because they cannot interview members for firsthand opinions about key issues. Some methods of analysis can partially compensate for the inevitable distance between historians and their subjects; cumulative scale analysis is such a tool, and its application was central to the definitions of maverick and conformist. Political scientists and historians originally borrowed scale analysis from sociologists who studied attitudes revealed in survey research. Loosely speaking, roll-call votes in a legislature became a kind of parallel to individual responses on an opinion-gathering questionnaire. Thus even though long-dead legislators cannot be quizzed directly about their ideas, the historian can describe with some precision the range of support—and each member's relation to that range—within a particular legislature for selected issues on which appropriate roll-call votes were taken.

The findings in *Sectional Stress and Party Strength* rested partly on cumulative scale analysis. Its results—information about the range of positions on key issues in the thirteen Congresses between 1836 and 1860—were described with the help of thirty-four scale tables. Each table presents the distribution of congressmen over a range of positions taken on related votes, with the pattern for each of several party and regional divisions in Congress depicted separately within the table. Most of the scale tables describe voting patterns for economic and slavery-related issues, illustrating the overwhelming tendency toward conformity within the House. Nevertheless, for almost every issue (that is, on almost every table), a few members differed from their closest colleagues. Even on sensitive issues relating to slavery, the tables show an occasional southerner voting with northerners, or, to use another example, on economic issues, a rare northern Democrat voting with Whigs. Although the tables in *Sectional Stress and Party Strength* presented only aggregate figures for voting by party and region, Alexander provided the underlying individual-level data from which the names of congressmen voting in the expected patterns and those deviating from them were determined.

These, then, were the initial conditions that defined maverick and conformist within the terms of Alexander's study: every congressman who almost always voted with the majority from his party and region was labeled a conformist; and every congressman who deviated significantly from the majority for his party and region on at least two sets of issues (that is, on two scale sets) was labeled a maverick. After legislators were identified and categorized in this manner, all congressmen who failed to serve two terms in the House were deleted, making workable the analysis of those remaining.

Having employed Alexander's study for the initial selection of mavericks and conformists, this work departed from the specialized methods of scale analysis. There are, to be sure, descriptive tables in this chapter and in Chapter 3, but the reader will find nowhere a further quantitative explanation for the presence of mavericks and conformists. Cumulative scale analysis has significantly enlarged historians' knowledge about voting patterns in antebellum Congresses, but it cannot explain why an individual congressman (or senator) voted as he did with party and section. What was the force of party to an individual? He might have felt its influence in many ways, including pressure from party leaders, loyalty to a common ideology, concern for national institutions, or desire for party success. How was sectionalism felt? Its influences could also assume varied forms; they might involve a strong sense of community or place, commitment to a sectional ideology, moral conviction about slavery, or keen awareness of a constituency's preferences. In addition some congressmen must have had private motivations for their votes—hidden interests or even unconscious inclinations. Given these complexities, what kinds of logical beginning assumptions can be made about the differences between mavericks and conformists? Can the limited definitions based on roll-call voting patterns be broadened logically?

From common patterns some common motives may be inferred. Without assigning any particular configuration to the interior nature of sectional and party influences, it can safely be said that the interests of national parties often competed with regional loyalties. Since conformists voted alike, it seems reasonable to assume that they interpreted the interplay of these influences in similar ways. Partisan conformity resulted largely from the overt cues of leaders or from caucus decisions, but the influences upon sectional voting were often more obscured. Conformists, then, either cooperatively weighed the relative importance of these competing influences or they independently reached common decisions about voting because they possessed extremely similar standards of evaluation.

There were less common patterns to unite mavericks. Like conformists, mavericks reconciled the interests of party and region, sometimes conforming to the majority voting pattern. Mavericks and conformists were exposed to similar influences, and each type had to secure some approval from colleagues and constitutents to remain politically successful. Each maverick, however, was unique, neither deviating nor conforming in precisely the same way as any other congressman. Clearly, then, mavericks evaluated cooperation and success by different standards than did conformists. To learn something about those standards, as well as to understand better the interior nature of the influences of sectionalism and partisanship, this study has focused on what maverick and conformist congressmen said about themselves, their work, and their environment.

It should not be surprising that mavericks said a great deal more about themselves than did conformists. The common-sense definitions of maverick and conformist have some relation to the quantitatively derived ones. Cumulative scale analysis does not relate roll-call votes to each other because their connections were explicitly recognized in the legislature. It rests upon the fact that congressmen voted as if relationships existed, but it cannot be assumed that those relationships were openly identified or even identifiable. On the other hand, Alexander's analysis included important votes on most of the key issues that the antebellum House confronted. It is thus highly likely that astute congressmen—the kind of men who counted votes before the roll calls began—could identify mavericks and conformists with some accuracy. Party leaders, therefore, often called upon mavericks to explain the reasons for their nonconformity, and many responded enthusiastically.

It would be naive to expect that mavericks' explanations for their conduct contain comprehensive revelations of their motives. Since this study is based in large part upon what mavericks said and wrote, its purpose cannot be to offer an exhaustive explanation of why mavericks voted as they did. While mavericks surely attempted honesty in some of what they wrote about themselves, perhaps more importantly they examined the world around them in the process of explaining themselves. Their interpretations thus offer new insights about the evolving political culture of the antebellum United States.

Given its purposes, the methods used in this study were traditional and largely nonquantitative. What mavericks said on the floor of Congress was recorded in the *Congressional Globe*, and therein the words of mavericks and conformists could readily be compared. Beyond that, every published source by or about each maverick or conformist that was available in the Library of Congress was read; the lists included pamphlet speeches, collections of speeches and writings, poetry, fiction, biographies, recollections, and autobiographies. Those congressmen about whom no material was available in the Library were eliminated from the study, producing finally a manageable group of 84 mavericks and 171 conformists.

Clearly, this body of 255 men cannot be considered typical of legislators in the antebellum period. Most congressmen in the early nineteenth century did not serve two full terms, and the bulk of them came and went without leaving a significant imprint of their presence upon the national scene. In contrast to them, mavericks and conformists were relatively successful and articulate politicians; since they were atypical, their experiences and observations cannot be extended to conclusions about the whole House. The tables in the pages that follow, as well as tables in Chapter 3, should therefore be understood only as descriptions of the characteristics of mavericks and conformists.

With that caveat in mind, mavericks and conformists can be described with reference to their regions, parties, and the thirteen Congresses between 1836 and 1860. Mavericks, the major characters in this study, sat in every Congress in those years, representing states within both the northern and southern regions and belonging to each of the major parties (See Table 1; Appendix II identifies each maverick by state, party, and scales on which he deviated).[4]

Mavericks were not distributed evenly across the various regional and party groupings. They were least evident among northern Whigs and Republicans, whether viewed in regard to their total numbers or as a percentage of the total groupings.[5] Only in four Congresses did the proportion of mavericks in these groups climb above 5 percent, and never did it reach 10 percent. Cultural homogeneity among northern Whigs may partially account for this lack of nonconformist presence. Other reasons appear to lie in the nature of the maverick political character and its relationship to Whig ideology and values, matters to be explored in later chapters.

Southern delegations usually had more mavericks than northern ones. In six Congresses the mavericks among southern Whigs or Democrats were 20 percent or better of the total of one of the two party groups, and rarely did their weight fall below 10 percent, a proportion at least partly attributable to the longevity of service of southern maverick congressmen in the antebellum period (See Tables 2, 3, and 4). The mean term of service for southern Democratic mavericks was 5.09 terms, more than ten years in the House; and the mean for southern Whig and Republican mavericks was 3.89 terms, or better than seven years in the House. Given that most congressmen in the antebellum period served less than two terms, these figures are significantly high. This pattern cannot be explained solely in terms of regional differences, because for both Whigs and Democrats in the South, mavericks served longer than conformists. The presence of elitism in southern politics may have contributed to the longer terms, as the ideal of rotation was associated with the new democratic politics; but that this or other factors did not operate evenly for southern mavericks and conformists can perhaps partly be explained in terms of the maverick political character to be examined in later chapters. The larger possibility—that maverick politicians were more acceptable to southern electorates than to northern ones—could only be explained in the context of a study considerably less restricted than this one.

The preceding pages have sketched a skeletal image of the presence of mavericks as well as their conforming colleagues. Mavericks cannot be understood, however, without reference to some essential features of antebellum culture and politics that provided a rudimentary foundation for their existence. Although the interpretive summary which follows draws partially upon evidence about the character of mavericks to be presented in later chapters, it should help the reader flesh out the image of mavericks. Mavericks were not simply deviants who failed to follow consistently the patterns of party or regional voting patterns. They

Table 1
Mavericks in the 24th through the 36th Congresses, as a Raw Value and Percent of All Congressmen by Region and Party

Congress	Democrats				Whigs or Republicans			
	Northern		Southern		Northern		Southern	
	No.	Percent of all N. Dems.	No.	Percent of all S. Dems.	No.	Percent of all N. Whigs or Reps.	No.	Percent of all S. Whigs or Reps.
24 1835-37	4	4.6	2	3.7	2	3.8	5	11.6
25 1837-39	3	3.7	3	6.4	2	3.0	9	16.7
26 1839-41	3	3.9	4	8.0	3	4.5	10	20.4
27 1841-43	7	12.7	7	4.9	4	4.4	10	18.5
28 1843-45	12	14.6	8	3.3	2	3.7	6	21.4
29 1845-47	9	12.0	10	4.7	3	5.2	3	12.5
30 1847-49	10	16.9	9	6.4	4	5.0	4	11.1
31 1849-51	8	14.8	11	7.8	7	7.8	6	21.4
32 1851-53	8	9.8	11	9.0	5	8.0	6	20.0
33 1853-55	7	7.5	11	7.2	3	6.0	3	23.5
34 1855-57	5	18.5	14	5.0	4	3.4	4	13.3
35 1857-59	6	12.8	15	0.0	4	4.3	5	33.3
36 1859-61	6	18.0	7	1.0	2	1.7	3	12.5

Table 2
Mean Terms of Service for All Mavericks and Conformists in the 24th through the 36th Congresses

Group	No. in Group	Total Terms Served	Mean Terms Served
Mavericks	84	319	3.79
Conformists	171	453	2.65

Table 3
Rank Ordered Mean Terms of Service for All Mavericks and Conformists in the 24th through the 36th Congresses, by Region and Party

Group	No. in Group	Total Terms Served	Mean Terms Served
Southern Democratic Mavericks	22	112	5.09
Southern Whig/Rep. Mavericks	19	74	3.89
Northern Whig/Rep. Mavericks	12	45	3.75
Southern Democratic Conformists	37	110	2.97
Northern Democratic Mavericks	31	88	2.84
Northern Whig/Rep. Conformists	92	245	2.66
Southern Whig/Rep. Conformists	16	38	2.38
Northern Democratic Conformists	26	60	2.31

Table 4
Rank Ordered Mean Terms of Service for All Mavericks and Conformists in the 24th through the 36th Congresses by Region

Group	No. in Group	Total Terms Served	Mean Terms Served
Southern Mavericks	41	186	4.54
Northern Mavericks	43	133	2.96
Southern Conformists	53	148	2.79
Northern Conformists	118	305	2.58

were men who perceived the political environment in terms of cultural predispositions acquired in their larger experiences as nineteenth-century Americans. Some notion of the particular aspects of the antebellum culture that linked congressional mavericks to other independent-minded Americans is now appropriate.

NOTES

1. Alexis de Tocqueville, *Democracy in America*, ed. by Phillips Bradley (New York: Random House, Vintage Books, 1961), II:82. Tocqueville contrasted his low opinion of the House with his favorable perception of the Senate as a body of ''eloquent advocates, distinguished generals, wise magistrates, and statesmen of note'' (ibid., I:211). In defense of Reynolds, it should perhaps be pointed out that his remarks were offered during a long debate over apportionment in which the conduct of the House had been severely criticized by some congressmen, senators, and the press (*Congressional Globe, Appendix*, 27th Cong., 2d Sess., 345).

2. Some readers may wish at this point to consult Appendix I for a slightly fuller description of Alexander's methods and the application of its results to the selection process.

3. Thomas B. Alexander, *Sectional Stress and Party Strength: A Study of Roll-Call Voting Patterns in the United States House of Representatives, 1836–1860* (Nashville: Vanderbilt University Press, 1967); and Joel H. Silbey, *The Shrine of Party: Congressional Voting Behavior, 1841–1852* (Pittsburgh: University of Pittsburgh Press, 1967).

4. In Table 1, mavericks are counted for each Congress in which they served, whether or not their voting behavior was maverick-like in that Congress.

5. Cohesion levels among the northern Whigs were often quite high; but, on the other hand, where mavericks appear in large numbers in Table 1, cohesion levels were also high. Obviously if all mavericks in a regional and party group had voted as mavericks on every issue and roll-call vote, this could not have been the case. See cohesion tables in Alexander, *Sectional Stress and Party Strength*, pp. 20–22.

CHAPTER 2

The Cultural Dimensions

If a man does not keep pace with his companions, perhaps it is because he hears a different drummer. Let him step to the music which he hears, however measured or far away.

Henry David Thoreau, *Walden*

Congressional mavericks, like their conformist counterparts, were working politicians, fully engaged in the party life of the antebellum era and in the legislative tasks they were elected to assume. Mavericks did, however, analyze and reflect upon their work. While they helped build parties and shape the legislature, they were critical about contemporary politics. In particular they worried about the limitations on independent judgment imposed by the increasingly sophisticated collective processes by which the parties and the Congress operated. Plainly, they felt a tension between the conformity demanded by progressive institutions and the individualism widely proclaimed as fundamental in the American character. Certainly these concerns were not unique to congressional mavericks. Among the many observers of the American scene who decried the tendency to conformity, none spoke more forcefully than Henry David Thoreau, the transcendental critic. Through his imaginative perspective, the cultural tensions centrally involved in the character of mavericks may be elucidated.

From his symbolic retreat at Walden Pond, Thoreau rhetorically attacked the deadening conformity of mass society. Testily observing that "wherever a man goes, men will pursue him and paw him with their dirty institutions, and, if they can, constrain him to belong to their desperate odd-fellow society," he urged his sleeping countrymen to wake up, resist, and act as individuals.[1] Thoreau, who never held a steady job and never married, seems not to have regretted his decision to stand outside of the ordinary world in order to try and move it; but most people were willing to tolerate the conformity of society in order to advance.

Though Thoreau was an intellectual extremist and a relentless maverick, he understood how far his radical idealism removed him from his contemporaries. At the same time, he believed he had an audience in antebellum America. He knew that liberty, independence, and individualism were important social ideals, regardless of the "quiet desperation" of the masses.[2] In speaking as a "different drummer," Thoreau hoped that he addressed dormant mavericks in every walk of life.

Thoreau's individualism was nurtured by nineteenth-century romanticism, which had a wide influence in the United States. Like the rationalists of the eighteenth century, romantics turned to nature for the grounding of their ideas, but the nature they conceived was organic rather than mechanistic.[3] Romantics assailed the mechanical aspects of eighteenth-century natural law; they saw oppressive mechanism in burgeoning institutions as well as in the material workings of the industrial revolution. These ideas affected every western nation, but in the United States there was a special importance to the romantic protest against mechanism. Since the revolutionary era, the American mission had been largely defined in terms of political institutions shaped by the Enlightenment ideals of the founders. Its authors had seen the mechanical arrangements of the Constitution as a safe means of assuring free government.[4] In James Madison's famous words, the structure offered "a republican remedy for the diseases most incident to republican government."[5] Thus individual liberty, America's gift to the world, was secured by mild institutional restraints. When Thoreau tried to link his credo "that government is best which governs not at all" to the Jeffersonian dictum "that government is best which governs least," he demonstrated his own awareness of the eighteenth-century roots of his extreme individualism.[6]

The small scale of society and the natural abundance of America had disguised paradoxes in eighteenth-century ideas about individuals and their institutions. But if experiences of the colonial period had encouraged early republicans to believe that aristocratic institutions could be discarded and progress stimulated by individual efforts—restricted only by the gentle mechanics of natural law— it became quite evident to most nineteenth-century people that more thorough-going organization was essential to American progress. Implicitly, Americans enacted the process Alexis de Tocqueville described in *Democracy in America:* "Among laws controlling human societies there is one more precise and clearer, it seems to me, than all the others. If men are to remain civilized or to become civilized, the art of association must develop and improve among them at the same speed as equality of conditions spreads."[7] To the dismay of romantics like Thoreau, his contemporaries busily improved the "art of association," whether they sought private wealth or public welfare. He could only hope that many quietly carried forward with them in their progress some of the same concern expressed in *Walden* about the relationship between individual and society.

In many respects, Thoreau's warnings that the driving force behind the transformation of the republic was the desire for gain echoed similar fears voiced by creators of the national experiment.[8] It was abundantly clear by the 1840s that the United States was not going to become Sam Adams' Christian Sparta or Thomas Jefferson's pastoral Arcadia. Instead, as Americans incessantly pursued wealth, the countryside was marked with more complex economic institutions that drew people together for profit.[9] As early as the opening decades of the nineteenth century, banking, transportation, and manufacturing began to lead in the increased use of the corporate form of business enterprise. Simultaneously, the newly devised factory system organized the production of some manufactured goods. Noting the human costs of rationalized mass production, Thoreau caustically commented about New England's textile mills that "as far as I have heard of or observed, the principle is, not that mankind may be well and honestly clad, but, unquestionably, that the corporations may be enriched."[10] Less skeptical Americans hoped to gain inexpensive clothing while the corporations grew.

The growth of urban workingmen's associations indicated that the laboring classes recognized the advantages of collective action as often as did corporation owners.[11] While independent craftsmen still dominated their fields, they were determined not to become, in Thoreau's words, "the tools of their tools."[12] The impact of the industrial revolution was most felt in the urbanizing Northeast, but wherever the newer modes of production were introduced, individuals resorted to the "art of association."

Outside of the industrializing towns and cities of the Northeast, the quest for economic progress less visibly altered traditional patterns of living; but, often imperceptibly, agriculture was also being affected by the growing market economy.[13] Technological advances, most particularly the development of the steamboat and the railroad, extended the scope of commercial agriculture into the interior of the nation. As Thoreau correctly predicted, technology heralded the destruction of the "pastoral life."[14] Encapsulating the instruments of change into the symbol of the railroad, he described a subtle but pervasive alteration: "The startings and arrivals of the cars are now the epochs of the village day. They go and come with such regularity and precision, and their whistles can be heard so far, that the farmers set their clocks by them, and thus one well-conducted institution regulates a whole country."[15] Unlike Thoreau, most farmers welcomed the railroads and steamboats, mechanical regularity notwithstanding. If they sensed that their participation in the market economy undermined the special status of the independent yeoman in American culture, that awareness did not generally stand in the way of their ambitions.

Bankers, manufacturers, urban workingmen, and even farmers willingly participated in the gradual transformation of the United States. Ironically, while they nostalgically looked backward to the Golden Age of the Republic, they destroyed its pastoral foundations.[16] Probably most acted unconsciously, without intellectually comprehending the significance of their actions. Thoreau's anxieties about the fate of individual men in a highly organized society were, however, quite consciously shared by many intellectuals and reformers, who clearly articulated their concerns for the American public.

Writers of the American Renaissance that began in the 1820s focused much of their attention upon national versions of the ancient conflict between man and his social institutions. As R. W. B. Lewis has demonstrated in *The American Adam*, they wrote of the quest for a new paradise in which man and society would be harmonized with nature.[17] From the beginning, their hopes were impelled by the belief that natural freedom and abundance might provide a "second chance" for humans to reshape their society. It was, at best, a tenuous chance. The advent of the industrial revolution generally stimulated renewed hope; but, like Thoreau, most writers came to fear that the organized energies of the emerging machine age would suffocate individual freedom.[18] No major writer of the antebellum years ignored these issues, though their conclusions were far from unanimous. The Jacksonian enthusiast George Bancroft exalted the expansive future; but the most important prose works of the period—Herman Melville's *Moby Dick* and Nathaniel Hawthorne's *The Scarlet Letter*—display a pessimism far more profound than Thoreau's about human possibilities in the new age.

The multitude of reformers who organized to improve society in the middle years of the nineteenth century were philosophically more optimistic than Melville or Hawthorne.[19] Although many were influenced by romantic or transcendental ideas, most active reformers were not radical individualists like Thoreau. Certainly they were conscious of the conflict between individual freedom and organized social action, and they heatedly debated how to create the proper relationship between institutions and individuals.[20] Yet, regardless of their goals, they also illustrated the tendency to rational organization that pervaded other progressive aspects of nineteenth-century American society. Whether they intended it or not, they often helped to move that society into more complex modes of collective action as they sought to improve it.

Thoreau was skeptical about the impact of organized reform. "Doing good," he wryly noted, "is one of the professions which are full."[21] More plainly, he was horrified by the moral impact of American politics. His eloquent *Civil Disobedience* bitingly described how the massive machinery of majority rule nullified the importance of individual morality. "Let your life be a counter friction to stop the machine," he urged his readers.[22] He surely knew how difficult that action would be, as Thoreau recognized that the conflict between individual and institution was written into the political system at its inception and was only aggravated by the changes of the nineteenth century. In politics, as in other areas of public life, progress seemed to lead inexorably to the development of more coherent and complex forms of organization—forms which limited the autonomy of independent-minded political men. Not surprisingly then, mavericks in politics revealed anxieties similar to those of other intelligent observers of American life.

The eighteenth-century framers of the Constitution had been ambivalent about the political effects of individualism. On the one hand, they respected intellectual independence, and they believed that strong leaders of wisdom and virtue were essential to republican life.[23] On the other hand, they feared the innate human urge for power, so they tried to prevent its concentration. By diffusing power throughout the nation's political structure, they tried to rid the republic of the danger of factionalism based on narrow self-interest or passion.[24] They hoped that the delicately balanced mechanism would prevent self-aggrandizement while encouraging the pursuit of enlightened self-interest. They believed the system might attract to the state rational philosopher/statesmen responsive to the public good but prohibit the rise of demagogues who pandered to the public passions. On the basis of experience as members of the colonial elites, they thought it possible to construct government which reconciled the private ethical ideals of leaders with the principle of majority rule.

The extra-constitutional development of political parties in the 1790s partially disrupted the balance between individual and majority will, while making possible the consolidation of power across the branches of government and the coordination of efforts throughout the states.[25] Critics like John Randolph noted that parties quickly began to limit personal independence and circumscribe the influence of philosophical statesmen.[26] Ironically, however, these changes were not initiated by the kind of demagogues loathsome to the founders but were set in motion by men like Jefferson and James Madison, true philosopher/statesmen, who helped to create the first party in the nation.[27] The pragmatic demands of power thus produced the impulse for organization, whatever its long-range consequences for political individualism.

At the same time that political power supplementary to constitutional forms was being organized through parties, the government itself was groping toward patterns of institutional organization.[28] Federalists and Republicans alike contributed to the growing complexity of government in order to rule effectively. Federalists, following the administrative genius of Alexander Hamilton, structured the judiciary and executive branches, and they tried to stimulate national growth in the private sector of the economy. Jeffersonians, less enthusiastic about the size of national government, nevertheless did not dismantle the Federalist creations; and under the pressures of war they also found it necessary to increase governmental power.[29] Without regard to party, politicians responded to the changes following the War of 1812 with new roles for government, as the rapid advance into the West and the continued expansion of the economy caused greater national interrelatedness.[30] By twentieth-century standards, governmental institutions remained minuscule, but the direction of change seemed unmistakable.

Expansion of the suffrage occurred along with the slow growth of the government.[31] Despite conservative fears, no revolution in the nature of government followed. Insofar as political choices were focused upon partisan options which reflected the public will, this ostensible democratization brought more power to the common man. It can also be argued that the new democracy merely masked a new elitism of professional politicians no more responsive to popular leadership than the propertied elite which preceded them.[32] In either case, the older notion of virtual representation that had influenced the creation of American political institutions was thoroughly repudiated by the majority of politicians and voters by the 1830s. After the rise of the second party system of Democrats and Whigs in that decade, it was an uncommon political figure who dared flout the expressed will of his constituents, with an opposition party ready to exploit his act for its political profit.

The new Democratic and Whig parties which dominated national politics after 1836 were each united by broad common principles, but they are as well known for their development of organizational skills devoted to gaining and holding office as for their ideological consistency.[33] In the light of universal white male suffrage, it was essential that party leaders defer ostensibly to the will of the majority, but "wire-pullers" were also learning to direct that will. Key workers in the new parties were becoming skilled at the interpretation and manipulation of public opinion by using expanded modes of mass communication. Party leaders commonly relied upon the use of symbols and images to project to the mass of sometimes semi-educated or illiterate voters the necessity for supporting a particular candidate. Through their newspapers and local organizations, parties provided essential support for congressional candidates, strengthening the candidates' personal appeal with the addition of images designed to appeal to particular groups within the electorate.[34] A strong candidate with significant private resources might forego the aid of a party, but on the whole the relationship between party and congressional candidate was a reciprocal one of great importance to successful politicians.

A newly elected congressman found parties at the center of life in the nation's capital. Through caucuses and informal power groups and through the committee structure of the House of Representatives, parties played a significant role in ordering congressional business. At the national level, party organization still rested largely upon officeholders, rather than upon behind-the-scene power brokers in a formal bureaucracy. Still, the pressures for compliance with the wishes of party leaders could be focused efficiently when need be, as John Tyler learned in 1842 when he refused to cooperate with his Whig-dominated Congress. The patronage system, an important cement of national party organization, could also be used to encourage conformity or punish rebels, as James Buchanan attempted to do to Stephen Douglas in 1858.

For a national party to use its power effectively, consensus and compromise were essential. In this respect, party welfare was often in conflict with particularist demands from local constituencies and with ideological intensity from any source. Madison had argued in No. 10 of *The Federalist Papers* that the pluralistic character of an extended republic would prevent selfish factions from destroying the nation. He could not have foreseen the extent to which the major parties would absorb factions and blunt reform impulses of any sort. Despite enormous diversity in the composition of American society and despite the plethora of reformist (or counter-reformist) ideologies of the era, congressional parties were more noted for social homogeneity than heterogeneity and more inclined to orthodoxy than to innovation.

In the House of Representatives, the rapid turnover of membership may have reinforced the power of party leaders.[35] The great majority of congressmen came to Washington with previous political experience, but most did not serve long in the House. Although the educational level of congressmen was above that of the general population, many congressmen were not well-educated by modern standards. Congressmen knew the interests of their politically active constituents, but many probably did not know a great deal about legislative issues unrelated to their central concerns. Under these circumstances, for a congressman to take his cues from party leaders was perhaps sensible. Party positions on major policy issues were clear; they may have provided the inexperienced members of Congress with a simple source of stability in an unstable legislature.[36]

Whether he were a Democrat, Whig, or Republican, a congressman typically reconciled his ideas with the broad ideology of his party and his votes with the policy orientation identified by party leaders in the House. If a man could not agree with his party, it was certainly possible to switch; some congressmen did so, most notably during the period of realignment in the 1850s. But because the functional considerations that created the need for partisan conformity affected all national parties, there was no permanent escape from the forces encouraging intraparty consensus and compromise throughout the life of the second party system and into the third.

Of the two parties of the second two-party system, the Democrats were the first to coalesce. Originally building unity around the personality and image of Andrew Jackson, the Democrats ostensibly spoke for the common man. In the popular view, and in many modern historical interpretations, Democrats have been associated with the West, out of which Jackson came, with the small farmers of the South, with common laborers and immigrants in the urban areas, and with the lower classes in general.[37] Middle- and upper-class support of the Jacksonian party has been attributed to the entrepreneurial image projected by the economic policies of Jackson.[38] Concrete positions taken by the Democrats tended to cluster around the concept of protection of the common man against the financial and industrial interests, typically eastern. Specifically, the Jacksonian Democrats' policies included opposition to the Bank of the United States, which Jackson effectively wrecked; a currency policy supposedly favorable to small farmers and debtors, which in Jackson's interpretation meant opposition to the use of paper money and bank notes; extreme economy in government; careful guarding of the prerogatives of the states; and opposition to the protective tariff and to federal aid for internal improvements. These ideas had national appeal, and the early Democratic party attracted voters in every major section of the nation.

The Whig party was formed out of the diverse elements which stood in opposition to Andrew Jackson, the core being the old National Republican party led by Henry Clay, whose policies became the nucleus of the Whig appeal.[39] Clay's "American System"—a protective tariff designed to articulate the nation's economy, generous federal aid to internal improvements, and a national bank—outlined the basic goals of many Whigs, in addition to their fortuitous opposition to the executive powers of "King Andrew" and his followers. Although historians in the past have taken at face value the Jacksonian accusation that the Whigs represented the moneyed interests and have stressed the middle- and upper-class origins of the Whigs, it is now generally agreed that both parties had a broad base of support in the lower classes and that upper- and middle-class preferences were mixed as well.[40] The idea that Whigs were more likely than Democrats to come from Anglo-American backgrounds has not yet been proven for the national electorate, but it does seem to have merit for some regions or locales.[41] In any case, the early Whigs existed throughout the nation and among most major segments of the population.

As economic developments in the various sections of the country took increasingly divergent paths and as the territorial expansion of the nation brought the slavery question into greater national prominence, the two-party system of Whigs and Democrats was altered.[42] The Democratic party gained strength in the lower South and lost critical votes in the North as a consequence. To a growing southern self-consciousness, there were some fundamental aspects of Democratic policy which made it attractive, in particular the party's laissez-faire and state's-rights leanings.[43] However it appeared in the days of Jackson, it was apparent to many southerners after the Mexican War that a minority section could only be protected in a national structure with severely limited powers. To admit the right of a national government to tamper with internal state matters in the field of transportation must lead to the development of ever greater power of the national government over other domestic institutions. In addition, many citizens of the lower South believed that the direction of economic policy advocated by Whigs and Republicans from the industrializing North would mean ruin to the agrarian South. Consequently, the Whig party in the lower South withered and finally almost disappeared as an organized entity in the years after 1852. Because the then augmented southern wing of the Democratic party exerted a strong leadership in national councils, many northern Democrats were accused of alliance with the slave power, a position difficult to defend against growing antislavery sentiment. Thus some Democrats in the northern states drifted out of the party ranks into one of the splinter parties and finally into the ranks of the Republicans. If their numbers were not great, their influence was because they provided not only increased congressional strength for the new party but also the crucial margin of victory in the election of 1860.

The Republican party which emerged as a national force in the congressional elections of 1854 represented in large part the continuation of the Whig appeal in the North.[44] Although its identification with the antislavery position made it anathema to southerners, probably for many northern voters the antislavery position was not more significant than the other economic and nationalistic concepts which Republicans advocated.[45] The party slogan—Free Soil, Free Labor, Free Men—indicated Republican recognition of the broad base of its appeal and reflected an affirmative attitude toward national politics much like that of the earlier Whig party, but with the addition of antislavery. The ideological picture of a free, industrializing, prosperous North helped Republicans win voters in the late 1850s, but national leaders strategically played down any definition of issues that might alienate voters and attempted instead to capitalize on their positive image and loyalty of former Whigs or anti-Democratic voters.

The Democratic party in the late 1850s also found itself relying strongly on voter loyalty and projection of images rather than clear commitment to issues. It was increasingly the party of opposition—to antislavery agitation, to economic interference by the government, to moralism in politics, to tariffs—and almost the only things the party could be clearly identified as for were Manifest Destiny, expansionism, and an attitude of belligerent patriotism.

By 1860 sectional issues dominated the national political agenda. As the emergence of the new two-party system after the 1820s was an index to the extent of national feeling present in the expansionary optimism of that era, so the literal division of the parties into sectional segments in the 1850s was a final testament to the breakdown of national unity before the Civil War.[46] The impact of the sectionalization of the party system can readily be observed in the voting patterns of the House of Representatives, where regional delegations within each party differed markedly on sectional issues and to a lesser degree on other issues of the late antebellum years. For individual congressmen this meant that the demands of party had to be more carefully balanced with local interests than ever before. In one sense, this might allow an individual space to adjust for his personal views within the nebulous range of region and party congruence; but frequent intensification of emotional issues and the consequent disruption of party stability contributed to each man's awareness that a misstep might be fatal to his ambitions.

Thus the inherited tension between individuals and institutions had been perpetuated and aggravated by the antebellum era. Most politicians, like most Americans in general, ignored or mastered these crosscurrents as they searched for success. For many men being caught between individual preference and the pressures of party and constituency was an acceptable part of the reality of political life. Others were, however, more clearly disturbed about the threat to self-reliance posed by nascent political institutions. There was no room in workaday politics for a Thoreau, whose political morality dictated to him such anti-institutional behaviors as his refusal to pay taxes for the Mexican War and his support of John Brown. But some of the maverick-like spirit of Thoreau, which after all reflected the ideals of other thinking Americans, did live in antebellum politics. It can be found in such opposite men as antislavery spokesmen and southern fire-eaters, among men who achieved real power, and among able men who were political failures. The political environment, like the society at large, produced important observations about the human response to nineteenth-century material progress. Maverick politicians, like mavericks elsewhere, cautioned that the price of success might be very high in personal terms. Like others, they, too, often chose to pay the price, despite their anxieties.

"What are we to come to, and what is to come to us?" a congressional maverick plaintively wrote.[47] He defined his predicament in terms Thoreau would have appreciated: "I confess I am at some loss whether to maintain principles without men, or men without principles."[48] To follow pragmatic party leaders meant the sacrifice of his valued philosophical independence to the demands of the moment; to oppose party leadership might be political suicide.

If we follow any of these fellows who have set themselves up as leaders of our little host we run against the posts of their selfish ambition at every turn, and must ramble and grope with them through the zodiac of their change. If we stand aloof from the dirty scramble for high office, and say as patriots that the "play is not worth the candle" to the people, then we are denounced as exclusives and impracticable theorists, behind the spirit of the age.[49]

For politicians, then, this summarizes the difficult position of a maverick: the maintenance of a personally acceptable balance between private values—moral, intellectual, or emotional—and the pressing demands of political groups for conformity to their interests. Given the stresses of antebellum politics, it was a delicate balancing act, often doomed to failure.

NOTES

1. Henry David Thoreau, *Walden and Other Writings*, ed. by Brooks Atkinson (New York: Random House, Modern Library Editions, 1937), p. 155.

2. Ibid., p. 7.

3. Intellectual histories which trace this transformation with attention to its implications for American politics include Vernon Parrington's classic *Main Currents in American Thought*, 3 vols. (New York: Harcourt, Brace and World, Harvest Books, 1927); and Charles A. Barker, *American Convictions: Cycles of Public Thought, 1600–1850* (Philadelphia: J. B. Lippencott Co., 1970). Although Thomas Jefferson is often viewed as a transitional figure, his mechanistic view of nature is brilliantly interpreted in Gary Wills, *Inventing America: Jefferson's Declaration of Independence* (New York: Random House, Vintage Books, 1979), esp. in "Part Two: A Scientific Paper," pp. 93–164. Also replete with insights for political implications of the shift from rationalism to romanticism is John William Ward, *Andrew Jackson: Symbol for an Age* (New York: Oxford University Press, Galaxy Books, 1962), esp. pp. 48–50, 72–78.

4. The development of the "kinetic theory of politics" embodied in the Constitution is thoroughly explored in Gordon S. Wood, *The Creation of the American Republic, 1776–1787* (New York: W. W. Norton & Co., Norton Library, 1972).

5. James Madison, No. 10 of *The Federalist Papers*, ed. with an introduction by Clinton Rossiter (New York: New American Library, Mentor Books, 1961), p. 84.

6. From the opening lines of his *Civil Disobedience*, included in Thoreau, *Walden*, p. 635.

7. Tocqueville, *Democracy in America*, I:118.

8. Wood, *Creation of the American Republic*, esp. pp. 570–574, treats the anxieties of John Adams. Jefferson's concerns were plainly revealed as early as the 1780s in *Notes on the State of Virginia*, particularly in the queries on commerce and manufactures; see pp. 164–169 in the convenient paperbound edition which has a very helpful introduction and notes by William Peden (New York: W. W. Norton & Co., Norton Library, 1972).

Drew R. McCoy, *The Elusive Republic: Political Economy in Jeffersonian America* (New York: W. W. Norton & Co., 1982) lucidly describes the Jeffersonians' attempt in the early nineteenth century to reconcile the developing economy with their early republican ideas.

9. The economic changes after 1830 are treated in Stuart Weems Bruchey, *The Roots of American Economic Growth, 1607–1861: An Essay in Social Causation* (New York: Harper & Row, 1965); Arthur M. Schlesinger, Jr., *The Age of Jackson* (Boston: Little, Brown & Co., 1945); George Rogers Taylor, *The Transportation Revolution, 1815–1860* (New York: Holt, Rinehart & Winston, 1957); Frederick Jackson Turner, *The United States, 1830–1850: The Nation and Its Sections*, with an introduction by Avery Craven (Gloucester, Mass.: Peter Smith, 1958); and Glyndon C. Van Deusen, *The Jacksonian Era, 1828–1848*, The New American Nation Series, ed. by Henry Steele Commager and Richard B. Morris (New York: Harper & Row, Harper Torchbooks, 1963). The viewpoint of the "new economic history" is reflected in Peter Temin, *The Jacksonian Economy* (New York: W. W. Norton & Co., 1969); and Douglass C. North, *The Economic Growth of the United States, 1790–1860* (New York: W. W. Norton & Co., Norton Library, 1966). The nature of the rate of growth of the economy is hotly debated; see W. W. Rostow, *The Stages of Economic Growth: A Non-Communist Manifesto* (New York: Cambridge University Press, 1960); Henry Rosovsky, "The Take-Off into Sustained Controversy," *Journal of Economic History* 25 (June 1965):271–275; and Thomas C. Cochrane, "The Paradox of American Economic Growth," *Journal of American History* 51 (March 1975):925–942.

10. Thoreau, *Walden*, p. 24.

11. Ideas associated with the movement are explored in Edward Pessen, *Most Uncommon Jacksonians: The Radical Leaders of the Early Labor Movement* (Albany: State University of New York, 1968).

12. Thoreau, *Walden*, p. 33.

13. Surveys of agricultural development include Percy Wells Bidwell and John I. Falconer, *History of Agriculture in the Northern United States* (Washington, D. C.: The Carnegie Institution of Washington, 1925); and Lewis C. Gray, *History of Agriculture in the Southern United States to 1860*, 2 vols. (Washington, D. C.: The Carnegie Institution of Washington, 1933). The influence of the market is stressed in North, *Economic Growth of the United States*; pp. 122–125 treat the changes resulting in South and West. An interpretative approach to the total impact of economic changes on traditional ways of living is Richard D. Brown, *Modernization: The Transformation of American Life, 1600–1865*, The American Century Series, consulting ed., Eric Foner (New York: Hill and Wang, 1976).

14. Thoreau, *Walden*, p. 111. Thoreau's reactions to the beginnings of industrialization in America are creatively explored in Leo Marx, *The Machine in the Garden: Technology and the Pastoral Ideal in America* (New York: Oxford University Press, 1964), pp. 242–265.

15. Thoreau, *Walden*, p. 107.

16. The nostalgic tendency in Jacksonian Democracy is discussed in Marvin Meyers, *The Jacksonian Persuasion: Politics and Belief* (Stanford, Calif.: Stanford University Press, 1957).

17. R. W. B. Lewis, *The American Adam: Innocence, Tragedy and Tradition in the Nineteenth Century* (Chicago: University of Chicago Press, Phoenix Books, 1958). Other important studies which relate literature to cultural change include Fred Somkin, *Unquiet*

Eagle: Memory and Desire in the Idea of American Freedom, 1815–1860 (Ithaca, N.Y.:
Cornell University Press, 1967); Ernest Lee Tuveson, *Redeemer Nation: The Idea of
America's Millennial Role* (Chicago: University of Chicago Press, 1968); Perry Miller,
Nature's Nation (Cambridge, Mass.: Belknap Press, 1967); Major L. Wilson, *Space,
Time, and Freedom: The Quest for Nationality and the Irrepressible Conflict, 1815–
1861*, Contributions in American History, No. 35 (Westport, Conn.: Greenwood Press,
1974); Lawrence J. Friedman, *Inventors of the Promised Land* (New York: Alfred A.
Knopf, 1975); and two works by Paul Nagel, *One Nation Indivisible: The Union in
American Thought, 1776–1861* (New York: Oxford University Press, 1964); and *This
Sacred Trust: American Nationality, 1798–1898* (New York: Oxford University Press,
1971).

18. The theme is stressed in Marx, *Machine in the Garden*. Also useful are Perry
Miller, *The Life of the Mind in America From the Revolution to the Civil War* (New
York: Harcourt, Brace & World, 1965); and Robert Ernest Spiller et al., *Literary History
of the United States*, 3 vols. (New York: Macmillan Co., 1948).

19. A comprehensive survey of the reform movement is Alice Felt Tyler, *Freedom's
Ferment: Phases of American Social History from the Colonial Period to the Outbreak
of the Civil War* (New York: Harper & Row, Harper Torchbooks, 1962). Three collections
which contain a number of essays linking the reform movement with cultural changes
are David Brion Davis, ed., *Antebellum Reform* (New York: Harper & Row, 1967);
Martin Duberman, ed., *The Antislavery Vanguard: New Essays on the Abolitionists*
(Princeton: Princeton University Press, 1965); and Lewis Perry and Michael Fellman,
eds., *Antislavery Reconsidered: New Perspectives on the Abolitionists* (Baton Rouge:
Louisiana State University Press, 1979).

20. Particularly useful in this light are David Rothman, *The Discovery of the Asylum:
Social Order and Disorder in the New Republic* (Boston: Little, Brown & Co., 1971);
and Aileen L. Kraditor, *Means and Ends in American Abolitionism: Garrison and His
Critics on Strategy and Tactics, 1834–1850* (New York: Random House, Vintage Books,
1970).

21. Thoreau, *Walden*, p. 65.

22. Ibid., p. 644.

23. Interpretive histories which treat the development of political ideas in the early
republic include Louis Hartz, *The Liberal Tradition in America: An Interpretation of
American Political Thought Since the Revolution* (New York: Harcourt, Brace & World,
1955); and Ralph H. Gabriel, *The Course of American Democratic Thought: An Intellectual History Since 1815*, Ronald Series in History, ed. by R. C. Binkley and Ralph
H. Gabriel (New York: Ronald Press Co., 1940).

24. A major theme of Madison's famous No. 10 and many other of *The Federalist
Papers*; diffusion of power in "The Federalist Persuasion" is brilliantly analyzed in
Wood, *Creation of the American Republic*, pp. 519–564.

25. Books which treat the development of the first two-party system include William
N. Chambers, *Political Parties in a New Nation* (New York: Oxford University Press,
1963); Roy F. Nichols, *The Invention of the American Political Parties* (New York:
Macmillan Co., 1967); James S. Young, *The Washington Community, 1800–1828* (New
York: Columbia University Press, 1966); Rudolph M. Bell, *Party and Faction in American
Politics: The House of Representatives, 1789–1801* (Westport, Conn.: Greenwood Press,
1973); Noble Cunningham, *The Jeffersonian Republicans in Power: Party Operations,
1801–1809* (Chapel Hill: University of North Carolina Press, 1963); and essays in Arthur

M. Schlesinger, Jr., gen. ed., *History of United States Political Parties*, 4 vols. (New York: Chelsea House Publishers in association with R. R. Bowker Co., 1973). An influential article that denies that the first two parties constituted a system is Ronald P. Formisano, "Deferential-Participant Politics: The Early Republic's Political Culture, 1789–1840," *American Political Science Review* 68 (June 1974):473-487. Formisano treats the transition between the first and second party eras in *The Transformation of Political Culture: Massachusetts Parties, 1790s–1840s* (New York: Oxford University Press, 1983).

26. A useful summary of antiparty ideas in the early republic is Richard Hofstadter, *The Idea of a Party System: The Rise of Legitimate Opposition in the United States, 1780–1840* (Berkeley: University of California Press, 1969).

27. Cunningham, *The Jeffersonians in Power*.

28. Patterns of organization are described in the first two administrative studies of Leonard White, *The Federalists: A Study in Administrative History, 1789–1801* (New York: Macmillan Co., 1948); and *The Jeffersonians: A Study in Administrative History, 1801–1829* (New York: Macmillan Co., 1959).

29. Noble Cunningham, *The Process of Government under Jefferson* (Princeton: Princeton University Press, 1978).

30. The relationship between economic and political changes is interpreted in George Dangerfield, *The Awakening of American Nationalism, 1815–1828*, The New American Nation Series, ed. by Henry Steele Commager and Richard B. Morris (New York: Harper & Row, Harper Torchbooks, 1965).

31. The standard history of suffrage extension is Chilton Williamson, *American Suffrage: From Property to Democracy, 1760–1860* (Princeton: Princeton University Press, 1960).

32. This point of view is specifically argued in Edward Pessen, *Jacksonian America: Society, Personality, and Politics*, rev. ed. (Homewood, Ill.: Dorsey Press, 1978), pp. 150–170.

33. The development of the new parties is treated in Wilfred E. Binkley, *American Political Parties: Their Natural History*, 4th ed., enl. (New York: Alfred A. Knopf, 1964). A more recent interpretation is found in Richard P. McCormick, *The Second American Party System: Party Formation in the Jacksonian Period* (Chapel Hill: University of North Carolina Press, 1966). The significance of parties in the political life of the nation is treated in Silbey, *The Shrine of Party*; and in Alexander, *Sectional Stress and Party Strength*. An essay which takes different positions is David J. Russo, *The Major Political Issues of the Jacksonian Period and the Development of Party Loyalty in Congress, 1830–1840*, Transactions of the American Philosophical Society; New Series, Vol. 62, Part 5 (Philadelphia: American Philosophical Society, 1972). See also Schlesinger, *History of Political Parties*. The literature on the Jacksonian era is discussed in Richard P. McCormick, "New Perspectives on Jacksonian Politics," *American Historical Review* 65 (January 1960):288-301; Charles G. Sellers, Jr., "Andrew Jackson Versus the Historians," *Mississippi Valley Historical Review* 44 (March 1958):614-634; Alfred A. Cave, *Jacksonian Democracy and the Historians* (Gainesville: University of Florida Press, 1964); Ronald P. Formisano, "Toward a Reorientation of Jacksonian Politics: A Review of the Literature, 1959–1975," *Journal of American History* 63 (June 1976):42-65; and the excellent bibliography in Pessen, *Jacksonian America*. Studies which evaluate different aspects of Jacksonian politics include Van Deusen, *Jacksonian Era*; Meyers, *Jacksonian Persuasion*; Lee Benson, *The Concept of Jacksonian Democracy: New York as a Test Case* (Princeton: Princeton University Press, 1961); Robert V.

Remini, *Martin Van Buren and the Making of the Democratic Party* (New York: W. W. Norton & Co., 1959); Leonard White, *The Jacksonians: A Study in Administrative History, 1829–1861* (New York: Macmillan Co., 1954); Jean H. Baker, *Affairs of Party: The Political Culture of Northern Democrats in the Mid–Nineteenth Century* (Ithaca, N.Y.: Cornell University Press, 1983); and Pessen, *Jacksonian America.* Ideological differences are stressed in the interpretation of Michael F. Holt, *The Political Crisis of the 1850s,* Critical Episodes in American Politics Series, ed. by Robert A. Divine (New York: John Wiley & Sons. 1978), Ch. 2, "The Second Party System in Operation," pp. 17–38. Ideological differences between Whigs and Democrats are described in Rush Welter, *The Mind of America, 1820–1860,* Part 3, "Politics" (New York: Columbia University Press, 1975).

34. Robert Kelley, *The Cultural Pattern in American Politics: The First Century* (New York: Alfred A. Knopf, Borzoi Books, 1979), pp. 160–184, conveniently summarizes the content of the reference group appeal for Whigs and Democrats. The ethnocultural homogeneity of Whigs as opposed to Democrats is dealt with in Benson, *Concept of Jacksonian Democracy*; Ronald P. Formisano, *The Birth of Mass Political Parties: Michigan, 1827–1861* (Princeton: Princeton University Press, 1961); and Michael F. Holt, *Forging a Majority: The Formation of the Republican Party in Pittsburgh, 1848–1860* (New Haven, Conn.: Yale University Press, 1969). For a constructive critique of ethnocultural interpretations see Richard L. McCormick, "Ethno-Cultural Explanations of Nineteenth-Century American Voting Behavior," *Political Science Quarterly* 89 (June 1974):351–377.

35. See Allan Bogue, Jerome M. Clubb, Carroll R. McKibbin, and Santa A. Traugott, "Members of the House of Representatives and the Process of Modernization, 1789–1960," *Journal of American History* 63 (September 1976):275–302.

36. It is worth noting here that both mavericks and conformists in this study served longer than the typical congressman, and mavericks generally longer than conformists. Length of service may have encouraged mavericks' independence, but they would have argued that independence won them long service. In any case, length of service did not make conformists independent.

37. Frontier influences are stressed in Frederick Jackson Turner, *U. S., 1830–1850.* A restatement of the Turner emphasis is found in Richard Latner, "A New Look at Jacksonian Politics," *Journal of American History* 61 (March 1975):943–969. The major work which argues the influence of labor is Schlesinger, *Age of Jackson.*

38. The emphasis upon entrepreneurial aspects of the Jacksonian movement is best represented by Bray Hammond, *Banks and Politics in America from the Revolution to the Civil War* (Princeton: Princeton University Press, 1957). A contrary interpretation is Shaw Livermore, Jr., *The Twilight of Federalism: The Disintegration of the Federalist Party, 1815–1830* (Princeton: Princeton University Press, 1962), which finds Jacksonians willing to receive old Federalists.

39. Whigs have been the subject of somewhat less historical attention than the Democrats, although they are generally treated in at least some detail in most of the Democratic studies. See, however, E. Malcolm Carroll, *Origins of the Whig Party* (Durham, N. C.: Duke University Press, 1925); and Arthur Charles Cole, *The Whig Party in the South* (Washington, D. C.: American Historical Association, 1914). Glyndon Van Deusen, in "Some Aspects of Whig Thought and Theory in the Jacksonian Period," *American Historical Review* 63 (January 1958):305–422, stresses the common ground of the two

parties. The most important recent study is Daniel Walker Howe, *The Political Culture of American Whigs* (Chicago: University of Chicago Press, 1979).

40. A thoughtful discussion of historians' views on the question of "Who were the Whigs?" is found in Pessen, *Jacksonian America*, pp. 233–260.

41. For example, New York, Michigan, and Pittsburgh in the works of Benson, Formisano, and Holt mentioned in n. 34 above. Kelley uses these and other state and local studies to make the generalization for the nation in *Cultural Pattern in American Politics*.

42. See Roy F. Nichols, *The Disruption of American Democracy* (New York: Macmillan Co., 1947); Chaplain W. Morrison, *Democratic Politics and Sectionalism: The Wilmot Proviso Controversy* (Chapel Hill: University of North Carolina Press, 1967); Eric Foner, "The Wilmot Proviso Revisited," *Journal of American History* 61 (September 1969):262–279; Frederick J. Blue, *The Free Soilers: Third Party Politics, 1848–1854* (Urbana: University of Illinois Press, 1973); and Richard H. Sewell, *Ballots for Freedom: Antislavery Politics in the United States, 1839–1860* (New York: W. W. Norton & Co., 1976).

43. William J. Cooper, *The South and the Politics of Slavery, 1828–1853* (Baton Rouge: Louisiana State University Press, 1978), emphasizes the influence of slavery throughout the antebellum period but agrees that not all southerners were equally quick to see the relationship between slavery and other issues; when the connection was made clear, it favored the Democratic party.

44. See Eric Foner, *Free Soil, Free Labor, Free Men: The Ideology of the Republican Party before the Civil War* (New York: Oxford University Press, 1970); and Holt, *Political Crisis of the 1850s*, for different interpretations of these events.

45. See Robert F. Durden, "Ambiguities in the Antislavery Crusade of the Republican Party" in Duberman, *Antislavery Vanguard*, pp. 362–394.

46. The extensive bibliography in the latest edition of James G. Randall and David Donald, *The Civil War and Reconstruction*, 2d ed., rev., with enlarged bibliography (Lexington, Mass.: D. C. Heath & Co., 1969), is perhaps the most useful guide to literature on the background to the Civil War. The crises which led to the war are related in Alan Nevins, *Emergence of Lincoln*, 2 vols. (New York: Charles Scribner's Sons, 1950); and *Ordeal of the Union*, 2 vols. (New York: Charles Scribner's Sons, 1947); and in David M. Potter, *The Impending Crisis, 1848–1861*, completed and ed. by Don E. Fehrenbacher, The New American Nation Series, ed. by Henry Steele Commager and Richard B. Morris (New York: Harper & Row, 1976).

47. Thomas Gilmer to his brother, George W. Gilmer, in December 1838, in L. G. Tyler, *Life and Times of the Tylers* (Richmond, Va.: Whittel and Shepperson, 1884–1896), II:699.

48. Ibid., II:700.

49. Ibid.

Part II

THE CONGRESSIONAL LEADERSHIP OF MAVERICKS AND CONFORMISTS

Conformists and the Regularization of the House

I know not how better to describe our form of government in a single phrase than by calling it a government by the chairmen of the Standing Committees of Congress.

Woodrow Wilson, *Congressional Government*, 1885

The antebellum House of Representatives was by no means as well organized as it would become by 1885 when Woodrow Wilson assaulted the covert power of the committee chairmen.[1] Only gradually did the House become "institutionalized" and develop regularized modes of operation for its constantly shifting membership.[2] In that process, conformists in the major political parties between 1836 and 1860 seem to have played a positive role. Sensitive to the demands of party organization and heedful of the contribution that legislative efficiency could make to partisan power, leading conformists encouraged the businesslike conduct of the nation's affairs.

Visitors to the galleries of the House of Representatives saw relatively little of the primitive machinery through which the legislature was learning to act. The floor of the House was often a stage for high drama, or low comedy; and although there were rules that restricted speakers to the subject at hand and confined them to rather impersonal manners in debate, there was no uniform adherence to these rules. Famous orators might entertain the galleries by the hour. Not infrequently the floor would erupt into violent argument over a critical issue, or, perhaps as often, over some point of detail that caught the attention of an active legislator. Most congressmen said little on the floor, speaking only once or twice each session to have something in print for their constituents; but the leadership was quite active in mustering support for bills, pushing committee decisions through the whole House and attempting to quickly move through Congress measures of particular importance to their party. An attentive observer might identify some chairmen by their commanding airs or frequent remarks. On the whole, however, the daily floor activity of the House did not reveal much of the power infrastructure that commanded it.

Unlike the gallery visitor, the twentieth-century student of the antebellum Congresses has no sights and sounds to lend reality to a reconstruction of the business of the House. Yet out of the enormous variety of congressional activities that offer themselves for study through the pages of the *Congressional Globe*, the historian must search for patterns, if the welter of names and words is to be rendered meaningful. Unfortunately, however, there is not much systematic information about nineteenth-century Congresses. Contemporary observers and party leaders, like historians since, have counted votes and made some basic categorizations. Mavericks and conformists were initially defined here in terms of the patterns of their voting behavior in relationship to the influences of party and section. The very notion of their conformity or nonconformity rested upon the existence of a set of shared standards—explicit or implicit—among the individuals in each Congress. Cumulative scale analysis, used to identify both types, defines a scale of related votes about particular issues and ranks individuals along the scale; thus mavericks were separated from conformists with the assurance that mavericks were actually deviating from a kind of normative behavior for their sectional and party grouping. No such convenient quantitative device as scale analysis exists for behaviors other than voting; but it is possible, using the record provided in the *Globe*, to distinguish some other patterns in the participation of congressmen. In regard to some of these other patterns, as in regard to their voting behavior, mavericks and conformists were different. In some respects, at least, it is likely that their distinctiveness marked them for their fellow congressmen as well as for the careful reader of the *Globe*.

Variety in the legislative style of antebellum congressmen was a logical consequence of the pluralism of American society. Obvious cultural differences probably resulted from regional attachments or economic and social backgrounds. Many variations may have been the consequence of length of service in the House or of the power position of the individual congressman. Other distinctions were surely attributable to personal idiosyncrasies. It is regrettable that, despite an enormous amount of writing about the antebellum Congress, no survey of patterns in legislative style exists. Political scientists have, as a rule, concerned themselves only rarely with the history of the legislative body.[3] Historians have been able to apply the findings and methods of political scientists and other social scientists only in a limited fashion to the Congresses of the antebellum period, most importantly in the analysis of roll-call votes.[4] All historians of the House do know is that a great diversity of behavior was characteristic of the nineteenth-century Congress; what they do not know is what was "normal."[5]

Without a backdrop of regularity against which to project the political styles of mavericks and conformists, patterns for mavericks and patterns for conformists can only be compared. Even this comparison is made difficult by the fact that the majority of them were hardly noticeable to the public view. Most voted, occasionally offered a one- or two-sentence opinion, or suggested a routine motion, but otherwise failed to leave any record of politically significant participation other than voting.[6] The few who did speak frequently necessarily became the focus of a quest for the patterns which they displayed in the *Globe*. As it turned out, most of those men who spoke frequently on the floor of the House also held formal positions of leadership. It is, then, in their styles as committee chairmen or Speakers of the House that mavericks and conformists can most effectively be compared.

Although some of Woodrow Wilson's disapproving analysis of the hidden features of congressional government does not apply to the period before the Civil War, one basic point—the power of the committee chairmen—seems to have had considerable relevance to the House at least as early as the age of Jackson.[7] James S. Young, author of *The Washington Community, 1800–1828*, one of the few works to analyze the internal operations of the Congress in the early nineteenth century, observed that "by 1825 the committee system had taken on most of its modern features—seniority rule and the House Rules Committee excepted—and had absorbed broad powers of initiative, amendment, and quasi-veto in legislation, as well as supervision of executive administration."[8] The lack of extensive written records for the antebellum period makes study of the internal workings of the committees difficult, at best, and there is not an extensive study of the committee system in print. Interactions of committee chairmen with the other members of the House, however, can readily be observed in the pages of the *Globe*.

Although these chairmen did not exercise power in the same fashion or degree that their counterparts of a century later would do, some comparison with the twentieth century may illuminate the pre–Civil War period. In the antebellum period, committee chairmen were often chosen for reasons unrelated to seniority or even to party; furthermore, they probably took a far more active role in managing floor debate than their latter-day counterparts.[9] As there were no party whips then, the task of organizing the passage of bills fell to the committee chairmen, who were chosen by the Speaker of the House in the years before the War. Absence of any formal seniority system made these important men somewhat more responsive to the power arrangements in the House, since retention of their offices depended upon the goodwill of the Speakers. Precisely what considerations influenced the choices made by the Speakers are unknown; factional alignments, personal qualities, bargains (corrupt or otherwise), regional distribution, and party regularity were probably involved. Variations over time in these factors appear with different Speakers, but no evident increase in regularity or standardization of selection is apparent.

Twentieth-century selections for House leadership are much more regularized, although outside observers may not be entirely aware of them. The seniority system largely determines which members of the majority party will chair standing committees; once assigned to a major committee, a member whose tenure is long stands a good chance of gaining power. Potential members for key committees, therefore, are screened carefully for their desirability. According to political scientist Nicholas Masters, author of an influential article on committee assignments, "legislative responsibility" is the primary consideration in the analysis of a member's qualifications.[10] Masters' description of that quality is as follows:

According to the party leaders and the members of the committees-on-committees, a responsible legislator is one whose ability, attitudes, and relationship with his colleagues serve to enhance the prestige and importance of the House of Representatives. He has a basic and fundamental respect for the legislative process and understands and appreciates its formal and informal rules. He has the respect of his fellow legislators, and particularly the respect of party leaders. He does not attempt to manipulate every situation for his own personal advantages. In the consideration of issues, he is careful to protect the rights of others; he is careful to clear matters that require clearance; and he is especially careful about details. He understands the pressures on the members with whom he cannot always agree and avoids pushing an issue to the point where his opponents may suffer personal embarrassment. On specific issues, no matter how firm his convictions and no matter how great the pressures upon him, he demonstrates a willingness to compromise. He is moderate, not so much in the sense of his voting record and his personal ideology, but rather in the sense of a moderate approach; he is not to be found on the uncompromising extremes of the political spectrum. . . . In short, a responsible legislator is politically pliant, but not without conviction.[11]

The kind of responsibility Masters describes was probably one factor in the assignment of positions of power in the antebellum Congresses. Moreover, it furnishes a useful standard against which to project alternative patterns of leadership for maverick and conformist chairmen. There are alternative styles of leadership in twentieth-century Congresses, and this was certainly the case in earlier years.[12] The youth of the constitutional system and the variety of regional subcultures led to acceptable variations in the ideals for statesmanship, as is demonstrated by the multiple roles of mavericks and conformists.

A large group of mavericks and conformists whose writings form the basis for this study comprised slightly less than one-third of all standing committee chairmen in the thirteen Congresses between 1836 and 1860 (see Table 5). Mavericks served in sixty-three chairmanship positions; conformists served in fifty-nine. There were twice as many conformists as mavericks who served in these Congresses and were therefore available for leadership positions, but the average length of service was longer for mavericks than for conformists.[13] While in any given Congress there were more conformists than mavericks present, the longer terms of the mavericks who were present may have given them some edge in attaining desirable places. There is considerable variation over time in the proportion of mavericks and conformists who served for one Congress as chairmen; but no trend in the balance between the two is evident, except insofar as the relationship reflects the partisan and regional distribution of mavericks and conformists described in Chapter 1.

Seniority, measured in terms of experience in the House, not experience on a particular committee, does seem to have been a factor in choosing committee chairmen from this group of men, at least for the more important committees (see Table 6). On eleven committees the mean period of service for chairmen was at least three terms, or six years, served in Congress before being chosen as chairmen. These eleven committees were Ways and Means, Claims, Post Offices and Post Roads, Judiciary, Revolutionary Claims, Manufactures, Naval Affairs, Foreign Affairs, Territories, Roads and Canals, and Accounts. The eleven committees for which the mean length of prior service for chairmen was less than two terms were Elections, Commerce, Public Expenditures, Private Land Claims, Agriculture, Revolutionary Pensions, Invalid Pensions, Revisals and Unfinished Business, Mileage, and Patents. Most of the committees in the latter group were less important than those in the first group, though not in every case. Because these figures are taken from only one-third of all chairmen of standing committees in the period studied, they do not support the generalization that most important committees were chaired by experienced members of Congress; but among this group of mavericks and conformists, some crude seniority system seems to have been at work.

Both mavericks and conformists chaired important committees; and although the rough seniority rule may account for the presence of more mavericks in proportion to their total numbers than conformists, that rule does not serve to explain their distribution across the committees. It may be understandable, in terms of twentieth-century legislative norms, that conformists, with greater regularity in their voting records, were more often Speakers of the House and chairmen of the Ways and Means Committee than mavericks, as these two positions were the most important in the House and usually the most directly related to party considerations. It may also be partially a consequence of the mavericks' propensity for philosophical concerns in general, and in particular for philosophical concerns about the meaning of the American experience, that mavericks outnumbered conformists as chairmen of the Naval Affairs Committee, the Foreign Affairs Committee, and the Judiciary Committee.[14] But beyond these general assessments, little can be said about possible reasons for chairmanship assignments except in particular cases, where often the reason can be understood in terms of the personal character of the individual or of special partisan circumstances related to that Congress.

In spite of the obvious presence of mavericks in the leadership ranks of most Congresses, a style of operation common to conformists seems to have prevailed in the House, among these chairmen. In floor leadership, as in voting, conformists tended to resemble rather closely the Masters' model of a responsible legislator. Most of the conformist chairmen took an active role in the daily business on the floor of the House. There were some low participators, generally the chairmen of minor committees. It is likely that some really important House leaders preferred to act exclusively behind the scenes, but their influence is difficult to evaluate without private records of the committees. The generalizations which

Table 5
Mavericks and Conformists Who Served as Speakers of the House or Chairmen

Standing Committees	Congress						
	24	25	26	27	28	29	30
Speaker of the House			R.M.T. Hunter	*J. White*			
Elections			*J. Campbell*	W. Halstead			*R. Thompson*
Ways and Means	C.C. Cambreleng	C.C. Cambreleng		M. Fillmore			
Claims		E. Whittlesey		*J.R. Giddings*	J. Vance	J. Vance	J.A. Rockwell
Commerce				*J.P. Kennedy*	I. Holmes		W. Hunt
Public Lands			T. Corwin	*W.C. Johnson*		*J. McClernand*	
Post Office & Post Roads				G.N. Briggs	*G.W. Hopkins*	*G.W. Hopkins*	W.L. Goggin
District of Columbia			*W.C. Johnson*	*J.R. Underwood*	*J. Campbell*	R.M.T. Hunter	
Judiciary		*J. Garland*	J. Sergeant				
Revolutionary Claims	H.A.P. Muhlenberg	H.A.P. Muhlenberg	H. Hall		D. King		
Public Expenditures			G.N. Briggs			R. Dunlap	*T. Clingman*
Private Land Claims						*J. Bowlin*	
Manufactures	*J.Q. Adams*	*J.Q. Adams*	*J.Q. Adams*	L. Saltonstall	*J.Q. Adams*	*J.Q. Adams*	*A. Stewart*
Agriculture							
Indian Affairs						J. Thompson	
Military Affairs							*J.M. Botts*
Militia							
Naval Affairs				*H.A. Wise*	*H.A. Wise*	I. Holmes	
Foreign Affairs		B. Howard	*F. Pickens*	*C. Cushing*	*C.J. Ingersoll*	*C.J. Ingersoll*	T. Smith
Territories						S.A. Douglas	C. Smith
Revolutionary Pensions						*R. Brodhead*	
Invalid Pensions						P. King	
Roads and Canals	C.F. Mercer	C.F. Mercer	C. Ogle		R.D. Owen		R. Schenck
Revisal and Unfinished Business		S. Mason					
Accounts							L. Boyd
Mileage					H. Cobb		
Public Buildings and Grounds			L. Lincoln			*Z. Pratt*	
Patents						*T. Henley*	

Italics Indicate maverick chairmen.

		Congress				Total Mav.	Total Conf.
31	**32**	**33**	**34**	**35**	**36**		
Cobb	L. Boyd	L. Boyd		J.L. Orr		2	4
	D. Disney	R. Stanton		T. Harris	J. Gilmer	3	4
	G.S. Houston	G.S. Houston	L.D. Campbell		J. Sherman	3	4
		A. Edgerton	J.R. Giddings	S.S. Marshall		2	6
		T.J.D. Fuller	E. Washburne	J. Cochrane	E. Washburne	3	4
↲lin		D. Disney	H. Bennett	W.R.W. Cobb		5	2
					S. Colfax	2	3
↲nge			J. Meacham			4	2
		F.P. Stanton		G.S. Houston	J. Hickman	4	1
						0	4
					J. Haskins	2	2
						1	0
						5	2
		J. Dawson		W. Whiteley		0	2
		J. Orr	B. Pringle	A. Greenwood	E. Etheridge	3	2
						1	0
						0	0
↲ton	F.P. Stanton					5	0
↲lernand			T. Clingman	T. Corwin		6	3
↲oyd	W. Richardson	W. Richardson		A.H. Stephens		1	5
				J. Hickman		2	0
	T.A.R. Hendricks	A. Oliver			R. Fenton	4	0
		J. Knox	G.W. Jones			1	6
	W.R.W. Cobb		A. Sabin			1	2
						0	1
↲itch	T.A.R. Hendricks					1	2
	R. Stanton		L.M. Keitt			2	2
	D.K. Cartter					2	0
						65	63

Table 6
Mean Terms Served in the House of Representatives Prior to their Service as Chairmen of the Standing Committees or Speakers of the House, for Mavericks and Conformists, by Committee

Standing Committees	Mavericks: Mean Terms Served Prior to Appointment as Chairman	Conformists: Mean Term Served Prior to Appointment as Chairman	Mavericks and Conformists Mean Terms Served Prior to Appointment as Chairman
Speaker of the House	3.50	4.75	4.33
Elections	1.67	1.25	1.43
Ways and Means	4.00	5.00	4.57
Claims	4.50	4.17	4.25
Commerce	1.67	1.50	1.57
Public Lands	2.20	3.50	2.50
Post Office and Post Roads	4.00	2.67	3.40
District of Columbia	3.00	2.00	2.67
Judiciary	3.50	6.00	4.00
Revolutionary Claims	—	3.00	3.00
Public Expenditures	1.00	2.50	1.75
Private Land Claims	1.00	—	1.00
Manufacturers	4.40	3.50	4.14
Agriculture	—	1.00	.50
Indian Affairs	2.00	2.00	2.00
Military Affairs	2.00	—	2.00
Militia	—	—	—
Naval Affairs	3.40	—	3.40
Foreign Affairs	3.00	3.67	3.22
Territories	7.00	2.80	3.50
Revolutionary Pensions	1.00	—	1.00
Invalid Pensions	1.25	—	1.25
Roads and Canals	7.00	3.80	4.28
Revisal and Unfinished Business	0	1.00	.67
Accounts	—	5.00	5.00
Mileage	0	0	0
Public Buildings and Grounds	1.00	3.00	2.50
Patents	1.00	—	1.00

"0" denotes no prior term served; "—" denotes no maverick or conformist served as chairman in the 24th through the 36th Congresses.

follow about the leadership styles of the conformists are drawn from evidence about the committee chairmen who did participate to a significant extent in the daily public routine.

Students of the antebellum House will recognize the names of many conformist chairmen as leaders in the second and third party systems. Belonging exclusively to no party or region, they enjoyed in their day the reputation of responsible legislators. They include several Speakers of the House and chairmen of the Ways and Means Committee—probably the most powerful men in their Congresses—as well as one chairman each from Foreign Affairs, Claims, Territories, Commerce, and Roads and Canals. The speakers were all from the South: Robert M. T. Hunter, a Whig turned Democrat, was from Virginia and served as Speaker in the Twenty-Sixth Congress; Howell Cobb, a Democrat, was from Georgia and served as Speaker in the Thirty-First Congress; and Linn Boyd, also a Democrat, was from Kentucky and served as Speaker in the Thirty-Second and Thirty-Third Congresses. The three chairmen of the Ways and Means Committee were all northerners: Churchill C. Cambreleng, a Democrat of New York, who served under Speaker James K. Polk in the Twenty-Fourth and Twenty-Fifth Congresses; Millard Fillmore, a Whig of New York, who served under Speaker John White in the Twenty-Seventh Congress; and Republican John Sherman of Ohio, who served under Speaker William Pennington in the Thirty-Sixth Congress. The other highly active chairmen were as follows: Benjamin Howard, a Democrat of Virginia, who served as chairman of Foreign Affairs in the Twenty-Fifth Congress; Elisha Whittlesey, a Whig of Ohio, who served as chairman of the Claims Committee in the Twenty-Fifth Congress; Stephen A. Douglas, a Democrat of Illinois, who served as chairman of the Territories Committee in the Twenty-Ninth Congress; Robert Schenck, a Whig of Ohio, who served as chairman of the Committee on Roads and Canals in the Thirtieth Congress; and Elihu Washburne, a Republican of Illinois, who served as chairman of the Commerce Committee in the Thirty-Sixth Congress.

Despite the relative youth of the party system, all of the top-ranking conformists accepted the ideology which legitimized it. They believed that parties were the proper vehicle for the expression of differing political opinions, and they thought that the organization of the House should reflect the distribution of power approved by the voters. They applied this latter principle early in the life of the second party system. In 1839, thirty-one-year-old R. M. T. "Bob" Hunter was elected Speaker of the House by the Democrats, although he had only recently followed his mentor, John C. Calhoun, into the ranks of the Democracy. Hunter, for all of his career a far more enthusiastic party man than Calhoun, explained his position in regard to the committee appointments he controlled: "The party upon which it naturally devolved to propose a question [i.e., the majority] ought to have the power to present its proposition in the shape for which it is willing to be responsible."[15] In his view, responsibility rested upon a system that focused power effectively and consistently; his justification for partisan organization was less ideological than pragmatic.

Similar ideas were espoused in a later Congress by Georgian Howell Cobb, another southern Democratic Speaker who, like Hunter, would one day serve the Confederacy as Secretary of State. The good-natured Cobb, who argued in 1848 for "The Necessity for Party Organization" in the House, was elected Speaker in 1849, helped lead the southern forces for compromise in 1850, and worked diligently to defend his party against division through the remainder of the decade.[16] Cobb rarely engaged in floor debate, except to expedite business; and his usual method was to appeal to fellow Democrats to support him, not to debate the issues at hand. There was perhaps no greater master of the mechanics of lawmaking than Cobb. Significantly, however, his successor as Democratic Speaker, Linn Boyd, who served two terms from 1853 to 1857, possessed similar qualities, indicating that the Democrats recognized the need for order and efficiency in the face of divisive uproar.[17]

Given the simplicity of organization in the House, Speakers directed most formal party activity, relying heavily upon the stacked committees for support. Conformist chairmen therefore counselled careful attention to the committee structure of the House, and they were demonstrably annoyed when less responsible legislators sought to argue detailed points of business on the floor rather than in committee. John Sherman, whose moderate views were to become a mainstay of Republican regularity, spoke to the theme of committee utility in the Democratically controlled Thirty-Fifth Congress. Deploring the amount of time the House was wasting in wrangles over minor claims, he insisted that

under the rules of the House they ought to have been referred to the Committee of Claims. That committee is organized for the express purpose of examining this kind of business. It is composed of lawyers. They have no doubt adopted certain rules by which they will be enabled to give to the reports from the Court of Claims, the speedy, minute, and thorough consideration which they deserve.[18]

Sherman's concern was not for the welfare of the Democratic majority on the Claims Committee. His impatience reflects, instead, the general belief of conformists that committee regularity was the only method of achieving efficiency in the cumbersome House.

Conformist leaders resisted assaults on the status and power of the committees they controlled, sometimes to the extent that they stifled discussion in the interest of reaching a decision preordained by committee vote. This was true even of foreign policy debate, which was ostensibly nonpartisan despite usual party unity on roll calls. Debates over foreign policy were usually broad and protracted; this was especially the case when former Secretary of State John Quincy Adams was a participant. On one such occasion in the Twenty-Fifth Congress, Adams rather high-handedly tried to bring into public view the internal divisions about Texas within the Foreign Relations Committee. His method was to poll the individual committee members on their opinions; confident of his superiority, he wanted to force discussion by the whole House. Understandably, the Democratic leadership was adamant in refusing to allow the polling. Chairman Benjamin Howard took refuge in the sanctity of committee prerogatives and indignantly asserted that Adams was being "disrespectful" to the dignity of the committee.[19] It may be safely presumed that Adams was also endangering the security given to committee decisions by the cloak of secrecy which covered its private sessions, a security all the more essential to party leaders when sectional controversy pressured representatives in diverse directions.

Howard's difficulties managing Democratic foreign policy under attack from Adams may serve to highlight another point of importance in the leadership pattern of conformists: compliance with the restraining influence of House rules prescribing politeness and impersonality in debate. Adams commonly employed his unusual intellect with wit and sarcasm to belittle his opponents as well as to stimulate more pertinent discussion. Howard, early in the Texas debate, appealed to his colleagues for sympathy because he "felt himself continually fettered in his remarks, by being obliged to keep constantly present to his mind the conformity of what he was about to say with the rules of the House."[20] For leaders like Howard, personal confrontations only distracted legislators from the flow of important business, while endangering the reputation of the legislature as a body devoted to responsibly conducting the nation's affairs.

The routine business of the Congress occupied center stage for conformist leaders during most sessions of the House, and they repeatedly expressed their sense of duty for expediting basic matters such as revenue bills, which had to originate in the House. Prominent Jacksonian Churchill Cambreleng frequently voiced his frustration over that duty during his service as the Chairman of the Ways and Means Committee in the Twenty-Fourth and Twenty-Fifth Congresses. In the middle of a wandering, philosophical debate over foreign affairs (with discussion dominated by Adams), Cambreleng attempted to "draw the attention of the House not only to the nature of the question itself, and the imperative necessity of acting upon it promptly, but also of the great mass of public business of a character almost equally urgent, remaining to be acted upon."[21] Unimpressed by the request for regularity, Adams ignored Cambreleng's plea, denying that "any haste was necessary," and refusing to rush.[22]

No Congress more clearly manifests the conflict between the regularity of conformist leadership and the disruptive influence they perceived in mavericks than the Twenty-Seventh, which was presided over by an unremarkable maverick Speaker, John White. The most influential Whig leader in the House was the chairman of the Ways and Means Committee, Millard Fillmore, the epitome of antebellum political moderation. In his efforts to help construct Whig economic legislation, Fillmore had the misfortune not only to have to cope with the opposition Democrats but also with the intense factionalism within his own party, which was nearly in ruins after the death of President William Henry Harrison and succession of the states'-rights Vice-President, John Tyler of Virginia. Fillmore, in spite of his difficulties, usually maintained his composure and a cooperative stance. Repeatedly he assured the House Whigs that he was willing to frame a bill to meet their collective desires; but the "corporals guard" were not willing to cooperate with him.[23] Acerbic Henry Wise, Tyler maverick from Virginia's eastern shore, constantly took verbal pot shots at Fillmore, when Wise was not engaged in the running battle with Adams that both seemed perversely to enjoy. Although the lackluster Fillmore is not an especially sympathetic figure, it is hard not to feel for his dilemma when, in desperation over the Adams–Wise display, he appealed to "the House . . . to ask the sober part of this House whether this matter had not gone far enough."[24] Fillmore failed to check the fray; and the Twenty-Seventh House continued in considerable disarray, perhaps not incidentally because six chairmen of important committees were mavericks and he had the support of only three conformist chairmen.

Conformists were not all alike in the manner in which they approached their colleagues; variations among them are evident when all fifty-nine chairmen are surveyed. Some, like Stephen Douglas and Robert Dale Owen, were more inclined than the rest of the group to offer set speeches; this may have been a result of their oratorical abilities as well as their relatively strong theoretical commitment to democratic politics.[25] New England Whigs especially were rather dignified or "respectable"—as they might have put it—in addressing the floor; this was certainly the case for George N. Briggs and Levi Lincoln of Massachusetts, for example, who were chairmen of Post Office and Post Roads and Roads and Canals, respectively, in the Twenty-Fifth Congress. Westerners, whether Whigs or Democrats, tended to label themselves as such, and they were often quite aggressively partisan without personal rancor. The more outspoken southern Democrats orated in a flamboyant style on sectional issues; but that style seems to have applied only to sectional conflicts, not to the larger pattern of their leadership. Despite individual, partisan, or regional varieties, the conformists as chairmen seem to have approached consensus in their concept of the Congress and their role concept of leadership; and the strength of the concepts they shared appears to have overridden other differences.[26]

The attempt of the conformist chairmen to infuse some efficiency into the conduct of congressional business through their leadership was on the whole consistent, even though they operated under stress. Utilization of the regular committee structure appears to have been one method of achieving that goal; self-restraint in debate was another. Regardless of their ambitions, they saw their legislative responsibilities primarily in terms of the institution and its goals. The distinction between this perception of conformists and that of many mavericks was explicitly clarified in a debate during the Twenty-Seventh Congress between conformist Richard Thompson, who later served as chairman of the Elections Committee, and maverick Charles Brown of Pennsylvania. Arguing about the proper size of the House under the terms of the decennial reapportionment, the two men asserted conflicting ideas about the very purpose of the institution. Thompson summed up their differences:

That gentleman, he contended, was for a talking number, while Mr. T. was for a business number. He was willing the gentleman and himself should be taken as fit specimens of what each would have the House composed of. The gentleman had spoken forty items during the session, while Mr. T. had scarcely ever intruded himself upon the House.[27]

A "fit specimen" of a House member interested in business, not talking, Thompson saw discussion on the floor as an intrusion of self into the routine of the legislature.

In light of evolving democratic ideas, the implication of Richard Thompson's comparison is significant. The patrician concept of statesmanship that described legislators as enlightened guardians of the public good was being rejected for a notion more suitable for the pluralistic society of post-Jacksonian America. If legislators truly stood for their constituents, not for themselves, the essential work of making laws could be performed by balancing interests systematically, without extended rational debate of issues. Efficiency, not enlightenment, was the goal. Thompson and other ambitious conformist leaders were pragmatic men who implicitly accepted the democratic model for legislators. They sought to become masters of the developing political machine and in the process to make more predictable the least stable element of the American constitutional system.

NOTES

1. Woodrow Wilson, *Congressional Government: A Study in American Politics* (Boston: Houghton Mifflin Co., 1885), p. 82.

2. Useful for an overview is George Galloway, *History of the House of Representatives* (New York: Crowell, 1953). Three excellent collections of articles on the Congress which provide some limited historical perspective are Ralph K. Huitt and Robert L. Peabody, eds., *Congress: Two Decades of Analysis*, Harper's American Political Behavior Series, ed. by David J. Danelski (New York: Harper & Row, 1969); Samuel C. Patterson, ed., *American Legislative Behavior, a Reader* (Princeton: D. Van Nostrand Co., 1968); and Robert L. Peabody and Nelson W. Polsby, eds., *New Perspectives on the House of Representatives*, 2d ed. (Chicago: Rand McNally & Co., 1969). The most useful single contribution of political scientists to an understanding of the development of the House is Nelson W. Polsby, "The Institutionalization of the U. S. House of Representatives," *American Political Science Review* 62 (March 1968):144–168. Polsby's contribution is discussed in a thoughtful essay about the status of historical studies of the legislature in Robert Zemsky, "American Legislative Behavior," in *Emerging Theoretical Models in Social and Political History*, ed. by Allan G. Bogue, Sage Contemporary Social Science Issues, vol. 9 (Beverly Hills and London: Sage Publications, 1973), pp. 57–76. Also useful is Bogue et al., "Members of the House of Representatives and the Process of Modernization, 1789–1960." Every student of Congress can benefit from the contribution of Robert U. Goehlert and John R. Sayre, *The United States Congress: A Bibliography* (New York: The Free Press of Macmillan Co., 1982).

3. Polsby's "Institutionalization of the House," which surveys the entire life of the body, is a notable exception.

4. For the antebellum period, Alexander, *Sectional Stress and Party Strength*; and Silbey, *Shrine of Party* are standard works.

5. Donald R. Matthews, *U. S. Senators and Their World* (New York: Vintage Books,

1960), perceptively discusses legislative norms in the twentieth century, but there is nothing comparable for the nineteenth century. There is a useful comparison between the mid-century condition of organization in the House and Senate in Frank Joseph Tusa, "Congressional Politics in the Secession Crisis, 1859–61," (Ph.D. diss. Pennsylvania State University, 1975), 5–70.

6. Page references for remarks on the floor of the House made by mavericks and conformists were taken from the index to the *Congressional Globe* for the thirteen Congresses studied. For most congressmen high participation was not the rule. It was immediately evident, moreover, that comparing the number of times mavericks and conformists spoke did not reveal significant differences between the two types, since the page entry might refer to a simple motion, to an extended debate, or to the beginning of a long speech. To give an example, John Quincy Adams and Churchill C. Cambreleng were two congressmen who spoke quite frequently in the Twenty-Fifth Congress, yet there is little resemblance in the kind of contributions they made. Counting page references alone would have placed them in the same category. For each congressman, then, an attempt was made to read as far in the *Congressional Globe* as was necessary to establish the existence of a pattern of behavior on the floor. Once a pattern seemed clear for each maverick or conformist, the collective interaction of all congressmen was followed through the text of the relevant volumes of the *Globe*. For most men there were too few entries in any session to make an assessment of congressional style. Reading did reveal, however, that most chairmen of committees were high participators; thus the final analysis in this chapter rests on the behavior of the chairmen. A small group of mavericks and conformists—six mavericks and seven conformists—were not in formal leadership positions during the thirteen Congresses but were very active. References to their behavior on the floor and outside of the House will be made in later chapters.

7. Randall B. Ripley, *Party Leaders in the House of Representatives* (Washington, D.C.: The Brookings Institution, 1967), deals with the subject after the Civil War. Norman Ornstein, ed., *Changing Congress: The Committee System*, in *The Annals of the American Academy of Political and Social Science*, ed. by Richard D. Lambert, Vol. 411 (January 1974), contains essays useful for understanding the committee system, but few of the essays have historical perspective. An overview of the early committee system is found in Joseph Cooper, *The Origin of the Standing Committees and the Development of the Modern House*, Rice University, *Studies*, LVI, no. 3 (1970).

8. Young, *Washington Community*, p. 202. The most useful analysis for the early years of the nineteenth century is in Noble Cunningham, *The Process of Government under Jefferson*; see esp. Ch. X, "The Anatomy of Congressional Committees."

9. Polsby, "Institutionalization of the House," 156–158; and Cunningham, *Process of Government under Jefferson*, pp. 276–278.

10. Nicholas Masters, "Committee Assignments," in Peabody and Polsby, *New Perspectives on the House of Representatives*, pp. 227–252; originally published as "Committee Assignments in the House of Representatives," *American Political Science Review* 55 (June 1961):345–357.

11. Ibid., pp. 240–241.

12. The importance of alternative models in the twentieth century is noted in Ralph K. Huitt, "The Outsider in the Senate: An Alternative Role," in Huitt and Peabody, *Congress: Two Decades of Analysis*, pp. 159–178. Huitt's analysis of Senator William Proxmire's role in the Senate effectively makes the point that maverick behavior can be

an excellent means to achieve the goals of a political figure and that such behavior is accepted as legitimate within the Senate whether it is popular or not (p. 171).

13. See Table 3. On the other hand, mavericks changed party more often than conformists, which might be expected to have negatively affected their usefulness as chairmen.

14. See, Chs. 6, 8, and 9.

15. *Congressional Globe*, 26th Cong., 2d Sess., 284. Hunter's cousin, James M. Garnett, wrote him in 1838:

I think you utterly wrong in the notion which you seem to entertain, that to be useful in public life, a man *must* join some political party or other. . . . I much fear the effect of our apparent belief, that all men must be either drones, or nonentities in political life, unless they will fall into these ranks, and be led or driven, as party politics require.

Quoted in Charles Henry Ambler, ed., *Correspondence of Robert M. T. Hunter, 1826–1876*, Vol. II of *Annual Report of the American Historical Association for the Year 1916* (Washington, D.C.: American Historical Association, 1918), pp. 28–30.

16. Howell Cobb, *Necessity for Party Organization. Speech of Mr. Howell Cobb, of Georgia, in the House of Representatives, Saturday July 1, 1848*. (Washington, D.C.: Congressional Globe Office, 1848). Cobb's career as a successful partisan is described in John Eddins Simpson, *Howell Cobb, the Politics of Ambition* (Chicago: Adams, 1973). See also Joel H. Silbey, "Parties and Politics in Mid–Nineteenth Century America: A Quantitative and Behavioral Examination," *Capitol Studies* 1 (Fall 1972):27.

17. Cobb and Boyd are compared in Holman Hamilton, *The Compromise of 1850* (New York: W. W. Norton & Co., 1966), pp. 35–36. Cobb was characterized by an opponent who served as Clerk of the House while he was a member as a man who "never persecuted the men of his party who refused to endorse extreme measures; yet he was most resolute in behalf of his State and section"; see DeAlva Stanwood Alexander, *History and Procedure of the House of Representatives* (Boston: Houghton Mifflin Co., 1916), p. 22. Alexander, himself a Republican congressman, did not altogether avoid bias in his assessments, but because he did attempt to evaluate all major leaders of nineteenth-century Congresses, his work is useful.

18. *Congressional Globe*, 35th Cong., 1st Sess., 321.

19. Ibid., 25th Cong., 2d Sess., 453.

20. Ibid., p. 63.

21. Ibid., p. 193.

22. Ibid.

23. The wreckage of the Tyler administration is surveyed in Robert J. Morgan, *A Whig Embattled: The Presidency under John Tyler* (Lincoln: University of Nebraska Press, 1954).

24. *Congressional Globe*, 27th Cong., 2d Sess., 173–177.

25. This commitment is described in Robert W. Johannsen, *Stephen A. Douglas* (New York: Oxford University Press, 1973) and Robert Dale Owen, *Threading My Way: An Autobiography* (New York: G. W. Carleton & Co., 1874; New York: Augustus M. Kelley, Publishers, 1967).

26. For some conformists, the leadership role may have been more difficult than for others. It almost comes as a surprise, for example, to find Democratic conformist Lawrence Keitt, the South Carolina fire-eater, urging the House to "facilitate business." But Keitt was clearly aware of the limits to personal preference placed upon him by the responsibilities of his status. Having failed to study a measure available to him for nearly a

year, he lectured those of his colleagues who wished to postpone consideration because of their similar neglect: "It was my fault; and I shall not come here and ask the members of this House who may have done their duty, to suspend the public business of the country, because I had not done mine." The hot-tempered Keitt performed his duties as chairman of the Committee on Public Buildings and Public Grounds, admittedly a minor responsibility, in a routine fashion, reserving his ire for sectional matters. See *Congressional Globe*, 33d Cong., 2d Sess., 66, 80. Also revealing is the debate in this same Congress over the use of a special committee to investigate rival patent claims for the Colt revolver. See esp. the remarks of conformist Alfred Edgerton, chairman of the Claims Committee, pp. 553, 557, and 651; in the latter instance he was baited by maverick Thomas Clingman but refused to be drawn into "any personal controversy."

27. Ibid., 27th Cong., 2d Sess., 436. Both Brown and Thompson were reasonably active in this session of the Twenty-Seventh Congress, Brown speaking over fifty times and Thompson about thirty times. The quality of the remarks, however, was quite dissimilar, as Brown was consistently disruptive and Thompson consistently businesslike.

CHAPTER 4

Mavericks and the Elevated Stage of Politics

> Standing on the elevated stage we occupy, every example for good or for evil, passes down throughout all the avenues of society, and affects, with a fearful responsibility, the public morals and public liberty.
>
> Robert Barnwell Rhett,
> Speech in the House of Representatives, 1839

Barnwell Rhett had little respect for democratic institutions, so it is no wonder that his view of the House had an olympian tone. Concern for his "fearful responsibility" to protect the masses by "passing down" a proper example seems anachronistic in the era of the popular slogan "the voice of the people is the voice of God."[1] To note that such a paternalistic vision of the legislature is sharply at odds with the "business" model of the leading conformists is perhaps to state the obvious. While the radically conservative South Carolinian did not speak for all mavericks, most shared some of his republican ideas and questioned aspects of the more modern style adopted by successful conformists.

It is accurate to characterize the conformists' concept of legislative responsibility as pragmatic and functionally oriented. Mavericks, however, did not exhibit a common behavior pattern, and their attitudes toward the House reflect much more personalized ideas about responsibility. Many viewed the House less as an institution with important legislative functions than as a means for exercising exemplary popular leadership or as a stage for their ego display. Some acted clearly in ways conflicting with the efficient exercise of legislative power. By-passing the committees and other regular channels of action, especially on questions of importance to them, mavericks sometimes appeared to stand almost outside of the institution, even in antagonism to it. Most mavericks understood the need for acting under the House rules and were cooperative at least some of the time. But also, for most of them, a root inclination for egocentric leadership prevented any consistently cooperative or conforming behavior.

Because of the variety among mavericks, it is, for the most part, difficult to describe their leadership in a summary fashion. Interestingly, however, the difficulty is least troublesome in dealing with the four mavericks who held the most important positions in the House between 1836 and 1860. These are the two Speakers (John White, a Whig from Kentucky who held the office in the Twenty-Seventh Congress, and James L. Orr, a Democrat from South Carolina, who presided over the Thirty-Fifth House) and two chairmen of the Ways and Means Committee, George S. Houston of Alabama, the Democratic chairman in the Thirty-Second and Thirty-Third Congresses, and Lewis D. Campbell, the Whig/Republican of Ohio, who chaired the committee in the Thirty-Fourth Congress.

At these very top levels of House leadership, it is important that differences between mavericks and conformists blurred. The highest ranking mavericks met many of the same behavioral expectations that conformists seemed to have perceived. Like conformists, mavericks in the top positions were rather like the responsible legislators of the twentieth century. This suggests that role expectations for the key positions were fairly well defined and that success in those positions may well have been a partial function of the degree to which individuals were willing or able to meet those expectations. On the other hand, the most important maverick leaders were not equally successful. According to one historian of the House, Speaker John White typified the "violence and irregularity" of the Congress in the 1830s,[2] but it was White's misfortune to preside over the Whig debacle in the Twenty-Seventh Congress, which no leader could have controlled adequately. Caught between the southern states'-rights Whigs and nationalists like conformist Millard Fillmore, whom he appointed as chairman of the powerful Ways and Means Committee, he appeared to share the economic views of the latter. Consequently, his decisions from the podium were frequently contested by both Whig factions and by the Democratic minority.[3] A Democratic maverick, delighted at the Whig confusion, described the situation cuttingly: " *'Quem deus vult perdere, prius dementat,'* Whom the gods would destroy, they first made mad. (Laughter)"[4] Probably the beleaguered Speaker did not join the laughter. All in all, White appears to have done less to lead the fractious Whigs than Fillmore, supposedly his subordinate.[5]

Maverick speaker James Orr fared much better in the Thirty-Fifth Congress, but then his Democratic party was strongly united in the face of growing Republican power. Not strongly partisan, Orr was fundamentally a congenial and philosophically moderate man.[6] As Speaker and chairman of the Indian Affairs Committee in the Thirty-Third Congress, he worked hard and effectively for his party, resembling a conformist leader. A controversial figure in South Carolina politics, he joined the Republican party during Reconstruction.[7] In his moderation and toleration, Orr met standards for responsible leadership. In his intellectual orientation and later independence from party, he had more in common with other maverick leaders.

Alabamian George S. Houston was a powerful figure in the House in the 1850s, serving twice as chairman of the Ways and Means Committee and once as chairman of the Judiciary Committee. Often ill tempered in arguments, Houston pushed mightily for his legislation and for Democratic policies, by this time being framed largely to suit southern standards.[8] Although his leadership was not irregular in those respects, Houston's style of debate was unusual, "sometimes baffling and frequently bewildering men of greater knowledge."[9] Like other mavericks, he took seriously the intellectual quality of debate while also paying heed to the effectiveness of practical business, more often attended to by conformists.

Houston was succeeded as Chairman of the Ways and Means Committee by one of his favorite opponents, Lewis D. Campbell, a Whig maverick who had become a Republican and was made chairman of the committee in the first Republican controlled House, the Thirty-Fifth. During his first term in Congress, Campbell had spoken so infrequently that when he rose, it was to address his constituents:

Although I have, at all times, during the present session, been in my seat ready to vote, I have not consumed one minute in discussion. . . . I have recently received a letter, in which I am informed that, in consequence of my *silence* here, some of my constituents inquire whether I am dead? They will now learn that I am still "alive and kicking."[10]

In later Congresses, Campbell began to assert himself in rather typical western form, taking an active roll in floor discussions. Campbell could not, however, exert leadership in a consistent direction because his views coincided fully with those of neither party. An opponent of slavery, he argued fiercely with southerners, perhaps most notably with Alexander H. Stephens, another former Whig maverick.[11] But he strongly disapproved of the radical course of Joshua Giddings and of the higher law doctrine of William H. Seward which he said would lead to "bloody revolution—to civil war—to anarchy."[12] As a westerner, he was in favor of internal improvements, but he was generally opposed to the expansion of the federal government; fittingly, he ended his career as a Democrat. These ideological variations from party positions created his problems. As he later in his life acknowledged: "I am a very poor follower of party when I consider it in error, and . . . I should make a very inefficient leader."[13]

Possessing energies and abilities of varying degree, the mavericks did not make outstanding leaders in the House positions they filled; on the other hand, none was known primarily for his individuality. The same cannot be said for the mavericks in the less important leadership positions, where there was probably more latitude to be independent and where it is possible that there was less filtering of potential appointees and less party pressure for conformity. Here congressmen who were mavericks in voting behavior displayed a wide variety of leadership patterns, some of which bear little resemblance to any concept of responsible leadership. An attempt to categorize the individualistic mavericks runs the risk of oversimplification, but for the sake of clarity a few subgroups can be tentatively identified.

Two outstanding mavericks often stood together in an unpopular position of antagonism to the regular business of Congress. Although they were respected by many of their colleagues for the consistency of their ideas and their moral stance, John Quincy Adams and Joshua Giddings were among the most disruptive of all antebellum congressmen, especially in pursuit of antislavery goals. Giddings, oddly enough, served as chairman of the Claims Committee twice, in the Twenty-Seventh and the Thirty-Fourth Congresses, acting in a position of considerable responsibility with a formally businesslike manner. But Giddings acting in behalf of Claims and Giddings on any issue touching remotely upon a slavery matter were two different leaders.[14] It is paradoxical that a man who openly expressed his contempt for the Congress could perform his committee role with effectiveness, but it seems to have been the case. Even the Democrats, who certainly did not like Giddings' general disruptiveness, retained him as a member of the Claims Committee twice, perhaps because he was less destructive to their aims there than elsewhere, perhaps also because he could by virtue of his experience make some practical contribution.

Adams likewise was retained on the Committee on Manufactures in both Democratic and Whig Congresses, serving as chairman of the committee four times in the Democratic controlled Twenty-Fourth, Twenty-Fifth, Twenty-Sixth, and Twenty-Eighth Congresses and also in the Whig dominated Twenty-Seventh Congress. But Adams was not a congressman with a committee orientation; his attention ranged over the entire business of Congress, and no matter was too minute for his consideration. Adams' disregard for the rules of Congress and for the feelings and pride of his fellow congressmen was often apparent. As he remarked in response to an attempt by the Speaker in the Twenty-Fifth Congress to call him to order for persisting in discussion on the gag rule: "I was merely giving notice of my intention to move to rescind that infamous resolution. I do not submit to that resolution, any more than I am obliged to submit to the power of the House."[15] Adams and Giddings were almost unequalled in their abilities to turn the calm atmosphere of the House on a quiet day into a snarling melee, yet they were kept in positions of responsibility. Their combined impact was certainly not insignificant.

Other maverick chairmen shared with Adams and Giddings a personalized view of politics and broadly intellectual concepts of congressional business; some were almost as disruptive, despite their positions of responsibility. Three whose self-consciously intellectual orientation was especially noticeable were Frederick Stanton of Tennessee and Charles J. Ingersoll of Pennsylvania, both Democrats, and Caleb Cushing of Massachusetts, a Whig who became a Democrat after the Tyler administration.[16]

Stanton and Ingersoll were both interested in foreign relations from a scientific and philosophical point of view. Ingersoll was chairman of the important Foreign Affairs Committee in the Twenty-Eighth and Twenty-Ninth Congresses. Stanton chaired the Naval Affairs Committee in the Thirty-Second Congress, having served on it for the three previous Congresses; he also chaired the Judiciary Committee in the Thirty-Third Congress. Stanton, even in his first Congress when he recognized himself as "inconsequential," spoke on a wide range of issues.[17] In addition to speeches on Oregon and internal improvements—key issues—he participated in the debate about the Smithsonian Institution's future, spoke in defense of printing a naval almanac with Ingersoll and Adams, and became involved with mavericks Adams, George S. Houston, Isaac Holmes, and other Whigs in what the *Globe* reporter described as a "very long scientific debate in relation to the theory of storms, the Baconian philosophy, and the utility of Mr. Espy's researches."[18] This pattern of broad involvement was typical of Stanton's congressional career; and although the subject of debate often related to his leading interests in naval affairs and the progress of science, he could by no means be described as a legislative specialist.

Stanton let his attention range far more widely than was likely to encourage the expediting of congressional business, but he was courteous and contained in his style of debate. Ingersoll, on the other hand, was one of the more unrestrained debaters in the House, a favorite target of John Q. Adams and sometimes his equal in disruptiveness. Declaring in his first term that "he did not know how parties stood here. He did not know, and he did not care, how they were to vote on this question," he regarded his judgment as superior to party considerations.[19]

How little bound by House norms of personal behavior Ingersoll was can readily be seen in his interaction with Adams over the international slave trade, a subject about which both believed themselves to have authoritative knowledge. Ingersoll wished to "uphold freedom of the seas," a view which Adams attacked intemperately.[20] Ingersoll responded acidly: "As usual, the gentleman chooses to indulge his passions, and play the termagant whenever anything is said which does not happen to suit his senile notions."[21] To the laughter of the other members, Adams responded by imitating Ingersoll's "peculiar manner" of speaking.[22] The debates carried over to the next day, when Adams attacked not only Ingersoll but also his hometown, Philadelphia, and Ingersoll rose to "repel and retort the blackguardism of the Member from Massachusetts."[23] Later in the session, Ingersoll even attacked the merits of Adams' poetry.[24] These displays of temper may have brought some personal satisfaction to the participants; the antics may have entertained the galleries; but in regard to the business of the House, neither member was being responsible.

Caleb Cushing, Adams' home-state opponent, was often as offensive in debate as Adams and Ingersoll and was certainly as intellectual in his approach, particularly to the subject of foreign affairs, about which he considered himself an authority. Cushing spoke enthusiastically and long-windedly about every kind of subject; Adams called one of his efforts "metaphysical and hair-splitting," a description which might apply to the more arcane addresses of either New Englander.[25] Cushing believed strongly in the educational responsibility of the House, and he openly attacked the committee system and its secretive approach to business:

How long is this House to fold itself in the mantle of its dignity; covering itself up in dullness; refusing to utter its opinion, suppressing opinion and debate; disdaining, as it were to treat the people fairly, in the light of day manfully and honestly, as becomes their representatives.[26]

Closed committee sessions precluded public enlightenment on critical issues; partisan action based on committee decisions hurried measures through the House to further damage public knowledge. In an encounter with Churchill Cambreleng, who was trying in vain to close debate on a money bill, Cushing protested "the principle of regarding the appropriations bills as the only matter of public business worth attending," and he denounced the practice of "any one gentleman consenting to let other business be taken up only at his convenience."[27] For erudite mavericks like Adams, Ingersoll, and Cushing, the elevated stage of the House could serve the public interest only if organization and efficiency were sometime subordinated to enlightened discussion.[28]

Several Democratic mavericks were self-proclaimed representatives of the farming and western interests. Often speaking in a straightforward and unpolished style, they attempted to explain the views of the plain people. Six of this sort were John McClernand of Illinois, James Bowlin of Missouri, David K. Cartter and David Disney of Ohio, Alfred Greenwood of Arkansas, and Williamson R. W. Cobb of Alabama. Although some of these men were quite well educated, generally speaking they did not approach politics intellectually.

Cobb and Cartter were characteristically blunt and outspoken in their conduct. Cobb was a spokesman for the small farmers of northern Alabama, and he was, by reputation, something of a demagogue. Public land policy and railroads were his almost exclusive concern, and he served for five terms on the Public Lands Committee, once as chairman in the Thirty-Fifth Congress during his fourth term. Cobb characterized himself as a "clod hopper" and publicly prided himself on his common sense.[29] He fought aggressively for the public lands bills, often displaying his temper when things did not suit him, whether he was with the majority of his committee or not. Although he appeared to be efficient and more concerned with action than with speech making, he also had a definitely egocentric conception of congressional business, and he reacted sharply when his business was interrupted or his judgment on a measure was questioned.[30]

Cartter, like Cobb, was boastful about his "unsophisticated rustic opinion," which, he asserted, could not be "whipped out of me no how."[31] Cartter's floor behavior was often flamboyant and certainly highly individualistic. On one occasion he corrected the chairman of the Ways and Means Committee, a member of his own party, with the testy observation: "I make the point of order because he made one on me the other day."[32] Often Cartter softened his sharp words with humor, not always evident out of context, as when he observed that two fellow Democrats did not have "the power of defining what the Democratic party is, even if they have the ability."[33] Cartter's chairmanship of the Patents Committee in the Thirty-Second Congress was a probable consequence of his own enthusiasm for tinkering; a biographical sketch describes his inventions, including such useful household oddities as a device to hold bed covers off of the sleeper's feet.[34] Cobb and Cartter were not equal in importance in the Congress, as Cobb consistently exercised greater power, but their styles were similar, nonetheless, in their rough-hewn eccentricities.

The other four western spokesmen—McClernand, Bowlin, Disney, and Greenwood—were much more dignified and reserved in manner than Cobb and Cartter. Three were chairmen of the Public Lands Committee like Cobb: McClernand served on that committee in the Twenty-Eighth through the Thirtieth Congresses, acting as chairman in his second term on the committee; Bowlin was chairman in the Thirty-First Congress, his first on the committee; and Disney chaired the committee in the Thirty-Third Congress, his first term on that committee. Greenwood headed the Committee on Indian Affairs in the Thirty-Fifth Congress. These Democrats were not rough and tumble debaters but assumed a more elevated tone in public address. McClernand, for example, attributed his support of the small farmers to the theory that "cheap lands are the bulwark of republicanism."[35] He, like the others, was very active in debate through most of his service in the House. McClernand and Disney, both closely identified with the interests of Stephen A. Douglas, were also expert behind-the-scenes operators of significant skill, illustrating a combination of talents not uncharacteristic of many moderate nonconformists.[36]

No single thread of political philosophy or behavior unites the maverick chairmen from the Northeast or the West; but for eight southern mavericks the imprint of states'-rights ideas and early American republicanism is apparent in varying degrees on each chairman. Perhaps their common ground is a result of the attempt to reconcile national party and southern regional interests, although the ideological and philosophical similarities among them do not extend to the level of policy.

Two of these maverick chairmen from the South, James Garland of Virginia and Cost Johnson of Maryland, served in congresses before the Mexican War and both spoke in language reminiscent of the revolutionary generation about the politics of the Jackson period. Garland, a Democrat, chaired the Judiciary Committee in the Twenty-Fifth Congress; and Johnson, a Whig, chaired the Committee on the District of Columbia in the Twenty-Sixth and Twenty-Seventh Congresses. Garland, in a long speech for public distribution, attacked his own party for an attempt to destroy him politically during the very Congress in which he chaired the Judiciary Committee. Insisting that he acted upon duty rather than for party, he couched his protest in terms of the antiparty sentiments of the eighteenth century.[37] Johnson, like Garland, explicitly attacked his own party, asserting that "the proscriptive spirit of both parties was but a modified form of that crusade which drove half of Europe to lose its best blood on the dry sands of Asia."[38] Both congressmen were genial and orderly in their floor activities, though Johnson was inclined to wander with other mavericks through the often irrelevant debates of the Twenty-Seventh Congress. Given their antiparty feelings, however, it is probably understandable that they did not occupy top positions.

Three southerners of a less antique version than Garland or Johnson were Tyler supporters: Henry Wise, Francis Pickens, and John Campbell. Acid-tongued Wise chaired the Naval Affairs committee in the Twenty-Seventh and Twenty-Eighth Congresses; Pickens, later Governor of South Carolina at the time of the firing on Fort Sumter, chaired the Foreign Affairs Committee in the Twenty-Sixth Congress and served on important Ways and Means in the Twenty-Seventh Congress; Campbell, a less important Carolinian, was chairman of the Elections Committee in the Twenty-Sixth Congress and of the Committee on the District of Columbia in the Twenty-Eighth Congress. All three were Whigs in early Congresses but became Democrats during the Tyler years. Although they were joined in their support of some Tyler measures and opposed to the nationalistic Whigs of the North, they disagreed among themselves enthusiastically. Aware of their minority status, it seems clear that they were often deliberately disruptive, determined to prevent regular business if they could not control it. Campbell explained the behavior on philosophical grounds, "He was aware that delay in legislation was often caused by the House. Yet he thought the people had the intelligence to know that was one of the inconveniences which they had to suffer as the price they had to pay for their liberties."[39] Efficiency, in the interest of bad legislation aimed at party objectives, was less a virtue than full discussion, which could educate the public to its interests. Perhaps partially out of a sense of frustration, these maverick chairmen refused to accept the pragmatic standards of responsibility common to many other leaders.

Three other southern mavericks served in Congress from the Twenty-Eighth Congress to the Thirty-Fifth. Thomas Clingman of North Carolina, a Whig who became a Democrat, served as chairman of the Foreign Affairs Committee in the Thirty-Fifth Congress, his third term on that committee; Alexander Stephens of Georgia, a Whig who switched to the Democratic party in the mid–1850s, served also as a chairman in the Thirty-Fifth Congress, heading the Territories Committee; and George W. Jones of Tennessee was chairman of the Rules Committee in the Thirty-Second Congress (during which Congress he also served on the Ways and Means Committee), and he was chairman of the Roads and Canals Committee in the Thirty-Fifth Congress. There were a total of seven Democratic mavericks serving as chairmen in the Thirty-Fifth Congress; and James Orr, maverick from South Carolina, was the Speaker of the House. These Democrats, however, disagreed furiously among themselves.

Jones, who served on the Ways and Means Committee for four terms, was clearly in a leadership position for many years. But he in no way resembled the relatively quiet leadership exerted by the conformists who served on that important committee. Jones was often ill tempered and did not hesitate to display his anger on the floor, despite his insistence on one occasion that "I am no bully; I am no duelist; and with such I have nothing to do."[40] Jones often worked closely with maverick George S. Houston of Alabama, whose views and temperament seemed to resemble his, but characteristically they spent as much time arguing with fellow Democrats, and often with each other, as in exercising responsible leadership. For example, in the Thirty-Third Congress, Jones, Houston, and W. R. W. Cobb, all Democratic mavericks, consumed so much time in disputes over the public lands bill—each insisting that they were "friends" of the bill—that Cobb was moved to argue that "it has been the friends of the measure, and not the enemies, who have thus long delayed its passage."[41] The southern "friends" were not always a congenial group.

Alexander Stephens, later Vice-President of the Confederacy, did not serve in formal leadership positions for most of his sixteen years in Congress, perhaps partly because of his continuous poor health. Before his final antebellum term, however, he had served on many of the most important committees in Congress, including Ways and Means (twice), Claims (twice), Commerce (twice), Public Lands, Rules and Elections—and this despite the fact that he changed parties in the 1850s. It is evident that his abilities and power were recognized, but they were not the usual sort of political abilities. A man of great intelligence, Stephens was perhaps more fitted to serve behind the scenes than to lead other men in a formal manner.[42] He may have been too convinced of his own intellectual and moral superiority to cooperate with others, especially those with whom he disagreed, whom he was inclined to dismiss as inferior men.

Thomas Clingman of North Carolina was another unique figure in the antebellum Congresses. Whereas Stephens was gentlemanly, even if privately contemptuous of his fellows, the orator Clingman was belligerently self-assertive and assaulted those who dared disagree with him, as nearly everyone did at one time or another. He thought himself an intellectual and participated enthusiastically on topics concerning science, education, or philosophy.[43] His service as chairman of the Foreign Affairs Committee in the Thirty-Fifth Congress did not, fortunately, involve him in sensitive issues of major scope, because he was certainly unfit to handle them.

Clingman did not discriminate between Democrats and Whigs in his attacks; and though he served in both parties, he had seemingly little respect for either. In an extreme instance of his contempt for regularity, he suggested in a Democratic Congress, while serving on the Foreign Affairs Committee, that the Public Lands Committee, headed by a fellow Democrat maverick, David Disney, be abolished entirely because it was so worthless.[44] His choice as chairman of the Foreign Affairs Committee would appear utterly senseless, if it were assumed that any kind of responsibility to party, or respect for fellow congressmen, were a prerequisite. That Clingman followed in the footsteps of Francis Pickens, Caleb Cushing, and Charles Ingersoll strongly suggests that such characteristics evidently were not prerequisite.

Most of the remaining maverick chairmen served in less important positions than those sketched above. Many were perhaps not critically involved in congressional business. Maverick John Pendleton Kennedy, the southern Whig novelist and bonafide intellectual, served as chairman of the Commerce Committee in the Twenty-Seventh Congress; and although he brought dignity and moderation to a Congress that sorely needed those qualities, his real interests were not centrally political, much less partisan. Kennedy participated very little in floor debates and may have followed the leadership of his friend Millard Fillmore, the chairman of the Ways and Means Committee. Other examples of the less involved maverick chairmen include James Meacham, chairman of the Committee of the District of Columbia in the Thirty-Fourth Congress, who was an abolitionist and Congregationalist minister and an infrequent participant in debates, and Thomas J. D. Fuller, a New England Democrat who so poorly managed his Commerce Committee in the Thirty-Third Congress that his fellow Democratic members attempted to get a bill out of committee without his cooperation, an effort which he denounced on the floor.[45] Some of the less active maverick chairmen may have agreed with one of their kind, Democrat John Henley of Indiana, who described himself as ''utterly and entirely disgusted with the whole system of speech making, as it prevailed in the House of Representatives.''[46] In any case, none appears to have been a major figure in the antebellum Congresses.

The dramatic contrast between the generally moderate but partisan leadership of the outstanding conformists and the widely varied and sometimes extreme leadership of important mavericks can be viewed as the result of alternative responses to the institutional boundaries within which the men operated. Members of one group, the conformists, appear to have adapted themselves more readily to the restrictions inherent in the developing organization of the House. Mavericks, taking their behavioral cues from sources antecedent to or outside of their congressional experience, refused to be so easily shaped. Parliamentary procedure, House rules, the committee system, and regular party leadership all served to hedge in and define the pattern of an individual congressman's impact. These devices, intended to aid the efficient and effective exercises of congressional power, incidentally required a good measure of conformity; and some mavericks resisted that tendency in floor behavior as they did in voting.

Without a thorough study of committees and their significance in the Congresses of the antebellum period, it is impossible to assess fully the relative effectiveness of mavericks and conformists in their roles as leaders of the House of Representatives. The resemblance of conformist leaders to the Masters' model of responsible legislators suggests that they anticipated the development of future years and that the emergence of their common style was part of the institutionalization of the House. But in the face of persistent criticism about the effectiveness of the twentieth-century Congress, a judgment against the maverick individualism hardly seems fitting. Their often stated conviction that the House was to deliberate and discuss politics while each man acted with independent judgment probably has more relevance to the political theories of the revolutionary and constitutional period than to the broker theories of the mid–twentieth century; perhaps also their ideas were more suitable in the relatively homogeneous eighteenth-century republic than in the complex nineteenth-century nation on the brink of modernization.

To assess the congressional significance of John Quincy Adams and Stephen

Douglas—to personalize the mavericks and conformists with their giant figures—must rest ultimately on a judgment about the moral nature of democratic politics, an assessment surely beyond the necessary scope of the historian's work. The color and excitement—not to mention personal character—mavericks lent to the antebellum Congresses may have impeded the calm resolution of social and economic problems with critical sectional implications. But on the other hand, it is equally possible that the pragmatism of the conformist leadership so poorly reflected the significant emotional and ideological differences in the nation that their leadership was ineffective in the long run.[47]

NOTES

1. *Congressional Globe*, 25th Cong., 2d Sess., 508.

2. DeAlva S. Alexander, *History and Procedure of the House*, pp. 114–118.

3. For a good example, see *Congressional Globe*, 27th Cong., 2d Sess., 92.

4. Ibid., p. 735.

5. DeAlva S. Alexander, *History and Procedure of the House*, p. 27, calls White a "party tool." Glyndon Van Deusen dismisses White as "a Clay man with little else to recommend him," in his *The Life of Henry Clay* (Boston: Little, Brown and Co., 1937), p. 345.

6. His views on partisanship and practicality are stated in the *Congressional Globe*, 33d Cong., 2d Sess., 142. See also Nichols, *Disruption of American Democracy*, pp. 157, 354, and 356. DeAlva S. Alexander calls him the "best tempered of the able ultras of the South," in *History and Procedure of the House*, p. 19.

7. The vagaries of Orr's political career are recounted in Roger P. Leemhuis, *James L. Orr and the Sectional Conflict* (Washingtion, D.C.: University Press of America, 1979).

8. See, for example, *Congressional Globe*, 33d Cong., 2d Sess., 138, 840.

9. DeAlva S. Alexander, *History and Procedure of the House*, p. 121. Alexander also comments that Houston had "neither patience nor political tact," and asserts that Houston "simply knew nothing of the social temper which in this day insists that the first duty of a gentleman is to apologize for an unjust or offensive expression in debate."

10. *Congressional Globe*, 31st Cong., 2d Sess., 589.

11. Ibid., 33d Cong., 2d Sess., 58ff.

12. Ibid.

13. *The Tariff on Agricultural Products. Speech of Hon. Lewis D. Campbell, of Butler County, Delivered in the Senate of Ohio, Wednesday, Mar. 9th, 1870* (n.p., n.d.), p. 2. DeAlva Alexander noted: "For a man of marked ability, Campbell proved, perhaps, the most disappointing of floor leaders. His speeches, admirable for freshness and vigor, had given him great prestige . . . [but] his erratic views, backed with cynical frankness, soon disclosed weakness as a leader." DeAlva S. Alexander, *History and Procedure of the House*, p. 122.

14. A full study of Giddings' congressional career is in James B. Stewart, *Joshua R. Giddings and the Tactics of Radical Politics* (Cleveland: Press of Case Western Reserve University, 1970).

15. *Congressional Globe*, 25th Cong., 2d Sess., 64.

16. A less notable Whig who exhibited similar traits was Joseph Underwood of Ken-

tucky, a loyal Whig until the Civil War. Underwood served on minor committees throughout his four terms in Congress, chairing the Committee on the District of Columbia in
his last term. He did, however, participate enthusiastically in debate, especially in the
rowdy debates of the Twenty-Seventh Congress, where he sided with the national Whigs
as opposed to the Tyler group. Underwood even entered into the Wise–Adams debates
on the side of Adams, urging respect for the person of the former President, whose
abilities he admired. Ibid., p. 182. Underwood acted in this instance with another southern
maverick, John Minor Botts of Virginia.

17. Ibid., 29th Cong., 1st Sess., 199.

18. Ibid., p. 846.

19. Ibid., 27th Cong., 2d Sess., 128.

20. Ibid., p. 422.

21. Ibid., p. 423.

22. Ibid.

23. Ibid., p. 426.

24. Ibid.

25. Ibid., p. 879.

26. Ibid., 25th Cong., 2d Sess., 499.

27. Ibid., p. 406.

28. See Cunningham, *Process of Government under Jefferson*, pp. 268–272, for observations on the role of debate at the opening of the century.

29. *Congressional Globe*, 33d Cong., 2d Sess., 233.

30. Ibid., 633, 760, 869.

31. Ibid., 29th Cong., 1st Sess., 684.

32. Ibid., 31st Cong., 2d Sess., 630.

33. Ibid., p. 531.

34. Ruth Gertrude Curran, "David Kellog Cartter," *Ohio Archaeological and Historical Quarterly*, XLII, No. 11 (Jan. 1933):105–115.

35. *Congressional Globe*, 29th Cong., 1st Sess., 898.

36. For the Douglas relationship, see Johannsen, *Stephen A. Douglas*.

37. *Congressional Globe*, 25th Cong., 2d Sess., *Appendix*, 571.

38. Ibid., p. 581.

39. Ibid., 27th Cong., 2d Sess., 725.

40. Ibid., 33d Cong., 2d Sess., 46.

41. Ibid., p. 175.

42. Nichols, *Disruption of American Democracy*, describes Stephens as "the administration floor leader" in the Thirty-Sixth Congress (p. 184) and terms him the "most
skillful parliamentarian in the House" (p. 157). Johannsen, *Stephen A. Douglas*, also
treats Stephens' activities within the Democratic party and especially his cooperation with
Douglas to avert secession. Although there are several biographies of Stephens, no
biographer seems to have been able fully to capture the nature of the unusual southerner.
His own writings are perhaps most useful for insight into the ambiguities of his character;
fortunately, these are profuse.

43. See *Selections from the Speeches and Writings of Hon. Thomas L. Clingman of
North Carolina* (Raleigh, N. C.: J. Nichols, Printer, 1877) for a sampling.

44. *Congressional Globe*, 33d Cong., 2d Sess., 945.

45. Ibid., pp. 906–907.

46. Ibid., 29th Cong., 1st Sess., 905.

47. This is a central theme in William R. Brock, *Parties and Political Conscience: American Dilemmas, 1840–1850. KTO Studies in American History*, ed., Harold M. Hyman (Millwood, N. Y.: KTO Press, 1979).

Part III

PATTERNS OF CONVICTION:
THE POLITICAL IDEAS OF
MAVERICKS AND
CONFORMISTS

CHAPTER 5

The Democratic Conformists

[Our party is not] a church or lyceum. It is no part of its mission to set itself
up as an expounder of ethical or divine truth. . . . And it is because that party
sometimes will forget that it is the first and highest duty of its mission to
be the depository of immutable political principles, and steps aside after the
dreams of a false and fanatical progress—sometimes political, commonly
philanthropic or moral—that it ceases to be powerful and victorious.

Clement L. Vallandigham, 1855

During his often frustrating tenure as Vice-President of the United States, Thomas
Jefferson composed his famous *Manual of Parliamentary Practice*, one of the
most influential documents in the history of the organization of Congress.[1] That
Jefferson—perhaps the most important formulator of the republican ideology of
the early nation—was also instrumental in organizing his party and the Congress
is testimony to the breadth of his concept of statesmanship. Only later generations
would question the union of man of thought and man of action in one political
character.

Jefferson decried the use of standing committees, but in his own time the
development of the committee system marked the beginning of legislative specialization in the House, a process which would ultimately lead to greater efficiency in the popular body.[2] This early rationalization of functions within the
House was accompanied by some standardization of leadership styles, as particularly adept legislators served as role models for others to emulate. Analysis
of leadership styles has provided some evidence for the functional rationalization
of congressional responsibilities; more evidence can be gleaned from a study of
the political ideas contained in congressional rhetoric.

Mastery of the arts of persuasion was as essential a skill as any the mid-
century politician possessed. The political battles of the antebellum period were

wars of words, in which opposing warriors employed rhetoric to an extent not characteristic either of the more genteel era which preceded it or the era of mass communication which followed. Oratory was a much-admired art form, providing the most important link between professional politicians and the politically active public.[3] Through their respective ideologies, Democrats, Whigs, and Republicans reminded voters of their partisan loyalties.

Political ideologies are directive in their very nature.[4] Uniting rational and nonrational elements, they offer a coherent vision of what ought to be, giving political focus to the aspirations and anxieties of members of the society from which they arise or to which they are addressed. Broad human themes—religious, social, psychological—are related within the political nexus, providing a basis for collective identity and action. Compatible with the main elements in the larger cultural tradition from which they are drawn, ideologies unite those who would alter society in a particular way, sustaining cohesion which, in a democratic nation, can translate into political action.

All antebellum politicians used partisan rhetoric, but not all played the same functional roles in the creation and popularization of the ideologies associated with the mass-based party systems of the era. Numerous intellectual sources were combined to produce the content of Democratic, Whig, and Republican ideologies: political thought inherited from the ancient and more recent Western past; the sanctified republican ideas of the revolutionary and constitutional periods; and, to a lesser extent, the works of contemporary thinkers.[5] The content of these partisan ideologies has been thoroughly explored, but the collective process by which they achieved their coherence remains somewhat obscure. A comparison of the political ideas of mavericks and conformists sheds some light on the nature of that process in the House of Representatives. There, mavericks were often tailors of ideology, while conformists played a more passive intellectual role, communicating ideas assembled for them by others. This is not to assert that mavericks created the antebellum political ideologies, given the fact that many important politicians and thinkers were never House members. The mavericks' creativity does, however, indicate another kind of specialization in the legislative responsibilities of that era, perhaps foreshadowing the trend that would enable modern congressmen to employ "idea men."

As the following discussion should demonstrate, partisan ideologies had instrumental purposes for both mavericks and conformists; but mavericks exploited ideology for personal as well as political reasons, while conformists primarily used it for partisan purposes. This distinction is not an invidious one, as ideology may have masked laudatory or blameworthy motives for either mavericks or conformists; but the greater personal involvement of mavericks in rhetorical expression had functional significance. Conformists restricted their political speeches to the context of particular political situations, and they gave very limited consideration to the relationship between political ideas and the fundamental ground of those ideas in philosophy, religion, or social thought. Mavericks were more generally analytical, if only because though they were often at odds with their parties they nonetheless had to fit into the essential party framework.[6] While they, too, related ideology to particular political problems, they also explored the bases of ideology outside of politics, directly addressing the kinds of philosophical, moral, and social issues that concerned thoughtful Americans not centrally involved in politics. For mavericks, then, the integrative and inherently creative aspects of political ideology were part and parcel of their rhetoric. Their motives may have been as self-interested as those of conformists, but their intellectual contributions were considerably more substantial.

Lines of demarcation between practical conformists who espoused "immutable political principles" and provocative mavericks who adhered to more peculiarly personal positions run through all three of the major parties of the period between 1836 and 1860. For conformists, a "given" party ideology seems most strongly to have influenced their public expressions of political belief, though sectional variations are evident. Party identification seems to have been as important to them in this regard as in their voting behavior. In contrast, for mavericks' political thought as well as their voting behavior, purely partisan distinctions are not relevant. Mavericks did adhere partially to partisan ideology, but perhaps more significant is the fact that their concept of politics transcended party lines. Both in their tendency to speculative thinking about politics and in the content of their ideas, mavericks can be distinguished by their similarities from conformists. The characteristic patterns of the mavericks' political thought help explain why these congressmen conformed less consistently than others to the pressures for partisanship they confronted.

Most leaders of the powerful political parties after the time of Jackson agreed upon the need for subordinating moral and philosophical issues to the important goal of controlling the government, but conformists were far more consistent than mavericks in the application of this basic rule.[7] Moreover, those conformists who most commonly referred to their "immutable political principles" without reference to their foundation in ethical or philosophical ideas were found in the Democratic party. That party was the first in the history of the United States to conceive of its political responsibility in professional terms.[8] The Democrats' attitude about politics was essentially pragmatic: their evident concerns were with means, not ends. Their opponents therefore accused them of nihilism, frequently describing them as the "party of plunder," a characterization which still persists in historical treatments of the Jacksonians. If, however, the Democrats understood the necessity of ideological vagueness in a pluralistic society, the tactic of espousing only general principles may be tribute to their astuteness.

Certainly conformity in voting behavior promoted partisan success, and the majority of all Democrats were conformists in that respect: that is, each voted on important issues within boundaries established by other Democrats from their region. These voting conformists were virtually inarticulate about matters other than party politics, as a cursory analysis of the titles of their printed speeches indicates.[9] These conformists also constituted the greater proportion of nationally known figures among House party members.[10] Most mavericks were not successful as party leaders; the few who achieved national reputation were noted for their outspoken and independent behavior, not for party regularity.[11] This pattern reinforces the idea, suggested first by the distribution of House leaders, that while there were varied paths to political success in the antebellum period, within the Democratic party some selective process produced more conformists than mavericks at the very top positions. The highest ranking Democrats in the House were either not very much concerned with nonpolitical issues or were willing to subordinate other interests to the goal of party success, contributing thereby to the solidarity that the Democratic party maintained until 1860 in the face of significant stress from sectional interests.

The ideological principles upon which Democratic conformists united are familiar: faith in the capacity of all white men for self-government; belief in individual liberty and limited government; conviction that equal economic opportunity provided the best security for democracy; a devotion to personal mobility—geographical, social, economic, and political. Reference to these staples of Democratic ideology was common for conformists, but they rarely explored the foundations of their ideas. Instead, both southern and northern Democratic conformists were almost tediously anti-intellectual about politics. Their carelessness about fundamentals was reflected in the area which eventually divided southern and northern Democrats: the relationship between individual liberty and romantic nationalism, which both subsumed rhetorically under God's manifest will for America. The intellectual analysis of contemporaries pointed to conflicts in the interpretation of God's law revealed through nature, but conformists avoided those conflicts as if they did not exist.[12] It is possible that they did not understand paradoxes hidden in their rhetoric, but the persistent habit for Democratic conformists of repudiating political moralism or intellectualism may be evidence of their unease. For all Democratic conformists, the everyday reality of party politics defined a safe framework through which to view the political universe.

Almost no northern Democratic conformists treated political issues philosophically in the set of published writings which served as the basis for this study. The congressional leaders vocally addressed major issues but consistently repeated their antagonism toward speculation or abstraction in politics. A proper concern for legislative duties, practically considered, might eliminate the need for analysis of theoretical causes and effects on the House floor, where the one-hour rule generally prevailed. As Stephen Douglas put the matter on one occasion, every member knew how he was going to vote already, so the House should proceed to vote "without going into these abstract discussions."[13] But anti-intellectualism was broader in application than the Congress. Churchill Cambreleng, Jacksonian House leader and Van Buren appointee to Russia in 1840, had stated the basic premise early in his career, suggesting that a wide range of American endeavors would profit by a mundane approach:

If men would pay more attention to these changes in the world, as natural as day and night; and trouble their brains less for discoveries of fanciful causes and new systems;

we should all make better farmers, better merchants, better manufacturers and better legislators.[14]

Clement L. Vallandigham, the northwestern conformist famous for his partisan activities during the Civil War, insisted in 1864 that the beleaguered Democrats adopt as partisan dogma the disavowal of moral and divine truth for politics and the abandonment of any attempt to "square our political institutions and our legislation by mere abstract, theoretical, and mathematically exact, but impracticable truths."[15]

Northern Democratic conformists expressed unremitting hostility to mixing politics and philosophy, but they virtually ignored the potential theory through which pragmatic and anti-intellectual conformity could have been justified. Jean Baker, in *Affairs of Party: The Political Culture of Northern Democrats*, has suggested a Burkean influence upon Douglas, whom, she acknowledged, "did not so much sway public opinion as represent it."[16] The Burkean philosophy that "emphasized historical continuity and experience over abstract theory" could have functioned effectively as a rationale for Democratic action, but no House conformist developed the connection.[17] One northern Democratic conformist did explain his conformity in philosophical terms, though they could hardly be called Burkean. Indianian Robert Dale Owen, son of the famous British reformer Robert Owen, was a founder of the utopian community at New Harmony, advocate for many unpopular reform causes, including women's rights and the organization of labor, yet he was a consistent congressional conformist.[18] In an 1854 reform tract containing his ideas as well as those of the infamous Fanny Wright, Owen thoroughly explained why he thought it important to vote a straight party line during his congressional career, and he offered a cogent justification for a mirror theory of representation. In Owen's view, maverick behavior, however admirable it might appear to individualistic observers, in fact deprived the constituent of his fundamental democratic rights:

He himself [a maverick], in the given instance, might be considered as a legislator, or a guardian, or it may be a disinterested friend of the people; their *representative* he was not. The people, therefore, in so far as his decision was concerned, were not represented at all. They virtually lost, for the time, their rights of citizens, as completely as if they had been by force deprived of the elective franchise.[19]

Voters should choose representatives not on the basis of superior personal character but on the basis of their interests, which should be as nearly the same as those of the majority of the voters as possible. Parties organized along interest group lines would facilitate this congruence. For a maverick to interpose independent intellectual or moral judgment would only distort the reflective relationship. In Owen's model, the Congress would become a microcosm of the United States, with a pluralistic character; then each representative had only to follow his interests for good government to be achieved.

Owen's rational theory for the operations of democracy was as unusual among conformists as was the remainder of his career. One other conformist among the northern Democrats hinted briefly, however, at a more romantic theory in a speech to his troops extolling the Democratic participation in the Civil War:

Here [in the North] neither learned deductions nor speculative theories are the source of the auxiliaries of freedom. Its truths are instinctive, and its impulses unconscious in the American mind, and they are infallible, too. What each one likes best, he does; and the aggregation of these likes in an American community, is its liberty; their execution is its government.[20]

This kind of rationale for democratic government might have delighted a transcendentalist, but despite its internal consistency as a foundation for conformity, neither it nor any other philosophical speculation was expressed by the majority of northern Democratic conformists. Such beliefs were not relevant to their publically expressed ideology. The evidence suggests that northern Democratic conformists absorbed such ideas as part of the political culture of northern Democrats, employed their end results of pragmatic anti-intellectualism to unite other Democrats to action, and attended consistently to the legislative work at hand. With their preference for practicality over political theory, conformists contributed to a definition of legislator as man of action, and, in that sense, they were models for a theory; but the development of the theory which justified their behavior was left to another kind of political activist.

A similar interpretation may be ascribed to the northern Democratic conformists' rendering of the idea of America's Manifest Destiny. Democratic intellectuals such as George Bancroft explained the relationship between individual liberty and collective mission and advocated the Democracy as the mode of attaining both.[21] Democratic conformists from the northern states testified to their belief in mission—that God had given the world a great second chance to salvage the wreck of European civilization. They agreed that mission entailed the spread of democratic institutions across the continent. Like all politicians of the day, they believed that God had ordained America's future through the founding of the nation upon His principles; but they insisted that the accomplishment of the national destiny lay in human hands and that the methods to achieve it were political. Given the foreordained mission, which they neither questioned nor explored, Democratic conformists could deliver enthusiastic speeches on the glory of the United States but remain absolutely free to consider closely only practical legislation.

Specifically, this interpretation of American destiny could be equated with practical legislative responsibility. The lawmaker's frame of reference should be, in John Dawson's words, human "institutions in harmony with man's nature."[22] As this same northern Democratic conformist put it, anyone who understood "human nature practically" would agree that "if you wish to elevate the intellectual and moral condition of a people, you should first make them easy in their physical circumstance.''[23] No one explained the guiding principle more clearly than Stephen Douglas, whose devotion to his idea of American destiny was unquestioned:

The law of God, as revealed to us, is intended to operate on our consciences. . . . The Divine law does not prescribe the form of government under which we shall live, and the character of our political and civil institutions. Revelation has not furnished us with a constitution.[24]

For the politician, the laws of politics offered a sufficient guide.

The pragmatic attitude that characterized the Democratic conformists' concept of mission reinforced their highly partisan approach to politics. For most of them, party loyalty needed no complex justification: government was a practical operation, and party was a self-evident means of running the system efficiently. The repeated statements of party loyalty, combined with the concrete evidence of conformists' voting patterns, suggest that for northern conformists in the Democratic party partisan attitudes were as fundamental to politics as practicality. Party leaders made explicit the necessity for party organization; their constant efforts to maintain discipline helped earn them their deserved reputation as party professionals.[25]

As sectional tensions increased, the northern Democratic conformists seemed increasingly to rely upon pleas for party unity as the only salvation for the practical American mission. Since Republicans, and some Whigs before them, explicitly professed the need for morality in politics and the more radical ones recommended direct consultation of God's laws, the Democrats could picture themselves as "the only barrier to the success of treason and fanaticism.''[26] Moral controversy over slavery could be conveniently labeled as "a species of demogoguism, to enable men to get into Congress who otherwise never would occupy a seat here.''[27] To remain "powerful and victorious," Democrats should not allow the party to "set itself up as an expounder of ethical or divine truth" but should remain true to "immutable political principles.''[28] Thus mission, practicality, and party loyalty were combined in a code of action for conformists—a code which seems to have been accepted by southerners as well as northerners down to the eve of the Civil War. That the code failed the party (and the nation) was partially due to the efforts of less purely pragmatic people than the northern Democratic conformists. At the same time, the blindness of their compatriots, the southern Democratic conformists, to consideration of the real abstractions which threatened them may have also played an important part in the failure of the Democratic party.

Taken as a group, the southern Democratic conformists were less philosophical about political life than any other group in this study. Most of them did not publish speeches outside of the *Congressional Globe*, and only a tiny fraction of the total number published anything other than political speeches. Southern Democratic conformists were especially prone to making declamatory speeches with little or no abstract reasoning and with a repetitive character that must have bored antagonistic listeners. An attempt to derive political philosophy from their works is a frustrating exercise: they give the impression that the speeches were set pieces designed only to impress the speaker's constituents with his political "soundness."[29]

Several explanations can be offered for this pattern. Perhaps because the Democratic party became an umbrella for many different kinds of southern politicians, they were inclined to avoid abstractions which might provoke internal dissent. The disruptive presence of the great political metaphysician, John Calhoun, who threatened party unity, may have provoked Democratic suspicion about abstractions.[30] The conformists' tendency to load speeches with statistics rather than with reasoning functioned as a mechanism by which they could avoid confronting substantive issues through use of overwhelming and insignificant detail. In his impressionistic *Mind of the South* Wilbur Cash suggested that southern oratory was purely romantic and hedonistic, that the words were valued more for their sounds than for meaning.[31] In Cash's interpretation, southern politics and oratory were inseparable, neither reflecting reality. Cash's description in some respects delineates the southern Democratic conformists:

Thus the politics of the old South was a theater for the play of the purely personal, the purely romantic, and the purely hedonistic. It was an arena wherein one great champion confronted another or a dozen, and sought to outdo them in rhetoric and splendid gesturing.[32]

For Cash the intellectual content of southern oratory was less important than its value as personal display and community entertainment.

Altogether, these explanations have bearing on the theme of conformists as popularizers of ideology, whose rhetorical purposes had more to do with action than with ideas. Drew Faust, in a thoughtful article entitled "The Rhetoric and Ritual of Agriculture in Antebellum South Carolina," has characterized the addresses to agricultural societies in that state as "tediously repetitive, long-winded, stereotyped orations," which played an "important role in establishing . . . symbolic consensus and social solidarity."[33] Agricultural addresses, products of the planter-class struggle for social unity under their leadership, were effective partly because they were repetitive. Seen as ritual celebrations of a projected southern community, the addresses manipulated familiar rhetorical devices for social purposes hidden beneath their overt content. South Carolina agricultural addresses differed from the political speeches of southern Democratic conformists in that the former aimed at nonpartisan audiences and reflected long-range goals, not immediate political needs. Designed to unify the community at large, the addresses dealt with essential social, psychological, and religious themes. The narrowly political speeches of southern Democratic conformists extolled the existence of southern superiority by reference to given data, not social, psychological, or religious theory, but as summons to political action they exploited and reinforced two senses of community. They spoke on the one hand to southern

Democrats in the familiar language of Democratic political culture, and they spoke to other southerners who, though not Democrats, might be persuaded that the party served southern purposes. Lacking intellectual creativity, they were nonetheless politically effective because of the familiarity of the ideas they carried, not in spite of their lack of creativity. Though southern Democratic conformists' rhetoric may also have served as a facade for planter-class interests, it seems more useful here to consider their purposes for the special elite of southern Democratic politicians. Whatever the covert class interests of the speakers, these political speeches were obviously related to the aims of the southern Democratic party, which always sought immediate political success and, by the 1850s at the latest, achieved that success partly by posing as defender of the South.[34]

Its purposes aside, the "splendid gesturing" of the southern Democratic conformists drew the political world in black and white: on one side were the good Democrats, North and South, who stood for a pragmatic, laissez-faire theory of politics, one which would enable the South to protect and preserve its way of life; on the other side were the wicked northern Whigs and Republicans, joined by the traitorous Federalist remnants in the South. who together represented a moralistic, speculative political ethos, encouraged all sorts of meddling in the life of citizens, and opened the door to a whole host of "isms" which threatened American and southern ideals. In the context of this dramatic picture southern Democratic conformists defended the southern status quo with factual evidence which justified it. Thus their most characteristic defense consisted of pages of economic, social, and cultural statistics designed to demonstrate the *prima facie* superiority of the southern way of life.[35]

In this framework of defense, anti-intellectualism was both implicit and explicit; as for northern Democratic conformists, safety lay in practicality. The general principle was critical in light of the need for southern security. Outstanding conformist leader R. M. T. Hunter, Calhoun's aristocratic Virginia ally who had been the Speaker of the House early in his career, warned a Senate audience in 1860 of the danger to the great American mission:

Mr. President, are we to be disappointed of such a destiny as this in the mad pursuit of abstractions and universals, conjured up by moonstruck theorists and crazy fanatics? Has political science yet reached the dignity of a certain science? Can the politician, like the mathematician, reason to certain and to safe results from abstract formulae? Sir, the statesman is he who derives his philosophy from the experience of the world.[36]

The concrete world of practical politics might provide defense from the political metaphysics which threatened the South.

Coupled with anti-intellectual pragmatism in the southern Democratic arsenal for defense of the status quo was the states'-rights position from which they argued without theoretical inquiry. They accepted and applied the convenient ideological legacy but never explored its actual relevance to existing circumstances. Like northern Democrats they insisted that government was essentially negative, not responsible for "attaining the greatest ideal good" but for giving independent Americans the opportunity to achieve their own greatest goods.[37] Interfering legislation, "whether in the form of protective tariffs, fishing bounties, assumption of state debts, building roads, giving land to colleges, or furnishing homes under sweeping and unconstitutional laws," was held to be "at war with the true theory of a republic, destructive of its integrity, and dangerous to popular liberty."[38] Although it is difficult to date the point at which southerners began to link laissez-faire theory and the protection of slavery, certainly by the time of the Mexican War they were making the connection and insisting on no interference with political, economic, moral, or other aspects of southern life.[39] Because the national Democratic party stood for laissez-faire in government in the Jeffersonian and Jacksonian tradition, southerners were for a long time comfortable in that party and often dominated its councils.

For most of the twenty-five years before the Civil War the southern Democratic conformists insisted that the Democratic party was the best hope of protecting the southern way of life. As former Whigs moved into the party they tended to be somewhat more philosophical about the southern defense, but the most philosophical of the southern defenders were mavericks, Democratic or Whig.[40] As a rule, the former Whigs who became Democratic conformists shared the attitude of the long-time Democrats: loyalty to the party was a necessity for the preservation of southern rights.[41] This concern for party unity was generally grounded on the argument from necessity, not in political theory or metaphysics.

Perhaps the most outspoken of the advocates of party unity for southern protection was Howell Cobb of Georgia. Cobb was an active party leader, not only serving as Speaker of the House but also as Secretary of the Treasury in the administration of President James Buchanan. His 1848 speech, "The Necessity for Party Organization," seemed clearly designed to persuade men of different political beliefs to join with Democratic party members to protect the South. Cobb insisted at length that the proper basis of party organization was "fundamental principles" and not an explicit set of ideas.[42] "Fundamental principles" in his southern Democratic conformist rhetoric meant only one thing: an adherence to the states'-rights position in all matters.

The importance of party discipline among the Democrats was not only defensively stated, it was also proudly proclaimed as a positive virtue that could overcome sectional differences for the national good because it would divide southerners and northerners along party lines, not regional ones. George Dromgoole, southern Democratic conformist from Virginia and a member of the important Ways and Means Committee, urged his fellow Democrats to support the Sub-Treasury Bill:

They [Democrats] did not ask their political opponents to assist them in perfecting a measure under our particular care, and belonging to the Democratic party peculiarly. They wanted none of their aid. . . . We should pass this bill by a triumphant majority.

... It is a measure which brings together in harmonious and patriotic cooperation the whole Democratic party—a unanimity and cooperation which he believed to be a bright harbinger of the harmony to be exhibited on all future occasions.[43]

National Democratic party unity on the principles of limited government would simultaneously protect the South and unify the nation.

The pragmatic application of laissez-faire principles to any set of problems was thought by southern Democratic conformist politicians to be adequate political philosophy and sufficient protection for the southern way of life—until the emergence of the Republican party. That party appeared to them as the polar opposite of the southern position; furthermore, for the first time the southerners found themselves confronted with antislavery idealism combined with political professionalism. As one southern politician aptly said, "The Puritan and the Jacobin are in fearful propinquity."[44] The southerners correctly assessed this redoubtable combination as a real threat to the future of Jeffersonian principles in government. If the Republicans should gain political power, it would not suffice to proclaim a hands-off policy; in the face of their attack the southern Democratic conformists demanded positive protection of their way of life. Although they professed not to be at all clear about what motivated the Republicans (money, power hunger, and madness were common suggestions) and though they were not certain from what quarter the threat would materialize, nothing is more vivid from a reading of the speeches of southern Democratic conformists than their virtual state of panic in the late 1850s. One well educated, normally rational southern conformist, J. F. H. Claiborne, wrote that:

Jacobinism, social equality without regard to race, and universal emancipation—more irrational and revolting than the agrarianism imputed in the Romans began to be.... These monstrous doctrines—chimeras from the brains of infidels and assassins—came trooping, one after the other, like bloody spectres, across the Atlantic.[45]

Fearing social revolution, southern conformist leaders in the Democratic party demanded that their party grant them protection, even if the theory of negative government were violated. Having outlived its function, the theory could be abandoned.[46]

The southern Democratic conformists in the House, like their northern Democratic colleagues, appear to have become increasingly defensive in their stance during the 1850s. In the House it was the mavericks in the Democratic party who took initiative in directing the course of their party, helping to lead, ultimately, into its disruption. In the three Congresses of the 1850s in which the Democrats were able to organize the House, mavericks outnumbered conformists as chairmen of the standing committees seven to one in the Thirty-Second Congress, seven to three in the Thirty-Third Congress, and seven to five in the Thirty-Fifth Congress. While not all mavericks were uncompromising on the slavery issue or willfully destructive of national ties, few were moderate politicians, and none was devoted to the persistence of the Democratic party above other considerations. If, indeed, the cement that bound that party also bound the nation, it may have been unfortunate that conformist leadership in the House of Representatives did not prevail. But to the extent that conformist leaders ignored problems of national scope, avoiding sectional confrontation by applying laissez-faire principles or states'-rights dogma and pragmatic partyism, it seems unlikely that they possessed sufficiently statesmanlike vision to avoid drifting into catastrophe.

NOTES

1. Jefferson's contribution is described in Dumas Malone, *Jefferson and the Ordeal of Liberty*, vol. 3 of *Jefferson and His Times*, 6 vols. (Boston: Little, Brown & Company, 1948–1977), 3:452–458.

2. Jeffersonian theory and practice in regard to committees are discussed in Cooper, *The Origins of the Standing Committees*, part 1, "Jeffersonian Attitudes and Committee Practice: 1789–1809," pp. 3–40. See also Malone, *Jefferson*, p. 457.

3. Howe stresses oratory as art in *Political Culture of American Whigs*, pp. 25–27. How much influence political oratory had on the beliefs of the public is a controversial issue. Philip Converse makes a sophisticated argument that "belief systems" are imperfectly communicated to the public, and he uses the abolitionist ideas within Republican ideology as an example in "The Nature of Belief Systems in Mass Publics," in David E. Apter, ed., *Ideology and Discontent*, vol. 5, International Yearbook of Political Behavior Research (New York: The Free Press, 1964), pp. 206–261. For recent contrasting views about antebellum political ideologies and voters see Lewis O. Saum, *The Popular Mood of Pre–Civil War in America*, Contributions in American Studies, No. 46 (Westport, Conn.: Greenwood Press, 1980), which argues that ordinary people did not generally attend closely to political issues, see esp. pp. 143–166; and the opposing view of William E. Gienapp, " 'Politics Seem to Enter into Everything': Political Culture in the North, 1840–1860," in Stephen E. Maizlish and John J. Kushma, eds., *Essays in American Antebellum Politics, 1840–1860*, a compilation of the Walter Prescott Webb Memorial Lectures for 1981 (College Station: Texas A & M University Press, 1982), pp. 14–69.

4. A useful collection of essays treating the broad subject of ideology in politics is Apter, ed., *Ideology and Discontent*. Especially relevant are Apter's introduction (pp. 15–46) and Clifford Geertz's valuable "Ideology as a Cultural System" (pp. 47–76).

5. The best syntheses are in Baker, *Affairs of Party*; Howe, *Political Culture of American Whigs*; Welter, *Mind of America*; and Foner, *Free Soil, Free Labor, Free Men*.

6. The situational dilemma was important, but other reasons for mavericks' analytical traits are explored below, Ch. 11.

7. No one more forcefully argues for the subordination of principles to the task of control than Pessen in *Jacksonian America*, esp. ch. 9–11.

8. For further development of this point see Richard Hofstadter, *Idea of a Party System*, pp. 242–249. Hofstadter's interpretation emphasizes the constructive aspect of the professionalization of political parties. Ronald P. Formisano discusses the professional attitudes of Democrats in Michigan in *Birth of Mass Parties*, ch. IV, "Party, Antiparty, and Political Character." Perry M. Goldman, "Political Virtue in the Age of Jackson,"

Political Science Quarterly 87 (March 1972): 46–62, discusses the transition from legislator as "virtuous republican" to "democratic soldier."

9. The bibliography of maverick and conformist speeches is arranged according to the plan of the chapters which follow so that the reader may refer to it for the speeches and writings available for any man or party and sectional grouping of men. Even a cursory reading of titles for Democratic conformists reveals the almost exclusively political nature of their works. This exclusively political orientation is thoroughly evident in the *Congressional Globe*.

10. Democratic conformist leaders included, for example, Stephen A. Douglas, Clement L. Vallandigham, Howell Cobb, and R. M. T. Hunter.

11. For example, of the eleven Democrats who served in the Senate in the 1850s, and therefore might be expected to have worked their way up the party ladder, six were conformists. The other five, mavericks while in the House, were Richard Brodhead of Pennsylvania, an anti-Lecompton Democrat; Preston King, a Free-Soiler; Robert Toombs and Thomas Clingman, both Whigs until roughly 1850; and Barnwell Rhett. Obviously none of these men was noted for party regularity; none, furthermore, ever held any other major national office, appointive or elective, or was ever choosen by his party for leadership roles outside of the Congress. The six conformist Senators, on the other hand, included party leaders Hunter and Douglas, and three lesser party figures, two of whom also received diplomatic posts in the late antebellum period. Two Democratic conformists and one maverick served in the Cabinet during the 1850s. The conformists were known party men Jacob Thompson of Mississippi and Howell Cobb; the maverick was Caleb Cushing, a consistent nonconformist whatever his party affiliation. Only one of the 255 mavericks and conformists served on the Supreme Court before the Civil War—Nathan Clifford of Maine, a loyal Democrat all of his life. The dominance of Republicans in the executive branch after the War and the confusion in party identity in the South after Reconstruction make this kind of analysis for the years after 1865 nearly meaningless.

12. The conflicts inherent in American nationalism are best revealed in Yehoshua Arieli, *Individualism and Nationalism in American Ideology* (Baltimore: Penguin Books, 1966; Cambridge: Harvard University Press, 1964); and in Nagel, *One Nation Indivisible* and *This Sacred Trust*.

13. *Congressional Globe*, 29th Cong., 1st Sess., 898.

14. Churchill C. Cambreleng, *An Examination of the New Tariff Proposed by the Hon. Henry Baldwin, a Representative in Congress. By One of the People* (New York: Gould & Banks, 1821), p. 20.

15. "History of the Abolition Movement," in *Speeches, Arguments, Addresses, and Letters of Clement L. Vallandigham* (New York: J. Walter & Co., 1864), p. 128. Hereafter cited as "Abolition Movement." See for other examples the following: Speech of Stephen A. Douglas in defense of the course of Andrew Jackson at New Orleans in Clark E. Carr, *Stephen A. Douglas, His Life, Public Services, Speeches and Patriotism* (Chicago: A. C. McClung & Co., 1909), p. 152; Willis A. Gorman, *Boundary of Texas. Speech of Hon. W. A. Gorman, of Indiana, In the House of Representatives, Friday, Aug. 30, 1850, on the Texas Boundary Bill and Slavery Agitation* (Washington, D. C.: Congressional Globe Office, [1850]), p. 7; and Samuel Scott Marshall, *Speech of Hon. Samuel S. Marshall of Illinois, on the Insanity of the Times and the Present Condition of Political Parties. Delivered in the House of Representatives, Aug. 6, 1856* (Washington, D. C.: Congressional Globe Office, 1856), pp. 5–6, hereafter cited as *Insanity of the Times*.

16. Baker, *Affairs of Party*, p. 184. Baker acknowledges Douglas' vagueness, noting

that "he had neither the time, inclination, nor intellectual depth to refine his views into a systematic theory" (p. 187), but insisting that he was, nonetheless, "conservative in the Burkean mode" (p. 189).

17. Ibid., p. 178.

18. Arieli links Owen with American philosophical writers in *Individualism and Nationalism*, p. 292.

19. Robert Dale Owen et al., "The Cause of the People," in *Quarterly Beacon. Popular Tracts by Robert Dale Owen and Others; to Which Are Added Fables by Frances Wright* (New York: Beacon Office, 1854), p. 2. See another Owen speech dealing with the constructive role of parties in the *Congressional Globe*, 29th Cong., 1st Sess., 1133–1134.

20. Passage in a speech made to his troops in the Civil War, quoted by the author, Congressman John Cochrane of New York, in *Arming the Slaves in the War for the Union. Scenes, Speeches, and Events Attending It* (New York: Rogers & Sherwood Printers, 1875), p. 4.

21. Baker, *Affairs of Party*, treats Bancroft's linking of the Democratic party with American mission, pp. 119–125.

22. *An Address by Hon. John L. Dawson, before the Washington and Union L[iterary] Societies of Washington College: Delivered on Wednesday Evening, June 18th, 1856* (Washington, Pa.: Grayson & Hart, Printers, 1856), p. 16.

23. *Speech of Hon. John L. Dawson of Pennsylvania, on the Homestead Bill. Delivered in the House of Representatives on Tuesday, Feb. 14. 1854* (Washington, D. C.: Robert Armstrong, Printer, 1854), pp. 24–25.

24. Speech of Douglas at City Hall, Chicago, Oct. 23, 1850, in [Henry Martyn Flint], *Life of Stephen A. Douglas, with His Most Important Speeches and Reports. By a Member of the Western Bar* (New York: J. Dayton, Publisher, 1860), p. 27.

25. The party demanded discipline of "an almost military severity," according to Hofstadter, *Idea of a Party System*, p. 244. Roy F. Nichols, *The Disruption of American Democracy*, deals with attempts to enforce party discipline in the decade before the Civil War but makes little distinction between party regulars and others. Frederick Blue, *The Free Soilers*, skillfully contrasts the ideological and partisan responses to the problem of slavery extension and the resulting stress upon party organizations; see esp. Ch. 4, "The Free Soilers: Politics and Principles."

26. S. S. Marshall, *Insanity of the Times*, p. 8. John M. McFaul in "Expediency vs. Morality: Jacksonian Politics and Slavery," *Journal of American History* 62 (June 1975):24–39, appears to accept the Democrats' assertion that their refusal to treat slavery as a legitimate political issue was an effective barrier to disunion, at least in the 1830s.

27. Stephen A. Douglas in *Congressional Globe*, 29th Cong., 1st Sess., 559.

28. Vallandigham, "Abolition Movement," p. 92.

29. In *Oratory in the Old South, 1820–1860*, a volume published in 1970, a group of scholars analyzed southern political oratory. In the various essays, written by specialists in the study of speech and rhetoric, the oratory of several different types of southern politicians is studied: included are Nullifiers, Anti-Nullifiers, southern Whigs, moderate Democrats, Know-Nothings, Fire-Eaters, and southern Unionists. Although Democrats are included in four of the groups and not expressly excluded from any except the essays on Whigs and Know-Nothings, not a single southern Democratic conformist is treated at length in any essay. By contrast, most of the analysis is devoted to the speeches of mavericks, both Democratic and Whig, although there are thorough discussions of the

oratory of a few southern Whig conformists. The authors of the various essays were unaware that they were making any such distinction, but their choice of orators certainly supports the conclusion that southern Democratic conformists made speeches of such repetitive and tedious character that they were not interesting for analysis. See Waldo W. Braden, ed., *Oratory in the Old South, 1820–1860* (Baton Rouge: Louisiana State University Press, 1970).

30. Calhoun's disruptive role is a major theme in Cooper, *The South and the Politics of Slavery.*

31. Wilbur J. Cash, *The Mind of the South*, Vintage Books (New York: Random House, 1941), p. 53. A perceptive critique is C. Vann Woodward's "The Elusive Mind of the South," in *American Counterpoint: Slavery and Racism in the North–South Dialogue* (Boston: Little, Brown & Company, 1971), pp. 140–162.

32. Cash, *Mind of the South*, p. 54.

33. *Journal of Southern History* 45 (November 1979):541–568, quoted passages, p. 567.

34. Cooper argues that the tactic of achieving success in the South by defending slavery was the key mode of operation for both Whigs and Democrats from the inception of their histories. Other scholars have stressed the persistence of Whig nationalism; see, for example, Degler's *The Other South*, p. 99–123.

35. For examples of the statistical accumulations common to the southern method of proof, see the *Congressional Globe*, 28th Cong., 1st Sess., *Appendix*, 425; 33d Cong., 1st Sess., *Appendix*, 895; 34th Cong., 3d Sess., *Appendix*, 140, 188; 35th Cong., 2d Sess., *Appendix*, 199, 268.

36. R. M. T. Hunter, *Speech of Hon. R. M. T. Hunter, of Virginia, on Invasion of States. Delivered in the Senate of the United States, Jan. 30, 1860* (Washington, D. C.: Lemuel Towers, Printer, 1860), p. 15. See also similar remarks about the "uncertain billows of this beautiful but dangerous sea of political metaphysics," in L. Q. C. Lamar, Speech in House of Representatives, *Congressional Globe*. 36th Cong., 1st Sess., Feb. 21, 1860, 113–117. Lamar's usually practical approach to politics is described in James B. Murphy, *L. Q. C. Lamar: Pragmatic Patriot* (Baton Rouge: Louisiana State University Press, 1973).

37. J. L. M. Curry, *Speech of J. L. M. Curry, of Alabama, on the Bill Granting Pensions to the Soldiers of the War of 1812*. Delivered in the House of Representatives, Apr. 27, 1858 (Washington, D. C.: Lemuel Towers, Printer, 1858), p. 8.

38. Ibid.

39. Obviously the economic interests of much of the South were such that no federal interference with the economy was thought to be necessary in the years before the Civil War; unquestionably there were real differences in the interests of North and South which contributed to the antagonism between the sections. But most southerners recognized that it was the institution of slavery that formed the outstanding difference between North and South and that other economic differences were susceptible to compromise, or log rolling, and could be treated with less fear. The rhetoric of laissez-faire in the Congresses of the 1830s lacked the impassioned appeal of the speeches on the same issues in the 1850s. Calhoun recognized the fundamental unity of southern interests when he framed the doctrine of nullification, ostensibly to fight the tariff but in fact to protect the entire southern position. The same can be said of his early ally, Robert Barnwell Rhett, the maverick Democrat from South Carolina. Most southern conformists did not seem to see the connection until after the propagandists had made it clear. The positions of Calhoun and Rhett are discussed thoroughly in Charles Wiltse, *John C. Calhoun, Nullifier, 1829–*

1839 (New York: Sentry Co., 1931). Calhoun's efforts to persuade other southerners to his point of view are related clearly in Cooper, *The South and the Politics of Slavery*, see esp. pp. 103–118.

40. Outstanding Whig mavericks who were also mavericks after they moved into the Democratic party include Alexander H. Stephens, Robert Toombs, and Francis W. Pickens.

41. One former Whig, R. M. T. Hunter, expressed antiparty sentiments shortly after his party switch, but he never deviated from his new party's position. Hunter spoke in the House in 1838 of the "baneful influence of party spirit." which he said interfered between representatives and "the wishes and interest of their constituents." See the *Congressional Globe*, 25th Cong., 2d Sess., 438.

42. Cobb, *Necessity for Party Organization*, p. 1.

43. *Congressional Globe*, 29th Cong., 1st Sess., 593. The confusions in pronoun consistency are the fault of the *Globe* reporter.

44. J. F. H. Claiborne, *Life and Correspondence of John A. Quitman, Major-General, U. S. A., and Governor of the State of Mississippi* (New York: Harper & Bros., 1860), 2:272.

45. Ibid., p. 17.

46. Emory Thomas treats the later life of southern adherence to the theory of negative government, describing how persistently ideological mavericks like Robert Barnwell Rhett and Alexander Stephens fought in vain to keep the South ideologically pure in the face of practical needs for the nationalistic measures that he believes transformed the Confederacy. See Emory Thomas, *The Confederate Nation: 1861–1865*, The New American Nation Series, ed. by Henry Steele Commager and Richard B. Harris (New York: Harper & Row, 1979), p. 142 for Rhett, p. 139 for Stephens.

CHAPTER 6

The Democratic Mavericks

They [party leaders] presume to set up a standard of Democracy, and modestly require everybody else to conform to it. Of course these gentlemen usually take themselves for the measure, and if it happens not to fit others—if it be too small or too large—then those who have the misfortune to possess different mental proportions are to be denounced as unfaithful Democrats, or not Democrats at all. . . . Whether this Procrustean bed be constructed after the dimensions of the gentleman from Virginia [Jefferson], or of any greater men, I shall never consent to yield my independent judgment, and to have my convictions stretched here and lopped off there in order to make them fit the exact mould which may be presented. The Democracy which I have learned . . . encourages, rather than destroys, individuality and independence of thought.

Frederick Stanton, 1850

Mr. Stanton's protest notwithstanding, in terms of the issues of the 1836–1860 period, the mavericks in the Democratic party represented such a wide spectrum of politics that fitting them into one party may have involved Procrustean efforts. At one extreme of the political spectrum stood David Wilmot, antislavery congressman from Pennsylvania and author of the Wilmot Proviso; at the other end was the flamboyant fire-eater, Robert Barnwell Rhett, the "father of secession."[1] In between Free-Soilers and fire-eaters was a hodgepodge of Whiggish northern businessmen, Douglas supporters from the West, southern Unionists, northern "doughfaces," and other men who defy classification. General similarities in the political postures of these Procrustean bedfellows are not obvious.

Despite their policy differences, however, the rhetoric of Democratic mavericks reveals common grounds which distinguish them from conformists. Although they shared an ideological emphasis on laissez-faire, individual liberty, and American mission with Democratic conformists, mavericks had no faith that a proper framework of laws alone would assure the perpetuation of these values. While the liberation of society from artificial restraints which promoted inequality was necessary, the mavericks' examination of American experience persuaded them that it was insufficient. Mavericks did not consciously explore the intellectual tensions that scholars have discovered between the liberal Lockean and the neoclassical traditions in revolutionary ideology, but their rhetoric demonstrates a continuing concern with the reconciliation of freedom and civic virtue, of democratic and republican values. Mavericks were self-conscious heirs of the revolution, and as stewards of the national trust they sought to protect the intellectual as well as the material heritage.

The functional flaws in the intellectual heritage were becoming evident in the antebellum period. If Jean Yarbrough is correct in her reconsideration of early American republicanism, the founders had understood the potential tensions inherent in a polity which liberated individuals for self-interested pursuits yet rested upon a common moral commitment to the preservation of institutions devoted to public good; but they believed they could secure "the best of liberal democracy and republicanism" in the constitutional system. The public morality necessary to the maintenance of the Republic could be preserved through education and through the participation of citizens in civic life; thus democracy could indirectly encourage republican values. She argues retrospectively that they erred:

As Alexis de Tocqueville correctly foresaw, one great danger in a democratic and commercial republic is that the people will come to understand liberty and equality primarily in economic terms. The decline of civic virtue speeds up and intensifies this process, and Tocqueville is again right when he warns that once civic spirit is gone, laws alone cannot bring it back.[2]

As Democratic mavericks observed Tocqueville's American democracy, they saw a decline in civic virtue, a degradation against which they set themselves as statesmen. Their opposition was not primarily legalistic, but personal, and thus consistent with the libertarian tradition within which they acted. Through a concept of leadership identified with heroes of the Revolution, they attempted to redefine and reinvigorate the heritage of the Revolution to meet contemporary needs.

Because Democratic mavericks did recognize the disjunction between the expectations conjured up by revolutionary goals and the realities of the antebellum period and because they did assume responsibility for restoring (as they understood it) the harmony between ideals and reality, their ideological statements contained creative elements. Clifford Geertz's explanation of the central role of cultural strain—the dissonance in society between values and behaviors—in stimulating the development of new political ideologies is relevant to the ideas of mavericks:

It is, in fact, precisely at the point at which a political system begins to free itself from the immediate governance of received tradition, from the direct and detailed guidance of religious or philosophical canons on the one hand and from the unreflective precepts of conventional moralism on the other, that formal ideologies tend first to emerge and take hold. The differentiation of an autonomous polity implies the differentiation, too, of a separate and distinct cultural model of political action, for the older, unspecialized models are either too comprehensive or too concrete to provide the sort of guidance such a political system demands. Either they trammel political behavior by encumbering it with transcendental significance, or they stifle political imagination by binding it to the blank realism of habitual judgment. It is when neither a society's most general cultural orientation nor its most down-to-earth, "pragmatic" ones suffice any longer to provide an adequate image of political process that ideologies begin to become crucial as sources of socio-political meanings and attitudes.[3]

The "autonomous polity" of the United States was, of course, the product of the Revolution; but despite nominal continuity, the political system of the 1790s was not that of the 1830s, 1840s, and 1850s. Political parties had modified the system in fundamental ways, whether or not the alteration was recognized.[4] In light of the enormous difficulties associated with recreating ideologies for a pluralistic society and in the face of the considerable legislative tasks they confronted, conformists acted economically when they applied "received tradition" and resisted metaphysical innovations. Pragmatic anti-intellectualism was a convenient and reasonable retreat for ambitious politicians. Mavericks were also ambitious, and they were not deep political thinkers; but neither were they satisfied with the pragmatic application of ideology to politics without reference to the social changes they perceived. Democratic mavericks clearly observed cultural strain, and they consequently questioned and adjusted their inherited tradition. As Frederick Stanton insisted in the quote which heads this chapter, they would not construct their ideas to fit the dimensions of others, even if that meant repudiation of Jefferson or greater men.[5] Unlike Stanton, however, most Democratic mavericks failed to reconstruct essentially new ideologies. They lamented the decline of civic virtue and accepted responsibility for helping in its restoration. But, for the most part, their help went no further than presenting themselves as models or, failing that, as martyrs for a refurbished inherited faith.

One of the key ideological elements that connects Democratic mavericks to the self-conscious refurbishing of inherited wisdom is antiparty sentiment. Believing in the virtue of independent leadership, they asserted its importance on abstract bases, drawing from varying philosophical positions which refuted the primacy of party loyalty as a code for action. As members of the party which was coming to hold proudly a proparty ideology, mavericks did not always oppose partisanship, and many cooperated with party activities, however inconsistently. Some were erratically active in organizational circles and recognized their dependence upon party support, but they subordinated partisan considerations to others in their voting behavior and in the public proclamations of their political thought.[6] Almost every Democratic maverick at one time or another attacked parties as dangerous to the republic and offered some philosophical rationale for the antagonism.

In keeping with their inherited faith, Democratic mavericks tended to be paternalistic about their roles in politics. They believed statesmen to be responsible for leading society, not for representing its collective will. Without superior leadership, social goals would be unfulfilled. To use the distinction of the revolutionary period, mavericks believed in a kind of virtual representation; they did not completely accept the implications of direct representation.[7] The need for responsible leadership flowed from limitations in human nature; from the same source flowed the need for limited government. With Jeffersonian logic, Democratic mavericks argued that governmental power threatened liberty, even though people without government would be dangerous to themselves and others. Limited government was a safe middle ground. Through the exploration of such received wisdom, Democratic mavericks reached a laissez-faire position similar to that from which Democratic conformists departed.

A summary of the common ideas of Democratic mavericks gives them a clarity they lacked in their actual diversity. It is now necessary to illustrate that diversity within the shared political culture of the Democracy which bound mavericks and conformists. An extensive sketch of the ideas of each prominent Democratic maverick might best establish the verisimilitude of the summary, but since space prevents such an effort, a collage should suffice to indicate the variety which existed. Beginning with a large fragment—the eccentric ideas of Charles Jared Ingersoll of Pennsylvania—the odd coherence of the whole may be anticipated, for his peculiarities illustrate problems found in the political ideas of most Democratic mavericks.

The personal history of Ingersoll suggests the nature of his political difficulties. His father, Jared Ingersoll, was a member of the Continental Congress and the Constitutional Convention and was a Federalist Vice-President candidate in 1812. His brother, Joseph Ingersoll, was a Whig member of the House while Charles served there and was Minister to Great Britain during the Whig administration of Millard Fillmore. Charles was a man of many interests, the author of drama and history as well as a congressman and judge. Erudite, prolix, and controversial, this American "aristocrat" was an ardent Democrat who believed "the voice of the people to be the voice of God."[8]

Despite his enthusiastic democracy, Ingersoll saw its failings, but he explained that "even if the tendency of the democratic principle be downward, I for one prefer the despotism of democracy to that of monarchy or aristocracy."[9] His nostalgia for the republican past is clear; an approving character sketch of Thomas Jefferson praises his gentility, refinement, love of the arts, "superior talents," "good morals and unreproachable conduct," and especially his republican concern for education. The conflict between Ingersoll's anti-Democratic predispositions and his democratic theory is revealed as he contrasts the contemporary "self-made man" with Jefferson:

The half-educated upstart, boasting, among other still less educated, himself a self-made man, rarely equals the adult, who after school tuition, pursues his studies at college, and, when graduating thence, still, like Jefferson, continues them as long as he lives, not only for the most rational of his own enjoyments, but for the greatest good of the greatest number. For collegiate education is necessary to prepare teachers to manage schools, and every uneducated laborer, mechanic, or other workman of the toiling million, is instructed, improved, comforted, enriched, and otherwise benefitted by literary and scientific amelioration, imparted by learned men, like the genial sun enlivening every family and individual, in peace and in war supplying the aid, and comfort, and elevation much more needed by the poor than the rich, and the uninformed than the educated.[10]

Ingersoll's animus towards the "upstart" is as evident as his interest in the welfare of the abstract "workman of the toiling million," and the tension evoked by the juxtaposition of these two stereotypes is similar to that found in his admiration for "learned men" and his dismissal of the needs of "the rich." Ingersoll's own literary activities exhibit his identification with the model of Jefferson and underline his belief that the moral responsibility of the statesman was to provide intellectual leadership.[11]

This was not, however, the only responsibility of the modern statesman. Ingersoll greatly admired men of action, most notably Andrew Jackson, the leader of his own party, who, though "illiterate" himself, understood that "the discernment and attachment of the illiterate are less selfish and more reliable than those of the aristocratic." Jackson acted nobly but instinctively in behalf of the principle of equality because he knew the interests of the common people as "one of them himself."[12] As government must embody thought and action, so should statesmen, but Ingersoll found few models with the essential combination among his contemporaries.

In his rambling *Recollections*, written as Ingersoll approached his eightieth year and death, he reflected upon the deficiencies of modern statesmanship. The concluding chapter treats the decision of the Senate in 1803 to open floor discussion to press coverage for public information; the context of the event is Ingersoll's philosophical analysis of the "radical and immutable alteration" of American political institutions. The heart of the chapter is a mock debate between "veterans" of the "old times" in the Senate and "modern reformers" who respectively oppose and support public recording of their discussions.[13]

The chapter opens with a long quotation (in Latin with Ingersoll's personal translation) from Cicero, the model republican statesman, concerning the advantages of mixed government. Agreeing with Cicero that any pure form of government deteriorates, Ingersoll insists that mixed governments—like those of the United States and England—are likewise subject to degradation. The Senate, in opening its discussions to the press, has illustrated this fundamental principle operating in American politics. The "veterans," who speak "with fond recurrence to what they call the good old times of primitive politics," describe the consequences of the decision they oppose:

Senators, amenable only to that transcendent thing, a State, dragged by the licentious press from the secluded sanctuary of private independent deliberation into the flagrant glare, noise, and turmoil of public disputation before the despotic mass, are no longer conscientious sages, but creatures of ephemeral, often ill-got public favor. Instead of men tried by experience in responsible places, and there proved worthy by wisdom and virtue of preferment to the Senate, its seats, since deprived of sanctity, are canvassed and usurped by the young, ardent, and ambitious aspirants for the presidency. Eminent statesmen who, since the change, from the Senate move the country, influence its measures, and mould its policy, are more conspicuous for shining with the blaze of oratory than warming with the light of wisdom.[14]

Ingersoll's exaggerated language serves his satiric intentions, for although the "veterans" were exalted republican statesmen, their sense of their own superiority annoyed and amused him. Is it possible, then, to take seriously the "veterans' " main point: the transformation of senatorial character from statesman to demagogue?

Before the "reformers" are allowed to speak, the "veterans" more carefully focus upon the key to understanding the transformation of Senate character, the new style of political oratory resulting from public exposure. Because senators now will address an undereducated public instead of each other, the purposes and form of their discussions will change:

Universal vulgarized aptitude for fluency of speech, stimulated by the ubiquitous press to echo its ejaculations throughout the whole country, supplying their troops of supervising reporters, provided with special accommodations and privileges, engenders incessant and inordinate appeals, not to convince other Senators, but captivate the idle audience and far-distant public. . . . These lovers of the past furthermore asked whether senatorial divergence from private councils to public appeals had not even changed the character of congressional oratory to more popular invocations of the hearts instead of convincing the understanding of the nation?[15]

Ingersoll then alters the personae of the "veterans" by having them illustrate the new oratorical style with reference to his own contemporaries:

Hamilton, Madison, Burr, Marshall reasoned when they spoke, seldom addressing the mere passions of auditors. Ames, in his highly pathetic speeches, even when enlisting sympathies, was not merely declamatory. Whereas, of later ruling public speakers, Clay seldom argued, though his command of an audience was perhaps greater than that of the public; Webster, a powerful logician to be sure, always courted popular support; and Calhoun, bald and bare as his speeches were of imagery and illustration and strictly argumentative, nevertheless addressed them expressly to the people. The inordinate length, too, not only of modern speeches but of State papers, is attributable to the supposed necessity of proving all the most familiar postulates to the multitudinous auditory, supreme in judgment as in power.[16]

With that snide assault on popular sovereignty, the "veterans" two-and-one-half page diatribe is closed.

What follows is not what might be expected. The "modern reformers" do not defend the goodness of the masses, nor do they deny the change in the character of statesmen. Instead, "in answer to these antiquated imputations of senatorial degeneracy," they insist that "the step once taken can never be retraced and temperate conformity is the only wisdom." With three questions, they rest their case:

Would an American Senate, less accessible to the public than its original type, the British House of Lords, be tolerated or tolerable, sitting like that of Venice, in odious conclave incompatible with republican government? Would not the most licentious press and most desperate popular sovereignty be less dangerous to public welfare, or more propitious to peace and more conservative of property? Would irresponsible privacy in permanent stagnation be consistent with American development in its perpetual exigencies?[17]

At this point, having asked loaded questions which should reveal his bias, Ingersoll reenters the narrative in a serious vein and returns to his analysis of "this drift of democracy," leaving the "reformers' " questions unanswered.

Almost as an afterthought, Ingersoll then adds a three page "vindication of silent action without speech," explicitly his own view of the subject. Although the "vindication" tacitly lends veracity to the criticisms of the "veterans," it more obviously shifts the ground of the discussion from the fundamental issues they raised to an attack on the power of the press. In a paragraph more ambivalent than direct, Ingersoll first vindicates Senate secrecy:

Oratory, like warlike exploit, will always be puissant, often more effective than learning, sometimes than wisdom. Still, silence is a great faculty, if not the greatest. The Deity rules by acts, not words, The silent man seldom, like the speaker, says foolish or injurious things. The talent for public speaking misleads, even when handled by its greatest adepts; when by its innumerable American agitations of this common faculty it is oftener injurious than useful. A secret Senate, felt and known only by acts, may be impracticable in a free country. The multitude, inured to be told how to think and what to do, might not submit to Senators not asking their opinion. The press, a power next to warriors and orators, would no doubt insist on what it unjustly deems its right of animadversion. But if Franklin, Washington, Jefferson, and Jackson had ruled by policy explained not by executive acts but only in deliberate, written vindications, would the nation be worse governed than if ruled by the speeches of Clay, Webster, and Calhoun?[18]

With another question, the implied answer to which contradicts the implied answers to the "reformers' " three questions, Ingersoll moves to a discussion of the role of the press, that "privileged class or aristocracy" which tyrannizes through its "uncontrolled malediction of everything and everyone."[19]

By making the press a scapegoat for the evils of democracy, Ingersoll escaped the central intellectual dilemma he raised: how was it possible to reconcile republican statesmanship, which he admired and emulated, with democracy, to which he was equally devoted? For Ingersoll, the anti-Democratic implications of his paternalistic political model could not be reconciled with Democratic ideology. In this respect, his confused attempts at political analysis posed a problem felt by other Democratic mavericks. His efforts were typical in another respect because they were confused; no Democratic maverick created a systematic appraisal of his political situation or a thorough and philosophically grounded analysis of American politics. Finally, the example of Ingersoll is useful because he recognized the importance of the content of political oratory. Silence, he argued, was preferable to political rhetoric without learning or wisdom—a sad reflection for an old man whose career had been filled with polished rhetorical expression.

The oratory of most Democratic mavericks was more active than reflective, but it was not devoid of learning or wisdom. Mavericks believed they were obliged to serve as popular models, living examples of good political conduct, rather than to make laws which might limit American freedom. In their exemplary roles, mavericks could actively influence their society without undemocratically shaping it. The interest of a good number of maverick committee chairmen in discussion rather than in rapid passage of bills may reflect this kind of concern. Barnwell Rhett's admonition to his colleagues to act wisely in the light of the fact that "every example . . . passes down throughout all the avenues of society" surely highlights this conviction.

Seen in this exemplary light, the House of Representatives assumed a responsibility higher than that strict constructionists might otherwise assign it. Although he advocated limited government, Democratic maverick Isaac Holmes of South Carolina placed the House in the center of the American political universe:

Every man, who philosophically looked into the workings of our political system, must be convinced of the fact, that this House was *ipso facto* the Government; for there was no other Government in this Union than the Congress of the United States. The attempt of our fathers to make the Executive counterpoise the influence of the House of Representatives had signally failed.[20]

Importantly, however, Holmes assigned the House's responsibility to a general leadership function, not to extensive legislative powers. More explicitly, a northern Democratic maverick extolled this view of the House. In resisting attempts to draw up standardized procedures for resolving contested elections in the House, Charles Brown of Pennsylvania argued that:

The committee were attempting too much. They were trying to do what our fathers were never able to do—to get a free popular assembly to be like some clock or other machine, that would go of itself, with a mechanical regularity. It could not be done; and if it could, the vital informing soul of a free Government would have been destroyed.[21]

It is clear that the regularity sought by the Elections Committee might encourage the development of more efficient and businesslike settlement of frequent election disputes, while restricting the role of discussion central to Brown's concept of the "vital informing soul" of the House.[22] Along with other Democratic and Whig mavericks, Brown resisted gradual bureaucratization of the Congress. He rejected the idea of a machinelike legislature and, by implication, the notion that he should become a cog in the machine. He claimed a moral responsibility for government in the education of citizens, implicitly assuming for himself a superior status as well.

Democratic mavericks offered themselves as models for citizenship because they believed the American public was in sore need of models; they all agreed that the first half of the nineteenth century had witnessed a deterioration in the quality of republican institutions. Though few would go so far as to attack the new universal white manhood suffrage, their reservations about mass democracy are evident. To many, popularity and rectitude seemed incompatible; in the words of one: "Success makes patriots now-a-days, and in politics, owing to the degeneracy of the times in which we live, many politicians, I regret to say, prefer success rather than virtue."[23] The art of mass manipulation through rallies, torchlight parades, and the like, was practiced first on a large scale by the Jacksonians, but many Democratic mavericks disliked the practice, especially after it was turned on their party in the hoopla of 1840. Few were more graphic in their description of this election than John Wentworth, distinctive Chicago maverick:

This new system of electioneering in company with fugitives from justice and wretched outcasts of society, with drunken brawlers and vulgar songsters profaning the Sabbath and compelling ministers to dismiss their congregations with their obsenities [sic] and uproars, is one of the most mournful signs of the times, bespeaking vitiated tastes and the most wicked hearts. Establish the principle that a party resorting to such vile practices . . . shall bear sway in this country, and this glorious republic . . . is destroyed in the bloody anarchy of the French Revolution.[24]

The degradation of republicanism made the individual examples mavericks set as leaders all the more important. Blaming the decline on parties, most conveniently on the opposition party, Democratic mavericks partially absolved the common people from responsibility for the decline, though with some incidental reflection on the state of popular intelligence.

Maverick fears about the decline of republican institutions also fueled their concern about the growth of government. A profligate government could not reflect "the substantial simplicity" of a republican society, and it might well corrupt it thoroughly.[25] David Wilmot put the case directly in regard to the unprincipled scramble for federal funds for internal improvements: "This log-rolling system," he declaimed, "has done much to lower the tone and corrupt the political morals of our people."[26] With typical rhetorical extravagance, William "Extra Billy" Smith of Virginia assaulted a similar measure, urging the House to "pause over this system of recklessness, this palpable disregard of all the duties imposed upon us; and especially not to invite every harpy in the country to come here for encouragement in any wild scheme of speculation."[27] Later in the same Congress he attacked a bill to support steam service to Europe in equally dire tones:

Is it the policy of a republican people to build, and foster, and sustain these splendid ocean palaces? I say the system is demoralizing. I say it corrupts the tastes and habits of the country, and it engenders a spirit of rivalry, and extravagance of habit which is wholly at war with the simplicity which ought to belong to republican institutions. . . . An elegant simplicity is true taste, whether in public or private affairs.[28]

An interfering government (again the policy of the opposition) could be held responsible for the decline in civic virtue from ideals of "elegant simplicity" to "extravagance." William Smith did not pause to explain how "elegant simplicity" might characterize public affairs, nor did he acknowledge the source of his moralistic aesthetics; but he did directly connect the purity of society with the quality of government. And, like other mavericks, he placed himself in a position opposing the perversion of either society or government by the material progress of the nineteenth century.

In the antebellum era, as in the revolutionary one, the means to achieving simplicity in government were often negative means: destruction of the Bank of the United States, opposition to protective tariffs, and disapproval of federal aid to internal improvements. To the extent that they both sought to prevent these connections between government and the economy, both varieties of Democrats acted together. Too consistent an application of laissez-faire principles could, however, run afoul of party interests, and mavericks were sometimes unable to resist the impulse towards ideological purity at the expense of party welfare. Few issues illustrate this clash of principle and party more clearly than the opposition of some mavericks to their party's support of a public printer. Conformists in each party, when it was a minority in the House, customarily attacked the connection between the majority party and the printing. Some mavericks, approaching the problem more philosophically, attacked their own party for its interference with the free press, thus striking at an important element in the party machinery. Given their republican sentiments, many mavericks viewed the dissociation of government and press as too essential to liberty to be sacrificed to party interests. As one latter-day Jeffersonian said, "with a free press, and a pure press, virtue and morality will be preserved, and general intelligence so diffused, as to bid defiance to all the assaults, however potent, of tyranny and despotism upon the rights of the people."[29]

Understandably, Southern Democratic mavericks believed the success of abolitionism in northern politics to be the worst sign of the decline of republican institutions.[30] Because southerners believed the ideas of abolitionists to be incorrect, and even immoral, they often claimed that their popular reception was the result of devious means of persuasion. According to the 1850 view of aris-

tocratic Virginia maverick Muscoe R. H. Garnett, the northern political abolitionists intended to "govern the masses by money and corruption." With atypical
consistency, Garnett in the same pamphlet voiced opposition to pure democracy
because of the potential weaknesses of the majority, and he expressed preference
for the kind of benevolent oligarchy characteristic of colonial Virginia.[31]

Most southern Democratic mavericks believed that a strict devotion to the
Constitution would protect the minority from majority misrule. In the dramatic
phrases of Virginia maverick Sherrard Clemons, who spoke in the tumult of the
last years before the Civil War:

. . . we are verging every hour into the excesses of an unbridled popular licentiousness,
which in the hallowed name of the people, is repudiating the judgments of the highest
courts in the land; breaking through all constitutional restraints, and destroying all the
checks and balances our fathers formed . . . in this respect, the people *can* act in mass,
and in such cases they always act from their worst instincts and passions. The law is the
barrier which keeps both back.[32]

In both language and ideology, the concern of the southern and northern Democratic mavericks over the excesses of the new democracy seems to have been
influenced by the most conservative elements within the political ideas of eighteenth-century America. Their resistance to the modernization of politics was
couched in terms appropriate to the inclination; and it emphasizes the strong link
between mavericks and the political beliefs of an earlier period in American
history.

These echoes of the past were most often heard as Democratic mavericks
elevated the significance of their own roles in government; in this respect, the
views of northern and southern Democratic mavericks are similar. They disagreed, however, about other issues, where their personal interpretations of
political duty brought them into stubborn conflict, most notably as they disputed
the future direction of American society. The fundamental differences between
the Free-Soil and proslavery mavericks are an obvious example of this kind of
conflict. The maverick principle of reasoning abstractly about political action
led Democrats to oppose each other bitterly.

As was the case with most Americans who considered government philosophically, mavericks turned to the dictates of natural law for explanation of the
political world. Natural law justified for many mavericks the same kinds of
political positions adopted by conformists on less theoretical grounds. Few democratic mavericks were romantics; most sought the truths of natural law in
empirical observations. Almost all believed in an absolute minimum of political
interference with the laws of nature as they applied to society; they generally
defined progress in terms of individual human accomplishment. The mavericks'
concepts of natural law reflect variously eighteenth-century Enlightenment precepts, romantic influences from a more recent period, and even naturalism of
the sort synthesized by Herbert Spencer or by later popularizers of Charles

Darwin. Since few Democratic mavericks constructed complete or consistent political philosophies but were theoretical in their approach, they mixed theories with unwarranted confidence. Not surprisingly, then, natural law could justify anti- or proslavery views for mavericks, just as it did for other less politically involved Americans.

Northern Democratic mavericks who opposed the spreading of slavery emphasized the expansive influence of nature upon America's mission. Like their conformist counterparts, they promoted the idea of Manifest Destiny.[33] For conformists, this spirit was associated with imperialism; for mavericks the idea of mission had domestic implications, especially in regard to the future of slavery. As these mavericks saw their mission, they were to help uplift and purify the masses of Americans as well as those non-Americans who might be benefitted by incorporation into the nation. Unlike the Whigs, they did not see popular improvement occurring through the direct intervention of government but rather through the guarantee by government of the opportunity for self-improvement to all people. Resisting southern domination of the party, these northerners asserted a kind of reform goal for Democrats. Alexander Duncan of Ohio described the goal broadly, asserting that the great mission of his party was to promote "philanthropy, universal emancipation, and the happiness of the human family."[34] David Wilmot expressed similar sentiments: "It is the mission of that party to elevate man, to vindicate his rights, to secure his happiness."[35] Despite the broad objectives proclaimed in these statements, neither Duncan nor Wilmot advocated increased governmental power; they, like most Free-Soil Democrats, were firm supporters of the party's laissez-faire policies.[36]

In addition to the fact that their concept of mission contained social as well as political goals, antislavery mavericks were inclined to be moral absolutists, believing that the laws of God restricted human freedom, even in politics. Though they shared with conformists the conviction that natural law underlay American institutions, they perceived its operation as directly compulsive on Christian men, not as a vague subjective influence operating through different consciences in different ways. They viewed political right and wrong as objective absolutes, related to a wide variety of subjects. In an 1845 speech on slavery extension, Alexander Duncan pointed out that "it is the duty of every member of society to do his part to preserve that state of morals, public and private, which the Christian religion imposes."[37] The notion that Christian religion should impose public morality is more often associated with reforming Whigs than with Democrats, but it was not uncommon among maverick Free-Soilers.

Other Democratic mavericks from the North also argued in similar terms for different proposals. Speaking of the inequitable distribution of wealth, Richard D. Davis of New York insisted that "the institutions, customs, opinions, education and whole arrangement of society which produced such deplorable results must be wrong; radically, inherently wrong; and it must be right, morally, religiously, gloriously right, to go for their reform."[38] Pro-southern New Hampshire maverick Edmund Burke defended the laissez-faire principles of the Democratic party on the grounds that they were consistent with the "fixed and immutable laws" which "Providence has imposed on the physical, moral and social world."[39]

Such religious standards made maverick behavior a necessity for those who saw disagreement with the majority of the Democratic party as a lesser evil than violation of the will of God. In a speech in 1860, a loyal Democratic maverick expressed this sense of duty in unmistakable terms:

Not more certainly does gravitation tend to the centre than God punishes a violation of his immutable laws, no matter to what department of his Universal Kingdom they relate. ... He has manifested through all succeeding ages, a direct interposition in human concerns, and now, as well as at any other time, if we depart from the Christian principles of truth and right, which underlie all properly organized society and compose the base of all just Government, the penalty will follow.[40]

Fear of the penalty of God might be a powerful motivator for a congressman; certainly it would not often support partisan conformity. Unfortunately, as northern and southern interpretations of God's will and the national future diverged, mavericks led in drawing immoderate political positions.

Almost all southern Democratic mavericks, like southern Democratic conformists, were constant defenders of their region, but their defenses assumed different forms. Conformists declaimed the superiority of the South based on distorted evidence from the status quo; mavericks melded ideas with experiential evidence. For the most part, they borrowed from the philosophies of Jefferson, John Calhoun, or John Taylor of Caroline, differing from conformists in their independent application of abstract ideas to political issues but making limited original contributions. Four among the twenty-two southern Democratic mavericks went beyond that first step, however, and attempted to construct ideological positions which integrated their borrowed ideas into personal interpretations. Of those four, two were important leaders in the southern wing of the party. Thomas Clingman represented his North Carolina district for seven terms before ascending to the Senate just before the Civil War. Briefly a Whig, he was in many respects a southern moderate; his voting nonconformity was equalled by that of only one other southern Democratic maverick, yet he was a recognized spokesman on sectional issues. South Carolina's Robert Barnwell Rhett, on the other hand, was rarely moderate during his long service in the House and Senate, but was, with William Lowndes Yancey, one of the most implacable ideologues for the South. The loyalty of Clingman and Rhett to the interests of the South was shared, but their ideological contributions were quite different.

The perspective which Thomas Clingman brought to politics was scientific. Fundamentally an active man, who read widely and used his gleanings to support his bellicose inclinations, Clingman was deeply interested in theories of natural law and evidence from the natural sciences. A famous orator, his collected speeches contain such philosophical subjects as a discussion of the impact of

Darwinism and a Christian treatment of "The Follies of the Positivist Philosophers."[41] He also spent much of his life exploring and mapping the wilds of the
trans-Appalachian South, in recognition for which there is a mountain bearing
his name in the Smokies.[42] Clingman reasoned from the laws of nature as they
were concretely manifested in organic and nonorganic form. He extolled the
virtues of slavery on that basis, insisting that his version of natural law was the
only true "higher law" and that it taught in the "light of the nineteenth century"
that the Negro race was inferior to the white.[43] He argued from nature on other
subjects. In one of the more curious speeches among numerous oddities, he
justified the caning of Charles Sumner on the grounds of natural law, maintaining
that "in accordance with the system of the universe . . . there should be adequate
punishment for each offense. This is equally true as respects the moral, the
physical, and the organic laws."[44] Violence, struggle, and competition were the
laws of Clingman's nature and the basis for his political philosophy as well.

Barnwell Rhett, one of the earliest agitators for southern independence, opened
his career with a violently revolutionary antitariff speech, a speech so radical
that it won him instant notoriety and an ideological leadership he never relin-
quished.[45] He worked from time to time with the Calhoun forces, and he adopted
Calhoun's ideas of nullification; but he was never a dependable follower of the
older South Carolinian, whom he succeeded in the Senate.[46] Less intellectually
profound than Calhoun, he freely borrowed ideas but modified them to his more
radical purposes. Drew Faust has noted that the "men of mind" in proslavery's
"Sacred Circle" objected to the political uses of their ideas by Rhett, Calhoun,
and Yancey; the intellectuals' objections were well founded.[47] Rhett, even more
clearly than Calhoun, advocated a reversal of the political direction of the nation
from democracy to oligarchy. Like Calhoun, he argued that slavery was necessary
to insure a "conservative" democracy. The law of nature dictated that capital
would exploit labor, but slavery made the exploitation as mild as possible and
by insuring white solidarity promoted stable government.[48] Rhett's inflammatory
rhetoric was revolutionary, explicitly linking the southern cause with that of
1776, but he advocated revolution to assure the perpetuation of planter dominance
of the South under a mere facade of democracy. Although he was associated
with the Democratic party from his entry into the House until the party's division
in 1860, Rhett's goals were far less partisan than they were personal. His persistent pursuit of southern aims through direct political action and through the
pages of the Charleston *Mercury* gained him fame as the most intransigent
ideologue among the southern Democratic mavericks.

The remaining two of the four southern Democratic mavericks who developed
their ideas more systematically than others were Frederick Stanton and Muscoe
R. H. Garnett. They were more intellectually creative than Clingman and Rhett,
but they were also lesser figures within the party and the nation. Stanton, whose
objections to the Procrustean bed of his party have been noted, was a naturalist
like Clingman. A four-term Tennessee Democrat, he gained notoriety in the
South for his rejection of the Lecompton Constitution after his service as Bu-

chanan's appointed Governor of Kansas. Stanton based his political philosophy on evolutionary principles bearing marked resemblance to the Spencerian philosophy popular after the Civil War. In two speeches in 1854 and 1857 he outlined the thesis that civilization progressively improved in stages of struggle among races and nations.[49] He described the immediate past as being characterized by struggles through war but predicted that the new age would be marked by competition through industrialism. He also predicted a final stage of equilibrium, in which the struggle of man against man would cease. Like Spencer's, Stanton's naturalism justified laissez-faire principles. While he did not oppose reform, he believed it must be gradual, in keeping with the kind of change characteristic of nature:

Our own civilization is the legitimate product of the experience and struggles of former generations. If uncounted ages of physical commotion, whose history is not obscurely written in the fossil and the rock, have been necessary to arrange and stratify the materials of the earth we inhabit, a few thousand years of struggle and conflict among men have hardly sufficed permanently to organize the elements of human society.[50]

Through imitation of organic natural law, legislators could improve human institutions without unnatural interference. His conviction that his own actions were rooted in such principles may have supported Stanton in his opposition to the dominant proslavery faction within the southern Democratic ranks during the late 1850s.

Easily the most philosophical of the southern proslavery advocates in the House was Muscoe R. H. Garnett of Virginia, nephew of Robert M. T. Hunter, who was a leading Calhounite in the House and Senate and an outstanding conformist leader of the southern forces within the Democratic party. Garnett never attained the influence of his more famous uncle, but the two were very close from the time of the premature death of Garnett's father. While Garnett was clearly influenced by Calhoun, probably through his uncle, the younger man was much more philosophical than Hunter, and a man, according to one of Hunter's biographers, of "brilliant literary accomplishments."[51] Unlike Calhoun, Garnett was a southern romantic, exhibiting from his college days a penchant for romantic literature and philosophy but deriving from writers like Wordsworth and Coleridge a very different social philosophy than did the New England transcendentalists, the most famous American exponents of romanticism. Idealistically he asserted that:

The whole shape of our lives, and of the world around us, is moulded by the abstract ideas, and living thoughts, which former sages and poets evoked in their calm retreats. The statesman may govern his own generation, but to the philosopher belongs the next, and so great is the advance of learning, so rapid its diffusion that he now disputes the empire of the present.[52]

Merging philosophy with statesmanship, Garnett used his romantic ideas to justify laissez-faire government (in the transcendental mode); but he also supported the proslavery argument romantically. Somewhat illogically, he attacked the skepticism of the northern transcendentalists, attributing abolitionism partially to "one form of the disease" of skepticism;[53] at the same time, he attributed the moral impact of abolitionism to the persistence of Puritanism.

Whatever the illogic of Garnett's connections between skepticism, Puritanism, and abolitionism, his analysis led him to a clear perception of the problems of the South in regard to their combined impact. Unlike many southern mavericks, Garnett did not see abolitionism as a temporary aberration for the North. Indeed, he recognized that "the vast force of the moral sense of Christendom is directed to our ruin."[54] The abolitionist crusade would never falter: "These sons of the Mayflower will never rest easy under a conviction of their neighbor's sins, without aggressive efforts for his compulsory salvation."[55] By 1850, he saw only two possibilities for the protection of the South: either full equality in the nation or independence.[56] Though he was never an agitator like Rhett, Garnett recognized that the inevitable tide of events in the North would lead to the eventual end of slavery, so he ultimately reached Rhett's position on secession. Firmly convinced of the rightness of his romantic philosophy, he was as intransigent in the last analysis as the radical activist.

The frequent disruptiveness of the Democratic mavericks from North and South partly resulted from their theoretical approaches to political life and their social perspectives on political issues. Their paternalistic interpretations of republican principles led them to see themselves as models for correct behavior in a period of potential decline. Whatever their party might prefer, as they understood their roles, mavericks had to retain a modicum of independence. They justified this independence in terms of its influence upon their constituents, typically referring to historical, Biblical, mythical, or literary models for nonconformity, perhaps since so few were present in the contemporary congressional setting. An antislavery maverick drew upon Shakespeare in a speech to his constituents:

Our people are progressive, and they deserve to have in the council halls of the nation representing such a district, a man who is not a "scurvy politician" (cheers); a man who will not "bend the pregnant hinges of the knee that thrift may follow fawning."[57]

Posing as an unwilling victim of Procrustes, Frederick Stanton insisted he followed an older tradition of democracy, which "encourages, rather than destroys, individuality and independence of thought." Appealing to his constituents, he insisted that "any other principle would be a slavish one, which I could never consent to adopt, without feeling myself to be a disgrace to the intelligent and liberal people whom I have the honor to represent."[58]

Understandably, such appeals were not always successful. The weight of party could be overwhelming, and a maverick who differed too openly might court martyrdom, no common goal for politically ambitious men. An antislavery Democrat who broke with the Buchanan administration over Lecompton raised that spectre:

I will never barter truths for errors, knowing that I may support the latter by sophistries. I believe with Milton, that—"Truth is strong! Next to the Almighty she needs no policies, no strategems, no licensings to make her victorious." And I will follow her wherever she may lead. If from power, then I am against power. If from the mass, then I am against the mass. If from my friends, then I am against my friends. If into solitude and the desert, I will make her my companion forever.[59]

Pure truth, without policies or strategems, was a wholly unsuitable companion for a politician in the antebellum period, and none followed it exclusively. Democratic mavericks understood the necessity for compromise, and the successful ones among them practiced that necessity. In the last analysis, however, their successful leadership had more to do with ideological contributions than with building the machinery of party or government. Clearly, they perceived their roles differently than did conformists. Perhaps, on the political spectrum of the antebellum period they should be placed between Democratic conformists and Whigs. But in terms of their personal commitments to political leadership they do not fit on a conformist spectrum. Their role in the party and in the Congress was not exactly like that of conformists, at least in their own perception. Perhaps, moreover, they were not functionally alike from a historical perspective. Mavericks did offer a rationale for laissez-faire government consistent with the Democratic position in voting; conformists were relatively silent. The philosophical underpinnings of the maverick ideas may have been unacceptable to conformists had they noticed it, but of that there is little likelihood. Evidence suggests that the Democratic conformists had their eyes firmly fixed on the political environment in which they worked, not upon the philosophies which might support it.

NOTES

1. Frederick Blue attributes authorship of the Proviso to Wilmot, to two other Democratic mavericks, Preston King and John Wentworth, and to Jacob Brinkerhoff; see *The Free Soilers*, p. 28. According to H. Hardy Perritt, the title "father of secession" was first used in 1876 in a Charleston paper. Laura White, in her biography of Rhett, includes it as a subtitle. See Perritt, "The Fire-Eaters," in Braden, *Oratory in the Old South*, p. 242; White, *Robert Barnwell Rhett*.

2. Jean Yarbrough, "Republicanism Reconsidered: Some Thoughts on the Foundation and Preservation of the American Republic," *The Review of Politics* 40 (January 1979):85. The relationship of the American problem to past theory is treated in J. G. A. Pocock's concluding chapter "The Americanization of Virtue: Corruption, Constitution and Frontier," in *The Machiavellian Moment: Florentine Political Thought and the Atlantic Republican Tradition* (Princeton: Princeton University Press, 1975), pp. 506–552.

3. Geertz, "Ideology as a Cultural System," pp. 63–64.

4. That fundamental constitutional changes were largely unincorporated into the ideologies of antebellum politicians is a major theme in Richard P. McCormick, *The Presidential Game: The Origins of American Presidential Politics* (New York: Oxford University Press, 1982), esp. pp. 162–163, 205–206.

5. Frederick P. Stanton, "Appropriations for Scientific Purposes," *Congressional Globe*, 30th Cong., 1st Sess., *Appendix*, 709.

6. Antiparty sentiments were part of the revolutionary heritage of Americans. Most scholars have seen Whigs as troubled by the ethos of party more than Democrats. See, for example, Ronald Formisano's *Birth of Mass Parties*, and his "Political Character, Antipartyism, and the Second Party System," *American Quarterly* 21 (Winter 1969):685–688; and Howe, *Political Culture of American Whigs*, esp. pp. 50–55, where antipartyism is treated in the context of the ideas of John Quincy Adams, Whig maverick. The general partisan distinction is confirmed by the ideas of conformists described below; but antiparty sentiments were common among both Democratic and Whig mavericks. Mavericks recognized, however, the power and utility of parties. Ronald T. Takaki, in *A Pro-Slavery Crusade: The Agitation to Reopen the African Slave Trade* (New York: The Free Press, 1971), quotes James L. Orr, South Carolina Democratic maverick, as asserting that "no man now living in this Union . . . has power to accomplish any great measure or policy without the aid of party, and if you desire influence in a party, it is only to be attained by affiliating heartily in its organization" (p. 187).

7. The intellectual or practical content of the concept of representation is something neither political theorists nor politicians of the antebellum period nor twentieth-century political scientists seemed to have agreed upon. Although revolutionary Americans argued that direct representation implied a close relationship between the interests of the constituency and the actions of the representative, their repudiation of virtual representation was not thorough. For an excellent brief discussion of this point of difficulty, see Gordon S. Wood's *Creation of the American Republic*, pp. 162–196, 596–600; for a full treatment of the historical background to the American problem see J. R. Pole, *Political Representation in England and the Origins of the American Republic* (London: Macmillan; New York: St. Martin's Press, 1966) and *The Gift of Government: Political Responsibility from the English Restoration to American Independence* (Athens: University of Georgia Press, 1983). Samuel Patterson, *American Legislative Behavior, A Reader*, has collected some of the viewpoints of political scientists on this subject, with the warning that "the concept *representation* is still not entirely unambiguous" (p. 3). Two useful essays in this context are those by Charles E. Gilbert ("Operative Doctrines of Representation") and the modern classic "The Role of the Representative" (originally subtitled "Some Empirical Observations on the theory of Edmund Burke") by Heinz Eulau, John C. Wahlke, William Buchanan, and LeRoy C. Ferguson. The latter authors suggest that there has been new growth in the prevalance of what they term the "trustee" concept of representation because of the complexity of modern government; complexity presumably requires a new sort of elitism (see p. 242). They imply clearly that the "delegate" concept, associated with the development of popular democracy, was the predominant form in earlier United States political history. This view is stated explicitly in Alfred DeGrazia, *Public and Republic: Political Representation in America* (New York: Alfred A. Knopf, 1951), p. 140. It seems likely that these works understate the persistence of the trustee concept as a minority view, even in the Jackson period. Robert Dale Owen's forceful argument for the delegate concept (see above, pp. 87–88) may or may not have been shared by most other conformists. At least it is safe to say that most conformists did not publicly question the delegate concept, even if they did not share it, which their behavior strongly implies.

8. Charles J. Ingersoll, *A Communication on the Improvement of Government: Read*

before the American Philosophical Society, at a Meeting Attended by General LaFayette, Oct. 1st, 1824 (Philadelphia: Abraham Small, Printer, 1824), p. 24.

9. Quoted in William M. Meigs, *The Life of Charles Jared Ingersoll* (Philadelphia: J. B. Lippincott Co., 1897), p. 193.

10. Charles J. Ingersoll, *Recollections, Historical, Political, Biographical, and Social, of Charles Jared Ingersoll* (Philadelphia: J. B. Lippincott & Co., 1861), pp. 68–70.

11. His approval of the model of intellectual statesman is also evident in his biting attack on John Quincy Adams in Charles Jared Ingersoll, *Historical Sketch of the Second War Between the United States of America and Great Britain* (Boston: Lea & Blanchard, 1845), 2:245–248.

12. Ibid., 2:272.

13. Ingersoll, *Recollections*, pp. 431–438.

14. Discussion of Cicero, Ibid., pp. 413–414; "veterans," p. 432.

15. Ibid., p. 433.

16. Ibid., p. 434.

17. Ibid.

18. Ibid., p. 436.

19. Ibid., p. 438.

20. *Congressional Globe*, 27th Cong., 2d Sess., 436. Holmes made this argument in connection with the debate over reapportionment; he favored increasing the size of the body and thereby lowering the ratio of representation. See also Ibid., p. 622.

21. *Congressional Globe*, 27th Cong., 2d Sess., 846.

22. Nelson W. Polsby, in "The Institutionalization of the House," discusses the regularization of procedures for dealing with contested elections as an indicator of institutionalization, pp. 160–164. Lest the mavericks appear too prescient in their fears of loss of individual autonomy in the face of institutionalization, it should be noted that increased size of the House, which Holmes argues for, is seen by Polsby as one basic cause of the institutionalization process. Holmes' reason for the greater size was that it would afford a closer relationship between constituents and representative, not that it would increase efficiency; he would have abhorred the consequence Polsby suggests.

23. John B. Haskin, *The Course of Hon. John B. Haskin, in the XXXVth Congress, Its Own Vindication* (New York: Sackett & Cobb, Steam Book & Job Printers, 1858), pp. 16–17.

24. *Congressional Globe*, 28th Cong., 1st Sess., 510.

25. This assertion was part of a speech in which Charles Brown attacked the expenses of government and particularly the fact that the representatives were paid too much. *Congressional Globe*, 27th Cong., 2d Sess., 252.

26. *Congressional Globe*, 29th Cong., 1st Sess., 1184. The dignified Douglas Democrat, John McClernand of Illinois, unlike his mentor a maverick, spoke in the same vein about internal improvements:

Congress was now invested with an unlimited power of taxation as to amount: superadd now to this the power of unlimited taxation as to objects, and the republic becomes a practical despotism. It may retain the forms of freedom, but will in fact sink into the violence, injustice, and wrong of tyranny.

Congressional Globe, 29th Cong., 1st Sess., 3.

27. *Congressional Globe*, 33d Cong., 2d Sess., 479.

28. *Congressional Globe*, 33d Cong., 2d Sess., 755. Earlier in this speech Smith had

attacked a western Democrat for his conversion to federal aid by reading the Bible about Saul's conversion; Ibid., p. 754. When the westerner responded by asking how Smith got his nickname (a reference to his drinking habits), Smith attacked him as "not a gentleman." Ibid., p. 755.

29. James Garland of Virginia, speaking to the Democratic-controlled 25th Congress, *Congressional Globe*, 25th Cong., 2d Sess., 571. M. R. H. Garnett, another Democratic maverick from Virginia, described the connection as a system of "public plunder" in another Democratic Congress, the 35th. *Congressional Globe*, 35th Cong., 1st Sess., 512. Leonard White in *The Jacksonians*, Ch. 15 ("The Administration Press and the Public Printing"), has a full discussion of the issue and its resolution in the Buchanan administration.

30. Both southern mavericks and conformists shared fears of northern popular opinion, but maverick expression was more consistent throughout the two decades before the Civil War, not just on its eve.

31. M. R. H. Garnett, *The Union, Past and Future: How It Works, and How to Save It. By A Citizen of Virginia* (Washington, D. C.: Jus. T. Towers, Printer, 1850), p. 26.

32. Sherrard Clemens, *Speech of Hon. Sherrard Clemens, of Virginia, on the President's Kansas Message; Delivered in the House of Representatives, Feb. 18, 1858* (Washington, D. C.: Congressional Globe Office, 1858), p. 8.

33. Descriptions of the idea of Manifest Destiny are found in Frederick Merk, *Manifest Destiny and Mission in American History: A Reinterpretation* (New York: Alfred A. Knopf, 1963); and Albert K. Weinberg, *Manifest Destiny: A Study of Nationalist Expansionism in American History* (Baltimore: Johns Hopkins Press, 1935). Also relevent is Arieli, *Individualism and Nationalism in American Ideology*.

34. Alexander Duncan, *Speech of Mr. Duncan, of Ohio, in the House of Representatives, Feb. 19, in Committee on the Army Appropriations Bill* (Washington: n.p., 1845), p. 12. Hereafter cited as *Speech on Army Appropriations*. Duncan was a physician, a fact often reflected in his speeches.

35. From a speech at Herkimer, Pa., quoted in Charles Buxton Going, *David Wilmot, Free Soiler: A Biography of the Great Advocate of the Wilmot Proviso* (n.p.: D. Appleton & Co., c. 1924; Gloucester, Mass.: Peter Smith, 1966), p. 298. Hereafter cited as *David Wilmot*.

36. Wilmot was scaled in the weakest position on economic issues in the 31st Congress and in the strongest position on sectional issues. This pattern was common among antislavery mavericks. See Appendix II.

37. Duncan, *Speech on Army Appropriations*, p. 11.

38. Richard David Davis, *An Address Delivered before the Literary Societies of Geneva College, on the First of August, 1843* (Geneva, N. Y.: Scotten & Stow, 1843), p. 21.

39. Edmund Burke, *An Address Delivered before the Democratic Republican Citizens of Lempster, New Hampshire on the Eighth of January 1839* (n.p.: H. E. & S. C. Baldwin, Printers, 1839), p. 14.

40. Isaac N. Morris, *Speech of Hon. I. N. Morris, on the Status of the States and Questions Incidentally Connected Therewith. Delivered at the House of Representatives, Springfield, Ill., Jan. 11. 1867* (n.p., n.d.), p. 1.

41. The latter speech is listed in the Foner collection of the Library of Congress but was unavailable. Other examples of the variety of Clingman's interests included in his collected speeches and writings are "The Great Meteor of 1860," "Volcanic Action in

North Carolina," and a postwar speech entitled "Huxley, Darwin and Tyndall; or the Theory of Evolution." See Thomas L. Clingman, *Selections from Speeches and Writings*.

42. *BDAC*, p. 708.

43. Thomas Clingman, *Nebraska and Kansas. Speech of Mr. Clingman, of North Carolina, in the House of Representatives, Apr. 4, 1854* (n.p., n.d.), p. 6.

44. Thomas Clingman, *Speech of Hon. Thomas L. Clingman, of North Carolina, on the Resolutions Reported by the Select Committee to Investigate the Alleged Assault upon Senator Sumner by Mr. Brooks; Delivered in the House of Representatives, July 9, 1856* (n.p., n.d.), p. 9. Thomas Bowie, Democratic maverick from Maryland, a man of similarly violent propensities, put forth a like argument in the context of a dispute over a contested election: "Inherent powers belong to individuals, belong to man in a state of nature, and not merely to man, but to animals and plants—the power to protect themselves." *Congressional Globe*, 35 Cong., 1st Sess., 772.

45. White, *Robert Barnwell Rhett*, pp. 14–15.

46. Rhett was characterized as "too independent to be a good lieutenant," in Charles Wiltse, *John C. Calhoun: Sectionalist, 1840–1850* (New York: The Bobbs-Merrill Co., 1951), p. 52.

47. Drew Faust, *A Sacred Circle: The Dilemma of the Intellectual in the Old South* (Baltimore: The Johns Hopkins University Press, 1977), p. 126.

48. White, *Robert Barnwell Rhett*, pp. 49–50.

49. The two speeches delivered by Stanton were *Address Delivered by Mr. Fred P. Stanton, of Tennessee, before the Metropolitan Mechanics Institute, at the Opening of Its Annual Exhibition in Washington, D.C., Mar. 2, 1857* (Washington, D. C.: n.p., 1857), hereafter cited as *Metropolitan Mechanics Institute Address*; and *A Lecture Delivered by the Hon. F. P.Stanton, on the Navy of the United States, Before the Mercantile Library Association, Feb. 3, 1854* (New York: Samuel T. Callahan, 1854), hereafter cited as *Lecture on the Navy*. The description of his philosophy here is taken from both speeches.

50. Stanton, *Metropolitan Mechanics Institute Address*, p. 14.

51. Wiltse described the foundation of the Calhoun–Hunter relationship in *John C. Calhoun: Nullifier*, p. 407. The close relationship between Hunter and Garnett is described in Henry Harrison Simms, *Life of Robert M. T. Hunter: A Study in Sectionalism and Secession* (Richmond, Va.: William Byrd Press, 1935), p. 7. Quote is from James Mercer Garnett, *Biographical Sketch of Hon. Muscoe Russell Hunter Garnett*; reprint from July and Oct. Numbers (1909) of *William and Mary College Quarterly Magazine*, pp. 12–13.

52. M. R. H. Garnett, *An Address Delivered before the Society of Alumni of the University of Virginia, at Its Annual Meeting. Held in the Rotunda, on the 29th of June, 1850,* published by order of the Society (Charlottesville, Va.: G. S. Allen & Co., Printer, 1850), p. 4. Hereafter cited as *Alumni Address*.

53. Ibid., p. 31.

54. Ibid.

55. M. R. H. Garnett, *Speech of Hon. M. R. H. Garnett, of Virginia, on the State of the Union, Delivered in the House of Representatives, Jan. 16, 1861* (Washington, D. C.: McGill & Witherow, Printers, 1861), p. 7.

56. Garnett, *Union, Past and Future*, p. 29.

57. Haskin, *Course of Haskin*, p. 75.

58. Stanton, "Appropriations for Scientific Purposes," p. 709.

59. John Hickman, *Popular Sovereignty—The Will of the Majority against the Rule of a Minority. Speech of Hon. J. Hickman, of Pennsylvania, in the House of Representatives, Jan. 18, 1858* (Washington, D. C.: Congressional Globe Office, 1858), p. 8.

CHAPTER 7

The Whig and Republican Conformists

> I claim to be a Whig, . . . I started a Whig, I have always been a Whig
> without wavering or shadow of turning to the right or to the left. I have
> served that party when I had the strength to serve it, and now though as a
> party it may not exist, I cherish its principles with all the ardour of my
> nature.
>
> Richard W. Thompson, 1855

Among Whigs of the antebellum period, there appeared to have been such a
happy consistency between partisan principles and individual preferences that
Richard Thompson could proclaim his institutional and ideological loyalty with
no evidence of tension. The Whig party represented, in the opinion of most of
its leaders, the continuation of the colonial tradition of government by an elite
of wisdom and virtue. Theoretical egalitarian Ralph Waldo Emerson, who described the Whigs as "the most moderate, able and cultivated part of the population," concluded that "of the two great parties which at this hour almost
share the nation between them, I should say that one has the best cause, and the
other contains the best men."[1] Whigs took pride in their position as the "best
men;" although in the second party system few leaders were from families of
great wealth, Whigs did identify their interests with those of the largely Anglo-
American "respectable" classes.[2] While the pragmatic, laissez-faire partyism
of the Democrats made a perfect umbrella under which men of different cultural
backgrounds could unite, Whigs seem to have gathered together because they
perceived the world in the same way. Whig party ideology appears to have been
a natural outgrowth of the Whiggish world view, one which was shared with
remarkable consistency by a large group of Whig conformists.[3]

Unlike Democratic ideology, Whig ideology united a consistent social vision
with concrete policy goals. Democratic laissez-faire ideas allowed different com-

munities diversity in free growth; Whig ideas called for an active national government to harmonize the social and economic needs of diverse communities into a coherent whole. From conservative ideas about the nature of man and society, Whigs praised those leaders who personified the "best" in Anglo-American culture and set the standard for others to follow. Within the "political culture of American Whigs," the great majority of mavericks and conformists, northerners and southerners, shared these ideas and applied them to policy considerations. Even Edward Pessen, generally quite suspicious about the ideological honesty of the major antebellum parties, has acknowledged that "for all the diversity of Whig political behavior on national, state, and local levels, there is a significant degree of congruence between the party's theory and practice during the era."[4]

Separating Democrats and Whigs into distinct American subcultures is a useful tool for understanding antebellum politics. Within the institutional confines of the House of Representatives, however, Democrats and Whigs had many common legislative tasks and responsibilities, and in that special context Whig conformists and Whig mavericks divided functions in ways similar to Democrats. Conformists passed around the common currency of Whig ideology; mavericks created new ideas. In his graceful exposition of Whig political culture, Daniel Howe has warned that to distinguish "between the ideas or culture of intellectuals and those of other (sometimes called 'real') people . . . creates confusion" for understanding Whigs. But Howe's illustrative Whigs are not ordinary House Whigs. In fact, he includes among his models only three House Whigs who served two terms or more between 1836 and 1860—John Quincy Adams, Joshua Giddings, and Alexander Stephens—and all three are mavericks in the terms of this study.[5] This selectivity does not undermine Howe's main contention, but it supports the interpretation that the demands of legislative responsibility within the House sorted out men according to their talents.

Although the evidence suggests some specialization of roles among the House Whigs, the rhetorical usages of Whigs do not bear direct comparison to those of Democrats because Whigs did not draw the bounds of political life narrowly. Whigs were proud of their social, intellectual, and moral responsibility, and their rhetoric displayed the sources of their pride; yet Whig conformists scorned political metaphysics which disrupted party policy and excoriated political moralism which threatened party unity.

The ideology of Whig conformists wed pragmatism and principles into a seamless whole that sustained their confident leadership. "Whig democracy" advocated the elevation of the common people to a mildly elitist standard without derogating the capabilities of the Anglo-American lower classes.[6] Whig conformists assessed human nature cautiously, but not negatively. Popular rationality could be developed through the careful construction of social and political institutions that would channel public passions and interests in wholesome directions. Devoted to the Union, Whig conformists were not so much convinced that the political institutions of the United States were perfect as they were certain that radical change would not improve them. Constructive reformism under wise leadership would assure gradual progress without jeopardizing the accomplishments of the past. Although the Whig cohorts insisted that they lacked the iron discipline of the Democratic army, their shared principles promoted conformity.[7] To be sure, sectional issues prompted northern and southern Whigs to differ, but among conformists the ideological cohesion of the party is much more striking than its divisions.

Northern Whigs had some special concerns as residents of regions where cultural homogeneity was rapidly decreasing. Whigs believed that the troublesome aspects of human nature were unevenly manifested across the globe, surfacing least among people of English ancestry. Though they, much more than Democrats, had humanitarian sympathies for Black Americans and American Indians, they were noticeably less interested in the welfare of ethnic minorities who were politically involved. These beliefs were surely not unrelated to the tendency of those minority voters to support the Democratic party; in this case as in others, partisan concerns and Whig ideology were mutually reinforcing. Washington Hunt, a New York conformist, warned his fellows in 1845 of their duty, urging the Whigs, "the political majority of the House, on whom rests the responsibility, to guard and defend the elective franchise," and "to warn them [the people] of the dangers to which they are exposed from vice, ignorance, and the seductive arts of party politicians."[8] Convenient congruence between party interests and conservative ideology supported Hunt's assault on the partisan devices of his opponents.

The cultural homogeneity which apparently united many northern Whig activists and voters provided ample cushion for a cautiously moralistic approach within the framework of practical politics. Northern Whig conformists supported both political independence and party organization; their moderate views would not support either independence which threatened institutional stability or partisan proscription of mild deviation from Whig positions. The balancing of party interests, constituent pressures, and personal beliefs was undoubtedly an occasional problem; but most northern Whig conformists found the act tolerable. George N. Briggs of Massachusetts, whom James Russell Lowell described in the *Biglow Papers* as a "sensible man," never broke congressional party lines to any measurable degree, but he insisted privately that a congressman's first obligation was to his conscience:

... though his constituents may not always appreciate the motives of their agent, when his public acts do not conform to their wishes, yet he is certain, if honest, good intentions govern his course, that He who weighs conduct by motives will judge him in mercy.[9]

"Honest, good intentions" of an agent who shared most beliefs of his constituents and colleagues were not likely to produce conflict.

The willingness to compromise was seen for most Whigs as an important part of the moral obligation of a congressman. As one Ohio Whig expressed it: "I believe the National Legislature never could do anything with any great national question of public policy unless individuals should occasionally compromise, in some degree, their own opinions.''[10] The positive value attached to compromise, "in some degree," reinforced the unity of Whig conformists on a wide range of issues.

The happy harmony of political life which could be explained through Whig conservatism was also characteristic of the economy in the prevalent Whig view. For Northern Whig conformists, the advent of industrialism had not destroyed the moral basis of economic effort. The marvelous consistency between private interests and public good was glowingly extolled by one Massachusetts Whig:

The industry, and skill, and sagacity, which have been faithfully and judiciously applied to the accumulation of private wealth, now pour back their varied generous contributions for the improvement, the refinement, and adornment of that land, which has been at once the scene and the witness of those noble aims and efforts. Here indeed is the whole science of what is improperly called Political Economy presented in all its practical bearings, and in its fullest length and breadth. Individual fortunes created by well-directed individual energies; and then distributed for individual and social welfare, and to build up the intellectual, moral and religious character of the community.[11]

The judicious application of individual effort could uplift the whole community in the direction of the model of the men who ennobled it, demonstrating the "practical" truth of Whig political economy. A congressman who epitomized this revised doctrine of stewardship, wealthy textile manufacturer Abbott Lawrence, reiterated the importance of approaching political economy practically as he assaulted the Democrats, "I am tired of this everlasting speculation upon free trade. It means nothing. It is ideal, a mere phantom, and not to be entertained by practical men. It is a transcendental, utopian doctrine, that has no practical result."[12] In economics as in politics, practical morality would produce an improved common lot, but radical speculation would destroy social harmony.

Northern Whig conformists, most of whom personally opposed slavery, were quick to recognize abolitionism as a threat to the unity of party and country, and for both reasons they sought to prevent its entry into politics. Joshua Giddings' Ohio predecessor and friend Elisha Whittlesey, a member of Congress from 1836 to 1840, described the agitation as "impracticable" and "inexpedient," despite his personal dislike of slavery. Like other conservative Whigs he hoped that the "stability and intelligence" of the people, "guided by the wisdom of Him who overrules all things" would protect the Union against the emotionalism of abolitionists.[13] Less optimistic was Indiana's Richard Thompson, who accused the agitators of appealing to the baser instincts of the people. "Beneath the pretence of humanity and philanthropy" they hid their actual "treasonable designs" and sought to corrupt and transform the body politic. Reverting to the eighteenth-century language which revealed his essential conservatism, he decried the disruption of political harmony by selfish men who "have kept the cauldron of their passions continually boiling over by the heated fires of faction."[14] Loyal Whigs like Whittlesey and Thompson seemed clearly to believe that in defending their party they were defending their nation; true social conservatives, they placed the practical defense of established institutions above personal opposition to slavery.

Of course many northern Whigs fought the introduction of the slavery issue into politics for purely pragmatic reasons. One suspects this of the later Republican, Schuyler Colfax, who launched his Whig newspaper in 1845 with the proclamation that he would "be opposed to both Calhounism and Birneyism, viewing them both as ultraisms."[15] The checkered career of Colfax indicated little of moral constituency and points to the possibility that for some Whigs appeals to morality masked less than moral motives. But regardless of motivation, the political dilemma the Whigs faced when abolitionism invaded politics was a real one.

A loyal Ohio Whig conformist, Daniel R. Tilden, explored the dimensions of the problem fully in a public paper during the Presidential election of 1852. Responding to an assault upon him and his party by Whig antislavery maverick Giddings, he outlined the reasons he adhered to the party rather than to personal interpretations of antislavery principle. He insisted that political parties were but means to ends, necessarily tainted with human imperfection, but capable nonetheless of producing good:

If political organizations are but the means we employ to secure something beyond them, and there be no demerit in separating from them when other means are at command, which can be bettter employed for our purpose, then I am at liberty to enquire of you, why it is that if the Whig party sustain their former relation to this same old issue of slave extension, that we may not, without sacrifice of honor, again combine with them? You may answer, it is because they are so corrupt. I confess this answere [sic] is not satisfactory to me. I do not anticipate, myself, a speedy reign of the saints in this country, and you and myself are old enough, and have had experience enough of men generally, and of politicians in particular, to decide at once, that an efficient party—a majority party in this country, however it may be brought into being, must embody a vast amount of corruption.[16]

Tilden thus posed to Giddings two rhetorical questions which might be asked of all dissenting Whigs: if parties are only temporary and should be dropped when they are evil, why was the party not abandoned in 1848, or earlier, when the first antislavery parties appeared? If all parties are evil, why support the new ones? Tilden intended to suggest two possible answers. One, which he obviously favored, was that the new parties were merely instruments of ambition, not of principle. The other, which he rejected, was that the new parties could represent pure morality. Hoping that conservative voters would follow his logic, he insisted that practical morality dictated Whig loyalty:

Now, sir, I have made up my mind that if I am so fettered by the Constitution of the country, that I cannot, as a politician, be true to principle, I will, at least, in all matters pertaining to slavery, endeavor to make myself useful in practice.[17]

A great many northern Whig conformists shared this perspective, agreeing that there would be no "speedy reign of the saints," and supported the party of practical morality as long as it offered a way of being "useful in practice."

In this endeavor they were supported by southern Whig conformists, most of whom appear to have perceived the nature of American politics and society in a very similar fashion to their northern party brethren. This may partially account for the fact that among them there were many Unionists. Although Unionism was more likely for Whigs from the border states, some lower South Whigs also refused to give their devotion to the Confederacy. Even among the Whigs who became Confederates, their political attitudes were characterized by the same sort of conservative and practical morality as that of the northern Whigs.[18]

Southern Whig conformists believed in the necessity for guidance of the masses by the able few. Like northern Whigs, they saw their political role as part of the general responsibility that educated and intelligent people had toward their society. Politics, "the highest vocation known to civil society, the great art upon which the happiness, and welfare of the country and its teeming millions depend," was stable in a democracy only as long as the voters were themselves virtuous and recognized virtue in politicians.[19] Southern Whigs favored national improvement but opposed rapid or violent change. Many southern Whigs, for example, opposed the Mexican War because they feared that conquest would introduce into the body of the Republic large numbers of uneducated, allegedly immoral people. They wished to witness moral and economic progress but not physical expansion. One Whig conformist who actually participated in the War (because he could not avoid it "with honor") wrote home letters describing the "savage and vicious" character of the Mexicans he met.[20] Although he conceded that the better class had probably fled upon the advance of the army, he expressed the opinion that the country would never amount to anything because the Mexicans were incapable of progress. A less typical example of Whig concern for moral and political progress was the opposition of one southern Whig conformist to universal manhood suffrage on the grounds that it incorporated into the body politic "all the worthless, ignorant and corrupt mass of population, native and imported."[21] As for northern Whigs, partisan interest and personal ideology were mutually reinforcing southern Whig concerns.

In regard to slavery issues, however, this congruence was not typical. The Whig party, the party of "intelligence, substance, and respectability,"[22] held the loyalty of southern Whig conformists through the antebellum years because of its overall soundess, despite the implications for slavery of its activist philosophy of government. Democrats and dissenting Whigs warned them of the danger, but southern Whigs seemed to perceive the Democratic alternative as threatening to social stability even if safe on slavery.[23] One southern Whig

probably expressed the sentiments of many in regard to uniting with Democrats
to protect the South, describing the proposed cooperation as a sort of Trojan
Horse: "When we tell them that we desire Union with them on this vital question
of slavery, we mean a union of the South for the *sake of the South*, not for the
benefit of the *Democratic party*."[24] Even if they offered a guard against interference with slavery, most southern Whig conformists rejected laissez-faire principles of the Democracy. In words that Abbott Lawrence would have found a
comfort, one spoke in favor of the protective tariff: "There is no such thing as
free trade, and never will be, as long as mankind remains selfish, and governments require to be supported by money."[25] On a wide range of economic issues,
southern Whigs were in ideological agreement with the northern Whigs, and
they jointly opposed other southerners.

Southern and northern Whig conformists shared a model for pragmatic statesmanship: the politician "free alike from romantic and sentimental notions of
man's perfectibility and from distrust of his capacity, when properly instructed,
to comprehend what are called great matters of state."[26] Indeed, one Tennessee
Whig sketched a picture of statesmanship that conformists in both parties probably could have accepted. The leading quality of the statesman, he said, was
"good sense."

Good sense . . . though not so dazzling to the observer—not so lightning-like in its manifestations, as that other quality called genius, is infinitely more conservative in its
tendencies and effects. Genius may immortalize an individual, but good sense conduces
to the safety of nations. The one may reflect glory upon Empire, but the other can alone
ensure its repose and its duration.[27]

Many southern Whigs believed that the safety of the American nation was more
secure in the care of the party of Whiggish "good sense" than under the leadership of the southern ideologues who berated its caution.

Southern Whigs, like many northern Whigs and also like many Democratic
conformists, opposed both southern extremists and northern abolitionists. When
forced to choose between the two by the secession of the South, southern Whig
conformists made different choices, but the justification typically rested on the
same kind of conservative Whig philosophy. One Whig who defended slavery
as the only way to save the country from the "thousand destructive isms infecting
the social organization" of the North, refused nonetheless to support secession.
If slavery were a safe institution, it still was not sufficient justification for
disruption of the greater safety of the Union and for letting loose the passions
of war: "The issues are Union or Disunion. I am for the Union. Peace or War,
I am for peace!"[28] This southern Whig conformist, like many others, North and
South, feared the coming of war because of its destructive effect on social order.
Yet he, like many others, finally went with the South and fought in a war he
did not believe in, probably on the grounds of the same conservative priorities.
If a man's neighbors, friends, political supporters, and business associates were

all in favor of secession, however unwise he might personally think it, practicality would dictate cooperation rather than following the course of social martyrdom.

The fact that among the southern Whig conformists there were few outstanding national leaders may be attributed partly to the consistent difficulties they faced in reconciling protection for slavery with their Whig party membership. Many Whigs in the South were unwilling to change party allegiance, even when faced with the death of the national party in the 1850s. Although some prominent southern Whigs became Democrats and made significant contributions to the antebellum leadership of that party, most of these appeared as mavericks in either or both of the parties to which they belonged.[29] Perhaps most of the southern Whig conformists were unable to gain and hold office as the strength of the party in the South waned under pressure of the crisis over slavery. In essence, they followed their party into political oblivion.

A similar fate met the northern Whig conformists who had decried the entry of slavery into politics and were unable consequently to accept the Republican party. The outstanding example of this course is the truncated career of Millard Fillmore. In a suppressed portion of his presidential message to Congress in 1852, Fillmore warned of the dangers of abolitionism in national politics:

I speak not of the merits or demerits of the sentiment in which this agitation originates, but look only to its effects upon the body politic; and for all the purposes of this argument, it may be conceded that the great majority of those who entertain this sentiment are entirely sincere and honest in their convictions; but this sincerity, so far from lessening, actually increases the danger.[30]

Fillmore seems genuinely to have feared the effects of abolitionism upon the Union as well as the Whig party; but some Whig conformists, even some who originally opposed the Antislavery movement spoke more for devotion to party organization than to principle.

Most obviously, this concern for party and its impact on personal ambition is reflected in the attitudes of those Whigs who moved into the Republican party. Schuyler Colfax proclaimed in 1842: "I am an uncompromising Whig—Whig all over."[31] Abraham Lincoln's friend, Edward D. Baker, who served as Whig congressman from Illinois and later as Republican senator from Oregon, orated: "To the very last of my blood and breath, I am a Whig, constant and unchanging, now and forever."[32] Richard Thompson, "the persistent Whig," who stated in 1855 that he was a Whig "without wavering or shadow of turning to the right or to the left," followed his Whiggish principles through the American party and into the Republican organization in 1861.[33] It would certainly be consistent in a general sense for men who measured political morality in terms of practical considerations to achieve a shift in parties when it seemed dictated by the necessity of political survival. And most conformist leaders of the Whig party in the North were able to make the shift and survive.

Many conformist Whigs who joined the Republicans attempted to influence that party in the direction of moderation and practicality, as they perceived it.[34] Their antebellum influence is difficult to measure because the Republican congressional group in the six years before the Civil War was composed of men with diverse former political party affiliations.[35] Many former Whigs had arrived in the new party via one of the splinter party organizations of the fifties. Another group was composed of former Democrats, many of whom were mavericks in the Democratic party early in their careers. Still a third group was made up of young men who had no national political experience of any significance before the rise of the Republican party. Only for the sizeable group of former Whigs is it possible to ascertain a clear pattern of belief among Republican conformists; for the others either information is lacking or their numbers were not sufficient to warrant any generalizations about political ideology.

A number of the former Whigs in the Republican party have been noted for their moderate to conservative ties. These include party leaders such as Thomas Corwin, Schuyler Colfax, Richard Thompson, and John Sherman. More inclined to romantic rhetoric but equally moderate in policy orientation were Edward Baker and Anson Burlingame, both of whom achieved fame for actions outside of the congressional milieu.[36] In general, there was mutual distrust between the Whig moderates and the more radical ideologues of the new party. Tom Corwin, speaking for many moderates, publicly repudiated the higher law doctrine as "destructive in its tendencies and impractical in its results."[37] In a double-edged assault on the Biblical attack on slavery and the southern Biblical defense, he urged, "Let us not dissolve the Union upon conflicting constructions of the Bible."[38] More commonly, the former Whig conformists preferred to avoid the moral controversy and treat the subject of slavery politically, identifying southern attempts to make gains on slavery issues as a Democratic party plot. One conformist insisted that all efforts to extend slave territory were the result of political motives, the manipulation of "a *political* question, to increase and extend the unequal *political power* given to the owners of slave property."[39] Even as late as 1861 Republicans could insist in apparent sincerity that "the question is one of political power."[40] This conviction may help to explain the refusal of many Republicans to believe the sincerity of the southerners in their threats to secede.[41]

It was almost as if former Whigs among Republican conformists had so well convinced themselves of the moral necessity of a political and practical approach to the slavery question that they made the mistake of assuming that their southern opponents were doing the same thing. Their notions of morality were very much a product of their social environment—of religious education, of their upbringing, of their own models of leadership. For these reasons it is very understandable that as the respectable portions of the northern public moved to a position that refused to tolerate the perpetuation and extension of the institution of slavery, most northern Whig/Republican congressmen moved to the same position. Their opposition to the institution of slavery or to its extension was, by the time of the Civil War, rooted not only in their personal moral convictions but also in their accurate perception that the northern public shared these moral convictions.

On the other hand, their strong preference for social order and their devotion to the Constitution and Union as means of preserving that order could hardly have supported deliberate provocation of a Civil War for freeing slaves. It seems more likey that the role of the former Whigs in the Republican party in bringing on the Civil War was more the result of a failure to understand the southern position than it was the result of an intransigent majority's desire to achieve a moral victory.

It was not possible to construct a single ideological pattern from the speeches and writings of congressional Republicans who were formerly in the Democratic party. Only one of the Republican conformists in Congress in the Thirty-Fourth through the Thirty-Sixth Congresses had been a Democrat before 1854.[42] A few Democratic mavericks did make their way into the Republican party but were not in Congess after 1858.[43] Two more were in Congress but were mavericks in the Republican party.[44] The same lack of information pertains to the small group of men with no former national political activities before their joining with the Republican party. Although none of these men clearly stated anything like a philosophical position concerning his political behavior, it does appear clear that they differed in their attitudes toward the South and slavery from their Republican allies who were formerly Whigs. But whether their extremism on the question of slavery was a reflection of a genuine difference in political philosophy or only attached to that particularly sensitive issue was not clear from the writings of the small group. It does appear evident that former Democrats who became Republicans, the young and relatively inexperienced original Republicans, and the radical mavericks in the Republican party tried to spur the more conservative former northern Whig/Republicans to a stronger stance on the question of slavery and away from compromise with the South.

In sum, the convenient union between principle and partisan interest that charcterized the ideas of antebellum Whig conformists, who constituted the majority of their party, did not persist into the Republican party. That new party was riddled with factionalism—ideological and organizational—throughout its early years and well into the postbellum decades.[45] It seems likely that the unity of Whig conformists rested partially upon a social coherence which was destroyed not only by the sweeping changes of the prewar decades but also by the further stress of the war itself. Aspects of Whiggery endured as "Victorianism" or as Republican policy, but Whig ideology no longer spoke to the aspirations of a majority in pluralistic America.

The ideology of Whig conformists poses analytical problems because it comprises an intellectual fabric that offers few loose ends with which to unravel its component threads. By drawing explicit boundaries to contain speculation, Whigs mitigated its disruptive effects upon their party. Those same boundaries, combined with worldly attention to political business, prevented Whigs from publicly exploring the moral or intellectual foundations which underlay their ideology. The opinions of Whig conformists about the social context of politics are much more clearly defined than those of Democratic conformists, but the sources of those opinions can only be inferred. Furthermore, the similarity of attitudes among all Whig conformists casts doubt upon the possibility that each thought independently about social, moral, and intellectual issues in politics. It seems far more likely that Whig conformists were men who were comfortable with the general ideology they espoused, having borrowed its central context from more creative individuals, including the mavericks who acted with their party.

NOTES

1. Emerson, "Politics," *Selected Writings*, p. 428.

2. References to the "respectable" nature of the Whigs are frequent in speeches of the period. Wealthy leaders included Abbott Lawrence and several other prominent Massachusetts leaders; but men like Thomas Corwin, John Sherman, and Schuyler Colfax, who were active in both Whig and Republican parties, were from middle-class backgrounds. See the bibliographical essay in Pessen's *Jacksonian America* for a survey of the literature on economic interests of Democrats and Whigs (to 1978). Whether or not the rich were attracted to the Whig party more than the Democratic (and the question is still open), it is clear that "respectability" had appeal to many aspiring members of the lower and middle classes as well.

3. Among conformists, the Whigs were generally more inclined to publish their opinions about both political and nonpolitical matters than were their opponents in the Democratic party. For a total of 108 Whig and Republican conformists there are 253 bibliographical entries; for 62 Democrats there are 148 entries. However, only 101 Whigs and Republicans had to be excluded because there was no available material; 122 Democrats were excluded. Put another way, of a potentially usable 209 Whigs, over 50 percent had writings available; of a potential group of 184 Democrats, only about 35 percent had writings available. (These figures exclude congressmen whose writings could not be found but were listed in the L. C. catalogue.)

4. Pessen, *Jacksonian America*, p. 222.

5. Quoted passage, in Howe, *Political Culture of American Whigs*, p. 6. Howe explains his choice of "informants" for Whig political culture in the light of two considerations: "I wanted people who were influential in defining the activities and scope of the Whig party; I also wanted to pick those who would offer the most insight into Whig culture." He goes on to state his belief that "articulate, self-conscious spokesmen, while not always 'typical' of most Whig voters, would reveal the fullest development and elaboration of Whig culture." (p. 4) Given Howe's guiding principles, it is not remarkable that his "informants" in the House were mavericks.

6. The apt phrase is that of Washington Hunt, *Congressional Globe*, 29th Cong., 1st Sess., 107.

7. This unity is most notable among northern Whig conformists, the grouping which contained fewer mavericks and more conformists than any other regional and party combination.

8. *Congressional Globe*, 29th Cong., 1st Sess., 105–106.

9. James Russell Lowell, *Biglow Papers, First Series*, in *The American Tradition in Literature*, ed. by Sculley Bradley, Richmond C. Beatty, and E. Hudson Long (New York: W. W. Norton & Co., 1967), 1:1657; passage quoted in William C. Richards, *Great in Goodness: A Memoir of George N. Briggs* (Boston: Gould & Lincoln, 1866),

p. 197. See an excellent thumbnail sketch in Formisano, *Transformation of Political Culture*, pp. 299–301.

10. John Taylor, an Ohio Whig who was born in Virginia, was defending his votes in support of the Compromise of 1850. *Congressional Globe*, 33d Cong., 2d Sess., 601.

11. William B. Calhoun, *Addresses at the Dedication of the New Cabinet and Observatory of Amherst College, June 28, 1848* (Amherst, Mass.: J. S. & C. Adams, Printers, 1848), pp. 11–12.

12. Abbott Lawrence, *Remarks of Hon. Abbott Lawrence before the Convention of Manufacturers, Dealers and Operatives, in the Shoe and Leather Trade, Held in the Marlboro Chapel, Boston, Mar. 2, 1842* (n.p., n.d.), p. 7.

13. Elisha Whittlesey, *An Address Delivered before the Tallmadge Colonization Society on the Fourth of July, 1833*, published by the Society (Ravenna, Ohio: Office of the Ohio Star, July, 1833), pp. 10, 27.

14. Quoted in Charles Roll, *Colonel Dick Thompson, The Persistent Whig*, Indiana Historical Collections, vol. 30 (Indianapolis: Indiana Historical Bureau, 1948), p. 140.

15. Quoted in Williard H. Smith, *Schuyler Colfax, The Changing Fortunes of a Political Idol*, Indiana Historical Collections, vol. 33 (Indianapolis: Indiana Historical Bureau, 1952), p. 40.

16. Daniel R. Tilden, *Letter to Mr. Giddings, Giving His Reasons for Supporting General Scott* (n.p., n.d.), pp. 6–7. Giddings was a thorn in the side of Whig conformists from his earliest days in the House. Horace Everett, a Whig conformist from Vermont and a member of the House for fourteen years, expressed his "utter abhorrence of the firebrand course of the gentleman from Ohio," in the 27th Congress, by which Giddings was ultimately censured. *Congressional Globe*, 27th Cong., 2d Sess., 343.

17. Ibid., p. 7.

18. Whig conformists from the South were far more likely to express some political philosophy than southern Democratic conformists but remarkably less so than southern Whig mavericks. The conformists published few speeches or writings, although some did involve themselves in literary pursuits after their political careers had ended.

19. Horace Maynard, *Political Education. An Address, Delivered before the Social Union of Amherst College at the Annual Commencement Wednesday, Aug. 8, 1860* (Boston: Geo. C. Rand & Avery Press, 1861), p. 1.

20. William Bowen Campbell, *Mexican War Letters of Col. William Bowen Campbell of Tennessee, Written to Governor David Campbell of Virginia, 1846–1847*, with introduction and notes by St. George L. Sioussat, reprinted from *Tennessee Historical Magazine* (June 1915):6.

21. Charles Fenton Mercer, *The Weakness and Inefficiency of the Government of the United States of North America, by a Late American Statesman* (London: Goulston & Wright, 1863), p. 53.

22. Ibid., p. 89.

23. William J. Cooper describes the "effort made by southern Whigs between 1842 and 1844 to substitute the politics of economics for the politics of slavery" as the "great aberration of antebellum southern politics;" *The South and the Politics of Slavery*, p. 176. While it is clear that overall Whig unity varied over time as sectional conflict waxed and waned and as the party's status in Congress varied, ideologically, there was more consistent unity than disunity among Whigs from all regions. For emphasis on the conservative unity of Whigs see Thomas Brown, "Southern Whigs and the Policy of Statesmanship, 1833–1841," *Journal of Southern History* 46 (August 1980):361–380.

24. Edward Carrington Cabell, *The Slave Question. Speech of Hon. E. C. Cabell, of Florida, in the House of Representatives, Mar. 5, 1850* (Washington, D. C.: Congressional Globe Office, 1850), p. 3.

25. Daniel Moreau Barringer, *Speech of Mr. Daniel Moreau Barringer, of North Carolina, on the Tariff. Delivered in the House of Representatives of the U. S., July 1, 1846* (n.p., n.d.), p. 8.

26. Maynard, *Political Education*, p. 10.

27. Abram Maury, *Address of the Honorable Abram P. Maury, on the Life and Character of Hugh Lawson White, Delivered at Franklin, May 9, 1840* (Franklin, Tenn.: Review Office, 1840), p. 12.

28. Cabell, *Slave Question*, p. 4.

29. See Appendix II. Some southern Whig conformists moved into the Democratic party very early in their careers and are included with Democrats.

30. Millard Fillmore, *Millard Fillmore Papers*, in *Publications of the Buffalo Historical Society*, vol. 1, ed. by Frank H. Severance (Buffalo: Buffalo Historical Society, 1907), p. 317. Compare also with the example of Washington Hunt, a political supporter of Fillmore, who, unlike his mentor, became first a Republican then eventually a Democrat. He criticized the abolitionists strongly and in keeping with Whiggish moralism urged that "in national concerns, no less than the subordinate relations of men, moderation is the highest wisdom." Washington Hunt, *Speech of Washington Hunt, at the Union Meeting in New York, Dec. 19th, 1859* (New York: Hall, Clayton & Co., Printers, 1859), p. 12.

31. Smith, *Schuyler Colfax*, pp. 16–17.

32. Quoted in Joseph Wallace, *Sketch of the Life and Public Services of Edward D. Baker, United States Senator from Oregon* (Springfield, Ill.: Journal Co., Printers & Binders, 1870), p. 31.

33. Roll, *Colonel Dick Thompson*, p. 148. "Persistent Whig" is Roll's title for Thompson. Party affiliation is discussed, pp. 160–161.

34. Foner, Ch. 6, "Conservatives and Moderates," in *Free Soil*, includes discussion of these men.

35. In the bibliography of Whig and Republican conformists the distinction is made between former Whigs who turned Republican and those for whom no former party is known. Appendix II gives party changes for mavericks.

36. There is some question as to whether Baker's rhetoric represented genuine radicalism. He seemed to have the quality of appearing equally enthusiastic about varying positions. Biographers emphasize the dramatic qualities of his expressions in Wallace, *Sketch of Edward D. Baker*, p. 118; and in Harry C. Blair and Rebecca Tarshis, *Lincoln's Constant Ally: The Life of Colonel Edward D. Baker* (Portland: Oregon Historical Society, 1960), pp. xi–xiii. For Burlingame's rhetoric see Anson Burlingame, *An Appeal to Patriots against Fraud and Disunion. Speech of Hon. Anson Burlingame, of Massachusetts. Delivered in the U. S. House of Representatives, Mar. 31, 1858* (Washington, D. C.: Buell & Blanchard, 1858), p. 8.

37. Corwin, "Speech on the Slavery Question," in *Life and Speeches of Thomas Corwin, Orator, Lawyer and Statesman*, ed. by Josiah Marrow (Cincinnati: W. H. Anderson & Co., 1896), p. 390. Corwin's interaction with the radicals is described in Blue, *The Free Soilers*, pp. 39–41.

38. Ibid., p. 388.

39. Henry Bennett, *Kansas and Slavery. Speech of Hon. Henry Bennett, of New York.*

Delivered in the U.S. House of Representatives, Mar. 29, 1858 (Washington, D. C.: Buell & Blanchard, 1858), p. 5.

40. Thomas D. Eliot, *Address of Thomas D. Eliot, of the 1st Congressional District of Massachusetts, to His Constituents* (Washington, D. C.: H. Polkinhorn, 1861), p. 2.

41. According to the interpretation of David M. Potter, Republicans continued to suspect that southern threats of secession were a political ploy to win further concessions on slavery. See David M. Potter, *Lincoln and His Party in the Secession Crisis* (New Haven, Conn.: Yale University Press, 1942), and his *The South and the Sectional Conflict* (Baton Rouge: Louisiana State University Press, 1968), pp. 252–254.

42. Clark Cochrane of New York. *BDAC*, p. 714. If others were Democrats in state politics the information was not given in the *BDAC*.

43. Information on Democratic mavericks is in *BDAC* and biographical sources.

44. See Appendix II.

45. Two general works which summarize the efforts of Republicans to meld factions into unity before the war include Potter, *The Impending Crisis*, and Holt, *The Political Crisis of the 1850s*. Numerous works deal with factionalism in the war and reconstruction years, most notably Allan G. Bogue, *The Earnest Men: Republicans of the Civil War Senate* (Ithaca, N. Y.: Cornell University Press, 1981); and Michael Les Benedict, *A Compromise of Principle: Congressional Republicans and Reconstruction, 1863–1869* (New York: W. W. Norton & Co., 1974). Much less close analysis has been given persistent Democratic factionalism; an exception is Joel Silbey, *A Respectable Minority: The Democratic Party in the Civil War Era, 1860–1868* (New York: W. W. Norton & Co., 1977).

CHAPTER 8

The Whig and Republican Mavericks

Legislative action is of high moral character. It bears with great power upon the permanent interests of States, Nations, Mankind. The stream of its influence is perpetual. It runs on with successive ages. In all acts of legislation which involve the personal rights and moral duties of the governed, the great principle to be observed is that of righteousness, and not that of party predilections, nor sectional interests, nor political expediency.

Orin Fowler, 1852

Application of the principle of righteousness to legislation has so often led to bitter conflict—even to war—that the notion has had few proponents in the mainstream of American political life. Contrary to the Reverend Fowler's dictate, "party predilections," "sectional interests," and "political expediency" have governed far more legislative actions than not.[1] Perhaps because of the dominant pragmatic character of American politics, the mavericks in the Whig and Republican parties have often been portrayed as villains in the events which culminated in the Civil War, for these were men whose inability or unwillingness to subordinate their peculiar philosophies to practicality was most notable.

The Whig and Republican mavericks present an astonishing variety of political and nonpolitical activity. Included among them are a President of the United States, the Vice-President of the Confederacy, several cabinet members, two Congregationalist ministers, one Methodist minister, four authors of poetry, novels, or drama, seven writers of history, and several Civil War generals. Although all were classified as Whigs or Republicans at the time of their maverick voting behavior, these congressmen belonged to a variety of other parties during their careers; there were members of the American party, the Free-Soil and Liberty parties, and the Democratic party, some states'-rights Whigs of the Tyler type, and even two no-party men, who were elected as Whigs but refused to call themselves that. These mavericks did not vote as a group, although there were some alliances among them; in fact, the number of public disagreements among them was considerable.[2]

The Whig and Republican mavericks occupied a variety of positions along the antebellum ideological spectrum, and scholars have noted the influence of some of them. Several made important contributions to Whig ideology; this is clearly the case for John Quincy Adams and John Pendleton Kennedy, whose intellectual reputations have outlived them. During his long congressional career, Alexander Stephens was a formulator of the ideology of southern Whiggery and later was perhaps the most influential defender of states'-rights in the Confederacy. Henry Wise of Virginia, whom Clement Eaton has labeled a southern progressive, attempted to reconcile a Whiggish moral philosophy with democratic rhetoric as he moved from one party to another. His friend Caleb Cushing of Massachusetts filled volumes with efforts to lend intellectual respectability to his Whiggish Democracy. Joshua Giddings, the "conscience" for both Whig and Republican parties, helped move northerners to political antislavery by his rhetorical tenacity in the House. Henry Winter Davis and Frank Blair, Jr., both border southerners, contributed to the blending of Whig, Know-Nothing, and Democratic ideologies which characterized the early Republican party, though they did not blend together personally. No single chapter could possibly describe the ideas of each of these notables, but the fact of their influence is adequately documented in the work of other historians.[3]

Influence and innovation should not, however, be confused. Not all men who were creative about political ideas had an audience persuaded of the verity of their beliefs. Men with superior rhetorical skills, a substantial power base, longevity in politics, easy access to the press or journals, or men who nicely balanced ideological creativity with practical political ability led others to their ideas. But some Whig and Republican mavericks never captured a large audience. The virulent anti-Catholicism of Lewis Levin of Pennsylvania never earned him national fame and was too extreme to be incorporated into a major party's ideology, despite his persistent efforts in behalf of early nativism.[4] Thomas Gilmer, a compatriot of Wise and John Tyler, makes an excellent commonsense example of a creative maverick whose contributions were limited. Far more than most of his contemporaries, he understood the relationship between partisan controversy, political development, and constitutional principles, as his work for the House's Retrenchment Committee and his eloquent defense of Tyler's exercise of the veto power demonstrated.[5] But Gilmer was only a two-term congressman, and he is probably best known to historians outside of Virginia because he was killed in the *Princeton* explosion shortly after becoming Tyler's Secretary of the Navy. Joseph Underwood of Kentucky, whose balanced and learned speeches exploring centrist Whig ideas were admired in the House and Senate, was overshadowed by his colleagues Henry Clay and John Crittenden. For different reasons, the ideas of Levin, Gilmer, and Underwood did not have broad influence; but their creativity, which did not necessarily lead them in attractive directions, is unmistakable.

The ideas of Whig and Republican mavericks were inevitably affected by their relationships with the major parties. All political rhetoric is properly analyzed with some consideration for the audience to which it is addressed. Most importantly for antebellum congressmen, the audience consisted of political activists such as other politicians, party propagandists, and the knowledgeable public. Scholars disagree about whether or not the masses attended carefully to political discourse, and politicians probably made differing assumptions about the social depth of their audiences. But, in any case, mavericks and conformists spoke to people whom they assumed to be politically aware, and both types knew the utility of speaking in familiar terms that evoked favorable responses to reinforce personal approval of the speaker. Knowingly, they used the ideas and language of the political cultures within which they operated. If recent interpretations of American political culture are correct, the terms of debate for Democrats, Whigs, and Republicans were sufficiently different that mavericks who changed parties—and about half of the Whig and Republican mavericks did that—adjusted to audiences with different beliefs about the nature of politics and society. Moreover, even for mavericks who did not change parties, rhetorical reliance upon party ideology presented serious problems.

An excursion into the theory of political speech may clarify the nature of the problems faced by Whig and Republican mavericks. All mavericks were engaged in what British historian Quentin Skinner has called "untoward" politial actions. At the very least, their voting behavior marked them as deviant. Most Whig and Republican mavericks challenged party regularity in other ways: disavowal of a central party position, refusal to support a presidential candidate, or party switching. Nonetheless, their ideas and the language in which they were expressed had to simultaneously reflect the values acceptable to their listeners and justify untoward behaviors. In Skinner's theoretical terms:

> The task of an innovating ideologist is a hard but an obvious one. His concern, by definition, is to legitimate a new range of social actions, which, in the terms of the existing ways of applying the moral vocabulary prevailing in his society, are currently regarded as in some way untoward or illegitimate. His aim must therefore be to show that a number of existing and favorable evaluative-descriptive terms can somehow be applied to his untoward actions.[6]

Some solutions to the mavericks' problem of locating a useful "moral vocabulary" have been suggested by the ideas of Democratic mavericks. With all Americans, mavericks shared a revolutionary heritage which emphasized the national mission, the importance of civic virtue, and the model of republican statesmanship. They also shared a western tradition which validated moral integrity and Christian principles. When mavericks quoted Shakespeare or Milton in justification of their independence, they relied upon the resonance of ideas common to all educated Americans. Whig and Republican mavericks, like Democratic mavericks, could rely, then, upon values which transcended partisan subcultures to explain their untoward behaviors.

No successful politician could, however, afford to ignore the partisan cultures which conditioned the responses of politically active voters. The American electorate demonstrated a continuity in voting that afforded candidates (and congressmen were perpetual candidates) advantages too great to sacrifice lightly. For mavericks in the Whig and Republican parties, the nature of their parties' appeal presented them with special difficulties. Democratic mavericks, speaking to people who appreciated a pragmatism that bordered upon anti-intellectualism, did not have to justify their untoward behaviors on philosophical grounds, and most did not. Whig and Republican mavericks, whose parties insisted upon the relevance of morality and intelligence in politics, had to construct justifications with substantial ethical and intellectual content. Even had they not been so predisposed, the need for an appropriate moral vocabulary would have encouraged them to speculative or moralistic discourse. That they were so predisposed is fairly obvious; men of lesser intelligence and learning could not have performed the mental gymnastics common to the Whig and Republican mavericks.

The content of their rhetorical justifications presented Whig and Republican mavericks with a paradox from which they could or would not escape. With their creativity, they could convincingly explain independence from party loyalty, which was a kind of untoward behavior. Their innovations, rooted in moral and intellectual foundations, involved them, however, in another kind of untoward behavior. By relying upon ethical absolutism, speculative inquiry, or political metaphysics, they violated the cardinal rule of practicality to which the majority of congressmen in both parties agreed. Conformists did not appreciate either form of disruptive behavior, but the successful careers of Whig and Republican mavericks suggest that they were playing a useful and perhaps necessary role in the political life of antebellum America.

A retrospective view of the functional relationship between Whig and Republican mavericks and their parties imposes a common structure upon the actions of men who were usually perceived by their colleagues as they wished to be perceived—as distinctive individuals. Each maverick offered such a peculiar interpretation of political ideology that it is difficult to categorize the contents of their ideas and explain them summarily. It is possible to define the common Whiggish ground of Joshua Giddings and Alexander Stephens, but their differences are as important as their similarities; and if the analysis is enlarged to a trio by including Caleb Cushing, the set of shared ideas shrinks further. Diversity is the rule when considering the policy positions of mavericks or when analyzing the moral and intellectual assumptions that shaped policy. Yet in some fundamental ways, the beliefs of Whig and Republican mavericks about politics were similar. Whig and Republican mavericks painted a collective portrait of an American society in flux, a situation which created tremendous opportunities for achievement—moral, intellectual, economic, social, and political. In the center of every version of the American landscape stood the maverick—each, of course, with a different name and face but bearing a personal responsibility defined by moral or intellectual standards beyond political ethics. The man in the center was drawn larger than life as a man compelled to political leadership by extraordinary ambition or overwhelming mission. Though many Whig and Republican mavericks explicitly rejected philosophical or literary romanticism and nearly all drew upon the rationalist ideas of eighteenth-century political thinkers, their collective portrait is a romantic one, appropriate to the intellectual mood of the age in which they lived.

In 1835 a Whig maverick speaking to a local audience prophesied "a new era on earth," assuring his listeners that "the moral, religious, and intellectual excitement pervading Christian countries, presages the accomplishments of great works in which mankind are to be blessed."[7] Four years later, another Whig maverick viewed the new era with less confidence:

We are . . . in the midst of a revolution; not a revolution conducted by arms, accomplishing its purposes by the shedding of blood, but a great revolution in the opinion and feelings of a great people; a revolution not the less to be feared because it does not now call physical force to its aid, for it is moving the foundations of society, and it is impossible to say where its waves shall be stayed.[8]

The speakers were both moderate Whigs: Joseph Underwood of Kentucky and Henry Washington Hilliard of Alabama, oratorical ornaments of the southern wing of the party. No romantic reformer, Underwood spoke in behalf of African colonization; even less romantically, Hilliard sought to persuade his state's legislature to oppose the independent treasury scheme. Nonetheless, their perception of living in a revolutionary era connects them to other Whig and Republican mavericks, as does their mutual determination, in Hilliard's words, to "ride on the foremost billows" of the "current of the age," wherever its waves were moving society.[9]

Most congressmen in the antebellum period were evidently unaware of the scope and nature of the changes occurring in their environment. They extolled the progress of the age, but there is little evidence in their speeches and writings that the majority of conformists in the Whig, Republican, or Democratic parties believed that the entire fabric of American society was being disrupted. Whig and Republican mavericks, on the other hand, appear in their works as men in the midst of a great general motion. There is an agitated quality to their speeches and behavior which suggests significant sensitivity, perhaps even hypersensitivity, to the changes taking place in all areas of American life. This is partially indicated by their frequent discussion of nonpolitical matters on the floor of the House, where many of them displayed a lack of businesslike focus annoying to their conformist colleagues. For some Whig and Republican mavericks this perception of change produced enthusiastic excitement about the possibilities of improvement; for others it generated fear; for a smaller number of moderates it was received with more intellectual enthusiasm than political anticipation. In any case, however, every Whig or Republican maverick whose speeches and writings left any considerable record of his ideas indicated that he saw the possibilities and problems associated with the changing American culture.

One of the oratorical luminaries among northern Republican mavericks, Representative John A. Bingham of Ohio, did reflect the faith of some nineteenth-century romantics that the new age might witness the perfection of human society:

It is the high heaven of the nineteenth century. The whole heavens are filled with the light of a new and better day. Kings hold their power with a tremulous and unsteady hand. The bastiles and dungeons of tyrants, those graves of human liberty, are giving up their dead . . . the mighty heart of the world stands still, awaiting the resurrection of the nations, and that final triumph of the right, foretold in prophecy and invoked in song.[10]

Bingham's enthusiasm for the sweeping changes he foresaw was boundless, and he believed himself to be in the forefront of the battle.

Moderate Whig mavericks typically saw similar changes with guarded optimism. In 1854, John Pendleton Kennedy humorously attacked the excessive agitation of the reformers, decrying the "mysticism and fanatical arrogance" characteristic of the extremes. But he, too, believed that the upheaval was progressive:

I think that motion, though it tend to the eccentric—I will not say motion that tends to wilful mischief—is preferable to that dead repose which accomplishes nothing. Out of this fermentation of mind, there comes up, somewhere, life and action, aim and effort which tell of a generation aspiring to do something. . . . The world will gather no green slime upon its waters, while they are thus agitated; and although there may come up much froth and foam to the surface, these are generally the signs of a wholesome sparkling flood below.[11]

Kennedy, like the majority of the Whig mavericks, knew both the dangers and possibilities inherent in the changing environment, but he also believed that progress would occur under proper guidance.

A southern Whig maverick much more threatened by the direction of events than either Bingham or Kennedy was Francis W. Pickens, congressman from South Carolina and Governor of his state during the Fort Sumter crisis. In the middle of the turbulent decade before secession, he offered an oration "on the Influences of Government upon the Nature and Destiny of Man." Pickens warned that ordinary men were not capable of guiding the nation, yet insisted that improvement would occur if wise leaders discovered the underlying forces which moved men:

Let it be remembered that man himself is but little more than the creature of events. There is a destiny that shapes our ends. Notwithstanding all this, much may be avoided.

Governments are in the hands of men. True, circumstances to a great extent make them. But with wisdom, virtue and an energetic spirit, they may be guided and directed in proper channels.[12]

Picken's ambivalence was characteristic of other southern Whig mavericks. Intellectual analysis revealed to them the South's difficulty in maintaining slavery within the democratic spirit of the age, but their emotional commitment to the South was also powerful. The resulting conflict was often psychological as well as political.

This dilemma is writ large in the career of Alexander Stephens, probably the most influential of all southern Whig mavericks.[13] There is no question about his belief that the nineteenth century was an era of hopeful change: "Progress," he asserted in 1849, "is the universal law governing all things."[14] Convinced of the essential connection between material and moral improvement, he advocated early in his career a Whig program of national improvements; and he always saw public education as the key to social growth. In the 1840s he proclaimed that "Whig principles in Maine and Louisiana, in Ohio, Georgia, and Virginia, are the same."[15] But Stephens' confidence gradually waned. From his cautious statement in 1845 that "he was no defender of slavery in the abstract," he moved in 1861 to the offensive position that slavery was the "cornerstone" of the great Confederacy.[16] After opposing secession, he became Vice-President of the Confederacy, but his antagonism to the government late in the War reflected his inability to align his principles and his behavior. Stephens' tendentious *Constitutional View of the Late War between the States* completed his abandonment of Whig constitutional principles with its argument for the interpretation of the Constitution as a states'-right document. In one light, however, the *Constitutional View* can be seen as a continuation of his role as a Whig maverick. Its two volumes of tortured prose closed with a plea to all Americans, North and South, for the adoption of Stephens' constitutional principles as the only sure means of renewed fulfillment of the national mission. Whether this futile effort be seen as tragic or pathetic—and historians have been unable to decide which is the proper adjective—Stephens' attempt once again to locate himself in front of the national destiny is consistent with the common vision of Whig and Republican mavericks that such was their place in history.

Their personal interpretations of politics provided Whig and Republican mavericks with the directions they offered to social flux. For some mavericks, partisan ideologies yielded to forms of ethical absolutism. Philosophical absolutes were embedded in the ideas that justified American existence by the "laws of nature and nature's God," but those eighteenth-century ideas were usually combined with a conservative social perspective and rarely produced extremism. The evangelical awakening and romantic movement of the nineteenth century together reinforced and broadened the appeal of moral absolutes. As a result, Whig and Republican mavericks had an ample moral vocabulary with which to explain their independent positions.

A small group of northern mavericks were political radicals in two respects: they described an instinctive, direct appeal to divine truth as the source of political ethics, and they advocated root changes in American society. Among these were John Quincy Adams, Joshua Giddings, John Bingham, Orin Fowler, and James Meacham (the latter two being Congregationalist ministers). For these men, truth was visible in an organic form and was perceived as surely as the material objects of the universe. The most notorious of the radicals, Joshua Giddings, was so unpopular in Congress that he was censured by the House for his antislavery activities. Associated with abolitionist Theodore Weld and fellow maverick Adams in developing strategy for elimination of the gag rule, Giddings was an expert at "the tactics of radical politics."[17] He described the source of his inspiration as intuitive truth, far removed from the normal structure of political motivation. In a speech before the House, Giddings recounted his experience before a congressional committee, surely no occasion for the inspiration of moral truth to ordinary congressmen:

I was wholly unprepared to address the committee. I had taken no notes, nor had I before me books or papers of reference; but the committee appeared anxious to proceed, and I was compelled to put to sea, upon the wide ocean of this debate, without chart or compass, and with nothing to guide my course but the glittering star of truth, as it shines in the moral firmament, unobscured by political clouds.[18]

Bingham spoke of the higher law as "the beautiful form of goodness," which could be seen by all truly virtuous men.[19] Fowler insisted that the "great principle . . . of righteousness" govern all political action.[20] In each instance, the radical mavericks repudiated normal political guidelines and turned to the immutable principles of the universe for support.

To believe his diary, John Quincy Adams was more motivated by moral absolutes than any of his contemporaries. Adams' life and ideas have been thoroughly studied, but historians are unlikely ever to fathom completely the depths of his character, despite the volumes of information he left about himself.[21] It is clear that Adams' motives were often political, in the most pragmatic sense of the word, and that he sometimes masked self-seeking motives in self-righteous forms. Without accepting uncritically Adams' image of himself, however, the evidence of his political moralism is ample. Adams was a deep thinker—his ideas were complex, if not always original—and his prolific personal and public writings reveal a wide range of opinions about politics and the American destiny as well as Adams' view of his place in history.

Throughout his life, Adams wrote poems, which are more important for the personal insights they afford than for their literary quality. After his death, a collection of *Poems of Religion and Society* was published. One poem, set in the Capitol, offers a view of Adams' political inspiration:

To the Sun-Dial, Under the Window of the Hall of the
House of Representatives of the United States

Thou silent herald of Time's silent flight!
Say, could'st thou speak, what warning voice were thine!
Shade, who canst only show how others shine!
Dark, sullen witness of resplendent light
In day's broad glare, and when the moontide bright
Of laughing fortunes sheds the ray divine,
Thy ready favors cheer us—but decline
The clouds of morning and the gloom of night.

Yet are thy counsels faithful, just, and wise;
They bid us seize the moments as they pass—
Snatch the retrieveless sunbeam as it flies,
Nor lose one sand of life's revolving glass
Aspiring still, with energy sublime,
By virtuous deeds to give eternity to Time.[22]

The sun-dial challenged Adams to an heroic task, to political action sufficiently virtuous to "give eternity to time." The source of inspiration had little to do with politics or society; Adams' energy derived from a sublime source appropriate to the magnitude of his responsibility.

Adams predicted as early in his career as 1820 that there was an inevitable conflict between the North and South, and he foresaw the secession of the South in the face of a determined abolitionist crusade.[23] Although he believed then that his duty was to protect the Union, his antagonism to slavery grew. The consequences of his single-minded opposition to the gag rule and his subsequent leadership of the antislavery cause in Congress probably had the effect of shortening the peaceful life of the Union, or at least it must have seemed so to southerners. Nonetheless, the political moralist could hardly have behaved differently.

Most Whig mavericks were devoted to the Union, believing that it was founded on high moral principles. By mid-century, romantics had reified those principles, resulting in a form of nationalism that equated the nation with moral absolutes. Two mavericks, Henry Winter Davis and Lewis Levin, were as radical in their application of romantic nationalism as Adams and Giddings were in political moralism. Davis and Levin were both affiliated with the American party, although for the former it was only a temporary home; both romantically believed the American nation to be the incarnate spirit of the people.[24] Unlike the antislavery radicals, they thus valued the Constitution and laws of the United States as having an inherent moral character. Levin expressed this sentiment in advocating restrictive naturalization laws as the only way to make the nation "one in soul, one in spirit, one in action, homogeneous, and possessing perfect moral and political symmetry."[25] Whig nationalism had always been associated with a paternalistic ethics. In the hands of romantic mavericks, it assumed coercive implications which would finally be reflected in public policy.[26]

The radical position of ethical absolutism provided a clear and consistent moral vocabulary for the justification of political extremism. Most Whig and Republican mavericks were not, however, extremists, and they were also not philosophically consistent. With the materials at hand, they attempted to blend diverse and sometimes contradictory intellectual and ideological influences. Their original constructions lacked aesthetic coherence and contained paradoxes and tensions—problems appropriate to the efforts of practicing politicians to mix such conflicting elements as rationalism and romanticism, Whiggery and Democracy, traditional and modernizing values, and a dual inheritance of republican and liberal political theory.

Four interesting examples can illustrate the originality and inconsistency in the ideas of most Whig and Republican mavericks. By way of introduction, brief biographical sketches demonstrate that their careers manifested mixed loyalties. Frank Blair, Jr., the son of a founder of the Democratic party, was a long-time political writer and partisan activist.[27] Originally a Missouri Democrat, he and his family joined the Republicans in time to make it possible for a brother, Montgomery, to be given a place in Lincoln's Cabinet; but Blair ended his career as Democrat. Caleb Cushing from Massachusetts was an early "Cotton Whig."[28] The bitter enemy of John Quincy Adams and the source of the scorn of James Russell Lowell in the *Biglow Papers*, Cushing became a Democrat in the 1840s and served in the Cabinet of Franklin Pierce. After making an uneasy peace with the Republicans, he was nominated by Ulysses S. Grant for the position of Chief Justice of the Supreme Court, but he failed to win confirmation. At the end of his long career, he was appointed by President Rutherford B. Hayes as Minister to Spain.

A third maverick with a strange career was Alabama's Henry Washington Hilliard.[29] A defender of Whiggery in a state dominated by Democrats, Hilliard opposed southern extremism in a series of famous debates with William Lowndes Yancey, the fire-eating cohort of Robert Barnwell Rhett, but when the Civil War came he accepted an appointment as a general in the Confederacy. After the War he associated with the Republican party and was appointed by Hayes as Minister to Brazil, where he was active in that country's movement to abolish slavery. A novelist and Methodist minister, Hilliard was noted for his tolerance and good humor towards his political opponents.

The same could not be said of the fourth illustrative Whig maverick—the volatile Virginian Henry A. Wise.[30] Wise began his career as a Democrat, switched to the Whig party in the late 1830s, and went back to the Democrats after the Tyler debacle. He served as Minister to Brazil from 1844 to 1847 then returned to Virginia and was elected Governor in 1856. While Governor, he took a personal role in the trial of John Brown, publicly defending the decision to hang him. Following Virginia's secession, he became a general in the Confederate army, where he became notorious for his inability to get along with other generals.[31] After the war's end, Wise renounced slavery as having been a great weakness to the South. Four years before his death in 1876 he published a curious volume called *Seven Decades of the Union*, which related the history of the United States during the life of John Tyler and also served as a vehicle for the unusual philosophical observations of its author.

The diversity in the careers of these four Whig and Republican mavericks was paralleled by their intellectual differences. Frank Blair, Jr., presented himself as a paradoxical mixture of eastern and western influences. With his well-known Democratic heritage, Blair was instrumental in developing a Republican ideology that could attract voters from a similar background. To that task he brought the benefits of a Princeton education and a personal history in which he was surrounded by men of learning and ability. Blair identified the East with the intellectual aspects of experience and the West with practicality. He expressed preference for western facts, but he based political arguments on both theory and fact.[32] For example, one of his favorite projects was the transcontinental railroad, which he proclaimed essential to the fulfillment of the Manifest Destiny of the nation. In a congressional speech on the railroad he presented tables full of statistics and provided justification from science—geology, meteorology, engineering, and the like;[33] but he also advocated railroad building on romantic and nationalistic grounds. In perhaps his most famous speech, *The Destiny of the Races of This Continent*, Blair insisted that "successful art always pursues nature in the attempt to accomplish similar designs" and proceeded to compare the human body to a river system and then to the proposed railroad system.[34] The metaphorical linking of political economy, art, and nature was a familiar one to the former Whigs in his New England audience; and the romantic proclamation of an expansive national destiny echoed his Democratic past.

Blair's vision of the national destiny belonged to the middle classes. Despite the wealth of his own family, he repeatedly aligned himself rhetorically with the independent farmers and mechanics rather than with the artistocracy.[35] The mass of Americans were pure, he insisted, because their political faith derived from "an instinct in the hearts of the people of this country whose ken looks beyond that of the most acute intellect." He defined the great political struggles of the 1850s not in sectional terms but as a conflict between "those who contend for caste and privilege, and those who neither have nor desire to have privileges beyond their fellows." He depicted the political turmoil of the late antebellum years as entirely the result of a plot on the part of the slavocracy to despoil the innocent yeomanry of the North and South. Lodging his appeal firmly within the republican tradition, he compared the fall of the American nation with the decline of Rome, both a product of the failure of government to "cherish the people as landholders."[36]

Importantly, Blair did not make the analogy with Rome apply to the dangers of imperialism. In point of fact, he was an ardent expansionist, basing his imperialism upon the typical Democratic grounds that a superior form of government would have to spread.[37] His scheme of colonization handily reconciled imperialism with republicanism and racism with antislavery sentiment. Blair, like most Republicans, believed in the right of the slaves to be free, partly because their immortal souls entitled them to freedom and partly because their slave labor threatened white free labor. Once freed, however, he thought that they must be removed from the United States, since they would be unable to compete with whites because of the inferiority Blair attributed to them. He advocated transplanting the freed slaves to Central America, where they would take over the governments there by virtue of their superior civilization, having been Americanized during their period of slavery. In this way, the American system would be spread, the problem of racial antagonism would be solved, and the greater progress of humanity assured.[38]

Loyal to Jacksonian ideas about the white middle classes but imbued with the reform spirit of the industrial age, Blair was an anomaly in the postwar Republican party, which he eventually left. His antagonism to consolidated wealth and his commitment to the white farmers of the West, as well as the dictates of political survival in Missouri, brought him back to the Democratic party as Vice-Presidential candidate in 1868. Undoubtedly, he had never, in his own mind, wandered far from the "true Democracy" of the days of Jackson in all of his affiliations with the Free-Soilers and Republicans between 1848 and 1868. For Blair, adherence to true democracy was not merely a matter of partisan political ties, manipulator though he was, but a conscious determination to accomplish through a party his own ideals of government.

Caleb Cushing, whose New England constituents were accustomed to intellectual politicians, nevertheless reflected some of the same crosscurrents as his western colleague. A child prodigy, Harvard Phi Beta Kappa, prolific author of drama, history, and poetry, politician, diplomat, and international lawyer and judge, Cushing's inordinate ambition had intellectual and political focuses; and he consciously attempted to combine them effectively. The youthful politician confided to his diary in 1829, on the eve of a European trip:

If my time were devoted to the law, I should clearly attain a more profound knowledge. . . . How far is my application to literature consistent with professional interest? How far does it go to give the qualities valuable to the orator and publicist? . . . Policy would show that I must make my pursuits abroad minister to my main purpose, of intellectual advancement with a view to oratory, law and public pursuits: which may be considered so far kindred objects as to be compatible with each other, and capable of being jointly pursued.[39]

Cushing knew his chosen course would be difficult, but he believed that political action needed intellectual motivation. Cautiously, however, he insisted upon practicality as well. He reflected in his two-volume history of the French Revolution of 1831 that the statesman must never forget practical considerations:

To neglect or condemn these considerations is the error of the mere theorist, the political fanatic, the man of *one idea*, the visionary enthusiast, who sails over the tide of time, with his eyes fastened to some fixed point in his intellectual firmament . . . only awakened from his trance of infatuation to feel his frail bark dashed to atoms and its freight plunged into the raging sea. On the other hand, to deem too highly of such considerations is characteristic always of the *merely* practical man, often of the selfish one . . . regardless of *general* principle,—or reckless of *any* principle.[40]

Cushing's philosophy of politics was mildly romantic: he believed the ultimate source of political truth to be God and his plan for the world. This plan, according to Cushing, was for the gradual improvement of the mind of man through Christianity and democracy, but he oddly saw the true unfolding of this plan in terms of material progress. A thoroughgoing and optimistic materialism was the immediate reality of the world for Cushing, however much the ultimate might be God. In a letter to his parents, Cushing (at age sixteen) affirmed both ideal (ultimate) and material (immediate) realities of the universe. However much some might doubt God, He exists, wrote the precocious adolescent, and the proof is clear:

. . . in nature the evidence is full and decisive, not resting on human wisdom; the doubtful assertions of one man, or one nation; but stretching itself beyond denial, because indestructible; and beyond foundation, because infinite.

Besides, man was made for happiness. I do not believe that this goodly frame of the universe—this enchanting harmony of nature—this erect and godlike form of man . . . was placed here without an approach, as there is an obvious tendency, to the happiness of man. This being supposed, it follows that the pursuit of gratification, so far as it is consistent with the security of our fellows, is the first, the only object of our exertions.[41]

Identifying the "pursuit of gratification" as the process by which God intended human happiness to develop was not a first principle likely to place Cushing within the ranks of Whiggery, but his social philosophy was consistent with the youthful premise despite changing partisan affiliations. Cushing did not participate in the reform movements of the mid-century; especially, he attacked northern abolitionists who busied themselves with other people's affairs. Though he was opposed to slavery in the abstract, he believed it proper to let the South solve its own problems.[42] He did not believe in human perfectibility, but he asserted that man's capacities were such that if he were left alone to improve his material status, moral and intellectual progress would automatically follow.[43] This optimistic prediction rested on the fact of the great abundance of land in the United States. American greatness was the result of natural law, not the product of a particular political party's leadership or policy—appropriate position for a man who shifted party affiliations repeatedly.[44] Because the abundance of land was so essential to democracy, the United States must expand to "people, cultivate, and civilize this Continent."[45]

While he believed that nature promised America's destiny, Cushing was no primitivist. Both the natural environment and human art were essential components in his mind Utopianism. His naturalism was romantic, but he never abandoned man to nature. In a perfect expression of the "mid-pastoral" vision of American, Cushing described the West as "that unrifled garden of primitive luxuriance,'' which ''succeeding generations alone were enabled to reach in tranquility and plenty'' and ''achieve the secure fruition of its bounties.''[46] Man must tame wild nature through art, and he must tame the wild elements in himself; the process must copy nature's method, which Cushing saw as practical, gradual, reasonable, and pacific. The goal of social progress, achieved through a laissez-faire policy, was essentially Whiggish. Cushing's Harvard education and New England background led him in contradictory directions. His talents and interests were broad, but his ambition and inclination towards an independent and intellectual approach to politics made him a poor party man.

Henry Washington Hilliard was an Alabama Whig whose opponents believed that his heart was in New England. In many respects he was a perfect model of national Whiggery. His carefully cultivated oratorical style, his refined manners, his cosmopolitan connections, and an elevated tone (which opposition newspapers called pompous) were part of a personal style that marked his entire career. Like Alexander Stephens, whom he admired, Hilliard was a nationalist who loved the South; but his postwar association with the Republican party suggests a greater consistency in political ideas than that of the diminutive Georgian. Among his public writings, none reveals more of the complexity of Hilliard's ideas than the novel he wrote immediately before the Civil War, during a period when his nationalism was unpopular in his South Alabama district. The title alone reveals Hilliard's concern for social balance: *DeVane: A Story of Plebeians and Patricians.*[47]

DeVane is a novel without literary merit, but the nature of the characters and the structure of the plot display Hilliard's anxieties and hopes for American society. Relying upon a standard convention of sentimental fiction, the novel presents its themes through two romantic couples whose marriages will reconcile conflicting ideas. The more important pair are DeVane, a proudly intellectual Virginia aristocrat, and Esther Wordsworth, his humble, poor, and pure sweetheart. The secondary couple represents similar traits with reversed sexes. Waring, a simple and honest Methodist friend of DeVane, loves Hortensia Godolphin, the wealthy and romantic friend of Esther. DeVane, the hero of the novel and the main foil for the author's feelings, represents patrician manners, brilliant intellectual accomplishments, and the influence of European transcendental and romantic philosophies; but he has no religious spirit (and was, indeed, an Episcopalian).[48] Esther represents innocence, religious piety, lack of sophistication, and natural loveliness; but she lacks the realistic human sympathy that only firsthand experience with tragedy can bring.[49] Their marriage in the closing pages of the novel is explicitly offered as a perfect blend for both—each complementing the other's shortcomings, making a complete union where vital parts had been lacking.

Throughout the novel, Hilliard revealed the intellectual tensions that played upon his political ideas, but, despite the Georgia setting, the sectional conflict is not central. The author tried to blend in his fictional marriages the aristocratic qualities of high intellect, expensive taste, and cultural refinement with republican virtues of pious simplicity, sincerity, and devout religious conviction. He debated the conflict between romantic and utilitarian ideas in a conversation between DeVane and Waring over the propriety of building a bridge to serve the community across a ravine in a sublime landscape. Economic theories were contrasted in gentlemen's discussions which set fears of imperial "consolidation" against the need for material progress.[50] With all their social concerns, *DeVane*'s themes inform Hilliard's political ideas offered in a less reflective setting. On religious grounds, he flatly refused to defend slavery; he opposed the military excesses of the Mexican War and argued that American ideals should spread "by their own inherent moral power"; he spoke in behalf of reform (such as temperance) and against revolution (such as abolitionism); he praised the industrial revolution for encouraging national unity and supported railroad building on that basis; but he always declared himself a firm believer in the southern way of life.[51]

Hilliard's novel about "plebeians and patricians" centered upon his social values, most importantly upon the religious ideas of the former Methodist minister. Those values were directly reflected in his rhetoric and other political actions; and if he was capable of intellectualizing them, he rarely did so. Perhaps he revealed his motives in a speech before the House in 1849:

There is a domestic institution in the South which in some sort insulates us from all mankind. The civilized world is against us. I know it; I comprehend it; I feel it. . . . Our moral condition at the South resembles the physical condition of Holland. . . . If the South were in a commanding position I should be willing to concede much; but because of her very weakness, I shall stand by her to the last.[52]

Only late in his career did Hilliard openly admit the immorality of slavery, when he actively worked against its continuation in Brazil. Hilliard found a foundation for his political ideas in religious and intellectual sources, and he used those sources to support his political actions—except in regard to the most important issue of his generation. He illustrates, in that respect, the fact that the ideological creativity of southern Whigs was severely limited by the constraints of sectional politics.

Henry Washington Hilliard, a muted voice for the "other South," joined the Whig party in the early 1840s, just as Henry Wise, a hotheaded exponent of southern rights, was leaving its ranks. Superficially, Wise epitomized reactionary southernism; he was violently aggressive, extraordinarily sensitive to pressures about slavery, and flamboyantly oratorical to the point of demagoguery. Although he was a planter and a Negrophobe, Wise insisted that he spoke to defend republican ideals rather than slaveholding interests or slavery *per se*. Like Frank Blair, he preferred to identify himself with the plain people and their future in progressive American society.

Wise's background may explain his early association with the Whigs. Raised on the eastern shore of Virginia within a family tradition of public service, Wise was the son and grandson of Federalists. At Washington College in Pennsylvania, he was tutored by the school's president, Andrew Wylie, a Presbyterian minister who taught moral philosophy, political economy, and literature. Wise described Wylie's impact on his life: "he taught me—a wild, reckless, and neglected orphan, a self-willed boy—to love honor and truth and wisdom, and the standard of all these and to try to be virtuous for virtue's sake."[53] After graduating at the top of his class, Wise studied law with Henry St. George Tucker, from whom he acquired his permanent attachment to states'-rights principles. Those principles supported his affiliation with the Democracy, but elements of Wise's Whiggery remained constant. He viewed moral, social, and economic reforms as related aspects of progress, though he called for change through state support, not federal direction. At different times, he advocated temperance, colonization, agricultural reform, public education, railroad and industrial development, universal white male suffrage, and popular election of state officials. The peculiar mixture in his ideas confused friends and enemies. In 1851, when the Democratic Richmond *Enquirer* characterized the members of Virginia's constitutional convention according to their principles, it made a special place for Wise: "Conservatives, Radicals, Conservative Radicals, Radical-Conservatives, and Infinite Radical [Wise]."[54]

Wise would brook no outside interference with the South's peculiar institution, and he defended slavery as a system of racial control; but his republican principles set him against planter interests. Arguing against Virginia's mixed basis in the 1851 convention, Wise intemperately proclaimed that "if there is anything in God Almighty's earth that stinks in the nostrils of my mind, as well as my body, it is the monied aristocracy; the negro aristocracy stinks worst of all."[55] Speaking for universal suffrage and a white basis, he told Virginians:

Our political representation in the legislature—based as in part it is practically on *slaves*, who have no political voice or entity, on carriages, which are in many instances but extravagant luxuries, and on *licenses to sell whiskey*, which are human curses—is not only fundamentally aristocratic and anti-republican, but it has *proven utterly futile and fallacious* in protecting the state from an onerous debt . . . whilst it degrades our brethren in the western portion of the state by its invidious inequality.[56]

By 1867, Wise was insisting that slavery had been a weakness to society, and he called upon southerners to reconstruct their lives:

Pull off your broadcloths—bare your arms—blister your hands until blisters become callous, to plough and reap the plenty which earnest labor will surely bring home to pay debts and provide comfort and maintain manly independence! You have no longer the host of slavery's drones to feed and clothe; your expenses now are comparatively small. Only be self-denying, determined, and work.[57]

The rhetorical excesses in Wise's speeches can be explained by his emotional nature and by his determination to win the political support of the middle classes within his state, but the essential consistency of his social ideas remained after his retirement from politics.

It is ironic that the republican principles and middle-class interests for which Wise spoke were not served by the war for slavery he helped to provoke, and Wise may have seen that irony as he wrote his 1872 retrospective, *Seven Decades of the Union*. Organized around the conflicting tendencies in Wise's political thought, *Seven Decades* portrays the history of the nation in terms of a war between the "humanities and materialism." Each aspect of life was necessary, but their imbalance was dangerous:

We have not yet begun to discern that God's harmonizing government is the adjustment of the two parts of humanity,—the moral and physical, the mental and material. All now is physical force; and this is the dragon's tooth which sprouted the armed men of the Civil War, teaching us that Humanities must be restored; that something better must be studied than the curriculum of West Point.[58]

Wise identified the "humanities" with the localism of the South, with a simple style of life, and with the "honor and truth and wisdom" of Wylie's moral philosophy. Like Alex Stephens, Wise illustrates a southerner's conflict between "the competing claims of two value systems, one emphasizing self-discipline and the other the defense of honor;" and both men found the conflict insolvable.[59]

Blair, Cushing, Hilliard, and Wise exhibited a common tendency to search for reason in political behavior, to look behind events to the ideas that impelled them. They all rationalized their political activities, if they did not begin with philosophical motivations. All of them were acutely aware, because of their analytical habits, that there were a great many ways of looking at political problems; and although each adopted one particular perspective, he never lost sight of other possibilities. These four men, therefore, did not see politics from a partisan light. Rather, political behavior was for each of them a part of a complex pattern of personal attitudes to which he was attached with singular tenacity. In all of these respects, Blair, Cushing, Hilliard, and Wise are characteristic of the other Whig and Republican mavericks.

All Whig and Republican mavericks believed that independence was an identifying mark of a statesman. Generally, they hoped that others would accept their position because they believed in the republican virtue of the people and they were confident of the wisdom and morality of their actions. But in any case fear of public disapproval did not function as a deterrence to independence. Alexander Stephens frankly expressed his feelings before the House:

It is not true that, in my course as a member of this House, I look solely to what my constituents wish. The first question that addresses itself to my mind is, whether any measure presented here is right? I send no letters home to know what they think there about it; I never have and I never shall. I consult my own judgment, and act accordingly. ... Upon the merits of every question I am responsible to my constituents; and when I go home to them, an intelligent and patriotic people, if they do not approve my conduct, they can send another in my place.[60]

For any maverick in a difficult position, an appeal to public virtue might seem an appropriate way to validate his interpretation of political reality: "I demand . . . an adjournment of this whole matter from the arbitrament of maddened unrelenting politicians to all the people. . . . "[61] "The people desire quiet and repose; demagogues prefer a storm."[62] Politicians and demagogues had reason to fear popular opinion; the statesman, on the other hand, would find his course upheld.

   Whig and Republican mavericks understood the workings of the party system well enough to know that unlimited independence was not acceptable, even with the support of a faithful constituency. The paths they followed were often narrow ones, as a Tennessee Whig observed:

The line of duty for a good man is not often found in the yielding to the extreme opinions of either side. The path of wisdom, of safety, and of right, is not often strictly followed by those who feel, too strongly, the pressure of sectional or party demands.[63]

But those pressures were real ones, and mavericks resisted them with rhetorical expressions that indicate they felt the dangers they imposed.

   For Whig and Republican mavericks, the ultimate justification of independence was personal. A psychoanalyst might describe their statements as compulsive, and some mavericks were sufficiently neurotic that such an evaluation seems warranted. It seems sufficient to say, however, that most mavericks expressed a sense of compulsion, whether they were driven by inner motivations or prompted by circumstances that called for extreme language. For some mavericks, the inclination to independence stemmed from a strong sense of duty, as John Quincy Adams demonstrated in a short poem he wrote to Joshua Giddings in 1844:

When first together here we meet,
Askance each other we behold
The bitter mingling with the sweet,
The warm attempered with the cold.

We seek with searching ken to find
A soul congenial to our own;
For mind, in sympathy with mind,
Instinctive dreads to walk alone.

And here, with scrutinizing eye,
A kindred soul with mine to see,
And longing bosom to descry,
I sought, and found at last—in thee.

Farewell, my friend! and if once more
We meet within this hall again,

Be ours the blessing to restore
Our country's and the *rights of men*.[64]

A sense of persecution was expressed with some frequency by mavericks in the Whig and Republican parties, but it was always coupled with the conviction that persecution was inevitable for a just man:

Mr. Chairman, I am aware that I have uttered sentiments ill calculated to suit the public ear—I know sir, that I have uttered sentiments which forever cut me off from all hopes of favor from this Government, or with those who are destined to control it. But I stand here to speak the truth to my country. What is a man born for? Is it that, through deception and sycophancy, he may wind his way to power? Is it that, for the day, he may catch passing popularity, that miserable mushroom thing which springs up in the moisture and darkness of night, only to wither and die under the beams of the noon-day sun? No, sir, man lives that he may live hereafter, in the hearts and affections of his countrymen, for having vindicated their interests, their honor, and their liberties. This, in my opinion, is the highest destiny that awaits an earthly career.[65]

For Whig and Republican mavericks, the highest justification for independence was absolute duty, or even destiny, to act in accord with immutable truth or divine morality.

It should be clear that Whig and Republican mavericks did not despair about the problems of independence. If the duties were sometimes overwhelming, the rewards were personally as significant. Three well-known mavericks, Alexander Stephens, Joshua Giddings, and John Minor Botts, wrote of the private gratifications they felt about being right, however much maltreatment it gained them. Stephens wrote to his closest companion, his half brother Linton, that the secret motivation of his life was *"revenge reversed"*:

That is, to rise superior to the neglect or contumely of the mean of mankind, by doing them good instead of harm. A determination to war against fate; to meet the world in all its forces; to master evil with good, and to leave no foe standing in my rear. . . . My spirit of warring against the world, however, never had in it anything of a desire to *crush* or *trample*; no, only a desire to get above them, to excel them, to enjoy the gratification of seeing them feel that they were wrong; to compel their admiration. . . . This is the extent of my ambition.[66]

Stephens' desire for "revenge reversed" never allowed him a peaceful victory; such a large ambition could never be completely fulfilled.

Joshua Giddings, Stephens' political enemy, had the same sense of perpetual obligation. In the following letter to his wife in 1848 he wrote of being deeply moved by personal triumph after years of frustrating failure:

I have seen the foundations of the great deep of public sentiment broken up, and party names discarded, and thousands of good and virtuous citizens, throwing aside party prejudices, declare for freedom and humanity. When I have witnessed these things for the last four days, I have shed many a tear of gratitude and joy. . . . I have lived very fast during the past week. I have been amply compensated for all the toil and anxiety which I have suffered during my public life.[67]

The rewards of 1848 were not sufficient to afford Giddings a respite, and he continued to subject himself to public harassment to accomplish his duty of converting northern voters to political antislavery. Like other Whig and Republican mavericks, he seemed to carry with him a private commitment to right that was, in itself, sufficient reinforcement for his behavior. For men like this, public disapproval did not function as negative sanction; in many cases it only made them more sure of their rectitude. But among the mavericks there were few Ahabs willing to sink the ship of state for the sake of monomaniacal self-righteousness. Even when their constituents supported them, most mavericks displayed a deep sense of regret that their beliefs were not shared by more people, so that the goods they advocated could be accomplished through the will of the majority. Committed to republican values as much as to their own leadership, they were caught in a tragic position when the two were irreconcilable.

Some Whig and Republican mavericks in that position fell from public favor. John Minor Botts, the Virginia nationalist, recorded his fate in his *History of The Great Rebellion*. He had for years warned of the dangers inherent in the radical southern position, to no avail. On the day of the passage of Virginia's ordinance of secession, he was advised by his friends not to leave his house; but he stubbornly attended a public meeting only to find that upon his appearance the members of the audience departed, one by one. The persistent maverick described his return home:

I never felt more proud or stepped more boldly, for I felt the most comfortable and confiding assurance that I was *in the right*. . . . I walked home proudly and defiantly; but when safely pillowed under my own roof, my pride and defiant spirit both forsook me, and I involuntarily burst into tears over what I too clearly saw—the calamities that were in store for my country.[68]

There were many Whig and Republican mavericks who testified to the same mixed feelings of pride, disappointment, and fear: pride in their independence and judgment, disappointment in public failure, and fear that the public to which they felt obliged would suffer from the failures of politicans—mavericks or conformists.

It is difficult to assess the significance of the presence of so many strongly outspoken mavericks in the ranks of the Whig and Republican parties. Mavericks were not tragic heroes, despite their self-portrayal in that light. The historian's knowledge that a national tragedy was in the making inevitably colors any attempt to evaluate these men who demanded that they be heeded. It is difficult to be equally sympathetic to Joshua Giddings and Alexander Stephens, to John Quincy Adams and Henry Wise, or to Henry Winter Davis and Francis Pickens; and preference for the moderates—John Pendleton Kennedy, Caleb Cushing, Henry Washington Hilliard—renders the sectional leaders villains. Because of their diversity the significance of these mavericks cannot be measured by their impact upon issues and events but in terms of their import for the state of American political thought in the years before the Civil War. To view Whig and Republican mavericks in that perspective, they must be placed back in the context in which they acted along with their fellow congressmen.

Analysis of the political ideas of mavericks and conformists in the Democratic, Whig, and Republican parties in the years between 1836 and 1860 has revealed important differences in the manner in which these congressmen perceived their political environment. There are clear ideological distinctions among conformist politicians, perhaps not profoundly significant if measured against the broader spectrum of western political thought but important in the context of American politics. For mavericks in all three parties, however, partisan ideologies are less distinct. Mavericks looked at politics from the vantage points of very individualized concepts, which if consistently followed would prohibit purely partisan behavior.

The ideological differences between Democrats and Whigs can be readily summarized. Democratic conformists were generally optimistic about American society; they professed belief in limited government, equality of opportunity for white men, the right to self-government, and the primacy of an expansive American mission. Though they were consistent in expressing these ideas, they applied them with no intellectual rigor. The Democratic conformists' commitment to a pragmatic professional code of businesslike conduct prevailed over ideological purity.

Whig ideas had greater relevance to Whig conduct because their ideology integrated the political, social, economic, and cultural spheres. Their optimism about public morality was moderated by a concern for social balance. Although they agreed with Democratic conformists on the right to self-government and equal opportunity, they wanted government to protect republican principles by promoting economic security. Furthermore, their faith in the American mission, equal in intensity to that of Democrats, was more limited to a concern for improvement in the status of the existing citizenry. They questioned the desirability of extending American benefits to people of dubious moral character. Finally, the Whigs' professional code was less bounded by definitions derived from party organization than was that of Democrats, but they, too, scorned those politicians who interpreted political ethics by immoderate intellectual and moral standards.

Broad generalizations about the character of Republican thought could not be drawn from the material available for Republican conformists. Because of the party's youth, there was by 1860 no single Republican view but a mixture of ideas related to the political backgrounds of party members. At the same time, there was no evidence at all that conformist Republicans reflected upon political ideas as did mavericks. Insofar as evidence is available, Republican conformists were in that respect very much like conformists in the Democratic and Whig parties.

The similarities in the political ideas of mavericks in the Democratic, Whig, and Republican parties are not found among the particular ideological positions of the various men but in the kind of relationship each congressman perceived between himself and his environment. All mavericks saw the political world from a similar focus: the individual and his personal interpretation of political right. Independent in voting behavior and ideas, they all believed such independence was a prerequisite for sound political leadership. Most Democratic mavericks explained their independence with reference to the declining state of public virtue, drawing upon the intellectual heritage of the Revolution to justify their differences with the majority. The result was an ideological image of "the republic in peril" that had tremendous resonance in the larger society, as other political activists were discovering. Whig and Republican mavericks also drew upon the republican tradition, but they mixed it with a variety of other intellectual sources, including romantic literature and philosophy, evangelical religion, and southern particularism. Each had an audience—an advantage of pluralism—but their influences were diverse. However, all of the mavericks shared a common audience: their conformist colleagues.

Conformists repeatedly expressed their impatience with the mavericks' independence and disruptive ideas. Legislative efficiency, not to mention political safety, dictated a far more practical approach to politics. Yet no intelligent conformist could fail to notice the success of many mavericks, and there were many intelligent conformists. As political scientist Ralph K. Huitt has observed in his influential article "The Outsider in the Senate," mavericks are a model of one acceptable type of political style, with distinct advantages accruing to it.[69] The increasing complexity of legislative responsibilities, the short terms of congressmen, and their middle-class origins all combined to render it unlikely that the "new men of politics" in the House would be men of thought and action.[70] Conformists seem neither to have had the inclination nor ability to adopt mavericks' creativity, but a modernizing society could provide them the services of others with appropriate intellectual skills. Journalists, editors, novelists, even poets served the parties of the antebellum era. Political scientists have noted the absence of ideological responsibility in American political parties, a problem usually attributed to the pluralistic character of society and the awkwardness of the federal system. Another explanation may lie in the peculiar evolution of parties in the antebellum period, when ambitious politicians turned to others to do the tasks they could not themselves accomplish.

The most talented writers in America served the antebellum parties, and they were rewarded for their services in many ways. Because the creative arts were somewhat suspect, literary men could gain status by their association with practical politics. They could also receive "sinecures" within the patronage system. Some of them realized that there were costs to political activism. Nathanial

Hawthorne, shortly before he wrote his campaign biography of Franklin Pierce, reflected upon that cost in "The Custom-House" preface to *The Scarlet Letter*:

Uncle Sam's gold—meaning no disrespect to the worthy old gentleman—has in this respect, a quality of enchantment like that of the Devil's wages. Whoever touches it should look well to himself, or he may find the bargain to go hard against him, involving, if not his soul, yet many of its better attributes; its sturdy force, its courage and constancy, its truth, its self-reliance, and all that gives the emphasis to manly character.[71]

Hawthorne's warning, directed to officeholders like himself, spoke plainly to the problems of mavericks. They saw themselves as men of "sturdy force," "courage and constancy," "truth," and "self-reliance," but their ambitions to serve "Uncle Sam" placed them in situations where those qualities were not always valuable. Mavericks did not, however, see their successes as "the Devil's wages;" their own explanations suggest a far more positive understanding of what they were about.

Mavericks, through personalized and varied reasoning, rhetorically placed themselves in the center of the political universe. According to their calculations, it was necessary to the Republic that they exercise independent leadership. That they led in a dozen different directions with equal fervor was perhaps unfortunate for their parties, but those political consequences of their thought seemed less significant to mavericks than their loyalty to the image of themselves which their reflection produced.

NOTES

1. Orin Fowler, *Speech of the Hon. Orin Fowler, of Massachusetts, on the Legislation of Massachusetts—Our Government—the Disposal of the Public Lands—the Tariff—Constitutional Law—and Our Foreign Relations* (Washington, D. C.: Buell & Blanchard, 1852), p. 10.

2. John Quincy Adams, Joshua Giddings, and John A. Bingham were linked by their strong moral opposition to slavery and by the close working relationship between Adams and Giddings in early Congresses and between Giddings and Bingham in later Congresses. George W. Julian, Giddings' son-in-law and biographer, relates that "Bingham was a most genial companion, a fascinating speaker, a lover of poetry, and an extensive reader of books. . . . He loved him [Giddings] as devotedly as any son could love his father." See George W. Julian, *The Life of Joshua R. Giddings* (Chicago: A. C. McClung & Co., 1892), pp. 398–399. Caleb Cushing, Henry A. Wise, Thomas Gilmer, and Francis W. Pickens were all Tyler Whigs. Probably the two most famous disagreements between Whig/Republican mavericks were the ones between Wise and Adams over the gag-rule fight, in which the two well-educated and equally belligerent antagonists were repeatedly engaged, and the squabble between Henry Winter Davis and Frank Blair, Jr., and his family over the appointment of Montgomery Blair to the Lincoln Cabinet. See Adams' running comments in John Q. Adams, *The Diary of John Quincy Adams, 1794–1845: American Diplomacy, and Political, Social, and Intellectual Life, from Washington to*

Polk, ed. by Allan Nevins (New York: F. Ungar Pub. Co., 1969, [c. 1951]); Wise's reflections in Henry A. Wise, *Seven Decades of the Union: The Humanities and Materialism, Illustrated by a Memoir of John Tyler, with Reminiscences of Some of His Great Contemporaries* (Philadelphia: J. B. Lippincott & Co., 1872); and a discussion of the Blair-Davis fight in Reinhard H. Luthin, "A Discordant Chapter in Lincoln's Administration: The Davis-Blair Controversy," *Maryland Historical Magazine* 39 (1944):25–48.

3. Biographical studies are cited under the name of each congressman in the bibliography. Daniel Howe's analyses of Adams, Giddings, and Stephens are as perceptive as those of their biographers; *Political Culture of American Whigs*, Chs. 3, 7, and 10.

4. Billington, *Protestant Crusade*, p. 218.

5. For comments on Gilmer's efforts in behalf of retrenchment, see White, *The Jacksonians*, pp. 136–137, 151; the speech on the veto, *Congressional Globe*, 27th Cong., 2d Sess., 696–698.

6. Quentin Skinner, "Some Problems in the Analysis of Political Thought and Political Action," *Political Theory* 2 (August 1974):294. Gordon Wood delineates the evolution of meanings within the vocabulary of the revolutionary and constitutional ideology in *Creation of the American Republic*. A fine illustration of the continuing process of innovation that focuses upon the transformation of the key word "liberty" during the antebellum years is the work of a former student, Dana Gail Ridings, "The Contours of Liberty in Southern Political Philosophy, 1820–1860," (M.A. thesis, The University of Alabama in Huntsville, 1979), esp. pp. 52–61 for the role of Alexander Stephens.

7. Joseph R. Underwood, *An Address Delivered to the Colonization Society of Kentucky, at Frankfort, Jan. 15, 1835* (Frankfort: Albert G. Hodges, Printer, 1835), p. 3; hereafter cited as *Colonization Society*.

8. Henry Washington Hilliard, *Speeches and Addresses* (New York: Harper & Bros., 1855), p. 9.

9. Henry Washington Hilliard, *An Address Delivered Before the Erosophic Society at its First Anniversary, May 26, 1832* (Tuscaloosa, Ala.: Wiley, McGuire, & Henry, Printers, 1832), p. 16.

10. John A. Bingham, *The Lecompton Conspiracy. Speech of Hon. John A. Bingham, of Ohio. Delivered in the House of Representatives, Jan. 25, 1858* (Washington, D. C.: Buell & Blanchard, 1858). Ironically, Bingham did not remain in the forefront of Republican reformism; see Benedict, *A Compromise of Principle*, p. 36.

11. John Pendleton Kennedy, "The Spirit of the Age; False and True Progress," in *Occasional Addresses; and the Letters of Mr. Ambrose on the Rebellion* (New York: G. P. Putnam & Sons, 1872), p. 285, 284.

12. Francis W. Pickens, *Oration Delivered before the Euphradian and Clarisophic Societies, on the Influences of Government upon the Nature and Destiny of Man, by F. W. Pickens* (Columbia, S. C.: Steam-Power Press of Gibbes & Johnson, 1855), p. 20. Hereafter cited as *Influences of Government*.

13. No published biography does as much justice to the complexity of Stephen's character as the single chapter in Howe, *Political Culture of American Whigs* (Ch. 10). I am also, however, indebted to the analysis of one of my students, Gladys Falkner Williams, "The Divided Mind of an Antebellum Statesman: Alexander Stephens, the South and the Nation," (M.A. thesis, The University of Alabama in Huntsville, 1982).

14. Stephens qualified his optimistic assertion with the warning that progress would

occur in the United States only if the Union persisted; see Williams, "The Divided Mind of an Antebellum Statesman," p. 44.

15. Quoted in Howe, *Political Culture of American Whigs*, p. 242.

16. Stephens' speech in the House of Representatives on Jan. 25, 1845, quoted in Richard Malcolm Johnston and William Hand Browne, *Life of Alexander H. Stephens* (Philadelphia: J. B. Lippincott & Co., 1878), pp. 191–192. Stephens' exceptional defense of slavery in the famous "cornerstone" speech seems anomalous in the context of his entire career. For a comment on that speech's ideological significance see Emory M. Thomas, *The Confederate Nation*, p. 10.

17. The description is that of Giddings' biographer, James B. Stewart, *Joshua R. Giddings and the Tactics of Radical Politics*. Giddings' congressional activities against slavery are also described in Joshua R. Giddings, *The Exiles of Florida: or, the Crimes Committed by Our Government against the Maroons, Who Fled from South Carolina and Other Slave States, Seeking Protection under Spanish Laws*, a facsimile reproduction of the 1858 edition with introduction by Arthur W. Thompson (Gainesville: University of Florida Press, 1964).

18. Speech in the House of Representatives, May 21, 1844, in *Speeches in Congress* (Boston: John P. Jewett & Co., 1853), pp. 106–107. Giddings said on one occasion that he would not believe the decalogue to be "of divine origin" if it sanctioned slavery. Speech in the House of Representatives in Feb., 1844, in *Speeches in Congress*, p. 69.

19. John Armour Bingham, *State of the Union. Speech of the Hon. John A. Bingham, of Ohio, in the House of Representatives, Jan. 22, 1861* (Washington, D. C.: Congressional Globe Office, 1861), p. 6.

20. See headnote p.000.

21. Howe discusses the difficulties of interpreting Adams' character, *Political Culture of American Whigs*, pp. 44–47. Also see George A. Lipsky, *John Quincy Adams, His Theory and Ideas* (New York: Thomas Y. Crowell Co., 1950), p. 88. The author asserts that "Adams, in contrast with the typical political practitioner, made few concessions in theory and practice to necessity and opportunity" and that "he stuck to his philosophy."

22. John Quincy Adams, *Poems of Religion and Society* (Auburn & Buffalo, N. Y.: Miller, Orton & Mulligan, 1854), p. 38.

23. For a discussion of Adams' ideas on slavery at the beginning of his career see Samuel Flagg Bemis, *John Quincy Adams and the Union* (New York: Alfred A. Knopf, 1956), pp. 415–523.

24. Henry Winter Davis, *The War of Ormuzd and Ahriman in the Nineteenth Century* (Baltimore: James S. Waters, 1852), p. 344.

25. Lewis C. Levin, *Speech of Mr. L. C. Levin, of Pennsylvania, on the Bill to Raise a Regiment of Mounted Riflemen. Delivered in the House of Representatives of the United States, Apr. 7, 1846* (Washington, D. C.: J. & G. S. Gideon, Printers, 1846), p. 10.

26. Specifically, for an example in the case of Davis, in the form of the Wade-Davis bill of 1864.

27. The best treatment of Frank Blair, Jr.'s, career is found in William Ernest Smith, *The Francis Preston Blair Family in Politics*, 2 vols. (New York: Macmillan Co., 1933).

28. Though Cushing was a Whig before the Massachusetts party was seriously divided over slavery, the "cotton" appellation seems appropriate. The best source of information about Cushing is his own writing, of which there is a great deal, but there is also one scholarly biography by Claude M. Fuess, *The Life of Caleb Cushing* (New York: Harcourt, Brace & World, 1923).

29. See Miss Toccoa Cozart, "Henry W. Hilliard," reprint no. 12 from *Transactions of the Alabama Historical Society* 4 (1899–1903):277–299; Hilliard's own memoirs, *Politics and Pen Pictures at Home and Abroad* (New York: G. P. Putnam's Sons, 1892); and Johanna Nicol Shields, "An Antebellum Alabama Maverick: Henry Washington Hilliard, 1845–1851," *The Alabama Review* 30 (July 1977):192–212.

30. An old biography of Wise by his grandson contains valuable speeches and information. See Barton H. Wise, *The Life of Henry A. Wise of Virginia, 1806–1876* (New York: Macmillan Co., 1899). There is also an excellent essay on Wise in Clement M. Eaton, *The Mind of the Old South*, rev. ed. (Baton Rouge: Louisiana State University Press, 1967), pp. 63–81. The scattered sources of information about Wise, who has not had the benefit of a modern biographer, were rendered cohesive for me by one of my students, Elizabeth Walker Shown, "Henry A. Wise: Slavery and Defense of the South," (M.A. thesis, The University of Alabama in Huntsville, 1983).

31. An amusing account of General Robert E. Lee's difficulties in gaining cooperation from Wise in the early Virginia campaigns is found in Douglas Southall Freeman, *R. E. Lee*, 4 vols. (New York: Charles Scribner's Sons, 1934–1935), 1:579–603.

32. See, for example, the opening paragraph of Frank Blair, Jr., *The Destiny of the Races of This Continent. An Address Delivered before the Mercantile Library Association of Boston, Massachusetts, on the 26th of Jan., 1859* (Washington, D. C.: Buell & Blanchard, Printers, 1859), pp. 3, 6.

33. Frank Blair, Jr., *Pacific Railroad. Speech of Hon. F. P. Blair, Jr., of Missouri, in the House of Representatives, May 25, 1858* (Washington, D. C.: Congressional Globe Office, 1858).

34. Blair, *Destiny of the Races*, p. 15.

35. See, for example, Frank Blair, Jr., *Speech of Hon. F. P. Blair, Jr., of Missouri, at the Cooper Institute, New York City, Wednesday, Jan. 25, 1860* (Washington, D. C.: Buell & Blanchard, 1860), p. 6; and Frank Blair, Jr., *Speech of Hon. Francis P. Blair, Jr., of Missouri, on the Kansas Question; Delivered in the House of Representatives, Mar. 23, 1858* (Washington, D. C.: Congressional Globe Office, 1858), p. 8, hereafter cited as *Speech on Kansas*.

36. Ibid., pp. 3, 8, 5.

37. Blair, *Destiny of the Races*, p. 22.

38. Ibid.

39. Fuess, *Life of Cushing*, pp. 84–85.

40. Caleb Cushing, *Review, Historical and Political, of the late Revolution in France, and of the Consequent Events in Belgium, Poland, Great Britain, and Other Parts of Europe*, 2 vols. (Boston: Carter, Hendee & Co.; Newburyport: Thomas B. White, 1833), 1:348. Hereafter cited as *Review of Revolution*.

41. Quoted in Fuess, *Life of Cushing*, p. 33.

42. Caleb Cushing, *Speech of Mr. Cushing, of Massachusetts, on the Right of Petition, as Connected with Petitions for the Abolition of Slavery and the Slave Trade in the District of Columbia: Delivered in the House of Representatives, Jan. 25, 1836* (Washington, D. C.: Gales & Seaton, Printers, 1836), p. 4.

43. Caleb Cushing, *An Oration on the Material Growth and Territorial Progress of the United States, Delivered at Springfield, Massachusetts on the Fourth of July, 1839* (Springfield, Mass.: Merriam, Wood & Co., Printers, 1839). Hereafter cited as *Oration on Growth and Progress*.

44. Caleb Cushing, *Address. Delivered Sept. 26, 1850, at Salem, before the Essex Agricultural Society* (Salem, Mass.: Salem Gazette and Essex County Mercury, Printers, Dec., 1850), p. 17. Hereafter cited as *Essex Agricultural Society Address*.

45. Cushing, *Oration on Growth and Progress*, p. 25.

46. Caleb Cushing, "Eulogy, Pronounced at Newburyport, Massachusetts, July 15, 1826," in *A Selection of Eulogies, Pronounced in the Several States, in Honor of Those Illustrious Patriots and Statesmen, John Adams and Thomas Jefferson* (Hartford, Conn.: D. F. Robinson & Co. and Norton & Russell, 1826), p. 38.

47. Henry W. Hilliard, *DeVane: A Story of Plebeians and Patricians* (New York: Blelock & Co., 1865).

48. Ibid., p. 8–15, DeVane is introduced and described.

49. She is referred to as "a soul fresh as Paradise before a cloud flitted over it," (p. 60) and as "Eve yet in Eden," (p. 17), Ibid.

50. Ibid., pp. 411, 227.

51. Ideas taken from his speeches in *Speeches and Addresses*. The speeches covered a variety of subjects and were all from the antebellum part of Hilliard's long career. For his later opposition to slavery, see Hilliard, *Politics and Pen Pictures*, pp. 352, 440.

52. Hilliard, Speech in the House of Representatives in 1849, quoted in *Speeches and Addresses*, pp. 214–215.

53. Shown, "Henry A. Wise," p. 5.

54. Ibid., p. 90.

55. Ibid., pp. 88–89.

56. Barton Wise, *Life of Henry Wise*, pp. 144–145.

57. Ibid., p. 400.

58. Wise, *Seven Decades*, p. 69.

59. Howe, *Political Culture of American Whigs*, p. 241. The power of the code of honor for southerners has been persuasively argued in Bertram Wyatt-Brown, *Southern Honor: Ethics and Behavior in the Old South* (New York: Oxford University Press, 1982).

60. *Congressional Globe*, 33d Cong., 2d Sess., 55.

61. Emerson Etheridge, *State of the Union. Speech of Hon. Emerson Etheridge, of Tennessee, Delivered in the House of Representatives, Jan. 23, 1861* (Washington, D. C.: Henry Polkinhorn, Printer, 1861), p. 4.

62. William Cullom, *Speech of Hon. Wm. Cullom, of Tennessee, on the Nebraska and Kansas Bill, in the House of Representatives, Apr. 11, 1854* (Washington, D. C.: Congressional Globe Office, 1854), p. 11.

63. Emerson Etheridge, *The Assault by Mr. Brooks on Mr. Sumner. Speech of Hon. E. Etheridge, of Tennessee, Delivered in the House of Representatives, July 12, 1856* (Washington, D. C.: Congressional Globe Office, 1856).

64. Julian, *Life of Giddings*, p. 165.

65. Francis W. Pickens, *Speech of Mr. Pickens, of South Carolina; Delivered in the House of Representatives, May 23, 1836, the House Being in Committee of the Whole on the Fortification Bill* (Washington, D. C.: Duff Green, Printer, 1836), p. 16.

66. Johnston and Browne, *Life of Alexander H. Stephens*, p. 263.

67. Julian, *Life of Giddings*, p. 246.

68. John Minor Botts, *The Great Rebellion: Its Secret History, Rise, Progress and Disastrous Failure* (New York: Harper & Bros., Publishers, 1866).

69. Huitt, "The Outsider in the Senate," p. 171.

70. The phrase is from a chapter title in Pessen, *Jacksonian America*.

71. Nathanial Hawthorne, *The Scarlet Letter*, a Norton Critical Edition, ed. by Scully Bradley, Richmond Croom Beatty, and E. Hudson Long (New York: W. W. Norton & Co., 1961), p. 33.

John Armor Bingham of Ohio, 1815-1900. (Reproduction from the collections of the Library of Congress.)

Francis Preston Blair, Jr., of Missouri, (1821-1875. (Reproduction from the collections of the Library of Congress.)

Caleb Cushing of Massachusetts, 1800-1879. (Reproduction from the collections of the Library of Congress.)

Muscoe Russell Hunter Garnett of Virginia, 1821-1864. (Reproduction from the collections of the Library of Congress.)

Charles Jared Ingersoll of Pennsylvania, 1782-1862. (Reproduction from the collections of the Library of Congress.)

Preston King of New York, 1806-1865. (Reproduction from the collections of the Library of Congress.)

James Lawrence Orr of South Carolina, 1822-1873. (Reproduction from the collection of the Architect of the Capitol by the Photoduplication Service of the Library of Congress.)

Joseph Rogers Underwood of Kentucky, 1791-1876. (Reproduction from the collections of the Library of Congress.)

John Wentworth of Illinois, 1815-1888. (Reproduction from the collections of the Library of Congress.)

ENGRAVED BY A.B. WALTER PHILAD.

HON. HENRY A. WISE.
GOVERNOR OF VIRGINIA

Henry A. Wise
of Virginia.

Henry Alexander Wise of Virginia, 1806-1876. (Reproduction from the collections of the Library of Congress.)

Part IV

THE MAVERICK MENTALITY

CHAPTER 9

The Maverick Intellect

> Statesmen and legislators, standing so completely within the institution, never distinctly and nakedly behold it. They speak of moving society, but have no resting place without it. They may be men of a certain experience and discrimination, and have no doubt invented ingenious and even useful systems, for which we sincerely thank them; but all their wit and usefulness lie within certain not very wide limits. They are wont to forget that the world is not governed by policy and expediency.
>
> Henry David Thoreau, *Civil Disobedience*

The maverick was defined in the opening pages of this study in terms of a particular pattern of voting.[1] In fact, for the bulk of men classified as mavericks the word has a more general application: mavericks, in their political spheres, were men set apart from others. Conceiving of themselves as leaders in a special sense, they exerted their influences in the House in a variety of ways, but not consistently in manners predictable on the basis of their party or regional ties. They were unusual in their personal concept of leadership; they were marked by their nonconforming voting behavior; and they were different from the mass of conformists because they exhibited habits of thinking wholly uncharacteristic of these more typical congressmen.

Mavericks were surely not more intelligent than conformists. There is no reason to question the political intelligence of conformists like Stephen Douglas or Howell Cobb; the popular assessment might even be that such men were more intelligent than erratic figures like Henry Wise or Caleb Cushing. But if they were not more intelligent than conformists, mavericks were certainly as a group far more intellectual than conformists.

The distinction between intelligence and intellect is not a specious one. Richard Hofstadter in *Anti-Intellectualism in American Life* provided a description that may clarify the differences between maverick and conformist habits of thinking:

. . . intelligence is an excellence of mind that is employed within a fairly narrow, immediate, and predictable range; it is a manipulative, adjustive, unfailingly practical quality—one of the most eminent and endearing of the animal virtues. Intelligence works within the framework of limited but clearly stated goals, and may be quick to shear away questions of thought that do not seem to help in reaching them.[2]

Intelligence is a quality admirably suitable for the "responsible" legislator, and its usefulness within the context of the increasingly more regular and well-defined environment of antebellum party machinery and the gradually institutionalizing House of Representatives is obvious. Its limitations, however, may be as clear. An intelligence that accepted the immediate political environment as adequate for its purposes, that worked within its boundaries with little heed for external considerations, could and perhaps did blunder badly when political decisions had public consequences of considerable scope. The successful manipulation which preceded the passage of the Kansas–Nebraska Act and its evidently unforeseen consequences are perhaps indicative of both the strengths and weaknesses of the political intelligence of conformists in the antebellum period as represented in the person of one of their more able figures, Stephen Douglas.

Hofstadter continues:

Intellect, on the other hand, is the critical, creative, and contemplative side of mind. Whereas intelligence seeks to grasp, manipulate, re-order, adjust, intellect examines, ponders, wonders, theorizes, criticizes, imagines. Intelligence will seize the immediate meaning in a situation and evaluate it. Intellect evaluates evaluations, and looks for the meanings of situations as a whole.[3]

An intellectual approach to politics suggests, then, an orientation toward considerations other than the immediate environment, an almost universal characteristic of mavericks in at least some political situations. Analysis must rest upon a certain ability to stand outside of the situation and perceive its relation to exterior circumstances, a pattern of perception quite typical of maverick political attitudes. Certainly not all mavericks displayed a contemplative and imaginative side in politics; but the number who did is impressive, especially when contrasted with the almost complete absence of such traits among conformists. As successful politicians, mavericks had to be able to account for the practical realities of getting elected; none could be a cloistered intellectual. But to a remarkable extent they did exhibit intellect, both in their approach to politics and in a wider range of activities.

In addition to their generally intellectual orientation, mavericks shared a number of specific intellectual characteristics that few conformists possessed, characteristics which when taken as a group denote a type of intellect particularly appropriate for political leaders who conceived of themselves in the paternalistic role described in preceding chapters. The special marks of the maverick intellect combine to describe an image of an active, yet reflective mind, one possessing the education, awareness, and historical sense necessary to fix it in the center of the cultural developments which were taking place in mid-nineteenth-century America.

The first of these notable characteristics of the maverick intellect was concern for education—that of the individual and of the general American public, that which was formal and fixed, and that which was informal and continuous. A second important characteristic was the mavericks' familiarity with the ideas, writers, scholars, and philosophers taking on significance in their own time. Mavericks were interested in the ideas that they believed were going to help shape the future as well as in those that had helped shape the past. A third characteristic of maverick intellectual attitudes was the tendency to analyze the evolving American culture in terms of its mission for the world. Frequently set in context of the contrast between American and European experience, between the ideas of the historical past and those of the visionary future, or even between the contributions of civilization in the past and the naturally inspired gifts of America, they set forth varying outlines for the culture which they believed themselves involved in shaping.

THE MAVERICK CONCEPT OF EDUCATION

Education, in the mavericks' sense of the word, was not necessarily book-learning, even though many a maverick was well educated in the classics and possessed a degree from Harvard, Dartmouth, Yale, Princeton, or some other prominent American institution. Mavericks believed in and acted on the premise that education was a lifetime process and that the sources of learning were both formal and informal. In the words of John A. Bingham, the Ohio Republican maverick: "I learn from everybody. I have been all my life learning, and have never yet seen a human being from whom I could not learn something."[4] Henry Winter Davis, writing of his departure from Kenyon College in Ohio, used a familiar metaphor to describe his innocent state: "I knew something of books, but nothing of men, and I went forth like Adam among the wild beasts of the unknown wilderness of the world."[5] One of the most common manifestations of the mavericks' interest in education, broadly defined, was their sustained activity in a variety of informal associations. Many belonged to some of the well-known reform groups: Bible societies, temperance organizations, antislavery, or colonization societies. They were also active, however, in groups with a more obvious educational purpose: philosophical, agricultural, scientific, literary, or drama societies, for example. Mavericks in these groups were active participants, and they were characteristically found in such roles as organizer, speaker, or writer. Although their activity may have served political purposes by providing public exposure, the theme of the mavericks' involvement seems to have been the elevation of the American public to a higher level of intellectual and cultural awareness.

Examples of mavericks' participation in educational and reform associations are so profuse as to be tedious, but two very opposite illustrations may be useful.

"Long John" Wentworth, the Chicago maverick, was not at all an intellectual, despite a Dartmouth degree and a family pedigree the equal of any in Illinois. To all outward appearances, he was the paragon of a western rough-and-tumble politician.[6] Yet his interest in popular education and improvement was deep and sincere. He was a leading member of the agricultural societies of Illinois, a writer for agricultural journals on the subject of scientific farming, and owner of scientifically bred herds of cattle which regularly won prizes at fairs. During his congressional service Wentworth proposed establishment of a national agricultural school. He also, after his semi-retirement from political life, wrote a two-volume genealogical study of the Wentworth family in America and several pamphlets on the history of Chicago, collected volumes of material for the Chicago Historical Society, and published his own congressional reminiscences.[7] Never a scholar, Wentworth was involved throughout his life in informal education—his own and that of the people of his state.

Wentworth exemplified the maverick whose educational experience was partially informal, public in its orientation, and thoroughly democratic in application. Another maverick whose emphasis was on formal and private education also demonstrated the typical maverick's conviction that a broad and continuing education was a necessary public asset for Americans. James Meacham was a Congregationalist minister, professor at Middlebury College, and Whig maverick congressman from Vermont. In Congress, Meacham became involved in the dispute over the future of the Smithsonian Institution, picking up the fight where his predecessor, the erudite conformist George Perkins Marsh, had left it.[8] According to Marsh's biographer, David Lowenthal, the Smithsonian battle represented the first drawing in Congress of clear lines "between the scholars and the frontiersmen, the anti-intellectuals of that era."[9] Meacham, Marsh, Rufus Choate, and John Quincy Adams were leaders for the intellectuals; Benjamin Tappan and Robert Dale Owen were leaders for the opponents.

The anti-intellectuals wanted the Smithsonian to be developed into a research center for the applied sciences so that useful knowledge could be disseminated throughout the country. The "scholars" preferred that the Smithsonian serve as a center for scholars, with emphasis on the collection of books and other research materials to be used by any American desiring to further his own intellectual advancement. The public benefit from the plan of the scholars would be indirect although, in their minds, no less important.

Presenting the argument for the scholars, Meacham argued that "to increase knowledge in any department one must have possessed himself of the knowledge extant in that department," a position entirely in line with his scholarly background.[10] He went on, however, to refine his idea of what kinds of knowledge were most valuable for the public in America:

To us history is of peculiar importance. A new people working out the greatest problem of time—the true theory and practice of self-government—we wish to examine history for ourselves. . . . We wish to re-write it from our own viewpoint. . . . Our free institutions are not the offspring of ignorant blundering, and scholastic rashness. Our fathers—the Jeffersons, the Adamses—were men of study and thought. . . . The doctrines developed here are destined to spread—not by sudden outbursts of enthusiasm—not in the wild tramp of revolutions—so much as by the silent influence of what thinking and studious men will write and speak.[11]

The balancing of words and phrases in this passage is significant: "Theory and practice;" "ignorant blundering and scholastic rashness;" the mixing of statesmanship and philosophy characterized by Jefferson and the Adamses—all these indicate Meacham's conviction that scholarly knowledge in America was, properly understood, also useful to the public.[12] He was advocating neither inferior scholarship nor neglect of utility; the public good, as he saw it, would be best served by practical scholarship.

The mavericks' belief that the citizens of a democracy should be well educated did not necessarily entail devotion to traditional concepts of education. In fact, many mavericks were concerned lest the older forms of education—with firm grounding in the classical languages and ancient history—be inappropriate for Americans. While not all mavericks rejected the value of a classical education, there was considerable evidence that many were involved enough in the cultural changes of their day to question its sufficiency for the modern age.

The opposition to the continuation of "dead forms" in American education was often couched in anti-intellectual terms. Intellectual anti-intellectualism, like that of romantic writers and philosophers, was sometimes found among maverick congressmen. For example, James L. Orr of South Carolina, in an address to the literary societies of Furman University in 1855, analyzed the cultural changes of the period and concluded that the classics were not only irrelevant but dangerous. He derided attending to them at the expense of the natural and moral sciences; and he advocated more emphasis on the national culture. Of the prevalent curriculum he said, "The course commences and terminates with the dead languages; and graduating students are often familiar with a despicable and vicious heathen mythology, that brutalizes the imagination and moral sense, who are ignorant of the history and literature of their own country."[13] His conclusion was nationalistic and certainly narrow, but it was based on both his emotional preferences and an intellectual analysis of the problems of American culture and education. He did not attack the value of education and intellect, only those forms he believed inappropriate to the nineteenth century and American mission.

MAVERICK AWARENESS OF CULTURAL CHANGE

Mavericks' speeches and writings indicate that many of them were thoroughly familiar with the philosophical, literary, scientific, and religious ideas which were emerging in their own time. The cultural changes of the nineteenth century, like the social and economic changes which they accompanied, sounded the death knell for the relatively stable world of the preindustrial era. While mavericks and conformists alike filled their speeches with allusions to the classics, mythology, the Bible, history, and poetry, only mavericks commonly referred to the ideas of the modern writers. Whether they were overtly aware of it or not, mavericks were participating in the cultural revolution of the mid-century by giving currency to ideas that would alter the status quo irrevocably. The most widespread example of this sort of cultural awareness is the very common usage by mavericks of the ideas of nineteenth-century romantic poets, novelists, or philosophers. The mavericks' familiarity with nineteenth-century developments did not indicate that they merely read and noted what some particular author suggested; the fact that the ideas were put to use rather than quoted indicated that some mavericks were as much involved in the intellectual revolution as aware of it.

An outstanding example of the high level of maverick sensitivity to cultural currents is found in a letter of Joshua Giddings' to the *Anti-Slavery Standard* in 1857.[14] Giddings, an ardent reformer, was definitely not an intellectual in the eastern mode. Because of his association with the Antislavery crusade, he came to know personally most of the New England reformers and scholars, and the influence of their ideas on his work is clear in the following passages from that letter:

I think the time has arrived when some modern Luther or Calvin should erect the standard of a higher, a purer theology,—a theology in harmony with the laws of justice, of God; a theology in harmony with the teachings of the gospel; a theology approved by the philosophy, the judgment of enlightened men; a theology that acknowledges and proclaims the primal truths that life, that civil, religious, and spiritual freedom are the *gifts of God*; that every member of the human family has received from the Creator an equal and inalienable right to enjoy them; that such enjoyment is necessary to develop the intellect, elevate the soul, and prepare the individual for usefulness, for happiness here and here-after. . . .

For the protection of these rights and the encouragement of these duties all governments and associations should be adapted. Of all nations of the earth ours is the most favorably situated for carrying forward this great reformation. . . . The reformation has commenced, is in rapid progress. In all parts of the country men are awakening to the necessity of a more practical theology. . . . Men see that mere theories, bald forms of sectarian faith, are impotent and useless. Our old organizations are becoming inert, inefficient, worn out. Men long to lay them aside, to disconnect themselves from these theoretical technicalities, which retard the union of hearts upon those great and vital truths which elevate mankind.[15]

The call for a new religion (which would, of course, support the fight against slavery) reflects diverse influences: the Puritan emphasis on practical and useful living, the political ethics of the Declaration of Independence, the personal appeal of the nineteenth-century revivalistic religions, and the rhetoric of the abolitionists. The second paragraph rings more clearly with transcendental concepts: the image of men separated by outmoded social and religious forms, longing to unite on the basis of a union of the heart, is very similar to the philosophy expressed in "Self-Reliance," "The American Scholar," and other Emerson essays.[16] Giddings' use of the ideas of New England intellectuals was typical of the antislavery mavericks, who were apparently sympathetic to the intellectual as well as to the political ideas behind abolitionism.

The northern reform mavericks were not alone in their sensitivity to romantic currents in American culture. There is considerable evidence among the southern mavericks that the romantic aspects of their thought were not only indebted to English and southern conservative thought but also reflected their involvement in the cultural life of the nation. The outstanding example is John Pendleton Kennedy, the Whig maverick from Baltimore. Kennedy was a competent novelist who wrote three novels with southern historical settings: *Rob of the Bowl* was set in seventeenth-century Maryland; *Horse-Shoe Robinson* took for its subject the exploits of a Revolutionary hero; and *Swallow Barn* treated early nineteenth-century plantation life in Virginia.[17] All of the novels had romantic aspects, and *Swallow Barn* is usually described as one of the first romantic plantation novels, although it by no means presents an uncritical view of southern society.[18] In any case, whatever the source and manifestations of Kennedy's romanticism, he could hardly be taken as a typical representative of mavericks' thought. Although his example is not sufficient to prove southern exposure to current intellectual trends, it is significant that a man of his intellect and activity was a maverick and not a conformist. Although he was certainly the most talented literary figure among southern mavericks, he was not an isolated example. Despite the intellectual conformity of the South in the prewar years, some men were exposing themselves to "unsound ideas."[19]

A deep-South maverick who illustrates as well as Kennedy the sensitivity of southern mavericks to cultural changes is Henry Washington Hilliard, the Whig congressman from Alabama.[20] Hilliard's novel *DeVane* was previously referred to as illustration for the degree to which his political ideas showed a mixture of aristocratic and democratic elements, two elements found within Hilliard's native Alabama; but the intellectual attitudes which underlay his plot and characters display familiarity with ideas from far beyond the deep South, ideas not only unpopular in Alabama but probably even in some cases proscribed. Hilliard, a Methodist minister and former teacher of literature at the conservative universities of Alabama and Georgia, was thoroughly conversant with romantic poets, novelists, and philosophers of the nineteenth century. His novel, written on the eve of the Civil War though not published until 1865, was unquestionably written with a southern audience in mind. Perhaps that accounts for the fact that Hilliard mentions prominently only one northern writer, William Ellery Channing, in the entire book, which is otherwise filled with quotations from Wordsworth, Coleridge, Byron, Burns, a host of lesser English writers, the German transcendentals, Goethe, Schiller, and others.[21] In the tense atmosphere of the years immediately before the War, Hilliard might have feared that overt reference to other northern writers would damage the reception of the book.

His plot and themes clearly indicate that he was familiar with American as well as European writers. The major character of the novel, DeVane, is converted from English and Virginia aristocratic ways to humble American Methodist manners and thought by his relationship with the heroine, Esther Wordsworth. Several levels of symbolism in the relationship between the major characters are made explicit by Hilliard. Esther is named for the Biblical queen Esther, who saved her people, and for William Wordsworth, poet of the religion of nature.[22] She saves DeVane through her devotion to Methodism, but the vehicle is her own innocence. She is unquestionably the Eve of the novel, though she offers not expulsion from the Garden but entry into it.[23] Although in a sense the salvation she represents for DeVane, and by extension for the southern people, could be expressed in terms of primitive or pure Christianity, it also is clearly American religion—democratic, simple, and well tainted with the reform ideas of the northern romantics.

In two separate conversations, DeVane reveals his philosophical conversion to Esther. The first concerns his own political ambitions, for DeVane, like Hilliard, wanted to be a leader of the people:

I am not unambitious, but I trust that the passion with me is an honest and honorable one. I desire distinction, but it must be earned—not inherited; earned, too, by a career of usefulness—not bought with money, nor obtained by the mean arts which degrade so many public men. I am satisfied that the dearth of high qualities which we must all acknowledge, is the result of the conventional rules of life, now becoming so strong in this country. Vigor and manliness are disappearing. Wealth is worshipped. The high places of the Republic are looked to as the rewards of the abject followers of some petty popular potentate, and the very road to the unseen world which we are assured awaits the good, is hedged in by aristocratic forms, which make no provision for the poor and the outcast. I wish to be a man. I will not consent to be dwarfed by the forms of society.[24]

Like Giddings, Hilliard, in the person of DeVane, employed the contrast between conventional forms of society and the vigor of natural manliness in his critique of American society. Although Hilliard's language was conventional, the theme of self-reliance expressed by DeVane owed more to romantic thought than to any aspect of southern conservatism.

In another, perhaps more politically significant passage, DeVane applied the doctrine of self-reliance to the problem of southern plantation society. Before the War, Hilliard did not publicly criticize the institution of slavery, but DeVane's remarks reveal the impact of Hilliard's exposure to romantic ideas:

With my views of life, to compel me to sit down upon a plantation in Virginia and see my slaves toil for my benefit, adding year after year to the increase of an estate already too large, would be intolerable. . . .

I firmly believe that some degree of labor is essential to happiness. For my own part, my mind is quite made up to make my own living.[25]

DeVane was gradually converted to Esther's religious and social views; Hilliard suggested that it was as if Eve had helped Adam to regain paradise.[26] Given the Biblical Esther's relationship to her people, a relationship that Hilliard reminds the reader of, it would seem more than likely that Hilliard was trying to point out that southern society needed to become simplified and reformed. The novel closes with the marriage of Esther and DeVane, and the author observed that they were as suitably matched as any couple since "that happy hour when our first parents stood in Eden, hand in hand, and looked up through the stars to praise their Maker."[27] There is no evidence in *DeVane* that Hilliard perceived in the 1850s the revolutionary nature of his ideas when applied to southern society; but he personally must have worked the ideas through after the war, since by 1878 he was involved in the campaign to end slavery in Brazil.[28] There was not a caustic word in Hilliard's novel; but the criticisms of southern society are clear, and the basis from which they arise is plainly the romantic, democratic, and religious sentiment of a man whose ideas stretch beyond the intellectual confines of his section.

A great many mavericks were neither as creative in their intellectual activities as Hillard nor as committed to public awakening as Giddings, but they exhibited nonetheless a persistent concern for keeping up with the ideas of the current generation. One Democratic maverick, Edmund Burke of New Hampshire (who, although he disagreed with his party in Congress, was a loyal Democrat till his death in 1883), was a newspaper editor, like Wentworth an amateur scientific farmer, and the Commissioner of Patents from 1846 to 1850.[29] Included in his library catalogue published after his death were 1,453 separate entries, many of which included several volumes and in which were listed many American and European writers of the period of his lifetime.[30] The listing reflected Burke's interests in science, philosophy, literature, art, and the history and politics of his own country, and it included such names as Louis Agassiz, Matthew Fontaine Maury, Theodore Parker, and William Ellery Channing from the United States and Jeremy Bentham, Thomas Carlyle, Auguste Comte, Charles Darwin, Thomas Henry Huxley, Charles Lyell, Immanuel Kant, Joseph Priestly, and Herbert Spencer (twenty volumes) from Britain and continental Europe. The list of fiction and poetry in Burke's collection was also varied. He owned twenty-six volumes of the works of James Fenimore Cooper, a holding which probably reflected interest in Indian history as well as approval of the Democratic sentiments of Cooper. There were also works by another Democrat, Nathaniel Hawthorne, by Whig poets James Russell Lowell and John Greenleaf Whittier, and by the romantic southern poet Edgar Allan Poe. From non-American sources, the wide variety of writings included works of Honoré de Balzac, Robert Burns, Lord Byron, and Samuel Taylor Coleridge. Burke's collection of political writings reflected in part his Democratic and pro-southern leanings: he owned the works of John C. Calhoun, many volumes of proslavery arguments, books by fellow maverick Caleb Cushing, and histories by George Bancroft. Less apparently congenial to Burke's politics but nonetheless included in his library were writings of the New England reformer Horace Mann. An odd, late addition to his political collection was Henry George's *Progress and Poverty*, published only four years before Burke's death.

Burke was a New England Democrat and yet his position on slavery was almost consistent with the southern one; his views on economics were radically laissez-faire. His library, however, contained writings from almost every possible sort of intellectual influence an American might have met; and his own published writings indicate that he was broadly read, although of course there is no way of demonstrating that he read any, most, or all of the books that he owned. Although he had no college education, his collection of books, as well as his newspaper work, his agricultural interests, and his interest in science and technology testify to the breadth of his education and to his familiarity with modern as well as classical or historical learning.

The interest of many maverick congressmen in the field of natural sciences was part of a historical pattern in American culture.[31] John Quincy Adams spent many hours late in his career working on an address to the Astronomical Society in Cincinnati on the subject of the role of science in American life.[32] Numerous mavericks like Wentworth and Burke were concerned with the application of science to agriculture. The scientific interests of Frederick P. Stanton (Tennessee Democratic maverick) and Thomas Clingman (North Carolina Democratic maverick) have already been discussed in the context of political theory.[33] In the years before the war, both men were using the philosophy later to be called social Darwinism, and both applied science to politics. Stanton was probably more consistent in this interest than Clingman, whose electicism was matched by a lack of depth on most topics; and Stanton's scientific philosophy seemed to have been also the matrix for a concurrent interest in romantic ideas. In an address delivered to the Alumni Association of Columbian College (later George Washington University) in 1852, entitled "The Character of Modern Science, or, the Mission of the Educated Man," Stanton exhibited his familiarity with a wide range of scientific and scholarly ideas.[34]

Dealing first with the character of educated man, Stanton spoke in a spirit of romantic reform and declared that

A generous and self-sacrificing spirit, looking to higher aims than mere personal aggrandizement or selfish enjoyment, and therefore seeking association for that development of good, is the characteristic of that man whose mind has been awakened by the electric touch of truth, to behold nature, physical and moral, in all the sublime simplicity and benevolence of her divine laws.[35]

Stanton saw the independent thinker as superior to the man who had merely formal education and asserted that the man who "pursues his own investigations by the light of that torch which God has placed in his own reason" had "in a thousand instances, outstripped his brother in the race of intellect, though the latter may have been tutored by the best masters and with the most assiduous and unwearied care."[36]

Stanton turned next to the substance of the mission of educated man—the development of science to the benefit of man. Like James Orr and others he believed that the educational curriculum should be reformed to begin with physical sciences; since the physical senses were developed before the moral sense, they should be educated first. Learning to follow nature's laws, man would be able to unravel the secrets of the universe, ultimately escaping even the limitations of man's finite sense of time and space. Stanton predicted that the use of machines capable of solving problems like men but more efficiently would enable man to discover the size of the universe and promote unbounded education in science.

A further accomplishment he predicated for the educated man of the future was the ability to tame the energy of the universe. Stanton insisted that all energy was of one sort and that the energy that caused men to live was the same as motor driven energy, which in turn was the same kind of energy that bound the universe together. This energy, which he called *ether*, was originally derived from God and served as the soul and spirit of the universe, but it had independent existence—the base of the universe was not, in Stanton's mind, an ideal one. The secret of the power of the universal ether would, according to Stanton, be revealed to the educated man in the future, and it would enable him to play an even greater role in guiding the course of human history.

Believing as he did that society was like a living organism, Stanton did not think any one man had the capacity to radically alter the course of history, but he did believe that change should be guided by educated men. Great men, he said, "must become the representatives of the general will and inclination, or of the general capacities and undeveloped energies of the mass of men, to whose exertions and purposes they propose to impart any particular direction."[37] Only through understanding the basic laws of universal change could a man be great enough to lead the people to higher levels of civilization.

Stanton's ideas outstripped those of most congressmen in their relationship to scientific knowledge, but they did not serve him well in the realm of practical politics. He was altogether unsuccessful in his attempt to tread a middle path between North and South, and he retired from active political life at the time of the Civil War. He lived until 1894 and probably gained considerable satisfaction in watching the growth in popularity of the scientific and philosophical views which he had espoused.

MAVERICKS AND AMERICA'S CULTURAL MISSION

Frederick Stanton believed that because of the freedom available in America the mission of the educated man was especially promising. He shared with other mavericks described in this chapter the conviction that cultural development had greater potential in the United States than in Europe. Giddings, in his letter, contrasted the new theology of America with the old forms of European religion. Hilliard relied on the tensions between European aristocracy and American democracy for the social aspects of his plot. As men acutely aware of cultural changes, mavericks participated in that typical nineteenth-century intellectual pastime—the attempt to define what was peculiar or distinct in the American culture. Like most intellectuals of their generation, mavericks centered their analysis around the fundamental contrast between American and European civilizations. Although for some mavericks the discussion of the American mind was subordinate to their interest in human experience in general, the approach to the subject was quite often framed in terms of the conflict between American freedom and European order. Other contrasts employed in the mavericks' analyses included the pairing of American material prosperity with European philosophical or mental culture, the practicality of Americans with the scholasticism of Europe, or the naturalness of America with the overrefinement of European society. Clearly, maverick politicians saw their own significance in terms of the magnitude of the mission of the country. In making American culture the hope of the future, they granted to themselves roles of special importance.

How each maverick perceived the uniqueness of American culture, the relative weight which he assigned to conflicting elements, conformed closely to the balance in his political ideas. Conservative Democratic mavericks were most likely to stress the influence of environment as guiding the development of American culture and to call for the unimpeded growth of the mind—a position thoroughly consistent with their laissez-faire economic policies and their states'-rights tendencies. Two similar speeches by Democratic mavericks, Charles Jared Ingersoll of Philadelphia and Muscoe Russell Hunter Garnett of Virginia, illustrate that approach to the history of American culture.[38]

Ingersoll's adddress was called *A Discourse Concerning the Influence of America on the Mind* and was delivered as the annual oration of the American Philosophical Society at the University of Philadelphia; Garnett's address was untitled and delivered to the alumni of the University of Virginia, but its subject was the development of the mind in America and the South.[39] Ingersoll's *Discourse* stressed the free development of the various aspects of American culture: "unfettered by inveterate prepossessions, the mind, on this continent, follows in its march the new spirit that is abroad, leading the intelligence of all the world to other pursuits."[40] Among the subjects covered in Ingersoll's catalogue of American cultural innovations are the unity of the American dialect, the practical orientation of America literary productions, the breadth of American education (at the necessary expense of depth), the tremendous quantity of printed material published in the United States because of the cheapness of publication, the quality of American newspapers, American mechanical science, advances in American medicine because of the dictates of necessity, the genius of Americans for functional politics, and theories suited to the workaday world.[41] Ingersoll's method was to explore the popular details of American culture and examine their origins rather than to elaborate any philosophical explanation for the development, yet his very method and his devotion to the ordinary as opposed to the exotic indicated a strong bias that was almost doctrinaire.

Muscoe R. H. Garnett's approach was quite different: he recognized the philosophical foundations of his position and stated them as such. His basic argument was that nature had created in America the causes for great literature and that the proper course for society and goverment was to leave man as free as possible to develop his genius.[42] Only unfettered minds could develop fully in Garnett's philosophical outlook:

Our thoughts acquire precision and accuracy, our ideas are properly limited and bounded, only when they have been tested by discussion with those who differ in opinion. They are never full, and their manifold connection with universal truth is never brought out, until they have been regarded by many different minds, each from its own peculiar point of view; and all the various aspects of the subject, thus obtained, every one true, but partial, are combined into one whole. Reason is continually assimilating all existing differences of opinion; it not only corrects error, but shows that views and facts, which seemed before contradictory, are really the same truth, as seen from opposite sides. It discovers to us more and more of the unity, which binds together all the parts of knowledge; and of the absolute truth, which contains and reconciles all finite thought. . . . Such is the free working of Nature, ever creating infinitely various opinions and characters, but at the same time, tending towards unity and likeness.[43]

The "free working" which created "infinitely various opinions and characters" revealed to Garnett a master plan which was determining the ultimate goal; although Ingersoll did not delineate the goal, he wrote just as persuasively of the unity of American culture achieved through its diverse aspects.[44]

Garnett went on in his address to deliver a stinging critique of northern society and the tendency he saw in it to leveling and conformity: "In Philosophy, Pantheism swallows up everything else. . . . Poetry becomes a mystic worship of Nature; vice and virtue are equally indifferent, for whatever is, is right; and a deadly fatalism poisons the springs of human action."[45] To Garnett, northern society had taken a path leading to the uniformity of socialism; his solution was to suggest that at least the South should preserve free society and the unhampered progress of the race. As a fellow southern maverick put it, the recourse for the South was to "cultivate poetry, arms and eloquence," to perpetuate and protect the principles of limited government which alone would insure greatness.[46]

Similar to Ingersoll and Garnett in their enthusiasm for material and moral progress but less doctrinaire about no federal participation in material development and less intellectual about its moral consequences were a group of western Democratic mavericks, which included John McClernand of Illinois, James Bowlin of Missouri, and David Cartter of Ohio. Although different in many respects, each of these mavericks moderately supported federal aid to economic development, and each couched the need for this aid and their defense of other political issues in terms of a positive vision for American growth. All contrasted the aristocratic features of European society with free American institutions; each with a certain amount of belligerence. In the words of Bowlin, the "despots of Europe" were the "natural foes" of the United States.[47]

McClernand, whose speeches on the floor of the House were consistently more

dignified and abstract than those delivered by most western Democratic conformists, was not an intellectual in comparison with eastern mavericks. His life's
activities were primarily political, but the focus was as often theoretical as
partisan. For example, in opposing his mentor Stephen Douglas over an Oregon
proposal, he stated that he would not "degrade a national question to a miserable
party level," and he voted with Democratic mavericks John Wentworth of Illinois, George S. Houston of Alabama, George Fries of Ohio, Thomas Henley
of Indiana, Joseph Hoge of Illinois, and Preston King of New York against the
party leadership embodied in the personalities of Howell Cobb and Douglas
himself.[48]

In a speech later in the same Congress he explained his views on the Oregon
issue, insisting that the strong assertion of American rights was a safe course
because of differences between the European aristocratic and American democratic systems. Even if national belligerence caused war, he proclaimed it would
be "a war not of force only, but also of systems—social, civil, moral, and
religious. It would be a war calling into action the impulse of civil and religious
liberty, the triumph of which would be only the more certainly secured by
resistance."[49] McClernand's service as chairman of the Foreign Affairs Committee in the Thirty-First Congress provided him with a prominent position from
which to explain his conviction that American national superiority fundamentally
rested on cultural genius.[50]

James Bowlin brought a similar orientation to his advocacy of price graduation
and cheap lands for the West.[51] Speaking as chairman of the Public Lands
Committee in the Twenty-Ninth Congress, Bowlin delivered a long and almost
completely nonpartisan speech in justification of his position, a speech which
began with the "origin of society" and traced through Rome, the feudal period,
and the early American colonies the influence of the man-land ratio on government.[52] In his conclusion he avowed that conquest of the West was the national
"fixed destiny" and described the western lands, owned by the mass of people,
as the "garden" of the world.[53]

These Democratic mavericks, none of whom could be characterized as intellectuals but who analyzed politics intellectually, represented a sort of middle
position between the extreme intellectual laissez-faire position of Ingersoll and
Garnett and the more doctrinaire interventionism and moral determinism of the
reform mavericks. These reformers shared with Garnett and Ingersoll a persuasion that the American mission was to offer the world a second chance, but that
mission was measured by them in terms of the victory of truth and ideas rather
than in the ascendancy of individualism. They were offended by the idea that
American freedom was better than the order of the divine or human mind. They
also disapproved of the deterministic linking of physical and moral progress.
Such views were typical of most mavericks with a strong reform bias, whether
they were northern or southern, Democrat or Whig. Adams and Giddings, as
well as the other northern Whig and Republican mavericks, expressed such ideas;
so did the free-soil Democratic and southern Whig mavericks. One such southern

Whig maverick, Joseph R. Underwood, will serve as an example for the reform maverick ideas on American culture in world perspective.[54]

Underwood was a Whig congressman from Kentucky, a senator from 1847 to 1853, and a Unionist Democrat by the time of the War.[55] Underwood was active in a variety of reform societies, and he praised the Temperance Society, Prison Discipline Society, Sunday School Society, Bible Society, Missionary Society, Colonization Society, and American Peace Movement.[56] He believed in the American mission, which would, he said, "regenerate the governments of the world, if our people will only do their duty."[57] To Underwood, the generation of his day was faced with great possibilities for improvement of the status of man both morally and materially. To accomplish this mission, Americans must study the past, which illustrated the relationship between environment and culture. Our institutions, he said, were based on "no fanciful Utopian notions, but resting upon principles identified with the nature of man, controlled to some extent by the circumstances in which the American people found themselves when they threw off the British yoke."[58]

In Underwood's moderate reformism America's mission included the ending of slavery. His analysis of the reasons that slavery should be gradually abolished reveals a clear mixture of practical and idealistic attitudes. He gave seven reasons for the predicted success of the colonization society:

1. The price of slavery is too high in terms of the value of the labor;
2. "Communities which have no slaves surpass those which have, in almost everything which renders life comfortable."
3. Slavery violates the Declaration of Independence;
4. Slaves are a disadvantage to children;
5. Slavery causes the out-migration of free white population;
6. Slave population grows faster than free, and therefore is racially threatening;
7. Slavery is a sin.[59]

Economic, political, cultural, racial, and religious influences were combined in arguing for reform in America. Underwood spoke in optimistic terms of American reform bringing to the world a "new era on earth,"[60] but his enthusiasm was tempered by the reservations of a practical man. To Underwood, the great second chance of the human race was an opportunity which could be just as easily muffed as the first had been, unless morality and intellect played their proper role.

A reformist maverick congressman even more certain that the role of America could be understood in terms of the guidance of God and truth was the Reverend Orin Fowler, who asserted that American history showed the "hand of God, scarcely less visible in the first settlement and subsequent prosperity of New England, than it had been, in planting his ancient covenant people in the land of Canaan."[61] Yet Fowler, like Underwood, was inclined to see progress in terms of both moral and material progress. In a New Year's day speech in which he waxed particularly eloquent on the subject of American mission, Fowler paid tribute to a wide variety of American accomplishments: "No other half century of the Christian era has unrolled such marvellous deeds—such stupendous changes—such throes of intellect—such reaches of discovery—such enlargment of thought—such improvements—such achievements—such progress."[62] He then proceeded to list the familiar catalogue of American material accomplishment—population growth, railroad mileage, agricultural output—and to urge the support of a national Post Office to be "a great machine for weaving a network of social, intellectual, and commercial intercourse, that would spread among all the people of the country."[63] Fowler's pride in American material growth and accomplishment was no less than that of Ingersoll or other seemingly more materialistic congressmen, but he saw the progress as part of God's plan not just for Americans but for all men. American material and spiritual progress was to serve as "a model for the human race" in the accomplishment of its God-ordained ascendancy over sin.[64]

Perhaps the most interesting of all mavericks who analyzed the interaction between American and European cultures were the two Baltimore Whigs, John Pendleton Kennedy and Henry Winter Davis. Two men could hardly have been more different in manner, intellect, and political careers. Davis went from the Whig to the American to the Republican parties, in each acting as orator, radical, troublemaker supreme; Kennedy was for all of his political career a Whig by conviction and an amiable party member, if independent in his ideas.[65] What is interesting is that both viewed the interaction between American and European culture from what might be described as an ironic point of view, assessing both the strengths and weaknesses of the American side, but always with affection for their country.

Davis presented a mixture of intellect and anti-intellectualism found more typically among Democratic mavericks than among Whigs. As he was keenly aware of public sentiments, it may be that his speeches reflect not his true opinions but his conviction that the voters had strong negative feelings about intellectuals; but in any case, his speeches were replete with derogatory references to speculative thinking. "The American people," he said, "place their faith, not in teachers of religion, or in speculative or traditional creed, but in the nature of man and the good inspiration of God."[66] In a speech at the commencement of the Female High School of Baltimore in which he praised women who stayed at home, Davis proclaimed the democratic life of the mind in America: "We first discovered the hidden value of the common mind. We first proclaimed that the impartial hand of the Almighty had sown his precious pearls of reason and affection in every vale as well as on the hills."[67] Even if this is discounted as inflated oratory, there remained in Davis' writings a strong sense of the inappropriateness of ivory-tower intellectualism to American life.

A striking example of Davis' ability to analyze ironically the contrasting cultures of America and Europe is found in an autobiographical sketch reproduced in a later biography.[68] Davis' descriptions of the attempt to cultivate intellect in a college on the frontier demonstrate a fine sense of humor as well as a rather hardheaded realism about the possibilities of classical education in the West:

The English origin of the college [Anglican], its church spirit and character and the admiration of the bishop for English forms, led to an attempt to naturalize the students' Oxford caps and gowns at Kenyon, but the gown was not a convenient garment to chop wood in, the silk tassels of the cap would make love to the boughs of the forest, its hard flat top rocked to and fro like a drunken man in every gust, and the impatient sons of the West were undergoing perpetual metamorphosis from a gownsman into a Buckeye in shirt sleeves—till the effort was abandoned as against the nature of the Western man.[69]

Keenly sensitive to the influence of these cultural paradoxes on the development of his character, Davis decried the result as "conservative, aristocratic, English in thought and view as much as one can be who lives in the woods and at the antipodes of everything English—a democrat in fact, an aristocrat in word—a contradiction which Southern origin and education tended to develop and conceal."[70] It might be added that Davis' obvious literary abilities seem as inappropriate to the associate of the Baltimore "Plug-Uglies" as the aristocratic forms to the western and southern man.

In the fervor of his youthful admiration for things English, Davis wrote a history called *The War of Ormuzd and Ahriman in the Nineteenth Century*, which concerned the struggle between the despotism of the East, represented by Russia, and the enlightened world of the West, primarily represented by England. In this story of the events surrounding the Crimean War, European civilization was given credit for at least helping to further the aims of Christianity and liberalism in the world setting.[71] The tone of the book, however, indicated Davis' view that somehow the English were fighting America's battle in Europe: the true accomplishments would be made in the United States.

Antagonized by what he saw as the reactionary attitude of the British upper classes during the Civil War, when Davis had become an enthusiastic Republican, he turned to attack England in much the same terms he had reserved for Russia in his youth. The following passage is taken from a bellicose speech called "No Peace Before Victory" made during the war days when northern public opinion was strongly anti-British:

I look with glorying to the day when the black regiments shall stream to the capital of the Montezumas, while the army of the Potomac, becoming the Army of the St. Lawrence, shall march to Quebec and Montreal . . . [and may even] live to hear of the explosion of the bombshells over the dome of St. Paul's, and of the arches of London bridge sent into the air. (great applause)[72]

It is difficult to conceive that the writer of *The War of Ormuzd and Ahriman* could have uttered the destructive sounding phrases of "No Peace Before Victory," even allowing for the difference in projected audience and for rhetorical

license. In Davis' understanding, however, the European phrase of the improvement of man had always been conceived as a passing one; the future belonged
to the United States.

A man of large intellect, Henry Winter Davis represents a primitively rough
version of the mind of the congressional maverick. Urbane, polished, sophisticated, balanced—these words more accurately describe John Pendleton Kennedy, the most literary of all mavericks in the Congresses before the Civil War.
According to his biographer, Charles H. Bohner, Kennedy's novels "were a
conscious attempt to contribute to a national mythology."[73] Thus in a strangely
different way, Kennedy and Davis were engaged in the same kind of intellectual
exercise in support of their political independence. Both saw clearly the revolutionary elements in the developing American culture, and both shared the hope
that this new culture would somehow redeem the world, though Davis was more
optimistic than Kennedy. And perhaps most significantly, the consequence of
the shared vision of American cultural greatness was to place each in his own
mind in the center of a vastly significant stage.

Kennedy's analysis and his fictional representations of the relationship between
the civilization inherited by the New World and its attempts to create a new
culture are certainly more detailed and more perceptive than those of most
mavericks. Nonetheless, his observations not only closely correlate with those
of the less articulate mavericks, but they also display the same sort of ambivalence
toward the tension between the two modes of thinking—American and European.
Unquestionably Kennedy wanted Americans to be aware of the importance of
American culture. In the 1851 preface to *Swallow Barn*, he explicitly addressed
the question:

An observer cannot fail to note that the manners of our country have been tending towards
a uniformity which is visibly effacing all local differences. The old states, especially,
are losing their original distinctive habits and modes of life, and in the same degree, I
fear, are losing their exclusive American character. A traveller may detect but few
sectional or provincial varieties in the general observances and customs of society, in
comparison with what were observable in the past generations, and the pride, or rather
the vanity, of the present day is leading us into a very notable assimilation with foreign
usages. The country now apes the city in what is supposed to be the elegancies of life,
and the city is inclined to value and adopt the fashions it is able to import across the
Atlantic, and thus the whole surface of society is exhibiting the traces of a process by
which it is likely to be rubbed down, in time, to one level, and varnished with the same
gloss.[74]

Kennedy sketched with genuine fondness the life of old Virginia, but it was not
an uncritical eye that guided his hand. He did not believe in worship of the past,
even if it were essential to understanding the present.

Reform, in Kennedy's opinion, was an important contribution of his own
generation and despite its excesses was performing valuable tasks. The "wholesome spirit of inquiry abroad in the land" had accomplished much but was

perhaps too enthusiastically accepted by many: "The result of this review has been to pull down, with an unscrupulous hand, the heavy lumber of antiquity, and in the place of cumbersome machinery by which man had heretofore wrought out his allotted task, to introduce the swift, powerful, and easy-working mechanism of our own times."[75] He saw progress, moral and physical, as a major contribution of his age.[76] He believed, too, that the physical improvements in the United States could bring about a more perfect moral and intellectual community.

Kennedy, however, had three important rules for the reformers that he deemed necessary in their efforts to improve American culture: they must avoid relying on the present at the expense of consideration of both past and future; they must recognize that instinct was an insufficient guide for human conduct; and they must take care not to damage valuable institutions in their zeal for progress.[77] Kennedy was not only skeptical about the excesses of the reformers but also skeptical about the excesses of the antireformers—the laissez-faire Democrats. In his *Quodlibet*, an 1840 political satire so biting that it was originally attributed to John Quincy Adams, he attacked the Democratic excesses of individualism. The leader of the New Lights (Democrats) orated:

We attend to ourselves—that is genuine New Light Democracy. We oppose Vested Rights, we oppose Chartered Privileges, we oppose Pledges to bind future legislatures, we oppose Tariffs, Internal Improvements, Colleges and Universities, on the broad democratic ground that we have nothing to do with Posterity.[78]

Kennedy also opposed the later Democratic position on Manifest Destiny. Despite enthusiasm for nationalism in cultural matters he had no use for militant nationalism, which he satirized with typical humor as "a new faith which sums up its creed in the three articles of—Manifest Destiny, Boundless Extension of the Area of Freedom, and Universal Annexation."[79] He marveled at the members of Young America who were fond of "holding that their tribe of mankind is master of all other tribes by law of nature. They boast that the Anglo-Saxon is, by instinct, a land-stealer, and, by pre-eminent right, Lord paramount of everything he can take; as if these were his inherited virtues."[80] Kennedy did believe in the virtue of American culture, inherited from the past, properly understood. In Bohner's words, "he expressed for Americans a view of their past commensurate with the prophecies the apostles of progress made for the future, and he adorned the present."[81]

The intellectual accomplishments of John Pendleton Kennedy were certainly not matched in quality by those of many other mavericks; yet, most others did similarly attempt to explain to themselves and to the public the significance of their activities in a broad intellectual framework. It would be impossible to ascertain whether for most mavericks the analysis of American education, culture, and mission preceded and served as impetus to their political activities or whether it followed and formed a convenient rationale. In many cases the development of political skills was perhaps accompanied by a growing intellectual sophistication, integrated as much as possible into a well-defined ego structure. Whatever the reasons for the appearance of the intellectual traits described above, the common pattern does clearly emerge from their speeches and writings: continuous interest in a democratic education; explicit concern for the evolutionary development of their culture; and a real conviction that the mission of that developing culture was the regeneration of the human spirit through the American example. And it is equally evident that this analysis lends considerable significance to mavericks' political activities by elevating their contributions above the immediate and partisan issues of the day into a mission of importance for humankind.

NOTES

1. While mavericks themselves would not have divided their lives into compartments, indeed would have protested strongly that such could be done, it is impossible for the historian to treat them as holistic units and describe anything more than an impression. It is appropriate, then, to point out that in this analysis the division of their lives into politics, intellect, and ego is something that does gross injustice to their own attempts to unify and give coherence to their lives. On the other hand, as they were analytical themselves and consistently engaged in examining their own self-concepts, perhaps mavericks would not frown upon an attempt to take apart their component characteristics in behalf of greater understanding of the whole. In any case, this entire division into maverick intellect and maverick ego should be clearly understood as a functional approach to the problem of analysis rather than as carrying any implication that maverick intellect and ego were actually separate parts of the men under analysis.

2. Richard Hofstadter, *Anti-Intellectualism in American Life*, Vantage Books (New York: Random House, 1963), pp. 24–25.

3. Ibid.

4. John A. Bingham, *The Treasury Note Bill. Speech of Hon. Jno. A. Bingham, of Ohio, in the House of Representatives, Feb. 4, 1862* (Washington, D. C.: Scammell & Co., [1862]), p. 3.

5. Bernard C. Steiner, *Life of Henry Winter Davis* (Baltimore: John Murphy Co., 1916), p. 40. Chs. I–III (pp. 7–63) are Davis' autobiography.

6. Don Edward Fehrenbacher, *Chicago Giant: A Biography of "Long John" Wentworth* (Madison, Wis.: American History Research Center, 1957), p. 242.

7. Ibid., pp. 209–212, 238–240.

8. James Meacham, *Report of Hon. James Meacham, of the Special Committee of the Board of Regents of the Smithsonian Institution, on the Distribution of the Income of the Smithsonian Fund, etc.* (Washington, D. C.: For the Smithsonian Institution, 1854). Hereafter cited as *Smithsonian Report*.

9. David Lowenthal, *George Perkins Marsh, Versatile Vermonter* (New York: Columbia University Press, 1958), p. 81.

10. Meacham, *Smithsonian Report*, p. 50.

11. Ibid., pp. 50–51.

12. It is perhaps worth noting that Meacham referred to "our fathers," meaning Jefferson and Adams, which was a little unusual. Most frequently that reference was

coupled with the name of Washington, and Meacham knew the familiar usage but substituted the more scholarly fathers. Although Washington was often referred to as a philosopher/statesman, to an intellectually inclined congressman Jefferson and Adams were more appropriately thus classified.

13. James L. Orr, *An Address Delivered before the Philosophian and Adelphian Societies of the Furman University, at Their Annual Meeting, Greenville, South Carolina, July 18, 1855* (Greenville, S. C.: G. E. Elford & Co., Printer, 1855), p. 17. Hereafter cited as *Address at Furman*.

14. Julian, *Life of Giddings*, pp. 400–401.

15. Ibid.

16. See Emerson, *Selected Writings*.

17. Kennedy's novels were republished in the 1960s. John Pendleton Kennedy, *Swallow Barn, or—A Sojourn in the Old Dominion*, introduction and notes by William S. Osborne, Hafner Library of Classics, no. 22 (New York: Hafner Pub. Co., 1962); *Rob of the Bowl*, ed. by William S. Osborne, The Masterworks of Literature Series (New Haven, Conn.: College & University Press, 1965); and *Horse-Shoe Robinson*, ed. with introduction, chronology, and bibliography by Ernest E. Leisy, Hafner Library of Classics, no. 23 (New York: Hafner Pub. Co., 1962). An excellent analysis of Kennedy's place in the national mythology is found in William F. Taylor, *Cavalier and Yankee*, esp. pp. 188–201.

18. The Hafner edition includes also an early draft of *Swallow Barn* which was much more satirical than the published version. Kennedy's published criticisms of southern society were generally mild and delivered with considerable warmth and humor, but they were nonetheless pointedly accurate. For example, his characterization of Squire Meriwether, the owner of Swallow Barn plantation is amusing but trenchant in critical observation:

The solitary elevation of a country gentleman, well to do in the world, begets some magnificent notions. He becomes as infallible as the Pope; gradually acquires a habit of making long speeches; is apt to be impatient of contradiction, and is always very touchy on the point of honor. There is nothing more conclusive than a rich man's logic anywhere, but in the country, amongst his dependents, it flows with the smooth and unresisted course of a full stream irrigating a meadow, and depositing its mud in fertilizing luxuriance. Meriwether's sayings, about Swallow Barn, import absolute verity. But I have discovered that they are not so current out of his jurisdiction.

Kennedy, *Swallow Barn*, p. 35.

19. See Degler, *The Other South*, for an extended treatment of this minority pattern.

20. For discussion of Hilliard's political ideas, see Chapter 8.

21. Reference to Channing, *DeVane*, p. 253; he is noted as the "great New England scholar." As an example of Hilliard's overloading of references to writers, in the three pages surrounding this reference, there are others as follows: a reading of a passage from Burke, described as "glorious" and "splendidly beautiful;" a paragraph or two on Bacon and his theories on poetry; a six-line quotation from the poetry of Swift; the paragraph on Channing which also evaluates Milton as poet; a comparison of Scott and Channing on Napoleon's life; the opinion of Byron on the worth of poetry.

22. Esther is compared to the Biblical queen, Ibid., pp. 561–562, and she refers to Wordsworth as "my namesake," Ibid., p. 166.

23. The parallel between Esther and Eve is used throughout the book; for example, DeVane reflects upon it, Ibid., p. 18, where he is also referred to as a fallen Adam.

24. Ibid., p. 201. Compare with "Man is the dwarf of himself." Emerson, *Nature, Selected Writings*, p. 39.

25. Channing, *DeVane*, pp. 273–274. The value of labor is extolled throughout the book.

26. Ibid., p. 396.

27. Ibid., p. 552.

28. Hilliard, *Politics and Pen Pictures*, pp. 426–440.

29. *BDAC*, p. 628.

30. Sullivan Bros. & Libbie, Auctioneers, comp., *Catalogue of the Private Library of the Late Edmund Burke, of Newport, New Hampshire* (Boston: W. F. Brown & Co., Printers, 1883).

31. See Morton G. White, *Science and Sentiment in America: Philosophical Thought from Jonathan Edwards to John Dewey* (New York: Oxford University Press, 1972); and George H. Daniels, *American Science in the Age of Jackson* (New York: Columbia University Press, 1968).

32. See Nevins, *Diary of John Quincy Adams*, pp. 557–559, for the importance Adams placed on the address. His comments on the completion of the job are thoroughly in character:

I have performed my task, I have executed my undertaking, and am returned safe to my family and my home. It is not much in itself. It is nothing in the estimation of the world. In my motives and my hopes, it is considerable. The people of this country do not sufficiently estimate the importance of patronizing and promoting science as a principle of political action. (p. 559).

33. See Ch. 6.

34. Frederick P. Stanton, *The Character of Modern Science, or, the Mission of the Educated Man. An Address Delivered before the Alumni Association of Columbian College, July 21, 1852* (Washington, D. C.: Robert A. Waters, Printer, 1852). Hereafter cited as *Modern Science*.

35. Ibid., pp. 5–6.

36. Ibid., pp. 6–7.

37. Ibid., pp. 24–25.

38. These themes are expressed by many other conservative mavericks; for examples, see Edmund Burke, *An Address before Democratic Republican Citizens*; Caleb Cushing, *Oration on the Material Growth and Progress*, and "Eulogy;" Charles Brown, *Remarks of Mr. Charles Brown, of Pennsylvania, on the Navy Appropriation Bill. Delivered in the House of Representatives, May 20, 1842* (Washington, D. C., 1842); and H. Wise, *Seven Decades*).

39. Charles Jared Ingersoll, *A Discourse Concerning the Influence of America on the Mind; Being the Annual Oration Delivered before the American Philosophical Society, at the University in Philadelphia, on the 18th Oct., 1823* (Philadelphia: Abraham Small, 1823), hereafter cited as *Discourse Concerning Influence of America*; and Garnett, *Alumni Address*.

40. Ingersoll, *Discourse Concerning Influence of America*, p. 9.

41. Ibid., dialect, p. 12; practical literature, p. 13; education, pp. 6–8; publications, p. 17; newspapers, pp. 22–23; mechanical discoveries, pp. 23–28; professions, p. 29; asssociations, pp. 30–31; necessity the mother of invention, p. 44.

42. Garnett, *Alumni Address*, p. 5.

43. Ibid., p. 7; compare with Emerson, "Herein is especially apprehended the unity

of Nature—the unity in variety—which meets us everywhere. All the endless variety of things make an identical impression." Emerson, *Nature, Selected Writings*, p. 24.

44. John P. Diggins, "Consciousness and Ideology in American History: The Burden of Daniel J. Boorstin," *American Historical Review* 76 (February 1970):98–118. This article deals with the ideological underpinnings of Boorstin's work, but the remarks would apply as well to Ingersoll's reasoning.

45. Garnett, *Alumni Address*, p. 30.

46. Pickens, *Influences of Government*, p. 30.

47. James Bowlin, Speech in U. S. Congress. *Speeches on the Oregon Question and on the Mexican War*. 29th Cong., 1st Sess., 1845–46.

48. *Congressional Globe*, 29th Cong., 1st Sess., 720. In contrast, Douglas consistently defended his Oregon position with reference to the Baltimore convention platform which called for 54°40′ ("sooner let his tongue cleave to the roof of his mouth than he would defend that party which should yield one inch of Oregon," Ibid., p. 497). This position left him painfully open to charges of inconsistency when he later shifted to support Polk's compromise (see Ibid., p. 686). In this instance, at least, the nonpartisan intellectualism of McClernand was politically safer than the partisan pragmatism of Douglas.

49. Ibid., p. 984.

50. It was perhaps no coincidence that in the two previous Democratic controlled Congresses (28th and 29th), Charles J. Ingersoll had held that position.

51. McClernand, who chaired the Committee on Public Lands before moving to Foreign Affairs, made exactly the same kind of association as did Bowlin. See above, Ch. 4.

52. *Congressional Globe*, 29th Cong., 1st Sess., 1059.

53. Ibid., p. 1062.

54. For further examples, see David Wilmot, "Speech on Freemasonry and Education, July 4, 1853 at Susquehanna Collegiate Institution," in Going, *David Wilmot*, pp. 727–731; William Cost Johnson, *Speech of William Cost Johnson, of Maryland, on Resolutions Which He Had Offered Proposing to Appropriate Public Land for Educational Purposes, to All the States and Territories. Delivered in the House of Representatives, Feb., 1838.* (Washington, D. C.: Gales & Seaton, 1838); in addition to the writings of Adams, Giddings, Bingham, Meacham, Hilliard, and others cited previously on reform.

55. BDAC, p. 1739. Underwood was the grandfather of Oscar W. Underwood (1862–1929), prominent Alabama congressman and senator.

56. Underwood, *Colonization Society*, p. 6.

57. Underwood, *Oration Delivered in "Parrott's Woods," Heights of Georgetown, D. C., By the Hon. Joseph R. Underwood, on the Fourth of July, 1842* (n.p., n.d.).

58. Ibid., p. 6.

59. Underwood, *Colonization Society*, pp. 19–20.

60. Ibid., p. 6.

61. Orin Fowler, *History of Fall River* (Fall River, Mass.: Almy & Milne, Printers, 1862), p. 8.

62. Orin Fowler, *Remarks of Mr. Orin Fowler, of Massachusetts, on a Motion to Reduce Postage on All Letters to Two Cents. Made in the House of Representatives of the United States, Dec. 31, 1850* (Washington, D. C.: Buell & Blanchard, Prnters, 1851), p. 7.

63. Ibid., p. 5.

64. Fowler, *Speech on the Legislation of Massachusetts*, p. 3.

65. Gerald Henig, *Henry Winter Davis: Antebellum and Civil War Congressman from Maryland* (New York: Twayne, 1973); and Charles H. Bohner, *John Pendleton Kennedy, Gentleman from Baltimore* (Baltimore: Johns Hopkins Press, 1961).

66. Davis, *Speeches and Addresses*. pp. 111–112.

67. Ibid., p. 105.

68. From the autobiographical portion of Steiner, *Henry Winter Davis*, p. 31.

69. Ibid.

70. Ibid. Davis in earlier passages had developed the theme that the southern character was a paradoxical mixture of types because of the combined influence of the frontier and the gentry or plantation ideal. His analysis of southern culture was marked by both humor and perspicacity.

71. Davis, *War of Ormuzd*.

72. Davis, *Speeches and Addresses,* p. 337.

73. Bohner, *John Pendleton Kennedy*, p. 3.

74. Kennedy, *Swallow Barn*, p. 9.

75. Kennedy, "An Address delivered on behalf of the Faculty of Arts and Sciences, on the Occasion of the Opening of the Collegiate Department in the University of Maryland, on the Third of January, 1831," in *Occasional Addresses*.

76. Kennedy, "The Spirit of the Age: False and True Progress. A Lecture delivered before the Mechanic's Institute, Baltimore, February 7, 1854," in *Occasional Addresses,* p. 275.

77. Ibid.

78. John Pendleton Kennedy, *Quodlibet: Containing Some Annals Thereof*, ed. by Solomon Secondthoughts (Philadelphia: Lea & Blanchard, 1840). Bohner comments that when the satire first appeared anonymously in September of 1840 "several newspapers attributed it to John Quincy Adams." Bohner, *John Pendleton Kennedy*, p. 136.

79. Kennedy, "Spirit of the Age," p. 280.

80. Ibid.

81. Bohner, *John Pendleton Kennedy,,* p. ix.

CHAPTER 10

The Maverick Ego

Be sure of this, O young ambition, all mortal greatness is but one disease.
Herman Melville, *Moby Dick*

The development of the second two-party system and the increased reliance of the House of Representatives upon standing committees to perform fundamental tasks of legislation probably inhibited the opportunities for any congressman to display his abilities and ideas in an individualistic fashion. Mavericks, however, found room even within the relatively structured roles of committee leadership to assert their individuality; and they certainly custom-tailored their political ideas and cultural analyses. Whatever the public scene in which they appeared, mavericks aggressively asserted their own concepts of themselves—their egos— not allowing functional or ideological pressures for conformity to create "selves" incongenial with their previously shaped concepts.[1]

The egos of maverick congressmen were not modeled after a single pattern. Mavericks like John Quincy Adams, Joshua Giddings, Barnwell Rhett, or Alexander Stephens, who combined unusual talents of intellect or analysis with an intense sense of mission, bear some resemblance to Melville's monomaniacal Captain Ahab. Others—Caleb Cushing, John Pendleton Kennedy, Charles J. Ingersoll, for example—combined equally keen intellects with more restrained views of their political missions; and they were as much interested in broadening themselves intellectually as they were concerned with egotistical self-assertion.[2] Many mavericks were less purely cerebral than these and much more characterized by emotional or even physical aggressiveness: John Wentworth, Henry Wise, Henry Winter Davis, and David Cartter were of this type.

The distinctiveness of the maverick ego as a congressional type consists in this: mavericks did not radically alter themselves to meet the demands of the political world; instead they either tried to shape politics to suit their desires or protested, perhaps futilely, the absorption of the individual of integrity by the mass of conformists. All shared a tendency to be preoccupied with testing their worth against the strength of the environment, political or otherwise, in a conscious measurement of the stature of their self-concepts.[3]

At the risk of making what might seem like an invidious comparison, it could be said that one of the prominent differences between the egos of mavericks and conformists was that conformists were typically ambitious to be something—congressman, senator, President—while mavericks were ambitious to be somebody. There is no evidence that conformists were less ambitious than mavericks; on the contrary, both groups contained men noted for their ambition and men who had succeeded as well as those who had failed. But the expressions of ambition by mavericks seemed to carry a more intense tone. Success or failure for a maverick was nothing more or less than success or failure of self, of the manhood and integrity of the entire character; consequently, it loomed large in his thinking. Failure for a conformist might mean no more than a shift in goals, a re-evaluation of the possible, if politics were then the art of the possible; failure for a maverick meant that he must reassess his worth as a man.

The comparisons of leadership roles and political ideas of mavericks and conformists underscore this difference in their political perspectives: the conformist orientation was practical and manipulative; the maverick frame of reference was more often personal and directive. For a conformist to be a success in politics required the approval of the public and the support of his coworkers. Mavericks certainly required this reinforcement at times, but they counted themselves successful only when they were fulfilling a personal concept of leadership, one which as often as not actually precluded consistent and extensive public or party approval. This "disease" of egocentric maverick ambition can be distinguished by a number of qualities not typical of conformists.

Several characteristics of the mavericks' self-concepts have been described in earlier chapters, but since they are relevant in the evaluation of the ego structure of mavericks, they bear repeating here. Mavericks believed that they functioned not merely as representatives of the people but as their leaders, exerting moral and political influence in a wide variety of public endeavors. Their concept of leadership included a strong reliance on independent judgment rather than adherence to party policy or position. Many mavericks were intellectually inclined or at least reflective in their evaluations of political life, the quality of the American experience, and their own role in the nation's future. Mavericks, moreover, were highly verbal about whatever they thought, expressing ideas that some conformists might have held but refrained from articulating.

The consistency with which mavericks exhibited in their speeches and writings the characteristics described in earlier chapters is in itself indication of an important feature in the maverick ego. Mavericks published more than conformists, if the holdings of the Library of Congress are reasonably representative of their total output, and there is a far greater amount of nonpolitical material available for mavericks.[4] The same pattern of inclusion of nonpolitical material is true for speeches and remarks on the floor of the House of Representatives. The existence of a greater amount of mavericks' writing and speech making could be attributed to their greater necessity for defensive measures; they were consistently on the spot, politically, so they spent more time justifying their "untoward" behaviors. But this does not fully explain the nonpolitical writing; philosophical and abstract matter, even if not considered irrelevant by the voters, certainly did not garner any substantial number of votes in most areas of the country. The absence of similar philosophical material in conformists' speeches and writings might suggest that they perceived it as nonfunctional, at the very least, and adds import to its presence in mavericks' speeches.

Given their concept of leadership, it seems likely that mavericks spoke as they did about nonpolitical matters because they perceived that as leaders of the people it was their obligation to instruct and elevate them. Furthermore, since they must have been aware of the sometimes unfavorable reaction of the public to their philosophizing, the hazard of inclusion was probably viewed by them as another of the forms of behavior dictated to them by their concept of themselves. In other words, mavericks had an ego structure acceptable to themselves and, despite contrary political wisdom, behaved according to that self-concept. In their own terminology, they were men of integrity first, politicians second.

Independence of character, the most prominent feature of the maverick ego, was often expressed in the context of the inappropriateness of following political party lines, as has been documented in preceding chapters. Mavericks contrasted their independence with the conformity of their colleagues in almost every vein imaginable. Angry assaults in which the invidious contrast was also accompanied by implicit testing of the mettle of the maverick was quite common among mavericks.[5] Less common, but not unusual, was the humorous stab at conformist malleability: "Why, I thought that consistency was decidedly an old fogy sentiment. I thought that at this day nobody prided himself on such an idea. I thought that it was completely voted down, out of the pale of the general circle of popular action now-a-days."[6] William Smith of Virginia, the maverick speaker here, aligned himself with tradition and independence in opposition to the modern popularity of his conformist opponents.

Independence of character was often identified with traditional moral values, but it was also associated with a more romantic concept of moral instruction. Humphrey Marshall praised a fellow Kentuckian for that "self-reliance which is the individuality of personal independence, and which proclaims him as a pupil whose instruction has been derived by communion in the solitude of the forest—in the great school of Nature—between his own conscience and his Creator."[7] Self-reliance in this sense, as in the transcendental philosophy, means not selfishness but reliance upon the common grounding all men have in the spirit of Nature and God, Creator, or Oversoul. Adherence to this concept of individuality rendered impossible easy adjustment to institutional norms unrelated to the philosophy of moral responsibility.

Another pattern typical in the distinctive ego of mavericks was their perception of themselves as heroes. Heroic egotism was not limited to politics but was often associated with a larger social or moral obligation. And very characteristically the mavericks were as much plagued by their failure to achieve heroic goals as they were certain of the necessity of attempting the accomplishment. A familiar example of the kind of extraordinary and perhaps impossible expectations mavericks set for themselves is found in the character of John Quincy Adams. There have been few major political figures in United States history whose relatives were more outstanding than those of Adams. Not only were the Adamses leaders of the Revolutionary movement and major movers in the political life of the new nation, but John Adams was among the major political theorists of the new Republic. These antecedents must have been the source of Adams' ambition to be not only an officeholder—President, congressman, secretary of state—but also a statesman and leader of the nation.

His ambition was unattainable in the bitter party struggles of the second quarter of the century, but the circumstances which caused his failure did not lessen his disappointment. The pages of his diary are filled with lengthy self-evaluation in which generally he finds himself lacking in some significant respect. The following reflection upon his early senatorial career is typical of the high standards Adams set for himself and also of the profound dissatisfaction consequent upon failure:

The year [1805] which this day expires has been distinguished in the course of my life by its barrenness of events. During its first three and last two months I was here attending my duty as a Senator of the United States. The seven intervening months were passed in travelling to and from Quincy, and in residence at my father's house there. The six months spent at Quincy were not idle. Indeed, I have seldom in the whole course of my life been more busily engaged. I gave some attention to my agricultural pursuits, but I soon found they lost their relish, and that they would never repay the labor they require. My studies were assiduous and seldom interrupted. I meant to give them such a direction as should be useful in its tendency; yet on looking back, and comparing the time consumed with the knowledge acquired, I have no occasion to take pride in the result of my application. I have been a severe student all the days of my life; but an immense proportion of the time I have dedicated to the search of knowledge has been wasted upon subjects which can never be profitable to myself or useful to others.[8]

As the accomplishments of Adams dwarf those of most mavericks, so do his morose reflections appear more extreme than those of the remaining mavericks. Yet if the more ordinary men among the mavericks were more moderate in goals and self-criticisms, they did exhibit unusually high self-expectations and generally an expression that they were unfulfilled.

Many mavericks established high goals of achievement quite early in their lives. Caleb Cushing, who was admitted to Harvard at thirteen and rivaled George Bancroft for top honors in his class, wrote home to his parents the following immodest assessment of his possibilities: "I do not wish to know a few things—to be a man of detail—a literary artisan, confined to this or that study without change or redemption. I believe it to be within the compass of man's powers, and the duration of his life, to know all, and much more, than is, or has been known."[9] In an attempt to realize his goal, Cushing by his mid-twenties estimated that he had published 1,655 pages of articles and books, covering a wide variety of subjects: a history of Personal Slavery, the witch trials of Massachusetts, drama, miscellaneous poetry, an article on longevity and physical education, a biography of the modern freethinkers, and many more. Cushing's biographer, Claude M. Fuess, commented on this listing that while Cushing's mind was "comprehensive and catholic in its tastes," it was likely that he "overestimated his literary genius."[10] Cushing never abandoned his attempt to achieve excellence, and some of the quirks in his shifting political career can be seen as the result of this pursuit.

Another maverick who set himself unusually high standards in his youth was Muscoe R. H. Garnett of Virginia. Garnett was a serious young man, explicitly aware of his own tendency to self-analysis and even concerned that he might be a little foolish in his seriousness.[11] He outlined at the beginning of his collegiate career at the University of Virginia a demanding plan of study:

I shall continue my general studies without reference to any particular profession for at least twelve months and probably longer. Of course, then, my three branches of study will be history, metaphysics, and Belle Lettres. I shall frame an extensive course of study in each, and the books may be in any of the five languages I am acquainted with . . . History I will study not as a mere amusement, but philosophically. I will study it in connection with Political Economy and the general doctrine of government, and as an illustration of the science of mind, in short, as "philosophy teaching by example."[12]

Though Garnett did not match the immodesty of Cushing, the program he designed for himself was pointedly planned for achieving excellence not only in scholarship but in political statesmanship. His college training was to be for nothing less exalted than a philosopher/statesman.

Another example of the magnified ambitions of young mavericks can be found in the journal of Alexander Stephens, written just after his graduation from college and at the beginning of his involvement in local Georgia politics. The frail and sickly Stephens, who could never decide whether he was far above the ordinary or grossly inadequate, was on this particular day feeling superior to the mass of conforming men:

I do detest vulgarity. Sometimes I almost have a contempt for the whole human race,— the whole appearing like a degenerate herd, beneath the notice of mankind, and the most brutish are the most honored. . . . Will I never find one whose company will please me? No; of this I despair. . . . My notion of merit is what is intellectual in its nature. I honor and long to be associated with the mind that soars above the infirmities and corruptions of human nature; that is, far out of the region of passion and prejudice; that lives and moves and has its being in the pure element of Truth.[13]

Stephens' disappointment at his own inability to accomplish the impossible was bitter, but in his lifetime he never ceased in his effort to prove to himself and the public that he was a superior person.

A maverick's reflection on ambition and ego in later life is found in the strange work, *The Great Rebellion*, of John Minor Botts of Virginia. Botts had heroic goals, and he alternately saw himself as success and failure. He did believe that he was faithful to his goals throughout the crises leading to the Civil War and throughout the War itself, during which he was imprisoned briefly for his Unionist sentiment.[14] He described his effort at historical writing as "one of the most important and interesting documents that has appeared in our history,"[15] an assessment which must match that of any of the mavericks for egotism. He insisted, however, that he acted not for his own satisfaction but to play a heroic role in the history of the nation. Contrasting his life with that of the more popular conformists, he asserted that the key to his career

was to protect, as far as I could, and *save* the Union; to prevent a civil war of an exterminating character, which I saw and knew must attend any effort at dissolution. Others there were who looked at these issues only to ascertain how far it would affect their personal popularity at home . . . while I claim to have paid no regard to the fact whether it kept either them or myself in place. The Union was the god of my idolatry on earth; and from its preservation I never permitted my eye to be turned for a moment.[16]

Botts was never at rest with himself or at peace with others; he fought with friends and foes alike. One of the most bitter moments in his life, according to his testimony in *The Great Rebellion*, was the public break between himself and his former friend, maverick Muscoe Garnett, over reconstruction policies when both had passed the peaks of their political careers.[17] In that dispute, as in all others, Botts was sustained by the conviction that he was correct and that his behavior was necessary to maintain his integrity and character.

Another aspect of the self-image of the mavericks which appeared with some frequency was the identification of manhood, of masculine integrity, with their course of action. Sometimes this occurred in passing reference and was for a particular speaker plainly no more than an incidental matter. But others appeared to exhibit unusual sensitivity to the threatening of their masculine independence and expressed this in terms which suggested that they felt their manhood assaulted.[18] The pattern of identification of manhood with a political position was most characteristic in one of several antagonistic situations: a disagreement over the position of the Negro in the United States; the conflict over the restriction of immigration into the country; and the more heated encounters between extreme northern and southern mavericks. In each instance the political issue was fraught with cultural implications which could have threatened traditional concepts of manhood.[19] In keeping with their roles as heroes of the people, the mavericks in their oratory aligned proper masculine role behavior with their own positions, so that a dichotomy was represented in which they took the side of the heroic males.

An example of a northern maverick who relied heavily on the rhetoric of manhood is found in a series of speeches by the antislavery Democrat John Hickman of Pennsylvania. In one, Hickman contrasts the masculinity of northern society with the lazy society of the South, which displayed "a sectionalism not of the farm and workshop, but of the lounge, the hammock, and the veranda."[20] He portrayed the impending Civil War as a conflict between the powerful North and the "ignorance, indolence, sterility" of the South.[21] Hickman also used similarly loaded epithets in his attack on Stephen Douglas for his shifting position on Kansas. He described Douglas as "a political hermaphrodite, a giant of the neuter gender, . . . [who] would not advise us to take sides with white labor, lest he should be thought a man, nor with black labor, lest he should be known as a woman."[22] Hickman's association of manhood with white labor and of female weakness with black labor revealed his cultural assumptions more clearly than it described Douglas.

Hickman's belief in white male superiority was also explicit in his defense of those who protested the Lecompton Constitution, whether in speeches or with guns in Kansas. A man who did not fight against slavery in Kansas, he said, "is not a true son, but a bastard. . . . Such a being would be far more servile, and destitute of manhood, than the negro slave himself."[23] From the manner of attack in many of his speeches it is clear that Hickman perceived himself as defending the rights of free white labor and the manhood of northern men. Furthermore, he identified his own course as the only virile one open given his definition of appropriate male role behavior. Anything less bold would cast on him the same imputations he cast on his opponents, in his own mind and in the public eye.

There were southern counterparts of the kind of masculine concern of Hickman. Francis Pickens of South Carolina, for example, urged in 1851 that if the South should yield to the North,

Our very women will condemn and despise us as a degenerate race, and they will look to others for protection. The first evidence of the corruption and decay of a people, is that the women begin to idolize foreigners. If the men become cowardly and luxurious, the women begin to look to others for that manliness which they so much admire. . . . *It may become our sacred duty to act alone and if so, we must walk the plank alone like men.*[24]

Pickens' rhetoric demonstrates his conviction that his course in following the strong fire-eater path was as much a function of his desire for manliness and integrity as a result of his ideas about politics. This kind of masculine appeal was characteristic of the extreme southern mavericks in their attacks on northern abolitionists.

Another example of one of the many instances of the use of the rhetoric of masculine integrity was found in the writings of the nativist newspaper editor and Pennsylvania congressman, Lewis Levin. The American party orators frequently referred to the concept of American identity (i.e., male identity) in their speeches, asserting that American manhood was endangered by the absorption of foreigners into the population. The contrast Levin employed between manly Americans and depraved Catholics had strong sexual undertones and suggested personal as well as cultural insecurity.

In a speech against the proposal to send a mission to Rome, the American party propagandist contrasted the heroic stature of the American freeman with the unnatural religion of Roman Catholics and called on American men to resist with him the subversion of American ways. First describing the American free- man in terms of heroic grandeur, he declared that "a republican . . . ought to have his whole soul expanded to the utmost bounds of liberality—free, daring, energetic, and boundless in its soaring flight; feeling no throb he feared to utter; burning with no thought he dare not express."[25] The American freeman was contrasted with the Pope, who was described as remote from nature and man on his throne:

A throne which extinguishes the fire on the altar of domestic love, in a form secular, fatal, revolting; snatching its votaries away from the homage of nature to the cold convent, the repulsive abbey, the gloomy cell of the anchorite, the horrid dungeon of the inquisition, and the demoralizing edict of celibacy.[26]

Finally, Levin called for the test of heroic manhood with the zeal of a true martyr: "How inscrutable are the ways of God to test our virtue and waken in our bosoms the divine emotions which led the noble men of other days to make such immortal sacrifices, when burning at the fiery stake, or dying under the tortures of the inquisition."[27] Levin probably represents an unusually immoderate position, even among mavericks; nonetheless, the sentiments of masculine identity as- sociated with political virtue are typical of many maverick speakers, if in less dramatic fashion.[28]

The identification of maverick behavior with heroic masculinity was part of the ego pattern of many mavericks; and testing of this ego structure was a pattern which seemed to be as pervasive as any among mavericks. The more reflective mavericks, frequently those who occupied positions in the middle of the political spectrum, were not nearly as inclined to engage either in explicit defense of their masculinity or in violent encounters with their political opponents. If they did participate in political scrapes, the method was nearly always verbal and some- times quite complex, as in the case of the satiric *Quodlibet* of John Pendleton Kennedy. For many mavericks, not as reflective as those who simply put on paper their antagonistic feelings, the strong sense of rightness they felt was manifested in a constant encounter with opponents—in the halls of Congress, in political infighting, and even in physical combat.[29]

Examples of the various ways in which mavericks put their heroic egoism to the test of conflict can be cited for a wide variety of behavior. The political polemic approach was characteristic of many and took a number of forms. Writers of satiric attacks included John Pendleton Kennedy, Caleb Cushing, and Henry

Winter Davis.[30] Mavericks who wrote more elevated literary, historical, or philosophical critiques of their opponents included Cushing, John Minor Botts, Henry Washington Hilliard, Alexander Stephens, Henry Wise, Joshua Giddings, and Muscoe R. H. Garnett.[31] Newspaper editors and writers among mavericks who were specially noted for their extreme language included John Wentworth, Edmund Burke, John McKeon, Lewis Levin, Henry Murphy, and Frank Blair, Jr.[32] The number of mavericks noted either by their opponents or in secondary sources as having been conspicuous for their oral invective is also long, including the famous pair of antagonists, Adams and Wise, as well as Robert Barnwell Rhett, Joshua Giddings, Henry Winter Davis, John Wentworth, David K. Cartter, Thomas Clingman, John A. Bingham, Francis W. Pickens, Robert Toombs, and a host of lesser figures.[33] In fact, of all of the major maverick congressmen, not one failed to make a reputation partly on the basis of his skill in fighting political battles. Whatever might be said for the influence of their defensive posture in relation to party and section in determining their belligerence, nothing is more clear from their writings than that their pugnacious behavior was not merely defensive but almost cheerfully offensive. The clear impression is that conflict, verbal and nonverbal testing of their self-image, was an integral part of the character of mavericks.

Scrapes on the floor of the House of Representatives between aggressive mavericks were a frequent feature of every Congress. Although sometimes the encounters were humorous, from the viewpoint of the efficiency of the House they could not have been desirable. Sometimes, however, they may have furthered the political ambitions of the maverick involved. For example, Williamson R. W. Cobb of Alabama pursued his interests with such singlemindedness that he often gave the impression that nothing other than his concerns were relevant to the House. In a fury over his failure to obtain passage of a railroad promotional bill for the benefit of his constituents, his tactics became clearly disruptive. "I object to everything," he protested, when his measures could not gain precedence.[34] An antagonist summed up the situation: "The Speaker has been 'Cobb-ed,' and I object to the House being 'Cobb-ed' too."[35] Although Cobb's methods may have been successful for his constituents, there is little question that much of his method was related not only to their interests but to his own egocentrism.

One of the more egotistical and disruptive of all mavericks was Edward Stanly of North Carolina. Stanly's invective was generally unrestrained; on one occasion he accused an opponent, maverick Charles Brown of Pennsylvania, of crowing "like a dung-hill chicken on a fence," for which he was ruled out of order; but he was allowed to continue when fellow maverick John Minor Botts came to his defense.[36] Stanly readily admitted his intemperate nature and acknowledged the disruptive effect it had upon the business of the House. He opened one speech before the House with an explanation of his behavior the previous day, when his attempts to speak had been thwarted:

I endeavored . . . to obtain the floor immediately after the gentleman from Virginia (Mr. Wise) concluded. I wanted it but ten minutes, but the estimable gentleman from Kentucky

(Mr. Underwood) saw fit to deny me, an act of courtesy seldom refused by the House. But, sir, I am satisfied. I was not in a humor to have said what I had to say in a mild or moderate way. I am generally easily provoked, I fear, by the assumption of audacious insolence; and probably more provoked than I should be.[37]

That Henry Wise was capable of "audacious insolence" is unquestionable; but the fact is that Stanly was provoked by much less than that on many occasions. Further, such egocentric explanations of behavior were neither necessary to nor characteristic of regular congressional debate, at least not insofar as it involved conformists.

The mavericks and their egotistical conflicts appear to have been most furious when two or more mavericks were involved, as in the instance above. Sometimes the scene took on an air of absurdity, as in the following exchange between Charles Brown and Henry Wise:

Mr. Charles Brown appealed to the gentleman from Virginia to withdraw the motion for the previous question; and not, by such a motion, to cut off a gentleman from reply who had been individually attacked by—

Mr. WISE. The gentleman well knows I made no attack.

Mr. C. BROWN. The gentleman talked about the children born in the sewers of Philadelphia.

Mr. WISE. I did not say that.

Mr. C. BROWN. You did.

Mr. WISE. I did not.

Mr. C. BROWN. You did; and I ask only ten minutes to show that up in its proper light.[38]

Wise had, in fact, made a reference to the "sewers of Philadelphia" and its inhabitants; and Brown, perhaps for reasons of ego and constituent interest would not let it pass. The encounter between Brown and Wise continued off and on for several days in the House, with Wise insisting that Brown was from the "faubourg St. Antoine" because of his urban democracy. Although Wise was a more famous congressman, Brown was certainly as irascible; even the fairly neutral *Globe* reporter described one speech of his as delivered with "more than his usual animation."[39]

Examples of the ego conflicts between mavericks could be multiplied indefinitely, but perhaps the basic relevance of the disruptive behavior of the congressmen can best be explained by one of them, Thomas Florence of Pennsylvania. In a routine motion to have the tellers count yeas and nays on a bill of interest to him, Florence was blocked by the speaker pro tem. Florence refused to cooperate with the ruling of the speaker, so Thomas Clingman, the feisty North Carolina maverick, suggested "Call the Sgt.-At-Arms." Florence's response evidences the attitude of egocentrism typical of the majority of the mavericks: "I do not care for the Sgt.-At-Arms; nor for any man in this House. . . . I am in order; and so long as I have a voice I shall lift it in demand for my rights."[40]

Mavericks did not always seek out conflict; but most of them appear to have made little attempt to avoid it. A maverick's inability to prevail, even in routine matters, often seems to have prompted a strong determination to exert his own individuality against the majority or against a strong opponent. This attitude toward congressional business was not political but personal.

A comparison with the behavior and writings of the outstanding conformists supports the contention that this pattern was much more characteristic of mavericks than conformists.[41] The method of most of the conformists seems to have been discreet manipulation rather than authoritative or directive antagonism. This is notoriously true, of course, for such party leaders as Stephen A. Douglas, Howell Cobb, Schuyler Colfax, R. M. T. Hunter, and Millard Fillmore.[42] Some of the conformists were noted as rough and tumble orators—Tom Corwin, Edward Baker, Anson Burlingame, and Richard Thompson, for example—but the conflict of their oratory was dramatic and political, rather than having the element of personal combativeness so characteristic of maverick oratory. Furthermore, secondary sources for the conformist orators who displayed the maverick-like characteristic of verbal invective revealed consistently that their behind-the-scenes behavior was predominantly manipulative and that many were active party workers.[43] In short, the oratory of the conformists was another tool to be used in the effective manipulation of the political environment, while for mavericks it was at least partly a means of character display.

This integral relationship between the character and oratory of mavericks was sometimes described explicitly. One of the more famous maverick orators, John A. Bingham, was responsible for an introduction to a manual for speakers, in which he was also featured as an example of the form at its finest. In his introduction, Bingham explained the proper relationship between the speech and the character of the speaker:

Unwritten speech is, in my judgment, the more efficient method of public speaking, because it is the natural method. . . . The essay delivered is but the echo of the dead past, the speech is the utterance of the living present. The delivery of the essay is the formal act of memory, the delivery of the unwritten speech is the living act of intellect and heart.[44]

Bingham further elaborated by quoting from Emerson's essay "Eloquence," stressing the integrity of the act of public speaking, properly understood: "God and Nature are altogether sincere, and art should be as sincere."[45] The theory of Bingham apparently matched the action of most mavericks, who in their verbal encounters with political opponents defended not a political position but their integrity.

Mavericks gave repeated verbal expression to their beliefs that their maverick behaviors were heroic and necessary to the preservation of their self-concepts even if they brought them into conflict with colleagues or constituents. Sometimes regretfully, but more frequently with pride, they pointed out the virtues. Henry

Wise, whose reputation as a caustic speaker was perhaps as notable as that of his favorite opponent Adams, reflected upon his own image:

I do not prize my fame for the faculty of saying severe things very highly, and he who is gifted with the power and constrained by the necessity of saying harsh things, or even of speaking out his mind and feelings strongly, however honestly, in this world, is not apt to be blessed with mild judgments of men himself.[46]

There is mixed pride and regret in Wise's words; he felt the stinging criticisms of his opponents and suggested loneliness but because of his "gift" and "necessity" felt he must go against the judgments of *this world*. The necessity might be political necessity, but the more likely real referent of the word is the necessity dictated by Wise's own self-image.

Other examples of the manner in which mavericks appealed to the idea of heroism as justification for an unpopular position or as justification for a belligerent stand have been cited throughout earlier chapters. It should suffice here to close with another immodest maverick's assessment of the worth of maverick behavior. The speaker was David Wilmot, who had first gotten in political trouble by his vote against the Walker Tariff and then antagonized a separate group of opponents by offering the Wilmot Proviso. In ill repute in many circles, Wilmot was undoubtedly a very defensive maverick. His description of true heroism, in which he does not mention himself by name but clearly by inference, can serve as a summary for the embattled and heroic self-image of mavericks:

The highest displays of heroism are not enacted on the fields of human butchery and carnage.... Steadfastness in truth; a firm maintenance of the right; an unwavering support of justice; a fearless denunciation of oppression and wrong—acts such as these, when performed at the expense of great personal interest belong to the truly heroic.[47]

For a politician in the middle of the nineteenth century, maintenance of these heroic standards could not always have been compatible with political success. Mavericks sometimes compromised. They were not heroes; they had heroic ambitions, but they were also politicians. The visible struggles to maintain and assert their individuality in the machinery of party and congressional organizations shed light upon the nature of the culture which produced them and upon the character of the emerging institutions.[48]

NOTES

1. The use of the word *ego* to describe that part of the behavior or personality of the subject which the subject perceived as self-concept or self-image is not meant to suggest a Freudian frame of reference. Robert K. Merton, *Social Theory and Social Structure* (New York: The Free Press; Revised and Enlarged Edition, 1957), has offered a useful interpretation of nonconformity as a form of reference group behavior in Chapter IX: "Continuities in the Theory of Reference Groups and Social Structure," problem 6. A

brief but thoughtful discussion which emphasizes the importance of attitudes upon behavior is found in Robert D. Putnam, *The Beliefs of Politicians: Ideology, Conflict, and Democracy in Britain and Italy* (New Haven: Yale University Press, 1973), pp. 1–7. A more extended treatment of the subject is Fred A. Greenstein, *Personality and Politics* (Chicago: Markham Publishing Co., 1969). For the historian wishing a clear and nontechnical introduction to the subject of role theory and in particular to the complexities of the relationship between individual and environment, Erving Goffman, *The Presentation of Self in Everyday Life* (New York: Doubleday Anchor Books, 1959), remains a delightful solution.

2. Henry Adams, the most literary of the talented Adams mavericks, in describing the difficulties the Adamses had with the emerging political machines of the late antebellum period, laughed at his own misunderstanding of Caleb Cushing's assaults on Charles Sumner as a "one-eyed" abolitionist; and he also commented on the clear distinction, even to a young man, between the "one-ideaed" politicians and Cushing's sort; see Henry Adams, *The Education of Henry Adams* (New York: Random House; Modern Library Edition, 1931), p. 49.

3. This description of the maverick ego should not be taken as historically exclusive. Many political and nonpolitical leaders in the history of the United States have shared the characteristics described here for mavericks; an obvious example might be the reform leaders of the same decades. Yet it can be demonstrated that the majority of conformists in the Congress between 1836 and 1860 did not possess the characteristics described here; and if a few did, they were not dominant features of their characters. On the other hand, there was not a single maverick who left a significant record of his ideas who did not clearly fit the description which follows. Scholarly biographies, to the extent that they exist for mavericks and conformists, completely support the distinction. For a listing of those, see the bibliography.

4. See bibliography, individual writings section.

5. See pp. 184–185.

6. William Smith, *Congressional Globe*, 33d Cong., 2d Sess., 34.

7. Humphrey Marshall, "Address of Col. Marshall upon the Life & Character of Capt. Ballard," in *Obituary Addresses Delivered upon the Occasion of the Reinterment of the Remains of Gen. Chas. Scott, Maj. Wm. T. Barry, and Capt. Bland Ballard and Wife, in the Cemetary, at Frankfort, Nov. 8, 1854* (Frankfort, Ky.: A. G. Hodges, State Printer, 1855), p. 52. Cf. also Cost Johnson, *Public Land Speech*, p. 15.

8. Nevins, *Diary of John Quincy Adams*, p. 27. Although a diary might well be considered a thoroughly private form of self-expression, it is highly doubtful that John Quincy Adams expected no one to read his reflections. If that had been the case, it hardly seems likely that his son, Charles Francis Adams, would have edited the completed *Memoirs* for publication.

9. Letter of November 11, 1816, quoted in Fuess, *Life of Cushing*, p. 32.

10. Ibid., p. 99.

11. See, for example, his letter home from the University of Virginia at age 19, in James Garnett, *Biographical Sketch of Garnett*, pp. 12–13.

12. Ibid., p. 8.

13. Stephens' journal in Johnston and Browne, *Life of Alexander H. Stephens*, p. 79. Journal date was May 23, 1834.

14. Botts was imprisoned without trial in Richmond in March of 1862 for a short period. See Botts, *The Great Rebellion*, pp. vii–ix.

15. Ibid., p. 317.

16. Ibid., p. 67.

17. Ibid., pp. 344–360. Garnett, whom Botts described as a "warm personal friend," one with whom "I had supposed sympathized in all my political views," publicly repudiated Botts (see p. 359).

18. The only conformist who appeared to rely as heavily as some mavericks on the concept of heroic masculinity was the southern fire-eater, Lawrence Keitt. Keitt's speeches, which were almost uniformly furious orations, ran the full gamut of southern emotional sectionalism and, while quite polished, do not seem to have represented so much a personal set of ideas as a refined expression of the more militant southern defense.

19. The relationship between cultural conflict and social role definitions for males is treated at least perpherally in David Bertelson, *The Lazy South* (New York: Oxford University Press, 1967); George M. Fredrickson, *The Inner Civil War: Northern Intellectuals and the Crisis of the Union* (New York: Harper Torchbooks; Harper & Row, 1965); Taylor, *Cavalier and Yankee*; Takaki, *A Pro-Slavery Crusade*; and Arieli, *Individualism and Nationalism in American Ideology*, especially Chapter XIV, "The Great Debate on the Nature of the American Ideal." It is a central theme in Wyatt-Brown, *Southern Honor*.

20. John Hickman, *Southern Sectionalism. Speech of Hon. John Hickman, of Pennsylvania. Delivered in the U. S. House of Representatives, May 1, 1860* (Washington, D. C.: Buell & Blanchard, 1860), p. 2.

21. Ibid., p. 3.

22. John Hickman, *Democracy–The Old and the New. Speech of Hon. John Hickman, of Pennsylvania, on the Battle Ground of Brandywine, Sept. 11, 1860* (Washington, D. C.: [Buell & Blanchard, 1860]), p. 3.

23. John Hickman, *Kansas Contested Election. Speech of Hon. John Hickman, of Pennsylvania, Delivered in the House of Representatives, Mar. 19, 1856* (Washington, D. C.: Congressional Globe Office, [1856]), p. 3.

24. Francis W. Pickens, *Speech of Hon. F. W. Pickens, Delivered before a Public Meeting of the People of the District, Held at Edgefield C[ourt] H[ouse], South Carolina, July 7, 1851* (Edgefield, S. C.: Advertiser Office, 1851).

25. Lewis Charles Levin, *Speech of Mr. L. C. Levin, of Pennsylvania, on the Proposed Mission to Rome, Delivered in the House of Representatives of the United States, Mar. 2, 1848* (Washington, D. C.: J. & G. S. Gideon, Printers, [1848]), p. 9.

26. Ibid., p. 16.

27. Ibid., p. 9.

28. For a brief description of Levin's life see Chapter 11. For examples of much milder nativism, but one which nevertheless expresses similar concern for identity, see several speeches on the subject of the American party in Henry Winter Davis, *Speeches and Addresses*.

29. An interesting point revealed by comparison of the seven names of southern congressmen involved in duels or near-duels in John Hope Franklin, *The Militant South, 1800–1861* (Cambridge, Mass.: The Belknap Press of Harvard University Press, 1956), pp. 52–53, is that of the seven, three were mavericks (Wise, Clingman, Edward M. Stanly), and two others appeared as mavericks on one scale set. The two others were conformists in their one term in the House, one of them being the flamboyant cohort of Rhett, William Lowndes Yancey. The Clingman–Yancey duel never came off. Yancey, a very colorful figure, also was involved in a famous speaking "duel" with Henry

Washington Hilliard over the question of the propriety of the secession of the state of Alabama in 1851.

30. Kennedy, *Quodlibet*; a semi-satirical attack on James Fenimore Cooper in Caleb Cushing, *A Reply to the Letter of J. Fenimore Cooper. By One of His Countrymen* (Boston: J. T. Buckingham, 1834); Henry Winter Davis, *An Epistle Congratulatory to the Right Reverend the Bishops of the Episcopal Court at Camden* (New York; n.p., 1853), which involves a peculiar church squabble in which Davis became embroiled.

31. Cushing, see the list in Fuess, *Life of Cushing*, p. 95; Botts, *The Great Rebellion*; Hilliard, *DeVane*; Stephens, *A Constitutional View of the Late War between the States; Its Causes, Character, Conduct, and Results. Presented in a Series of Colloquies at Liberty Hall* (Philadelphia: National Publishing Co., 1868–70); Wise, *Seven Decades*; Giddings, *The Exiles of Florida*; Garnett, *Union, Past and Future*.

32. Wentworth edited *The Chicago Democrat*; according to Fehrenbacher he "demonstrated such a mastery of vituperation and ridicule that he was soon one of the most feared and hated men in the region" (*Chicago Giant*, p. 25). Burke edited the New Hampshire *State Capital Reporter*; his attack on his former mentor Franklin Pierce and on Pierce's opponent Stephen Douglas was described as a "bitter assault" in P. O. Ray, "Some Papers of Franklin Pierce, 1852–1862," reprinted from *American Historical Review*, vol. X, nos. 1–2 (Oct. 1904–Jan. 1905):110. McKeon contributed to the *New York Weekly Caucasian*, a "white man's" newspaper (see John McKeon, *Peace and Union—War and Disunion. Speech of Hon. John McKeon, Delivered before the Democratic Union Association* (New York: Van Evrie, Horton & Co., 1863). Murphy was sometime editor and publisher of the *Brooklyn Daily Eagle* (*BDAC*, p. 1373); his problems with one of his editors, poet Walt Whitman, are related in Gay Wilson Allen, *The Solitary Singer: A Critical Biography of Walt Whitman* (New York: New York University Press, 1967), p. 210–211. Blair helped reorient the *Missouri Democrat* as an antislavery paper (with B. Gratz Brown) and was active as a propagandist for the cause in many other papers (see Smith, *The Blair Family*, vol. I, Chs. XXI, XXIII, XXIV, XXV for examples of Blair's style).

33. Most detailed histories of the political life of the period contain frequent references to the verbal encounters of the more well known of these men. In addition, the *Globe* references to their frequent debates and spats add humor to the task of reading the texts of the daily meetings of Congress. Beyond that, in most of their autobiographical works, mavericks refer to their differences with other mavericks.

34. *Congressional Globe*, 33d Cong., 2d Sess., 760.

35. Ibid., p. 796.

36. Ibid., 27th Cong., 2d Sess., 333. Stanly's career is described in Norman D. Brown, *Edward Stanly: Whiggery's Tarheel "Conqueror,"* Southern Historical Publication no. 18 (University, Ala.: University of Alabama Press, 1974).

37. *Congressional Globe*, 27th Cong., 2d Sess., 474.

38. Ibid., p. 653.

39. Ibid., p. 846.

40. Ibid., 33d Cong., 2d Sess., 1177–1178.

41. A systematic reading of the *Globe* turned up not more than two examples of conformists who were consistently disruptive or combative on a personal basis.

42. Douglas' manipulative abilities are described by his biographers in George Fort Milton, *The Eve of Conflict, Stephen A. Douglas and the Needless War* (Boston & New York: Houghton Mifflin Co., Riverside Press Cambridge, 1934); and Robert W. Johann-

sen, *Stephen A. Douglas*. Johannsen, in his preface, describes Douglas in terms wholly consistent with the picture of conformist character delineated herein. Also highly revealing are Douglas' letters; see Stephen A. Douglas, *The Letters of Stephen A. Douglas*, ed. by Robert W. Johannsen (Urbana: University of Illinois Press, 1961). Howell Cobb is described as "an adroit political manipulator" in John Eddins Simpson, *Howell Cobb, the Politics of Ambition* (Chicago: Adams, 1973), p. iii; see also Zachary Taylor Johnson, *The Political Policies of Howell Cobb* (Nashville: George Peabody College for Teachers 1929); Robert Preston Brooks, ed., "Howell Cobb papers," *Georgia Historical Quarterly* V–VI (Sept.–Dec., 1922); and U. B. Phillips, ed., *The Correspondence of Robert Toombs, Alexander H. Stephens, and Howell Cobb* in *Annual Report of the American Historical Association for the Year 1911*, vol. II (Washington, D. C.: American Historical Association, 1911). For Hunter, see Simms, *Life of Robert M. T. Hunter*; and Charles Henry Ambler, ed., *Correspondence of Robert M. T. Hunter, 1826–1876* in *Annual Report of the American Historical Association for the Year 1916*, vol. II (Washington, D. C.: American Historical Association, 1918). See Colfax's biography (Smith, *Schuyler Colfax*) for references to his skill at politicking. For Fillmore, see *Fillmore Papers*.

43. Burlingame, for example, used highly inflammatory political language but was not seemingly personally inclined to commit himself to defense of any position. One scholar concludes that he rose to prominence by virtue of three assets: oratory, opportunism, and personal political friendships. See Carl Francis Yeager, Jr., "Anson Burlingame: His Mission to China and the First Chinese Mission to Western Nations" (Unpublished Ph.D. diss., Georgetown University, May 25, 1950). He has been criticized, perhaps unjustly, for his role in the Sumner–Brooks affair. After the attack, Burlingame made a fiery House speech attacking the South and the behavior of Preston Brooks. Brooks responded with a challenge for a duel. Burlingame accepted, but the duel was never fought because the only site acceptable to Burlingame was Canada, while Brooks (also a conformist) refused to travel northward through perhaps hostile territory. One southern scholar concludes that Burlingame was "actively interested only in the pusillanimous purpose of getting where he could not be served with a challenge to fight." James E. Campbell, "Sumner, Brooks, Burlingame, or The Last of the Great Challengers," *Ohio Archaeological and Historical Quarterly* 34 (Oct., 1925):463. Burlingame's invective could be turned with equal enthusiasm upon Democrats. He said in Congress in 1858, "I think it is the first duty of Republicans to extinguish the doughfaces" (*An Appeal*, p. 6). He served during the Civil War as Minister to China.

44. William Pittenger, *Oratory Sacred and Secular: or, the Extemporaneous Speaker, with Sketches of the Most Eminent Speakers of All Ages*, introduction by Hon. John A. Bingham (New York: Samuel R. Wells, Publisher, 1868), p. 7.

45. Ibid.

46. Barton Wise, *Life of Henry Wise*, p. 59.

47. From a speech to a Free-Soilers' meeting, in Going, *David Wilmot*, p. 730.

48. Henry Adams' descriptions of his emerging awareness of the potential conflict between principled politicans and the new institutions are thoroughly to the point here. As he put it in *The Education of Henry Adams*, p. 49:

America and he began, at the same time, to become aware of a new force under the innocent surface of party machines. Even at that early moment, a rather slow boy felt dimly conscious that he might meet some personal difficulties in trying to reconcile sixteenth-century principles and eighteenth-century statesmanship with late nineteenth-century party organization.

CHAPTER 11

The American Congressional Maverick, 1836–1860: Causes and Consequences

I know I am solid and sound,
To me the converging objects of the universe perpetually flow,
All are written to me, and I must get what the writing means.
Walt Whitman, "Song of Myself"
Leaves of Grass

The maverick first identified only in terms of his voting behavior pattern must now be seen in a different light. No maverick was romantically formed out of the natural cosmos. His character was shaped, like that of other men, by the complex interactions between himself and his environment. Yet by the time he reached manhood, a maverick did have a "self" which, while it might thereafter have been altered somewhat by the demands of his political career, did not apparently undergo any basic transformation. That "self" remained to him the constant factor in a shifting world.[1]

In the most general sense, cultural conflict in pluralistic antebellum America produced the maverick political character.[2] The oldest American cultural traditions were rooted in rural and agricultural life and were predominantly elitist in social and political order. Newer patterns, clearly emerging by the 1830s, centered around urban and industrial institutions and reflected the influence of democratic ideas upon social and political structures. Mavericks shared with many western intellectuals an ambivalent response to these newer transatlantic developments. They believed that while material progress was obviously being engendered by the "modern age," exceptional individuals were in danger of being smothered by the rising masses and subjected to what Tocqueville aptly termed "the tyranny of the majority."[3]

Many mavericks and intellectuals agreed upon the ominous traits of the embryonic era: at the least it demanded rationalization and conformity; at the worst it threatened mechanization and dehumanization. Some despairingly maintained that men were about to become copies of the machines they were trying to master; and they vigorously insisted that the enthusiastic quest for efficiency through standardization was a deadly pursuit in human organizations, however appropriate for mechanical or industrial systems.

The concern that progress in the organization of human affairs might enervate individual efforts was surely at the center of the mavericks' attitudes towards their political situation. They were drawn towards this awareness by the force of tensions inherent in their being individualists in an increasingly group-oriented system; but their capacity to perceive the predicament in this way was established by earlier influences which had produced within the matrix of their own attitudes a sort of microcosmic cultural conflict. Strongly affected by the traditions of the eighteenth century and profoundly attracted to the vitality of the nineteenth century, mavericks rested consistently in neither cultural framework.

For mavericks this cultural tension was exacerbated by the fact that the House of Representatives also manifested the effects of cultural crosscurrents in the United States. Not only did its membership reflect the diversity of changing society, but the institutional growth pattern of the House dynamically embodied cultural tensions. Even without a full history of the House, the broad outlines of the development are evident, and they bear repeating here because of their relationship to the making of mavericks.

As American politicians had engaged in fleshing out the political structure designed by the elitist statesmen of the eighteenth century, they had consistently relied upon the "art of association." When political institutions administered by temporary associations proved inadequate to the demands of national problems and insufficiently responsive to the ambitions of office-seeking politicians, factions evolved into parties and ultimately into the two-party system, a "machine" which by the late antebellum period was beginning to possess some of the functional and rational characteristics associated with large institutions in mass society.

Furthermore, the efforts of the two parties after 1836 to create popular enthusiasm for partisan issues and therefore reap political profit from the problems of expansion and economic growth seem to have fostered an awareness among the conformist leaders of the clumsily large House that effective power could best be wielded by increased internal complexity and some rationalization of functions and roles within the legislature. The creation of the committee system, the practice of making partisan assignments to committees, some attention to seniority in choosing leadership for them, and frequent demands for regularity in debate and discussion—all appear to have been part of the process through which the young legislature developed a distinctive institutional structure.

Within the confines of this changing House of Representatives, leadership styles of ambitious and able men varied considerably. Conformist leaders were quite adept at mastering the machineries of the legislative body and the parties, and they were concerned for the welfare of the institutions as well as for their own ambitions. The identification of personal interest with that of party may have preceded widespread realization that the respectability of the House reflected upon the reputation of its members, but both tendencies were certainly prevalent in the attitudes of the leading conformist congressmen before the Civil War.

Mavericks did not generally perceive this kind of fortuitous coincidence between individual and group interests. According to their understanding of the political universe, all realities had to be evaluated by their own private standards. Personal philosophy took precedence over party ideology, and individual merit might lend luster to the House. The mavericks insisted that the world at large accept them as they saw themselves, as "solid and sound" men of integrity in a pluralistic and often amoral setting.

It was largely the cultural pluralism of the United States that afforded mavericks the opportunity for independence. In most parts of the country a fairly broad range of political behaviors was acceptable. The paternalistic elitism of the colonial and revolutionary period was a familiar model for statesmen like John Quincy Adams; Andrew Jackson's forceful plain style had demonstrated nationally the effectiveness of that political type; and the machine politician was becoming more familiar, particularly in the urbanized areas which sent forth men like Martin Van Buren. As far as the voters at home were concerned, mavericks could probably afford to be "themselves."

Maintaining political independence within the more restricted setting of the House was perhaps more difficult, for there mavericks met conflicting demands simultaneously. The *Congressional Globe* and newspapers carried home to voters the mavericks' daily behavior on the floor of the House. Party leaders encouraged them to represent the collective will of the party, whether in voting or in committee service. And some roles of leadership were acquiring stereotypical models, especially at the upper levels of service, so mavericks' freedom to operate independently was limited if they desired to climb the ladder of legislative success. In a sense, the immaturity of the House as a legislative body did offer greater freedom for individuals to assert their personal styles than may be possible in the twentieth-century body. On the other hand, this freedom also presented mavericks with the problem of numerous role conflicts, a situation made more precarious by their strong self-expectations and by their determination to be consistent at the core.

Although mavericks recognized that attempting leadership in the fluid world of antebellum politics might entail some loss of personal autonomy, they thought the risk worth taking. Most mavericks tried to maintain a tenable middle ground between the conformities expected by party or House groups and the independence they themselves desired. It was not often that a maverick defied all authority and stood as a "majority of one."[4] Frequent and consistent self-assertion generally stopped before political self-destruction occurred. In some instances this self-assertion resulted in public ostracism by party and congressional colleagues, even in political martyrdom; but at the other extreme, mavericks sometimes shaped, through their own determination and abilities, the attitudes of their fellows, extracting from a flexible situation the rewards of aggressive leadership.

Certainly to the extent that mavericks were able to mold the environment to suit their own desires, public life must have been rewarding. Other influences could also have encouraged mavericks in their independent courses, although the supportive character of some perceived incentives may have resulted from mavericks' private readings of events rather than from any political consensus about their significance. Constituent support, registered in a variety of public and private forms from voting behavior to letters and personal contacts, may have reassured mavericks that nonconformity was desirable. Working in a congressional milieu where brief tenure in office was the rule, mavericks may have interpreted their reelections to mean approval for their independence from party and sectional influences, whatever other factors may be seen retrospectively to have caused their victories. Popular respect and admiration for notable mavericks also may have given vicarious pleasure to those men who identified themselves as similarly independent. This process of gratification through identification seems clearly to have occurred in the case of John Quincy Adams and Joshua Giddings as well as for southerners Alexander Stephens and Robert Toombs, instances in which political identification was reinforced by the bonds of friendship.

Clearly, then, there were ways in which the antebellum House of Representatives and the active public supported the persistence of leadership patterns not fully congenial with the evolution of mass-based politics, though this support may not have been deliberate. It would seem likely, moreover, that the long tenure of some mavericks and their presence as chairmen of House committees indicates some congruity between public or congressional ideas about statesmanlike conduct and mavericks' own self-concepts. Their political experience could have and probably did thus encourage some mavericks to be more maverick-like; but this is distinctly not to say that mavericks were merely mutant creations of the political process. Conformity in voting behavior was so overwhelmingly the rule that mavericks must have entered political life with strong predispositions which enabled them to resist institutional pressures for conformity in this critical role and to seek out the rewards of individualism wherever they might be found.[5]

Speculations about the prepolitical causes of congressional behavior lead the scholar into the perplexing study of psychological motivation, an area that historians are increasingly willing to explore, if with mixed results. It is obvious that the responses of both mavericks and conformists to their political circumstances were conditioned by previous experiences; mavericks, however, frankly described the relationships between personal character and political action, while conformists did not. To speculate about conformists' motives would entail, therefore, an analysis of their unpublished personal records, a task (for 171 men) beyond the scope of this study. Yet in spite of the limitations of relying upon published sources, it seems clear that the primary clues for understanding conformists' congressional behavior lie within the political environment itself, to which they responded with remarkable flexibility and tolerance. Whatever their previous experiences, conformists were able to draw a line between public and private spheres and to resist inclinations to conform every action in one sphere to the standards of the other.

The nature of conformists' accommodations can be seen in comments made by one Maine Democrat in a letter to his wife shortly after his entry into the House in 1835. John Fairfield, a gregarious New Englander whose self-described goal was to be a "sober, industrious, and useful" legislator, observed the disjunction between personal principles and political expedience when a late-night Saturday session led him to work in the early hours of a Sunday morning, the day of rest. Fairfield handily resolved his conflict by attending without voting, but he acknowledged that he would have temporarily abandoned his religious principles had his vote been necessary for his party's victory. Without explaining the reasons for his personal decision, he described for his wife the circumstance which made it possible: "It is strange how soon we become accustomed to the habits of those with whom we happen to be placed and how readily we slide into their views and modes of thinking and feeling, however averse to them we might have been."[6] John Fairfield was a thoughtful and principled man who seems to have understood instinctively that his own effectiveness rested upon conformity to the rules of the legislative game. Conformity did not threaten his self-image, even as he observed the change it made in his "thinking and feeling."

Contemporary political scientists term this process of adopting special rules for legislative behavior "norm integration." Through the use of personal opinion surveys and interviews they have attempted to explain how twentieth-century congressmen adjust to institutional expectations and why some "slide into" new normative patterns more easily than others. Such studies have, by and large, been more successful in describing the prevalence of explicit norms in modern legislatures than in explaining the varying responses of individuals to those norms.[7] The standards by which conformists acted do resemble those found for modern "responsible legislators," and conformists may be identified as precursors of the contemporary type; but given the current status of research, speculation about why the type emerged would transcend scholarly bounds. An informed guess is that conformists will be understood better as historians know more about the significance for personal character of the broad economic changes of the nineteenth century. The findings of such diverse works as David Riesman's *The Lonely Crowd* and Richard D. Brown's *Modernization* suggest that congressional conformists belong to a larger body of Americans who learned to accommodate to their changing society without undue personal stress.[8]

Businesslike conformists were not inclined toward self-revelation, nor did they commonly speculate in public about the personal motives for their political actions; thus even a limited interpretation about the influences upon them rests upon inferences drawn from their actions and their environment, supported by a modicum of political theory. Mavericks explained themselves much more fully, thus inferences about influences upon them can be derived from slightly more sturdy evidence. Nonetheless, to reason backwards from what mavericks *did* say and from what conformists *did not* say imposes a double standard upon interpretation and may slight the possibility that conformists had the same experiences as mavericks but did not record their thoughts and feelings. Because of that double standard, the pattern of influences to be described for mavericks cannot be proved untrue for conformists.[9] What follows is an attempt to integrate within the context of current historical knowledge and theory what mavericks said about themselves with the biographical information available about their lives.

The first thing that should be noted about the cultural influences upon mavericks is that they were contradictory in operation and effect. The striking paradoxes in the attitudes of mavericks towards politics had their origins in the diversity of the influences which created them. One pole of attraction for mavericks was the culture of the eighteenth century and before. Especially in regard to political behavior, but generally as well, the standards of the mavericks were standards of eighteenth-century elites. Not only were mavericks educated, formally or imformally, in these elitist ideas, but they appear to have internalized these standards, most probably because of high familial expectations. Mavericks believed that it was their duty, perhaps even their fate, to act out the eighteenth-century model for statesmanship on a nineteenth-century stage.

The other pole of attraction for mavericks was the vital potential of the nineteenth-century world. There is a great deal of evidence suggesting that mavericks had brought home to them in very personal ways the social and economic changes of the first third of the century. In some cases this may have been an unpleasant experience; indeed, a few mavericks were probably driven by the pain of such encounters to reject the nineteenth century altogether. But most mavericks reacted more positively to the creative possibilities of change, and their reaction largely seems to have been a result of their knowledge of nineteenth-century developments in the arts, philosophy, religion, literature, science, and technology.

Thus mavericks were equipped at the outset of their congressional careers with a sort of split allegiance, culturally speaking, and the result was a persistent tension made stronger by their working within an institutional setting that mirrored the same kind of mixed nature. The specific ways in which mavericks were influenced by contradictory cultural forces can be tentatively sketched in a biographical pattern that fits the known facts of many mavericks' lives. For the sake of clarity, each aspect of the maverick history will be traced separately, although the influences upon the lives of mavericks were undoubtedly overlapping and intertwined as they actually occurred.

It is difficult to assign a date to cultural influences because of the evolutionary nature of cultural change. For American political culture, however, there is little doubt but that the years between the opening of the Revolution and the adoption of the Constitution represent a brief period of time in which various traditions were crystallized into the rather specific body of ideas and practices generally termed republican. It was this republican political culture that most clearly influenced the making of congressional mavericks.

Thomas Jefferson wrote to John Adams in 1813:

The natural aristocracy I consider as the most precious gift of nature for the instruction, the trusts, and government of society. And, indeed, it would have been inconsistent in creation to have formed man for the social state and not to have provided virtue and wisdom enough to manage the concerns of the society. May we not even say that the form of government is the best which provides the most effectually for a pure selection of these natural *aristoi* into the offices of government.[10]

The hopeful belief that in an orderly and just government leaders would be chosen from among the superior members of society was part of the conservatively democratic atmosphere of the early Republic; but that idea was fast losing ground in the businesslike world of politics after Jackson. The influence of this kind of political theory upon the mavericks is clear, although it would be incorrect consequently to describe most mavericks as old-fashioned. In point of fact, they were more likely than conformists to be aware of current intellectual trends, including trends in political theory. Much nineteenth-century thought was incorporated by mavericks into their ideas, but their concepts of personal responsibility for community leadership were basically derived from the republican theory of the founding fathers, rather than from the theory or practices of the nineteenth century. Mavericks would have been pleased to be counted among members of the "natural *aristoi*," designed to "manage the concerns of society."

The influence of eighteenth-century political ideas upon mavericks was of course not unique to them. Remnants of revolutionary ideology and rhetoric can be found in speeches of congressmen throughout the nineteenth and into the twentieth centuries. Especially among conservative Whigs, antiparty sentiments (generally in reference to the Democrats) and mildly elitist perspectives were not uncommon. But mavericks, Democratic, Whig, or Republican, gave eighteenth-century political philosophy a vitality not found in conformist rhetoric. It is found variously woven into the basic fabric of their ideas, and it stands as a basic part of their public expression of themselves. For these reasons it seems most likely that these ideas were absorbed by mavericks as part of their intellectual development in their formative years not added as window dressing to the oratory of practicing politicians. To this assertion of a logical relationship there can be added some evidence from the biographical material available for prominent mavericks.

Many mavericks learned the fundamentals of political theory at home. Among the outstanding mavericks there are a number of men whose fathers were either political leaders, teachers, or ministers—men who probably attempted to inculcate their standards in their sons. As most of them were children in that era, it is likely that mavericks' fathers accepted the prevalent republican view that leadership and social responsibility were inseparable. Furthermore, educated politicians, teachers, and ministers in the colonial or early national period were often drawn from something like Jefferson's natural aristocracy, if not from the aristocracy of wealth. It seems unlikely that such men would fail to pass on their ideas to their sons, and this kind of direct link to the traditions of the early Republic is evident for some mavericks.

Some examples of parental influence are so obvious as to require little elaboration. John Quincy Adams could not have grown up politically illiterate unless he had suffered from a mental handicap.[11] The same could be said of Frank Blair, Jr., who with his brother Montgomery, Postmaster General under Lincoln, reflected the strong imprint of ideas from their forceful Jacksonian father, Francis Preston Blair, Sr.[12] All of the Blairs were closely associated with the professional politicians of the Democratic and Republican parties, and they were experts themselves; but their enthusiasm for behind-the-scenes maneuvering was marked by a distinctly elitist attitude towards political leadership. Ability—intellectual and practical—qualified men for leadership in their revised western version of Jefferson's aristocracy of talent. Both the senior Blair and his sons plainly modified Jacksonian egalitarianism with a kind of "democratic elitism" and a pronounced sense of family pride.[13]

Other prominent mavericks who must have been influenced by political ideas directly received from the family environment were Caleb Cushing, whose family had been active in colonial politics in Massachusetts,[14] Charles J. Ingersoll, whose father was a member of the Continental Congress and Constitutional Convention of 1787,[15] Muscoe R. H. Garnett, whose family on both maternal and paternal sides had been active in Virginia politics since the colonial period,[16] and Robert Barnwell Rhett, who proudly counted among his ancestors the colonial leaders of South Carolina.[17]

Rhett was the leader of a reactionary family of South Carolina politicians who wanted to return to the presumably idyllic days of the colonial period, when their society prospered without the incubus of a national government to restrict local freedom. Barnwell and his brothers so closely identified themselves with the remembered past that they abandoned their surname (Smith) when they became adults, assuming the name of their prominent ancestors.[18] To the socially sensitive South Carolina elite, this must have suggested the kind of politics that the Rhetts preferred; and it seems a significant reflection of the kind of attachment they felt for the political standards of a past era.

Henry Winter Davis, an urban maverick, who like the Blairs was associated with machine politicians much of his life, also inherited his political ideas from his family. His father was an Anglican minister and president of a small Virginia college during Winter's childhood; but, according to Davis' recollections, he lost his presidency because of his Federalist leanings.[19] The father, clearly a maverick himself, engrained his aristocratic standards upon his son. The young Winter acquiesced in attending denominational school to study for the ministry but ultimately rejected the vocation. The Baltimore maverick's antipathy for everything associated with the Democratic party was as much a result of his father's political ideas and experience as it was a function of his own large political ambition.[20] The combination of urban machine politician and eighteenth-century philosopher/statesman that he represents stands as an extreme example of the anomalous maverick mixture of diverse cultural traditions.

For at least one group of mavericks, free-soil and antislavery men in both parties, the heritage of New England's Puritan culture was a marked influence. Something of the Calvinist sense of purpose and vocation appears in their ideas about government; the stark moral contrasts of Puritan theologians are echoed in the language of their political speeches; and New England's antislavery tradition probably shaped their own convictions. Obvious examples of this pattern are John Quincy Adams and the two Congregationalist ministers, James Meacham and Orin Fowler.

Other mavericks of New England ancestry represented areas outside of the center of Puritan culture but still bore the stamp of that pattern in their political ideas, language, and antislavery beliefs. Joshua Giddings' ancestors had appeared in New England in 1635 and migrated with waves of other New Englanders to Ohio's Western Reserve through the familiar path of western New York and Pennsylvania.[21] John Wentworth, politically a product of the young city of Chicago, boasted of two colonial Governors of Rhode Island in his direct family line.[22] David Wilmot's ancestors came to New England in 1641 and remained there for five generations before making the gradual move westward to Pennsylvania.[23] By all of these men, social responsibility in political life was seen as a moral obligation, whether they consistently met that obligation or not.

The association of leadership and social responsibility was part of the eighteenth-century political tradition, in and out of New England, and mavericks demonstrably were carriers of this tradition. It is clear that for many mavericks exposure to republican ideas came relatively early in life, if not in childhood, at least before the period of their congressional service. Since the revolutionary heritage of Americans was not an exclusive possession of mavericks' families, however, but was probably taught wherever young men were educated in the first third of the nineteenth century, some further influence must be sought to explain the zeal with which the mavericks defended that tradition as basic to the maverick ego.[24]

The precise cause of adult behavior patterns which had sufficient consistency to be commonly termed character or personality lie buried in the generally unrecorded childhood years of the congressional mavericks. Nonetheless, from the composite picture of the maverick ego it can reasonably be inferred that mavericks translated political ideas from early American culture into personal values because they were brought up to expect more of themselves than of ordinary people.[25] Most educated men in the antebellum United States admired the ideals of the founding fathers but believed that they were part of a Golden Age not to be recovered. If some conformists attempted to live the part of the philosopher/statesman, it was not centrally a part of their public images. None of the conformists revealed extensive self-doubts or any preoccupation with duty or his own adequacy to meet duty—which revelations might support the assumption that he had unusually high self-expectations and standards for personal achievement. The establishment of inordinately high goals for personal development does not seem to have been typical for conformists, regardless of their political ambitions.

Mavericks, conversely, openly acknowledged their personal striving for high self-expectations. This determination to excel, combined as it was with apprehensions about failure, strongly suggests that mavericks had familial expectations which required their constant efforts imposed upon them in childhood. The generally sound minds and healthy self-respect of most of the adult mavericks perhaps indicate that parental demands upon them were accompanied by ample affection, attention, or praise. The apparent intelligence of mavericks, surely a source of pride to their relatives, may also have imaginatively expanded the horizons of their aspirations far beyond the hopes of their parents. In any case, they seemed to have achieved enough personal satisfaction from their constant striving to make this striving a permanent feature of the maverick ego.

Biographical information indicates that mavericks were schooled in self-sufficient excellence by various instructors. For example, the young John Quincy Adams may have received inspiration from a variety of sources; but unquestionably both his father and mother taught him by example and explicit instruction to seek constant self-improvement. Muscoe Garnett lost his father when he was young, and the replacement figure was his uncle, conformist Robert M. T. Hunter.[26] Hunter worried about the seriousness of his nephew and about his tendency to take family responsibility too heavily. While part of that responsibility was represented in the kind of manly leadership Hunter himself exercised, Garnett also acquired from his mother a desire to excel in intellectual as well as political activities. Hunter wrote to his sister frequently about their mutual concern for the young boy Muscoe. In one letter he expressed concern lest the mother overburden her child with worry. "This mode of viewing your duties as sacrifices will never do," he counseled; and he urged her to "rule him [Muscoe] by love and be reasonable in your requirements of him."[27] Hunter clearly believed that his sister was demanding too much of her child, but the future of the young boy would suggest that she did not heed her brother Bob's advice—especially interesting because it represents a conformist's view of how to avoid making a maverick. By the time young Garnett entered college, he was designing a course of study that would satisfy family tradition and his mother's expectations, but by that time they had become his own standards.

Another example of high parental expectations is found in the youth of Alexander H. Stephens, whose father was a schoolteacher in rural Georgia, a man with little money but a community reputation as an honest and upright man.[28] His training of his son was so thorough that despite his death when Stephens was still young the father's example probably was the dominant influence upon the development of the young man. One biographer suggested, within a Freudian framework of interpretation, that the image of his father was the primary motivation for nearly everything Stephens tried to accomplish in later life.[29] At the least, it seems safe to assert that Stephens' father did teach his son the basic intellectual and moral orientations he carried with him later and that he set a standard for achievement in knowledge and integrity that the son never forgot.

Family influence may or may not have been the source of Joshua Giddings' high self-expectations. James B. Stewart, a twentieth-century biographer, writes that by 1830 "neither his beliefs nor his temperament left room for extended self-congratulation. Though he had attained his clearly defined goals, he still felt that there was simply no point at which a man could justly cease working toward higher levels of achievement."[30] But the reasons for this compulsive overachievement are not explained:

How much of this ethic Giddings drew from the conservative creeds of his social circle, and to what extent he created it to live in peace within himself, can never be known. Nevertheless, it is clear that by 1830 he had become emotionally unsuited to placid living. He languished to the point of physical pain when released from the tension of difficult tasks, a complaint which he called "hydrochondria."[31]

Giddings' father was a financial failure, and the young man was determined not to repeat that pattern. Although this strong motivation to succeed could have been implanted by the homogeneous standards of transplanted New England society, it is equally possible that either or both of Giddings' parents wanted their son to avoid the father's failures and thus encouraged his restless pursuit of expanding goals.

The pervasiveness of this characteristic in Giddings' life can be seen in his comments about the death of John Quincy Adams, the man in national politics whom he admired above all others. Giddings was deliberately left out of the funeral arrangements in the House, but he had been present at Adams' last moments.[32] In his *History of The Rebellion* Giddings quoted the elder maverick as saying before his death "This is the last of earth, but I am prepared."[33] There followed a note acknowledging that Giddings' version differed from the official version of Adams' last words: "The writer here gives the words as he then understood them, but the committee appointed to arrange the funeral ceremonies reported his last words to be, "This is the last of earth, but I am content." The word *content* the writer believes was seldom used by Mr. Adams."[34] Or by Mr. Giddings, one might add. The emotional bond between the two great antislavery advocates was more than a result of similar political beliefs. They shared a common perception of duty, so strong a commitment to its fulfillment in the face of political expedience that it must have been the result of a lifetime's belief.

A final example of the early establishment of high standards for personal accomplishment is that of John Pendleton Kennedy. Brought up with both literary and public interests, Kennedy's drive for excellence was thoroughgoing. His best biographer, Charles Bohner, points out that it touched even so small a detail as the boy's efforts to conquer his fear of the dark. Bohner sees this desire to eliminate the smallest imperfections in his character as a result of Kennedy's independence: "Where he was generous with other men's faults, he was ruthless with his own. His early inclination toward solitary pursuits bred in the depths of his character a healthy contempt for dependence in any form."[35] Kennedy seems to have adopted and perhaps exaggerated his parents' expectations at a very young age. His ultimate success in polishing his character was manifested in the attractive balance, wit, and intellect he exhibited as an adult maverick.

The rational balance Kennedy displayed in his personal manner and in his novels is strongly reminiscent of the model for eighteenth-century gentlemen. Not all mavericks were as poised or as gentlemanly as the Baltimore man of letters, but the compulsion to self-improvement was a part of all mavericks, and they also emulated the mythical statesmen of wisdom and virtue. The combined influence of these patterns created the fundamental prepolitical character of the congressional mavericks.

Stamped by childhood experience with the image of eighteenth-century statesmen and determined to live up to the standards that such an image evoked, mavericks grew to maturity in a society self-consciously aware that the Golden Age was past. Older social and economic arrangements persisted for a long time in some rural parts of the country, especially in the deep South, but nowhere were the marks of progress absent. Perhaps because of the firmness with which they clung to private and traditional expectations for themselves, mavericks were highly sensitive to what they perceived as revolutionary changes. Intellectually alert enough to realize the impact of particular advances upon society as a whole, mavericks anticipated the shape of things to come and attempted to insure the security of their own futures.

There is some evidence which suggests that successful attempts by the young mavericks to meet the demands of rapid alterations in their surroundings reinforced their commitment to their tradition-oriented self-concepts. That is, the youths who were taught to be independent and forceful in the accomplishment of their goals were compelled by circumstances to act in line with their training at an early stage in life, before their political careers were established. There are numerous cases, for example, of outstanding mavericks who were either orphaned in childhood or forced by some family catastrophe to move into another environment, sometimes as demanding as the first had been. The cases of Muscoe Garnett and Alexander Stephens have been mentioned. Henry Winter Davis' father's misfortune resulted in the temporary separation of the family, the young son going to live in Washington with the family of his cousin, future Supreme Court Associate Justice David Davis.[36] Rhett's father suffered severe financial reverses from which the family did not recover until the sons, led by Barnwell, remade the fortune; Rhett always regarded the decline with embarrassment.[37]

Henry Wise was orphaned at age six; and although he did not leave the small eastern shore community in which he was brought up, he was apparently expected to be especially active in living up to family standards, despite the death of his parents.[38] The Ohio maverick David K. Cartter was apprenticed to Thurlow Weed after the death of his father when he was only ten and received thorough training in politics and achievement from both sources. A judge of the District of Columbia Supreme Court after the Civil War, Cartter was noted for his inventions, for his tall tales, and for the invective which marked his politicking.[39] In all of these cases there is biographical or autobiographical evidence that the wrenching changes of youth or early manhood were the sources of considerable stress in the mavericks' development. If such episodes occurred in conformists' lives, they left no record of the significance of them. For mavericks, it appears likely that their emerging tendencies towards self-reliant behavior were reinforced by successful functioning in a new environment.[40]

Mavericks noted another pattern of disruption that seems to have been influential in shaping their attitudes of independence and leadership: the factor of societal change. This is not meant to suggest that maverick behavior was simply an irrational response to a loss of status or to cultural strain.[41] What is apparent is that for many mavericks social, cultural, and economic changes did contribute to the formation of that pattern of behavior which became an integral part of the maverick character and which consequently had political results.

A summary description of this process of development can provide the framework for explication of particular mavericks' experiences. Mavericks were taught from childhood to set high standards for their personal accomplishment and to conceive of those standards in terms of the model of the elite leaders of the early republic. These young men then found themselves confronted with social changes which they correctly perceived would inevitably affect the relevance of their standards for achieving success. Rather than abandoning their deeply ingrained rules of conduct, mavericks sought to influence the direction of anticipated social change. A broad social concern, not a narrow political one, was characteristic of their leadership model as well as appropriate to the circumstances they met. The fundamental aim of their efforts was to create out of social flux a community (local, state, or national) in which their leadership ideas would continue to serve them well.

Not all mavericks copied their personal versions of the good society from historical examples; often traditional ideals blended with contemporary social visions. The clumsy mixing of romantic philosophy and pietistic religious values in Henry Washington Hilliard's *DeVane* is an example of this crossing of two cultural strains by a deep South writer. "Long John" Wentworth's enthusiastic participation in the development of Chicago, as much as a model of the nineteenth-century city as the United States offered, while he still echoed the persistent moral values of his New England past exemplified the combining of two traditions in another way. Some mavericks, however, did borrow their inspiration and goals entirely from past societies, and they can perhaps be tagged reactionary; latter-day Jeffersonians like Cost Johnson of Maryland represent one moderate version of this nostalgic kind of perspective. Whatever the social ideal they held, mavericks responded with positive action; societal changes stimulated generally rational and sometimes well-directed efforts by these aggressive men to mold future society to their private standards.

There were elements of irrationality in the responses of some mavericks to nineteenth-century social and economic change. A clear example of the kind of irrational response that has become almost stereotypical in some historical writing is the case of Lewis Levin of Philadelphia. In the absence of extensive biographical material on the relatively obscure congressman, the story of his life is incomplete, but the information that exists suggests a strange career. Born and reared in Charleston, South Carolina, Levin moved to Mississippi in 1828 and taught school there. He then became a lawyer and practiced in several states, finally settling in Philadelphia in 1838.[42] There he was an editor of the Philadelphia *Daily Sun* and founder of the American party in 1842. The emotionalism of his rhetoric clearly indicates that his response to the supposed virtual inundation of the country by Catholic agents was irrational.[43] The glimpses of him provided in Ray Billington's *The Protestant Crusade* further support this impression.[44] It could readily be argued, though not proved from the insufficient biographical data, that the drifting lawyer, writer, and teacher was thoroughly frightened by the size of Catholic immigration. His speeches, with their nightmarish fantasy plots and sexual overtones, certainly indicate some form of fear. Whatever political motivations, ambitions, or plans may have prompted Levin's course, it also appears highly likely that the impact of the social changes in his life helped direct the shape of his whole personality, a fact in turn reflected in political behavior.[45]

The case of Robert Barnwell Rhett has been cited in previous historical writing as an example of the force of social and economic changes on the development of political ideas.[46] The Carolina Low Country from which the Smith/Rhett family came had undergone steady economic decline since the first decade of the nineteenth century, a decline which profoundly altered the lifestyle of Rhett's own family. His revolutionary call for a return to the kind of political structure, society, and economy characteristic of the eighteenth century probably reflected a desire to gain the cultural and social security he had learned of as a young man. Although in the context of the modern world which he hated Rhett's ideals hardly seemed rational, given his frame of reference they were logical, perhaps even attainable. There may, however, also have been irrational elements in Rhett's response to social and economic change. A possible manifestation of the unstructured aspect of his desire for change is the violence of his rhetoric and some of the flamboyance of his character. In any case, however distasteful Rhett's "reform" goals might appear to the twentieth-century reader, it must be admitted that he was as successful an agitator as any northern abolitionist. If the parallel strikes an offensive note to those readers who would discriminate between being an agitator for freedom and an agitator for slavery, it is perhaps a usefully grating comparison because it serves as a reminder that the behavior of both northern and southern political extremists should be at least partially understood in the light of the social and economic changes which shaped their actions.[47]

A northern parallel to the career of Rhett is provided by the case of Joshua Giddings. In the first place, there is for Giddings, as for Rhett, historical literature suggesting social and economic stress as a cause of his behavior, pointing to the Panic of 1837 as one cause of his antislavery zeal.[48] It is difficult to deny that the economic catastrophe had an effect on the course of Giddings' life. Even his son-in-law and biographer, George W. Julian (also a congressman and Republican Radical), testified to the impact of the Panic: "A distressing form of dyspepsia and an irregular action of the heart, which greatly troubled him in later life, made his condition wretched. . . . Hypochondria followed, and for months in succession, he kept up his fight with [against] Giant Despair."[49]

What apparently brought Giddings out of his "Giant Despair" was his conversion to the radical antislavery position and his increasing activities in that field. It is possible to postulate from this, as many have done, that the radicalism of his moral stance was a result of economic insecurity; but in fact, the whole of Giddings' work suggests that the relationship between his perception of economic and social change was much more complex, and in most respects, it was quite rational. That his New England conscience was jolted into action by the panic may have been the case, but it also is equally true that Giddings perceived the economic changes occurring around him as a part of a major world revolution, affecting especially the United States. He saw that revolution as full of potential for the human experience, not as threatening, despite his own personally unpleasant experience. For Giddings, physical and moral progress were linked in the great changes that were underway; if he perceived that the Panic was part of that change, he probably also justified it as a sign of movement or as a sign that the older ways were coming apart.

He was not, in any case, unaware that economic changes were related to the reform he advocated. For example, in this speech on New Mexico in 1850, he explicitly connected moral and industrial progress:

This progress in morals and in political intelligence, is in strict accordance with the law of our being, and cannot be prevented. The idea of setting bounds to the human intellect, or circumscribing it by statute law, is preposterous. Why not limit the arts and sciences by conservative legislation, as well as moral and political progress? . . . if we are to have conservative legislation, let us tear down the telegraphic wires, break up our galvanic batteries, and imprison Morse, and stop all agitation upon the subject of your "magnetic railroad of thought." Lay up your steamboats, place fetters upon your locomotives, convert your railroads into cultivated fields, and erase the name of Fulton from our history.[50]

Rather than attacking the economic system that had caused him distress, Giddings was pointing out to his opponents (who admired the economy) that the changes were irrevocable and progressive, just as were the moral changes he was trying to bring about. Rather than indicating an irrational attack on the scapegoat cause of his economic distress, Giddings' attitudes toward economic progress suggest that he perceived all of these changes as an opportunity through which he could exert his influence in bringing about the kind of environment he would prefer to have surround him.

Giddings' great indignation when he thought the Republican party in 1860 had lost sight of the moral goals for which in his mind it was founded also suggests that his motivation for antislavery activity was positive, not directed by a desire to hold the South responsible for his problems. There was nothing economically unsatisfactory about the Republican platform of 1860; nor did it fail to take a strong position on facing down southern extremism. What it did not originally include was the 1856 platform's positive statement in support of the principles of the Declaration of Independence; for this Giddings left the convention in anger and returned only when agreement was made to include his creed of faith.[51] Giddings, like Rhett, was an agitator, and both agitated in behalf of a way of life, a broad vision of what the society should be. In each case the impetus to action came partially from changes in the economic and social environment which suggested to them the possibility of shaping things to their desires. To a man imbued with concepts of community responsibility and leadership, what could be more likely than that he undertake to make a changing situation conform to his vision?

Levin, Rhett, and Giddings are cited as examples of mavericks to whom particular social and economic changes had special significance. Other such changes might have had impact without being either especially personal or unpleasant. Some urban areas of the United States were undergoing particularly rapid changes in the first half of the nineteenth century, and from these areas came a number of outstanding mavericks. Boston and its environs contributed Adams, Cushing, Fowler, and several lesser figures. New York City was the home of Henry Murphy and a number of other Democratic mavericks. Philadelphia was the home city of Levin and C. J. Ingersoll. New York and Pennsylvania were the two states outside of New England most directly affected by new trends in urbanization, industrialization, and immigration and provided a large number of mavericks. In the South a large proportion of the more outspoken mavericks came either from the cities—Kennedy and Davis from Baltimore, Botts from Richmond—or the more changing or northern-oriented areas of the upper South—Wise originally from the eastern shore of Virginia, Underwood from Kentucky, and Stanton from east Tennessee. In all of these places the revolutionary changes of the nineteenth century were taking place with a greater degree of visibility than in the hinterlands. To thoughtful and reflective men who were concerned with directing their destiny and that of the nation, these changes were especially evident.

It has been noted above that mavericks were remarkably sensitive to change. It should be further noted that mavericks were not only aware of change in the general cultural and economic sense but that they seemed to perceive its significance for them personally. They believed that the United States was beginning to become a mass society, not a country of neighbors, and the maverick plea for independence was an attempt to prevent that. They did not, for the most part, want to stop the clock; some southern mavericks saw industry as threatening, some nativists wanted to stop immigration, perhaps more of the mavericks worried about the influence of the cities, but undoubtedly the things which worried them most were not the economic and social changes but their cultural consequences. What they feared was the loss of the identity of moral, upstanding, independent men like themselves. In the words of Francis W. Pickens:

The tendency of all modern society is to aggregation, where the individual man is lost and absorbed amid the masses. . . . The question is no longer, are you right? but are you with the tide that flows on to power? The utilitarian doctrines of Franklin, expounded and enlarged by Jeremy Bentham, have the greatest good of the greatest number the supreme law of communities. Nothing is thought of but what is physically useful. Man is but a cog in the wheel and machinery of society. The heart is treated as a mere function of the body. . . . Under this system, imagination withers and all sentiment perishes and dies away.[52]

Pickens' speech, delivered in South Carolina in 1855, illustrates as well as any other a final influence, the impact of ideas upon the making of congressional mavericks. The mechanistic system of Bentham was an end product of eighteenth-century optimism about progressive social change under nature's automatic operation. Pickens' attitude to this mechanism reflects the anxieties about the future shared by nineteenth-century romantics and conservative liberals like Tocqueville. It does not have to be demonstrated that Pickens borrowed his ideas and metaphors, which is possible, to make the point that his reaction was that of a man aware of the spirit of the age.

Not all mavericks read widely in western philosophy and literature as Pickens may have. Some were more familiar with the ideas and philosophy of science; many were fascinated by popular speculative writings about the future of applied science and technology. Mavericks entered the world of nineteenth-century thought through different paths, but regardless of their particular interests most intellectually appreciated the interrelatedness of the cultural changes of their day. Maverick congressmen thus stand clearly as illustration of the impact of ideas upon historical development.

Mavericks have hitherto spoken about their ideas for themselves in this study; and perhaps their own words, profuse as they are, can constitute sufficient evidence of the diverse intellectual debts they owed to contemporary thinkers. Reading the speeches of maverick congressmen is an intellectual adventure not because of their aesthetic or philosophical significance but because they constantly jolt the reader with phrases so similar to more familiar ones that resisting the temptation to search for their sources is difficult. As with the passage cited from Pickens' speech, however, the significance lies not in the specific sources from which the mavericks may have borrowed but in their integrated use of familiar phrases and ideas. Speeches for mavericks were not strung-together plagiarisms but consistently structured expressions of their own basic ideas; and their ideas and behavior were closely matched. Ideas for mavericks became part of their independent integrity, the wholeness of the concept of themselves they expressed for the contemporary public and for posterity.

The dynamic combination of influences which seems to have produced the maverick political character was, in some senses, a fortunate one. Republican leadership concepts were becoming anachronistic by the 1830s; had they not possessed private determination to become leaders, mavericks might have abandoned public life in utter disillusionment with mass-based, democratic politics. Alternatively, maverick ambition without republican principles and intellectual acuity could have produced maverick demagogues. While it is true that some opponents characterized mavericks this way, scholarly biographers have generally found real conviction at the heart of maverick disregard for public opinion; this study supports that conclusion. Mavericks acted independently because they believed that they were more capable of acting in the interest of the people than the masses themselves. Their mistakes were not made in pursuit of narrow self-interest because they defined political success in terms of public welfare as well as personal accomplishment. Their equating of community needs with their own best judgment of those needs was not an emotional predilection or an *ex post facto* rationale for unpopular behavior. It instead rested on their basic belief that, as men who possessed wisdom and virtue, they should exercise leadership independently. This did not prevent colossal error in judgment, but it did usually preclude demagoguery.

Mavericks were involved at the intersection of ideas and action—less intellectual than the intellectuals and less political than other politicians, they moved in both the realm of ideas and politics; and the former gave force to the latter. It is not necessary to admire the goals of mavericks to recognize the effectiveness with which they acted as advocates. Adams, Giddings, Rhett, Wise, Stephens, Toombs, Wilmot, Cushing, Davis, Bingham, and the others were not passive actors in the drama that preceded the Civil War. They were in the thick of the fighting; and if their behavior had consequences which pushed the nation closer to war, it was not because they were unreflective or unaware of the dangers but because their ideas and attachments were so much shaped by the sectional differences of that day that they were a miniature of the national struggles. To take the sectional extremes, Rhett and Giddings are excellent illustrations of the power of ideas strongly held; while both envisioned a grand future, both surely influenced the course of the nation toward violence, not pacific solutions of differences. This was not because they were violent men but because their thorough commitment to two completely incompatible goals did not permit a compromise, especially given the maverick mentality.

Mavericks set for themselves extraordinarily high standards of leadership; did they meet their own expectations? Obviously the answer to this question would vary with the particular maverick, as their individual goals were different, but for the majority of mavericks the answer was probably framed in the negative. Of the mavericks, only a few were so devoted to their sectional interests that they actively agitated for sectional ascendancy. Most mavericks saw their success within the terms of the American national experience. If the democratic experiment was what had provided the opportunity for them to become leaders, it was likewise an important basis for their success. The disruption of the Union, except for the most chauvinistic mavericks—Pickens, Rhett, Toombs for the South; Giddings, Bingham, perhaps Wilmot for the North—was an indication of their failure. Its evident coming caused some to retire from politics; its actual occurrence was for many the central tragedy of their lives.

The success of the radical minority of mavericks was then the failure of the moderates—those mavericks who by voting behavior and temperament were in the center of the political divisions of the antebellum period. How was it that the center mavericks failed in their attempt to bring about peaceful solutions to the sectional differences? Their failure rests on a number of related foundations. An obvious answer is that the center mavericks were a tiny minority of the congressmen and politicians in the country, and most of them were from urban areas and border states rather than the several heartlands of the country.

Mavericks, moreover, were victims of their own determination to be leaders of the people who had elected them to Congress. Sectional differences were so exacerbated that leadership toward the national common ground could be provided only by men who were emotionally, intellectually, and politically committed to that common ground. The mavericks might have the latter two requirements, but emotionally they apparently were deeply committed to their homes rather than to the national community. The few border-state mavericks who chose to go with the tide outside of their section were rare. However much they tried to stay that tide, most chose ultimately to stand with their people. Mavericks in the middle were caught in a trap they had made: committed wholly to the concept of community leadership in the broadest sense, they had to keep the community, as they defined it, or lose faith in their self-concept. As in their voting behavior pattern, mavericks would in those circumstances choose a political deviation and remain loyal to the force of their own personal ambitions. It was in both cases far easier for them to shift political alignments, which were for them secondary commitments, than to admit failure to their own concepts of themselves as leaders of their people.

The failure of the moderate mavericks was not wholly a personal one. The foregoing analysis of the behavior and ideas of congressional mavericks between 1836 and 1860 suggests that some structural weaknesses in the political system of those years were also relevant. The flux of society that has since become a distinguishing feature of life in the United States was accelerating in the antebellum period, but the political structure was imperfectly adjusted. In part, the Civil War was a result of that lag. The second two-party system was disrupted, and its replacement system had yet to be refined. Whatever lines of alliance based on the new realities might have emerged have been obscured by the bitter sectional conflict.

The relative instability of parties in the late antebellum period may have lent to maverick activities of a kind of significance they would not have had in an older party system. Disagreements with party positions by men of unusual commitment and intellect can be a vital source of political progress; at the very least, intraparty debate over important issues is a sign of healthy openness in the democratic process. In the late antebellum period, unfortunately, party insecurity, compounded by sectional antagonism, seems to have engendered attempts to stifle dissent, transforming what might have been constructive discussion into impassioned argument. Rather than absorbing the criticism of mavericks, conformist party leaders reacted defensively and often isolated their nonconforming colleagues, inhibiting their effectiveness.

A similar influence upon the significance of mavericks within the Congress was caused by the lack of consistent institutional structure in the House. A large body of diverse individuals representing widely differing constituencies, the House was inadequately organized for efficient action. The selection of committees and committee chairmen was not regularized, despite the legislative importance of the committee system. Mavericks with longer tenure than the average congressmen and with personal qualities which were traditionally associated with leadership often were chosen for positions of power they were unsuited to hold. Where intellect and broad education were important and efficiency relatively unimportant, mavericks may have been constructive on the floor of the House. But where speed and order were more important than philosophical considerations, as in the framing of minor money bills and dozens of lesser items, maverick leadership impeded progress. Their insistence upon full discussion may have aired their important ideas, but it worked counter to the committee system, where most framing of bills occurred. Sometimes their personal aggressiveness and disregard for relevant issues in floor debate was purely disruptive. Despite the importance of some mavericks' ideas, they were largely rendered ineffective by the way in which their indifference or outright hostility to emerging patterns of congressional organization caused those ideas to be received.

The political structure of the United States militated against mavericks who might have worked for compromise and cooperation because it did not allow for the free play of ideas. Mavericks fought to make their ideas effective, but since the direction of their efforts ran against the grain of developing institutional forms, their attempts too often backfired. The pragmatic, ad hoc nature of the congressional government of the time was totally unequipped to frame solutions for nonpolitical problems which had political contingencies. Those men who did have the intellect and vision to see political questions in their broadest light were often cast in the role of spoilers by the institutional currents which produced the conformist leadership. The mavericks were a minority; the majority of congressmen gave no indication of the fact that their cultural antennae were functioning in any except the most limited sense. They rallied to slogans—to ideology dramatically presented—but not to the complexity of ideas at work in the society in which they lived. The ideas of some radical mavericks were indeed successful—successfully destructive of the political environment with which they were incompatible. The effective functioning of complex ideas within the political environment was notably absent in the years before the War, and this may partially account for the failure of Congress to steer clear of active belligerence.[53]

Some of these weaknesses may be inherent features of the constitutional system in America; it is true that political mavericks have been familiar figures throughout the nineteenth and twentieth centuries. Some of the contributing influences which shaped maverick behavior between 1836 and 1860 have been significant for other periods. In a society which is perpetually changing, as long as substantial segments of the American population retain commitment to social and cultural stability, mavericks who try to mold the flux of their ideas will exist. The antebellum mavericks were, however, products of the transformation of the old agrarian republic. Without the background of relatively stable political traditions dating from the colonial period their maverick posture might have been much more a function of general factors such as family environment and social strain and possibly they would have lacked the intellectual depth which marked many mavericks' ideas.

Mavericks represented the continuation in antebellum politics of a tradition older than the political institutions of the Republic. For them politics was a vocation—a calling—not a job to be carried lightly and shed at will. Whether this led mavericks to what their fellows might characterize as excessive zeal and intransigence or to political vacillations equally annoying to their colleagues, it also earned for them respect from their constituents for their personal consistency, a consistency of character, not of political position. They also embodied the principles of self-reliance issued to Americans from Emerson's Concord study: "Who so would be a man must be a nonconformist."[54] At once they reflected the persistence of American tradition and the determination to create a better society, both concerns of the nation at large. In their incessant attempts to define and assert their own characters, congressional mavericks mirror the constant hopes of Americans since their time that the material benefits produced by a society based on mass institutions will be accompanied by ample opportunity for individuals to achieve their differing private aspirations.

NOTES

1. This is not meant to imply that mavericks did not continue to develop their political styles; however, for reasons to be discussed, mavericks were perhaps less responsive to further socialization than conformists. Theoretical perspective on adult development is found in Orville G. Brim, "Adult Socialization," in John A. Clausen, ed., *Socialization and Society* (Boston: Little, Brown & Co., 1968); and Merton, *Social Theory and Social Structure*. Personal character and the political environment are treated in Greenstein,

Personality and Politics; and in Putnam, *The Beliefs of Politicians*. A useful summary of the literature on the subject of the relationship between environmental sanctions and conforming behavior is Charles A. Kiesler and Sara B. Kiesler, *Conformity* (New York: Addison-Wesley, 1969).

2. Although the discussion which follows focuses primarily upon two conflicting cultural traditions which seem to have been especially important to mavericks, this should not be interpreted as a statement that mavericks were exposed to two dichotomous cultural patterns and to no others. The historical pluralism of American society and culture was perhaps more noticeably diverse in mid-nineteenth century American than at any previous time. A warning against the dangers of a simplistic categorization of the change to "modern" society is sounded in Formisano's "Toward a Reorientation of Jacksonian Politics," pp. 51–53, 65. See also Brown, *Modernization*; and the excellent critique of his interpretation in James A. Henretta, "Modernization: Toward a False Synthesis," *Reviews in American History* 5 (December 1977):445–452. The fact of pluralism in nineteenth-century society is not inconsistent, however, with the perceptions of dualism found throughout the literature and popular writings of that period.

3. *Democracy in America*, vol. I, Ch. XV, XVI. Lawrence J. Friedman in *Inventors of the Promised Land* has thoughtfully criticized Tocqueville's concept in light of the findings of social historians about Jacksonian society; see Appendix A, "A Note on Tocqueville's 'Tyranny of the Majority.' "

4. Thoreau, "Civil Disobedience," in *Walden and Other Writings*, p. 645.

5. Legislative decision-making processes have been thoroughly studied by political scientists; and although there is a great deal of disagreement about the relative effects of pressures upon congressmen from constituents, party, and other sources, it is generally agreed that personal standards carry some weight. That some congressmen rely more heavily upon personal standards as a consequence of influential earlier experiences is argued effectively in Putnam, *The Beliefs of Politicians*; and in Huitt, "The Outsider in the Senate: An Alternative Role." The pattern is treated in the context of a review of different theories in Greenstein, *Personality and Politics*.

6. Letters of John Fairfield to his wife, Dec. 17. 1835, and Feb. 21, 1836, in *The Letters of John Fairfield*, ed. with an introduction by Arthur G. Staples (Lewiston, Maine: Lewiston Journal Co., 1922), pp. 34, 110.

7. See, for example, Herbert B. Asher, "Learning of Legislative Norms," *American Political Science Review* 67 (June 1973):499–513. Donald Gross, in "Representative Styles and Legislative Behavior," *Western Political Quarterly* 31 (Sept. 1978):359–371, warns against generalizations which relate differences in style (trustee, delegate, politico) with responses to legislative norms. The concept of norm integration has been applied to the nineteenth–century Senate by political scientist Dean Yarwood, "Norm Observation and Legislative Integration: The U. S. Senate in 1850 and 1860," *Social Science Quarterly* 51 (June 1970):57–69.

8. David Riesman, with Nathan Glazer and Reuel Denney, *The Lonely Crowd, a Study of the Changing American Character* (New Haven: Yale University Press, 1950), should be balanced by Seymour Martin Lipset and Leo Lowenthal, *Culture and Social Character: The Work of David Riesman* (Glencoe, Ill.: The Free Press, 1961); for Brown, see this chapter, n. 2. An excellent summary of problems associated with the treatment of the relationship between personality and historical change is Philip Gleason, "Identifying Identity: A Semantic History," *Journal of American History* 69 (Mar. 1983):910–931.

9. The explanation offered here is in no way an attempt to construct a covering law which under any similar circumstances would account for mavericks' behavior. Lack of consensus among psychologists about how human behavior is shaped and lack of historical information about mavericks and conformists are the two most important handicaps to any attempt at formulation of a law for the causes of maverick behavior, but these are by no means the only obstacles. Thoughtful discussions about the difficulty of applying covering law theories are found in Murray Murphey, *Understanding our Historical Past* (Indianapolis and New York: Bobbs Merrill, 1973), esp. Ch. III, "Historical Explanations"; and in Robert Berkhofer, Jr., *A Behavioral Approach to Historical Analysis* (New York: The Free Press of Macmillan, 1969), esp. Ch. 12, "The Role of Explanation in Historical Syntheses."

Reliance upon the description of mavericks about themselves gives to their self-analyses a credence some historians would question. Quentin Skinner, in "Some Problems in the Analysis of Political Thought and Action," has developed the argument that the rhetoric of the "innovating ideologist" does in fact help to explain his behavior; in his words, "any principle which helps to legitimate a course of action must also be amongst the enabling conditions of its occurrence." (p. 299) Mavericks did not completely explain their behavior, but their explanations are useful in a descriptive, if not an analytical, sense. Moreover, it does not seem likely that mavericks and conformists were equally influenced by circumstances to which mavericks attended frequently but to which conformists hardly attended at all. To take this position, however, is clearly to make assumptions about the rationality of both mavericks and conformists for which no proof will be attempted.

10. Thomas Jefferson to John Adams, October 28, 1813, in Gerald N. Grob and Robert N. Beck, eds., *Foundations (1629–1865)*, vol. I of *American Ideas: Source Readings in the Intellectual History of the United States* (New York: The Free Press, 1963), p. 201.

11. That Adams would become a maverick politician was not determined by his past but the influences towards entering politics were great, and the influences toward maverick behavior virtually determinant. Although perhaps the case of Adams is so unusually clear as to make it overdrawn, it is probably the most readily understandable example of the pattern of early childhood political influence.

12. See Smith, *The Blair Family.*

13. The phrase is from Kammen, *People of Paradox.*

14. Fuess, *Life of Cushing.*

15. *BDAC*, pp. 1104–1105.

16. Garnett, *Biographical Sketch of Garnett.*

17. David Donald comments on this aspect of Rhett's political theory in "Proslavery Argument."

18. Laura White, *Robert Barnwell Rhett*, p. 34, in a footnote cites an 1861 publication concerning the name changing and asserts that Barnwell was indifferent to the notion— the initiation of the project coming from his brothers. In light of his political ambitions and her own admission that Rhett was sensitive to questioning of his past, his indifference seems unlikely.

19. Davis describes his background, with particular attention to his father, in the Steiner biography, *Life of Davis*; see also Henig, *Henry Winter Davis*, pp. 17–19.

20. Steiner, *Life of Davis*, p. 41; Henig, *Henry Winter Davis*, pp. 17–18.

21. See Stewart, *Joshua R. Giddings*, pp. 4–5. Although Giddings' Puritan ancestry

"impressed him not at all" (p. 4), the influence of Puritan ideas and practices upon his political ideas was important throughout his career.

22. Fehrenbacher, *Chicago Giant*, p. 4.

23. Going, *David Wilmot*, pp. 1–2.

24. As political scientists have observed, children learn attitudes about themselves and their relations with others which fundamentally condition their political attitudes. Generally speaking, these youthful experiences are not overtly political at all, although it is possible that the political sensitivity within American families was especially high in the early years of the Republic. For the impact of politics on family life, see Linda Kerber, "The Republican Mother: Women and the Enlightenment—An American Perspective," *American Quarterly* 28 (Summer 1976):187–205. Jean Baker in *Affairs of Party* stresses childhood experiences in shaping partisan attachment but suggests no common pattern of influence for political activists. (Ch. 1, "Partisan Roots"). Useful introductions to the political science theory relating childhood and adult political experiences are Stanley Allen Renshond, ed., *Handbook of Political Socialization* (New York: The Free Press of Macmillan Co., 1977); and David Easton and Jack Dennis, *Children in the Political System: Origins of Political Legitimacy* (New York: McGraw-Hill Book Company, 1969).

25. There is a rapidly growing body of historical literature which treats the influence of childhood experiences upon adult public behavior; for the antebellum period, the best literature deals with abolitionists. Especially suggestive are Silvan S. Tomkins, "The Psychology of Commitment: The Constructive Role of Violence and Suffering for the Individual and His Society," in Duberman, *Antislavery Vanguard*, pp. 270–298; and several essays in *Antislavery Reconsidered*, the fine collection edited by Lewis Perry and Michael Fellman. More extended recent explorations of the psychology of abolitionism include Lawrence J. Friedman, *Gregarious Saints: Self and Society in American Abolitionism, 1830–1870* (Cambridge: Cambridge University Press, 1982); and Robert H. Abzug, *Passionate Liberator: Theodore Dwight Weld and The Dilemma of Reform* (New York: Oxford University Press, 1980). The works of Erik H. Erikson, especially his well-known *Childhood and Society* (New York: W. W. Norton, 1950), as well as the reflections collected in *Life History and the Historical Moment* (New York: W. W. Norton, 1975), and his biographies of Ghandi and Luther have influenced many recent explanations, though the psychoanalytical approach has been applied more successfully to individual psychobiography than to collective studies. An excellent essay review of recent efforts to apply psychological insights to abolitionist history is Richard O. Curry and Lawrence B. Goodheart, " 'Knives in Their Heads': Passionate Self-Analysis and the Search for Identity in American Abolitionism," *Canadian Review of American Studies* 14 (Winter 1983):401–414.

26. Simms, *Life of Robert M. T. Hunter*, p. 7.

27. Martha Hunter, *A Memoir of Robert M. T. Hunter* (Washington, D. C.: Neale Pub. Co., 1903), pp. 81, 83.

28. The best factual approach to Stephens' childhood is in Johnston and Browne, *Life of Alexander H. Stephens.*

29. A biography of Stephens by Rudolph von Abele gives a Freudian interpretation to the life of Stephens and makes the figure of his father the single dominant factor in the life of the politician son. Though the interpretation does stretch the imagination, it fits the facts rather neatly. See Rudolph von Abele, *Alexander H. Stephens* (New York: Alfred A. Knopf, 1946).

30. Stewart, *Joshua Reed Giddings*, p. 11.

31. Ibid.

32. Ibid., p. 150.

33. Joshua Giddings, *History of the Rebellion: Its Authors and Causes* (New York: Follett, Foster & Co., 1864), p. 280.

34. Ibid.

35. Bohner, *John Pendleton Kennedy*, p. 18.

36. See Steiner, *Life of Davis*, Chs. I–III, pp. 7–63.

37. White, *Robert Barnwell Rhett*, p. 4.

38. Wise, *Life of Henry Wise*, pp. 8–13.

39. See Curran, "David Kellogg Cartter," pp. 105–115.

40. It is possible that a new environment could be so hostile as to destroy any tendencies towards independence. But, to repeat, this argument is not meant to suggest that if one added up the influences described here, a maverick would be the result no matter what else the environment offered. The factor of a new and challenging environment does seem to have been important to these mavericks, whatever it might have done to a different sort of person.

41. The literature on the subject of social and cultural strains and their consequences is voluminous. An article which summarizes several different points of view, is William R. Hutchinson, "Cultural Strain and Protestant Liberalism," *American Historical Review* 76 (April 1971):386–411.

42. *BDAC*, p. 1214.

43. See quoted passages in "The Maverick Ego" (Ch. 10).

44. See Billington, *Protestant Crusade*, pp. 208, 217, 233, 431.

45. Ibid., p. 233. An interesting note which may have significance is that ten years after his death Levin's wife became converted to Catholicism, and his son also later became a convert. If his wife's attitude toward Catholicism were sympathetic during Levin's lifetime it may partially explain the emotional nature of his speeches.

46. See Donald, "Proslavery Argument." This should be balanced by Lee Benson's stinging critique of Donald's thesis, "Explanations of American Civil War Causation: A Critical Assessment and a Modest Proposal to Reorient and Reorganize the Social Sciences," in *Toward the Scientific Study of History: Selected Essays* (Philadelphia and New York: J. B. Lippincott Co., 1972), pp. 271–287.

47. See Donald, "Proslavery Argument."

48. Thompson, in the introduction to *The Exiles of Florida*, noted the prominence of this line of approach to Giddings' career (p. xv).

49. Julian, *Life of Giddings*, p. 35.

50. Giddings, *Speeches in Congress*, pp. 410–411.

51. Julian, *Life of Giddings*, pp. 350–352.

52. Pickens, "Influence on Government," p. 21.

53. Cf. Holt, *The Political Crisis of the 1850s*; and Brock, *Parties and Political Conscience*. Despite efforts of some radical Republicans, the resumption of politics as usual after the Civil War perhaps accounts for some of the intellectual disillusionment with politics in the Gilded Age. This disillusionment is nowhere more clearly expressed than in Henry Adams, *Education*, see esp. pp. 280–283.

54. Emerson, "Self-Reliance," *Selected Writings*, p. 148.

APPENDIXES

APPENDIX I

Method of Selecting Mavericks and Conformists

Mavericks and conformists were selected on the basis of their voting records as reflected in the scale analysis for *Sectional Stress and Party Strength*. For a full description of the cumulative scaling techniques applied in that work, the reader should consult Alexander's introduction.[1] Some features of that analysis having direct relevance to the selection of mavericks and conformists are summarized here.

Sectional Stress and Party Strength analyzes roll-call votes from the regular, or long, sessions of the 24th through the 36th Congresses, though data from two special sessions were also included. For each Congress, between 60 and 120 roll calls were selected for analysis from those relating to the important business of each session. Routine procedural roll calls and repetitive roll calls involved in the passage of a single measure were omitted. Once selected, the roll calls were described and analyzed using several techniques; for the present study, the results of the cumulative scale analysis were primary.[2]

Scale analysis provides historians with two important kinds of information about a legislative body. First, by means of a statistical test that determines scalability, associations among roll calls are revealed. These associations may be evident to the investigator, and they may have been obvious to the members who voted; but, regardless of those possibilities, the roll-call responses themselves have a logical and mathematical relationship that points to their scalability. Roll calls are scalable only when almost all legislators indicated (by their votes) that there was a progression among the meaures from those positions many congressmen found easy to support to those few were willing to support. Hypothetically, for example, most congressmen might vote for military funding to protect American troops already involved in combat, but many might be unwilling to vote additional monies to expand a war's scope. Once scalability has been determined, clusters of similarly supported measures may be ranked together and assigned a collective position number or name (for example, 0–10, or dove-moderate-hawk).

The second result of cumulative scale analysis that is useful to historians focuses upon members rather than their votes. Once scale positions have been developed for votes or for clusters of similar votes, the ranking of almost every member of the legislature in regard to those positions can be readily ascertained. So, to return to the hypothetical example, if one is interested in regional patterns, it may be found that ten midwestern congressmen are doves and only five are hawks. Or it can easily be noted that Congressman Jones was a dove and Congressman Smith, a hawk, if one is concerned about individuals. The results of scale analysis are often presented in table form describing the distribution of congressmen along a spectrum of opinion (as registered in votes) about the issues involved in a scalable set. Investigators employ different statistical methods to achieve these two results; a detailed description of Alexander's methods is provided in *Sectional Stress and Party Strength*.

The scale tables or scalograms in *Sectional Stress and Party Strength* describe patterns of voting for economic and sectional issues in every Congress from 1836 to 1860. For some Congresses there are other kinds of issues analyzed—partisan issues (for example, the choice of a public printer) being the most frequently included. The scale tables rank members in positions described by party and region. The regional subdivisions of the United States employed in Alexander's study were New England, Middle Atlantic, Northern Northwest, Southern Northwest, South Central, and South Atlantic states.[3] Appendix II provides identification for each maverick congressman with reference to the party and regional labels used in *Sectional Stress and Party Strength*.

The first step in borrowing quantitative data from Alexander's study consisted of examining the scale tables in his book to decide what constituted conformity within each region and party delegation. To clarify this process, an example of one table—the "Economic Scalogram" for the Twenty-Fourth Congress—is reproduced in Table 7.[4] In this scale table, Scale Position 0, containing one Democratic congressman from the South-Central region, represents a position of refusal to support any of the economic measures in the scalable set. Position 8, where two Democrats and six Whigs are located, is the position of those members who were willing to support all measures in the set. To identify conformists, the scale position containing the median member for each party and regional delegation was determined. In Table 7, the median Democrat is in Scale Position 4 and the median Whig is in Scale Position 6. In many instances, though not in this example, over half of a party's regional membership was grouped in the same position as the median member; members in that position were labeled conformists. When less than 50 percent of the members of a delegation were in the position of the median, as is the case here, the positions adjacent to that occupied by the median member were included in defining conformists on that scale. Thus, in Table 7, since Position 4 does not contain 50 percent of all South-Central Democrats, the adjacent Positions (3 and 5) were included in defining conformity; since Scale Position 6 does not contain 50 percent of all South-Central Whigs, Scale Position 5 with seven additional Whigs was also counted as defining conformity. By defining conformists as those members of a party/sectional grouping who voted with at least half of the other members of their party/section, the label reflected the dominant voting pattern for any area and party. For this scale, ten of the total fourteen South-Central Democrats and twelve of the total twenty South–Central Whigs were voting closely together by party and were counted as conformists. This kind of analysis was performed on every scale table in *Sectional Stress and Party Strength*. To insure that conformists were actually consistent in their voting patterns, no congressman was counted a conformist if he occupied a scale position that was *not* in or adjacent to the median member's position on any scalogram. No conformist, therefore, ever deviated significantly from the dominant voting pattern for his region and party as reflected in these tables.

A congressman was labeled a maverick on any scalogram if he were scaled two positions away from the median for his party/sectional delegation. On Table 7, therefore, among South-Central Democrats, congressmen in Scale Positions 0, 1, and 8 are mavericks. For

Table 7
An Example of Scale Positions Containing Mavericks and Conformists, Taken from *Sectional Stress and Party Strength*

(Number of Representatives)

Scale Position		South Central D	W
0		1	
1		1	
2			
3		3	1
4	Position of Median Democrat	4	1
5		3	7
6			5 Position of Median Whig
7			
8		2	6
(Total)		14	20

South-Central Whigs, congressmen in Scale Positions 3 and 8 are mavericks (the one member in Scale Position 4 was treated as ambiguous and not classified). If scale tables indicated unusual patterns of regional and party distribution—for example, if all congressmen were ranged evenly over seven positions—the scale, or the unusual portion of it, was not used in determining either mavericks or conformists. In cases of doubt, the scale-set data and subject descriptions for roll calls were analyzed for such matters as percent difference between scale positions and subject matter significance. To assure that mavericks were properly identified as such, a congressman was included in the set selected for the present study only if he appeared as a maverick on at least two scalograms in *Sectional Stress and Party Strength*. All mavericks and conformists served in at least two Congresses.

Historians and political scientists differ about many points of judgment involved in cumulative scale analysis. No two scholars would agree precisely about such matters as the selection of roll calls, the definitions of regions and party memberships, the standards for determining scalability, or the extent to which a member's deviance should be called significant. In selecting mavericks and conformists, defining characteristics were set at such levels that the possibilities of including "flukey" mavericks were reduced. It should be clear, however, that enough judgmental decisions were involved that the term mavericks—based on voting behavior alone—is merely descriptive of a particular voting pattern in a single quantitative study. The validity of the categorizations could be tested by the application of other methods of analysis. The qualitative findings of the present study do suggest, nonetheless, that the original categories were soundly conceived.

The process of selecting mavericks and conformists from scalograms in *Sectional Stress and Party Strength* produced a group of over a thousand congressmen belonging to one or the other category and serving in more than two Congresses. The size of the group to be studied was further reduced by eliminating those for whom no published works were available at the Library of Congress. The search for published material on which to base the qualitative assessments for *The Line of Duty* was limited to the Library of Congress for practical reasons that should be obvious. For similar reasons, unpublished sources were excluded. A limited number of manuscript collections (about two dozen) were scanned to ascertain if the conclusions made on the basis of published sources would be seriously contradicted by material in manuscript collections. While that was not found to be the case, it is true that some of the speculative conclusions offered in Chapter 11 could be more fully explored with the use of the manuscript collections available for 255 men throughout the country. That effort, however, is beyond the scope of the present work.

NOTES

1. Alexander, *Sectional Stress and Party Strength*, pp. 3–8.

2. A simple guide to some familiar roll-call analyses is Lee F. Anderson, Meredith W. Watts, Jr., and Allen R. Wilcox, *Legislative Roll-Call Analysis* (Evanston, Ill.: Northwestern University Press, 1966). A very sophisticated methodological appraisal is Duncan MacRae, Jr., *Issues and Parties in Legislative Voting: Methods of Statistical Analysis* (New York: Harper and Row, 1970).

3. See maps for each region in Alexander, *Sectional Stress and Party Strength*, p. 5. Alexander's scale tables also reflect an additional border South/lower South analysis not used in identifying mavericks and conformists.

4. Table 24–1, "Economic Scalogram," Ibid., p. 10.

APPENDIX II

Scale Positions for Mavericks

The information which follows can lead the reader to the correct scale table in *Sectional Stress and Party Strength*. Regions are the same as those used in Alexander's study, abbreviated here for convenience (NE = New England, MA = Middle Atlantic, NNW = Northern Northwest, SNW = Southern Northwest, SC = South Central, SA = South Atlantic). Scale table numbers correspond to the numbers given in his List of Tables (pp. xi–xiv); Table 24-1 designated the first table presented for the Twenty-Fourth Congress, and so forth. The last two columns provide information that can identify precisely where on a table the member is located, using the terms that define mavericks as described in Appendix I. Thus, for example, Nathaniel Borden, the first of the northern Democratic Mavericks in Appendix II, is located in Scale Position 5 on Table 24-1; the median member for all New England Democrats is located in Scale Position 2.

Representatives who made "errors" on any scale set were classified as non-scale types (see Appendix II, *Sectional Stress and Party Strength*, p. 279). "For a group of roll calls to form a satisfactory scalable set, it is necessary that for every possible pair of roll calls in the set, few if any members commit the 'error' of supporting a hard but rejecting an easier proposition." (*ibid.*, p. 7) These non-scale types were the few who made such "errors" on otherwise satisfactory scale sets.

Congressman and Congresses Served In	Region	Party	Scale Table	Member Position	Median for Region-Party
Northern Democrats					
Borden, Nathaniel B. (24, 25, D; 27, W; 1835-39, 1841-43)	NE	D	24-1	5	2
		D	24-2	4	2
		D	25-1	4	2
		D	25-2	4	1
		D	25-3	3	1
Brodhead, Richard (28, 29, 30; 1843-49)	MA	D	30-1	0	2/3
		D	30-3	1	3
Brown, Charles (27, 30; 1841-43, 1847-49)	MA	D	30-1	1	2/3
		D	30-3	2	3
Burke, Edmund (26, 27, 28; 1839-45)	NE	D	28-1	2	4
		D	28-2	1	5
Cartter, David K. (31, 32; 1849-53)	NNW	D	32-1	4	1
		D	32-2	3 (land policy)	0/1
Clark, Horace F. (35, 36; 1857-61)	MA	D	35-1	6	4
		D	35-2	3	1
		D	35-3	5	3
Davis, Richard D. (27, 28; 1841-45)	MA	D	27-5	5	0
		D	27-6	2	4
		D	28-2	7	4
Disney, David T. (31, 32, 33; 1849-55)	SNW	D	31-2	7	5
		D	32-1	3	5
Doty, James D. (31, 32; 1849-53)	NNW	D	32-2	7	5
		D	32-3	Non-scale type[2]	
Duncan, Alexander (25, 26, 28; 1837-41, 1843-45)	SNW	D	25-2	3	1
		D	28-1	4	2
		D	28-2	4	2
Florence, Thomas B. (32, 33, 34, 35, 36; 1851-61)	MA	D	32-1	4	2
		D	32-2	4 (land policy)	1
		D	33-2	1	3
Fries, George (29, 30; 1845-49)	MA	D	29-1	0	3/4
		D	30-1	0	2/3

Congressman and Congresses Served In	Region	Party	Scale Table	Member Position	Median for Region-Party
Fuller, Thomas J. D. (31, 32, 33, 34; 1849-57)	NE	D D	34-1 34-2	0 4	- -
Haskin, John B. (1857-61)	MA	D D D	35-2 35-3 35-4	3 5 7	1 3 2
Hendricks, Thomas A. R. (32, 33; 1851-55)	SNW	D D	32-2 33-1	7 (land policy) 2	5 4
Henley, Thomas J. (28, 29, 30; 1843-49)	SNW	D D	28-1 28-2	0 4	2 2
Hickman, John (34, 35, 36; 1855-61)	MA	D D	34-2 35-3	6 6	4 3
Hoge, Joseph P. (28, 29; 1843-47)	NNW	D D D	28-2 29-1 29-2	1 0 0	3/4 3 2
Ingersoll, Charles J. (27, 28, 29, 30; 1841-49)	MA	D D D D	27-3 28-2 29-2 30-3	2 2 0 2	0 4 2 3
King, Preston (28, 29, 31, 32; 1843-47, 1849-53)	MA	D D D	29-1 29-2 32-2	1 4 9	3/4 2 3
McClernand, John A. (28, 29, 30, 31, 36; 1843-51, 1859-61)	SNW	D D D	28-1 29-1 29-2	0 0 0	2 3 2
McKeon, John (24, 27; 1835-37, 1841-43)	MA	D D D	24-2 27-3 27-6	0 2 1	2 0 4
Morris, Isaac N. (35, 36; 1857-61)	SNW	D D	35-1 35-4	1 4	3 2
Murphy, Henry C. (28, 30; 1843-45, 1847-49)	MA	D D D	28-1 28-2 30-3	1 2 2	5 4 3
Parmenter, William (25, 26, 27, 28; 1837-45)	NE	D D D	25-2 26-2 27-5	3 4 3	1 2 0
Pendleton, George H. (35, 36; 1857-61)	SNW	D D	35-2 36-2	0 0	2 2

Congressman and Congresses Served In	Region	Party	Scale Table	Member Position	Median for Region-Party
Scott, Charles L. (34, 35, 36; 1855-61)	SNW	D	34-1	3	5
		D	34-2	6	4
		D	35-1	1	3
		D	35-3	2	4
		D	36-1	3	1
		D	36-2	0	2
Smart, Ephraim K. (30,32; 1847-49, 1851-53)	NE	D	32-2	Non-scale type	
		D	32-3	4	2
Ward, Aaron (24, 27; 1831-37, 1841-43)	MA	D	24-1	0	2
		D	27-1	2	0
Wentworth, John (28, 29, 30, 31, 33; 1843-51, 1853-55)	NNW	D	30-2	2	0
		D	33-2	2	4
Wilmot, David (29, 30, 31; 1845-51)	MA	D	31-1	0	4/5
		D	31-2	8	5

Southern Democrats

Congressman and Congresses Served In	Region	Party	Scale Table	Member Position	Median for Region-Party
Bowie, Thomas Fielder (34, 35; 1855-59)	SA	D	34-1	6	1
		D	35-1	4	2
		D	35-3	3	1
Bowlin, James Butler (28, 29, 30, 31; 1843-51)	SC	D	29-1	3	1
		D	30-1	3	0
		D	31-1	3	1
		D	31-2	4	1
Chapman, Reuben (24, 25, 26, 27, 28, 29; 1835-47)	SC	D	24-1	Non-scale type	
		D	27-6	5	3
		D	28-1	0	3
Clemens, Sherrard (35, 36; 1857-61)	SA	D	35-1	0	2
		D	35-4	3	1
Clingman, Thomas L. (28, 30, 31, 32, 33, 34, 35; 1843-45, 1847-58)	SA	W	30-3	5	3
		D	32-1	3	1
		D	32-2	3	1
		D	32-2	4 (land policy)	0
		D	32-3	3	-
		D	33-1	5	0
		D	34-2	4	2
		D	35-2	3	1

Congressman and Congresses Served In	Region	Party	Scale Table	Member Position	Median for Region-Party
Cobb, Williamson, R. W. (30, 31, 32, 33, 34, 35, 36; 1847-61)	SC	D	31-2	3	1
		D	32-1	0	4
		D	32-2	0	2
		D	34-1	Non-scale type	
Garland, James (24, 25, 26; 1835-41)	SA	D	25-1	5	3
		D	26-1	3	1
		D	26-3	2	0
Garnett, Muscoe R. H. (35, 36; 1856-61	SA	D	35-2	3	1
		D	35-4	3	1
Greenwood Alfred B. (33, 34, 35; 1853-59)	SC	D	34-1	5	1
		D	35-1	0	2
		D	35-2	0	2
Holmes, Isaac E. (26, 27, 28, 29, 30, 31; 1839-51)	SA	D	27-3	3	0
		D	30-1	Non-scale type	
Hopkins, George W. (24, 25, 26, 27, 28, 29, 35; 1835-47, 1857-59)	SA	D	24-1	5	3
		D	25-1	6	3
		D	26-3	2	0
		D	28-1	Non-scale type	
Houston, George S. (27, 28, 29, 30, 32, 33, 34, 35, 36; 1841-49, 1851-61)	SC	D	33-2	2	1
		D	35-2	0	2
Jones, George W. (28, 29, 30, 31, 32, 33, 34, 35)	SC	D	32-1	2	4
		D	32-2	0	2
		D	33-1	2	4
		D	33-2	2	1
		D	35-1	1	2
		D	35-2	Non-scale type	
		D	35-3	3	1
McMullen, Fayette (31, 32, 33, 34; 1849-57)	SA	D	32-1	3	1
		D	33-1	2	0
Orr, James L. (31, 32, 33, 34, 35; 1849-59)	SA	D	32-3	5	3
		D	33-1	Non-scale type	

Congressman and Congresses Served In	Region	Party	Scale Table	Member Position	Median for Region-Party
Phelps, John S. (29, 30, 31, 32, 33, 34, 35, 36; 1845-61)	SC	D	29-1	3	1
		D	34-1	Non-scale type	
		D	35-1	Non-scale type	
		D	35-2	0	2
Rhett, Robert Barnwell (25, 26, 27, 28, 29, 30; 1837-49)	SA	D	28-1	0	2
		D	29-2	3	1
Savage, John H. (31, 32, 34, 35; 1849-53, 1855-59)	SC	D	31-1	3	1
		D	32-1	2	4
		D	35-4	2	1
Smith, William (33, 34, 35, 36; 1853-61)	SA	D	35-1	4	2
		D	35-3	3	1
		D	35-4	3	1
Stanton, Frederick P. (29, 30, 31, 32, 33; 1845-55)	SC	D	29-1	3	1
		D	30-1	2	0
		D	32-3	0	4
Stanton, Richard H. (31, 32, 33; 1849-55)	SC	D	31-1	3	1
		D	32-3	0	2
		D	33-2	3	1
Watkins, Albert G. (31, 32, W; 34, 35, D; 1849-53, 1855-59)	SC	D	35-1	0	2
		D	35-3	0	1

Northern Whigs and Republicans

Congressman and Congresses Served In	Region	Party	Scale Table	Member Position	Median for Region-Party
Adams, John Quincy (24, 25, 26, 27, 28, 29, 30; 1835-48)	NE	W	26-1	3	5
		W	27-1	Non-scale type	
Bingham, John Armour (34, 35, 36; 1855-61)	NNW	R	34-1	3	5
		R	35-3	8	6
Campbell, Lewis Davis (31, 32, 33, 34; 1849-57)	SNW	W	32-3	7	5
		R	35-2	2	7/8
Cushing, Caleb (24, 25, 26, 27; 1835-43)	NE	W	27-4	1	4
		W	27-6	3	6
Fowler, Orin (31, 32; 1849-52)	NE	W	31-1	7	5
		W	32-3	7	6

Congressman and Congresses Served In	Region	Party	Scale Table	Member Position	Median for Region-Party
Giddings, Joshua Reed (26, 27, 28, 29, 30, 31, 32, 33, W; 34, 35, R; 1842-59)	NNW	W	32-1	Non-scale type	
		W	33-1	0	4/5
		R	35-3	8	6
King, George G. (31, 32; 1849-53)	NE	W	31-1	7	5
		W	32-1	0	2
Levin, Lewis Charles (29, 30, 31; 1845-51)	MA	W	29-1	5	7
		W	30-1	4	6
		W	30-2	3	5
Meacham, James (31, 32, 33, 34; 1849-56)	NE	W	32-3	7	6
		W	34-1	3	-
Nichols, Matthias H. (33, D; 34, 35, R; 1853-59)	NNW	D	33-1	2	4
		R	35-2	4	6
Oliver, Andrew (33, D; 34, R; 1853-57)	MA	D	33-1	Non-scale type	
		R	34-1	1	6
Van Dyke, John (30, 31; 1847-51)	MA	W	31-1	7	5
		W	31-2	Non-scale type	

Southern Whigs and Republicans

Congressman and Congresses Served In	Region	Party	Scale Table	Member Position	Median for Region-Party
Blair, Francis P., Jr. (34, 35, 36; 1855-61)	SC	R	35-1	6	
		R	35-2	7	
		R	35-3	9	
		R	35-4	6	
Botts, John Minor (26, 27, 30; 1839-43, 1847-49)	SA	W	26-2	3	1
		W	27-1	5	3
		W	30-3	5	3
Campbell, John (25, 26, 27, 28; 1837-45)	SA	W	26-1	1	4
		D	27-6	5	2
Cullom, William (32, 33; 1851-55)	SC	W	32-1	3	5
		W	33-2	6	2
Davis, Henry Winter (34, 35, 36; 1855-61)	SA	W	35-3	8	5
		[R?]	36-1	3	0
Etheridge, Emerson (33, 34, 35, 36; 1853-61)	SC	W	33-2	6	2
		W	36-1	4	1

Congressman and Congresses Served In	Region	Party	Scale Table	Member Position	Median for Region-Party
Gilmer, Thomas W. (27, W; 28, D; 1841-45)	SA	W W W W	27-1 27-3 27-4 27-6	0 0 1 3	3 5 3 6
Habersham, Richard (26, D; 27, W; 1839-43)	SA	D D W W	26-1 26-3 27-4 27-6	4 3 1 4	1 0 3 6
Hilliard Henry W. (29, 30, 31; 1845-51)	SC	W W W	29-1 29-2 31-2	Non- scale type 2 0	4 2
Johnson, William Cost (25, 26, 27; 1837-43)	SA	W W W	27-1 27-3 27-6	0 9 4	3 5 6
Kennedy, John Pendleton (25, 27, 28; 1837-45)	SA	W W	27-3 28-2	8 7	5 3
Marshall, Humphrey (34, 35; 1855-59)	SC	W W W	35-2 35-3 35-4	8 7 5	3 3 3
Pickens, Francis W. (24, 25, 26, W; 27, D; 1835-43)	SA	W W D	24-2 25-1 27-1	0 3 2	1 6 0
Stanly, Edward (25, 26, 27, 31, 32; 1837-43, 1849-53)	SA	W W	27-1 27-3	7 7	3 5
Stephens, Alexander H. (28, 29, 30, 31, 32, 33, W; 34, 35, D; 1843-59)	SA	W W W W D D	30-1 30-3 31-2 33-1 34-1 35-1	5 5 0 5 5 4	7 3 2 3 1 2
Toombs, Robert (29, 30, 31, W; 32, D; 1845-53)	SA	W W W W	29-1 30-1 30-3 31-2	5 5 5 0	7 7 3 2
Underwood, Joseph R. (24, 25, 26, 27; 1845-53)	SC	W W W	24-1 24-2 27-5	8 3 4	6 0 0

Congressman and Congresses Served In	Region	Party	Scale Table	Member Position	Median for Region-Party
White, John	SC	W	24-1	8	6
(24, 25, 26, 27, 28;		W	28-2	7	3
1835-45)					
Wise, Henry A.	SA	W	27-1	0	3
(24, 25, 26, 27, W;		W	27-3	1	5
28, D; 1835-45)		W	27-4	0	3
		W	27-6	3	6

Bibliography

PRIMARY MATERIALS

Published Sources for Mavericks and Conformists

Northern Democratic Conformists

ADRAIN, GARNETT B. (N. J.; 35, 36)*
———. *Speech of Hon. Garnett B. Adrain, of New Jersey, against the Admission of Kansas (Mar. 20, 1858).* Washington, D.C.: Lemuel Towers, 1858.
———. *Speech of Hon. G. B. Adrain, of New Jersey, on the Treasury Note Bill (Dec., 1857).* Washington, D.C.: Congressional Globe Office, 1857.
———. *State of the Union. Speech of Hon. Garnett B. Adrain, of New Jersey (Jan., 1861).* Washington, D.C.: Congressional Globe Office, 1861.
BINGHAM, KINSLEY S. (Mich.; 30, 31)
———. *The Rise and Fall of the Democratic Party. Speech of Hon. Kinsley S. Bingham, of Michigan. Delivered in the United States Senate, May 24, 1860.* n.p.: Republican Congressional Committee, 1860.
———. *The Slavery Question. Speech of Mr. Bingham, of Michigan, on the Admission of California. Delivered in the House of Representatives, June 4, 1850.* Washington, D.C.: Congressional Globe Office, 1850.
BISSELL, WILLIAM H. (Ill.; 31, 32, 33)
———. *The Slave Question. Speech of Mr. William H. Bissell, of Illinois, in the House of Representatives, Thursday, Feb. 21, 1850.* Washington, D.C.: Buell & Blanchard, 1850.
CAMBRELENG, CHURCHILL C. (N. Y.; 24, 25)

*Hereafter, all Congressmen's names will be followed by the name of the state from which they were elected and the numbers of the congresses in which they served between 1836 and 1860.

————. "*Eulogy,*" in *A Selection of Eulogies, Pronounced in the Several States in Honor of Those Illustrious Patriots and Statesmen, John Adams and Thomas Jefferson.* Hartford: D. F. Robinson & Co. and Norton & Russell, 1826.

[————.] *An Examination of the New Tariff Proposed by the Hon. Henry Baldwin, a Representative in Congress. By One of the People.* New York: Gould & Banks, 1821.

————. *Speech of Mr. Cambreleng, (in reply to Mr. McDuffie and Mr. Storrs,) on the Proposition to Amend the Constitution of the United States, Respecting the Election of President and Vice President. Delivered in the House of Representatives, Mar. 7, 1826.* [Washington, D.C., 1826].

————. *Speech of Mr. Cambreleng, of New York, in the House of Representatives, Feb. 11, 1835, on the Bill Regulating the Deposite of the Public Money in Certain Local Banks and on the Abuses and Corruptions of Government.* New York: Office of the Evening Post, 1835.

CLIFFORD, NATHAN (Maine; 26, 27)

Clifford, Philip Greely. *Nathan Clifford, Democrat (1803–1881).* New York: G. P. Putnam's Sons, 1922.

COCHRANE, JOHN (N. Y.; 35, 36)

————. *Arming the Slaves in the War for the Union. Scenes, Speeches, and Events Attending It.* New York: Rogers & Sherwood Printers, 1875.

————. *Speech of Hon. John Cochrane, of New York, on the Union and the Constitution. Delivered in the House of Representatives, Dec. 20, 1859.* Washington, D.C.: Lemuel Towers,[1859].

DAWSON, JOHN L. (Pa.; 32, 33)

————. *An Address by Hon. John L. Dawson, before the Washington and Union L[iterary] Societies of Washington College: Delivered on Wednesday Evening, June 18th, 1856.* Washington, Pa.: Grayson & Hart, Printers, 1856.

————. *Speech of Hon. John L. Dawson, of Pennsylvania, Delivered at a Democratic Mass Meeting in New Geneva, Fayette County, Pennsylvania, Sept. 1, 1860.* Washington, D.C.: Congressional Globe Office, 1867.

————. *Speech of Hon. John L. Dawson, of Pennsylvania, on the Homestead Bill. Delivered in the House of Representatives on Tuesday, Feb. 14, 1854.* Washington, D.C.: Robert Armstrong, Printer, 1854.

————. *Speech of John L. Dawson, of Pennsylvania, on the Bill Granting One Quarter Section of the Public Land to Actual Settlers. Delivered in the House of Representatives, Mar. 3, 1852.* Washington, D.C.: Congressional Globe Office, 1852.

DEAN, GILBERT (N. Y.; 32, 33)

————. *The Emancipation Proclamation and Arbitrary Arrests!! Speech of Hon. Gilbert Dean, of New York, on the Governor's Annual Message, Delivered in the House of Assembly of the State of New York, Feb. 12, 1863.* Albany, N. Y.: Atlas & Argus Printers, 1863.

DOUGLAS, STEPHEN A. (Ill.; 28, 29)

————. *The Letters of Stephen A. Douglas.* Edited by Robert W. Johannsen. Urbana: University of Illinois Press, 1961.

Carr, Clark E. *Stephen A. Douglas, His Life, Public Services, Speeches and Patriotism.* Chicago: A. C. McClung & Co., 1909.

[Flint, Henry Martyn]. *Life of Stephen A. Douglas, with His Most Important Speeches and Reports*. By a Member of the Western Bar. New York: J. Dayton, Publisher, 1860.

Johannsen, Robert W. *Stephen A. Douglas*. New York: Oxford University Press, 1973.

Milton, George Fort. *The Eve of Conflict, Stephen A. Douglas and the Needless War*. Boston & New York: Houghton Mifflin Co., Riverside Press Cambridge, 1934.

Wells, Damon, Jr. "Man in Motion: The Last Years of Stephen Douglas, 1857–1861." Ph.D. diss., Rice University, 1968.

DUNLAP, ROBERT P. (Maine; 28, 29)

————. *Address Delivered before the General Grand Chapter of the United States at the Triennial Meeting in the City of Hartford, Connecticut, Sept. 9, 1856*. [Portland, Maine: I. Berry, Printer], 1856.

EDGERTON, ALFRED P. (Ohio; 32, 33)

[————]. United States Civil-Service Commission. *Investigation of a Complaint against Collector Seeberger of the Port of Chicago, Charging Violation of the Civil Service Act, Apr. 11, 1887. Reports of Commissioners Edgerton and Lyman and Opinion of the Commission*. Washington, D.C.: Government Printing Office, 1887.

FAIRFIELD, JOHN (Maine; 24, 25)

————. *The Letters of John Fairfield*. Edited by Arthur G. Staples. Lewiston, Maine: Lewiston Journal Co., 1922.

FITCH, GRAHAM (Ind.; 31, 32)

————. *Speech of Hon. Graham Fitch, of Indiana, on the Constitution of Kansas; Delivered in the Senate of the United States, Dec. 22, 1857*. Washington, D.C.: Congressional Globe Office, 1857.

GORMAN, WILLIS A. (Ind.; 31, 32)

————. *Boundary of Texas. Speech of Hon. W. A. Gorman, of Indiana, in the House of Representatives, Friday, Aug. 30, 1850, on the Texas Boundary Bill and Slavery Agitation*. Washington, D.C.: Congressional Globe Office, [1850].

————. *Speech of Hon. W. A. Gorman, of Indiana, against Appropriations for Internal Improvements by the General Government. Delivered in the House of Representatives, Feb. 15, 1851*. Washington, D.C.: Lemuel Towers, Printer, [1851].

————. *Speech of Hon. W. A. Gorman, of Indiana, on the Admission of California. Delivered in the House of Representatives, Tuesday, Mar. 12, 1850*. Washington, D.C.: Congressional Globe Office, 1850.

"Life and Public Services of Hon. Willis A. Gorman. Compiled from Obituary Notices in the St. Paul Journals." Vol. III (1870–1880). *Collections*. St. Paul, Minn.: Published by the Minnesota Historical Society, 1880.

HARRIS, THOMAS L. (Ill.; 31, 34, 35)

————. *Letter of Hon. Thos. L. Harris, of Illinois, upon the Repeal of the Fugitive Slave Law*. Washington, D.C.: Jus. T. Towers, 1851.

————. *Speech of Hon. T. L. Harris, of Illinois, upon the Kansas and other Political Questions, and in Reply to Messrs. Foster, of Georgia, and Norton, of Illinois. Delivered in the House of Representatives, Aug. 9, 1856*. Washington, D.C.: Jus. T. & Lemuel Towers, 1856.

————. *The Tariff Question. Speech of Hon. T. L. Harris, of Illinois, in Reply to the Speech of Mr. Hampton, of Pennsylvania*. Washington, D.C.: Congressional Globe Office, 1851.

HASTINGS, JOHN (Ohio; 26, 27)

————. *Remarks of Mr. John Hastings, of Ohio, on the Tariff Bill. Delivered in the House of Representatives, July 9, 1842.* Washington, D.C.: n.p., 1842.

————. *Speech of Mr. John Hastings, of Ohio, on the Revenue, or Tariff Bill. Delivered in the House of Representatives, July 29, 1841.* n.p., n.d.

KELLY, JOHN (N. Y.; 34, 35)

————. *The Union of the New York Democracy—the Kansas–Nebraska Act Vindicated. Speech of Hon. John Kelly, of New York. Delivered in the House of Representatives, May 25, 1856.* [Washington, D.C.: n.p., 1856].

McLaughlin, J. Fairfax. *The Life and Times of John Kelly.* New York: American News Co., 1885.

MARSHALL, SAMUEL SCOTT (Ill.; 34, 35)

————. *The Real Issue—Union or Disunion. Letter of Hon. S. S. Marshall, on the Parties and Politics of the Day, to the Freemen of the Ninth Congressional District of Illinois.* Washington, D.C.: Union Office, 1856.

————. *Speech of Hon. Samuel S. Marshall of Illinois, on the Insanity of the Times and the Present Condition of Political Parties. Delivered in the House of Representatives, Aug. 6, 1856.* Washington, D.C.: Congressional Globe Office, 1856.

MUHLENBERG, HENRY A. P. (Pa.; 24, 25)

————. *The Life of Major-General Peter Muhlenberg of the Revolutionary Army.* Philadelphia: Carey & Hart, 1849.

OWEN, ROBERT DALE (Ind.; 28, 29)

————. *An Address on the Influence of the Clerical Profession. As Delivered in the Hall of Science, New York. To Which is Added a Tract and a Warning; Truth and Error; or the Fear of God.* London: J. Watson, 1840.

————. *Labor, Its History and Prospects. An Address Delivered before the Young Men's Mercantile Association of Cincinnati.* New York: Fowlers & Wells, Publishers, 1851.

————. *Texas, and Her Relations with Mexico. Speech of Robert Dale Owen, of Indiana, Delivered in the House of Representatives, Jan. 8, 1845.* n.p., n.d.

————. *Threading My Way: An Autobiography.* New York: G. W. Carleton & Co., 1874. Reprint. New York: Augustus M. Kelley, Publishers, 1967.

————. et al. *Quarterly Beacon. Popular Tracts by Robert Dale Owen and Others; to Which Are Added Fables by Frances Wright.* New York: Beacon Office, 1854.

Leopold, Richard William. *Robert Dale Owen, A Biography.* Cambridge: Harvard University Press, 1940.

PRATT, ZADOCK (N. Y.; 25, 28)

————. *Description of the Prattsville Tannery.* Prattsville, N. Y.: n.p., Nov. 27, 1847.

RICHARDSON, WILLIAM A. (Ill.; 30, 31, 32, 33, 34)

————. *Speech of Hon. W. A. Richardson, of Illinois, Delivered in Burlington, New Jersey, Tuesday Evening, July 17, 1860.* Philadelphia: Ringwalt & Brown, Printers, [1860].

SYKES, GEORGE (N. J.; 28, 29)

————. "The Accident on Board the U.S.S. 'Princeton,' Feb. 28, 1844: A Contemporary Newsletter." Edited with notes by St. George L. Sioussat. *Pennsylvania History* (July 1937).

VALLANDIGHAM, CLEMENT L. (Ohio; 35, 36)

————. *Speeches, Arguments, Addresses, and Letters of Clement L. Vallandigham.* New York: J. Walter & Co., 1864.

Vallandigham, Rev. James L. *A Life of Clement L. Vallandigham*. Baltimore: Turnbull Bros., 1872.

WELLER, JOHN B. (Ohio; 26, 27, 28)

———. *Speeches of Messrs. Weller, Orr, Lane, and Cobb, Delivered in Phoenix and Depot Halls, Concord, New Hampshire at a Mass Meeting of the Democratic Party of Merrimac County*. n.p., n.d.

WHITELEY, WILLIAM G. (Del.; 35, 36)

———. *The Revolutionary Soldiers of Delaware. A Paper Read by William G. Whiteley, Esq., Before the Two Houses of the Delaware Legislature, Feb. 15th, 1875*. Printed by order of the legislature. Wilmington, Del.: James & Webb, Printers, 1875.

Southern Democratic Conformists

ATKINSON, ARCHIBALD (Va.; 28, 29, 30)

———. *Speech of Mr. Atkinson, of Virginia, on the Oregon Question. Delivered in the House of Representatives, Feb. 7, 1846*. Washington, D.C.: Union Office, 1846.

AVERY, WILLIAM T. (Tenn.; 35, 36)

———. *Aggressions and Disunionism of the Republican Party. Speech of Hon. Wm. T. Avery, of Tennessee, Delivered in the House of Representatives, Apr. 23, 1860.* [Washington, D.C.]: Lemuel Towers, Printer, [1860].

———. *Letter from Hon. William T. Avery of Tennessee, to His Constituents*. [Washington, D.C.: n.p., 1860].

———. *Speech of Hon. William T. Avery, of Tennessee, in Reply to Hon. Emerson Etheridge. Delivered in the House of Representatives, Jan. 31, 1861*. [Washington, D.C.]: Lemuel Towers, Printer, [1861].

BEDINGER, HENRY (Va.; 29, 30)

———. *Speech of Hon. Henry Bedinger, of Virginia, on the President's Special Message. Delivered in the House of Representatives, Tuesday, Jan. 25, 1848*. Washington, D.C.: Congressional Globe Office, 1848.

———. *Speech* in the U. S. Congress. *Speeches on the Oregon Question and on the Mexican War*. 29th Cong., 1st Sess., 1845–1846.

BOYCE, WILLIAM W. (S. C.; 33, 34, 35, 36)

———. *Admission of Kansas. Speech of Hon. William W. Boyce, of South Carolina, in the House of Representatives, Mar. 25, 1858*. Washington, D.C.: Congressional Globe Office, 1858.

———. *The Annexation of Cuba. Speech of Hon. W. W. Boyce, of South Carolina, Delivered in the House of Representatives, Jan. 15, 1855*. Washington, D.C.: Congressional Globe Office, 1855.

———. *Kansas Contested Election. Speech of Hon. W. W. Boyce, of South Carolina, Delivered in the House of Representatives, Mar. 6, 1856*. Washington, D.C.: Congressional Globe Office, 1856.

BOYD, LINN (Ky.; 24, 26, 27, 28, 29, 30, 31, 33)

———. *Speech of Mr. Linn Boyd, of Kentucky, in Reply to the Hon. John White, Relative to the Charge of Bargain between Messrs. Adams and Clay, in the Presidential Election of 1824–25. Delivered in the House of Representatives, Apr. 30, 1844*. Washington, D.C.: n.p., [1844].

———. *To the Citizens of the First Congressional District in the State of Kentucky*. n.p., 1843.

Kentucky. General Assembly. *Speeches and Proceedings upon the Announcement of the Death of the Hon. Linn Boyd, in the Senate and House of Representatives of Kentucky, Tuesday, Dec. 20, 1859*. Frankfort, Ky.: Yeoman Office, 1860.

BROOKS, PRESTON S. (S. C.; 33, 34)

Campbell, James E. "Sumner, Brooks, Burlingame, or The Last of the Great Challengers," *Ohio Archaeological and Historical Quarterly* 34 (Oct. 1925):435–473. [Columbus, Ohio: F. J. Heer Printing Co., 1925].

CHASE, LUCIEN BONAPARTE (Tenn.; 29, 30)

————. *English Serfdom and American Slavery: or Ourselves—as Others See Us*. Reprint. Miami, Fla.: Mnemosyne Pub. Co., 1969.

————. *History of the Polk Administration*. New York: George P. Putnam, 1850.

————. *Speech* in U. S. Congress. *Speeches on the Oregon Question and on the Mexican War*. 29th Cong., 1st Sess., 1845–46.

CLAIBORNE, JOHN FRANCIS H. (Miss.; 24, 25)

————. *Life and Correspondence of John A. Quitman, Major-General, U.S.A., and Governor of the State of Mississippi*. 2 vols. New York: Harper & Bros., 1860.

————. *Life and Times of Gen. Sam. Dale, the Mississippi Partisan*. New York: Harper & Bros., 1860.

————. *Mississippi, as a Province, Territory and State, with Biographical Notices of Eminent Citizens*. Jackson, Miss.: Power & Barksdale, Publishers & Printers, 1880; Baton Rouge: Louisiana State University Press, 1964.

Riley, Franklin Lafayette. "Life of Col. J. F. H. Claiborne." Reprinted from *Publications of the Mississippi Historical Society* 7 (n.d.):217–244.

COBB, HOWELL (Ga.; 28, 29, 30, 31, 34)

————. *Great Speech of General Howell Cobb, delivered in Atlanta, Georgia, July 23, 1868*. Augusta, Ga.: Specially reported for and published by the Chronicle and Sentinel, [1868].

————. *Necessity for Party Organization. Speech of Mr. Howell Cobb, of Georgia, in the House of Representatives, Saturday, July 1, 1848*. Washington, D.C.: Congressional Globe Office, 1848.

————. *Remarks of Mr. Cobb, of Georgia, Delivered in the House of Representatives, Dec. 31, 1855, on the Organization of the House*. Washington, D.C.: Congressional Globe Office, 1855.

————. *A Scriptural Examination of the Institution of Slavery in the United States; with Its Objects and Purposes*. Georgia: Printed for the Author, 1856.

Brooks, Robert Preston. "Howell Cobb and The Crisis of 1850." *Mississippi Valley Historical Review* 4 (Dec. 1917):279–298.

————, ed. "Howell Cobb Papers," *Georgia Historical Quarterly* 5–6 (Sept.–Dec. 1922).

Johnson, Zachary Taylor. *The Political Policies of Howell Cobb*. Nashville: George Peabody College for Teachers, 1929.

Montgomery, Horace. *Howell Cobb's Confederate Career*. Confederate Centennial Studies, edited by William Stanley Hoole, no. 10. Tuscaloosa, Ala.: Confederate Pub. Co., 1959.

Phillips, U. B., ed. *The Correspondence of Robert Toombs, Alexander H. Stephens, and Howell Cobb*. Vol. II, *Annual Report of the American Historical Association for the Year 1911*, Washington, D.C.: American Historical Association, 1913.

Simpson, John Eddins. *Howell Cobb, the Politics of Ambition*. Chicago: Adams, 1973.

CURRY, JABEZ LAMAR M. (Ala.; 35, 36)

————. *Admission of Kansas. Speech of Mr. Jabez L. M. Curry, of Alabama, in the House of Representatives, Feb. 23, 1858, on the Admission of Kansas as a State under the Lecomptom Constitution.* Washington, D.C.: Congressional Globe Office, 1858.

————. *Civil History of the Government of the Confederate States with Some Personal Reminiscences.* Richmond, Va.: B. F. Johnson Pub. Co., 1901.

————. *The Constitutional Rights of the States. Speech of J. L. M. Curry, of Alabama, in the House of Representatives, Mar. 14, 1860.* [Washington, D.C.]: T. McGill, Printers, [1860].

————. "Difficulties, Complications, and Limitations Connected with the Education of the Negro." *Occasional Papers*, no. 5. Baltimore: Published by the Trustees of the John F. Slater Fund, 1895.

————. *Principles, Acts, and Utterances of John C. Calhoun, Promotive of the True Union of the States.* Chicago: University of Chicago Press, 1898.

————. "The South in Olden Times." *Publications of the Southern History Association* 5 (Jan. 1901):35–48.

————. *Speech of J. L. M. Curry, of Alabama, on the Bill Granting Pensions to the Soldiers of the War of 1812. Delivered in the House of Representatives, Apr. 27, 1858.* Washington, D.C.: Lemuel Towers, Printers, 1858.

Rice, Jessie Pearl. *J. L. M. Curry: Southerner, Statesman and Educator.* New York: King's Crown Press, 1949.

DAVIS, REUBEN (Miss.; 35, 36)

————. *Speech of Hon. Reuben Davis, of Mississippi, on His Resolution for the Acquisition of Cuba. Delivered in the House of Representatives, Jan. 31, 1859.* Washington, D.C.: Lemuel Towers, Printer, 1859.

————. *Speech of Hon. Reuben Davis, of Mississippi, on The State of the Union; Delivered in the House of Representatives, Dec. 22, 1858.* Washington, D.C.: Congressional Globe Office, 1858.

DROMGOOLE, GEORGE C. (Va.; 24, 25, 26, 28, 29)

————. *Speech of Mr. Dromgoole, of Virginia, on the Bill to Separate the Government from the Banks.* Washington, D.C.: n.p., 1838.

GREEN, JAMES S. (Mo.; 30, 31)

————. *Naval Appropriation Bill. Speech of Hon. J. S. Green, of Missouri, in the Senate of the United States, Feb. 12, 1861.* Washington, D.C.: Congressional Globe Office, 1861.

————. *Speech of Hon. J. S. Green, of Missouri, in Favor of the Admission of Kansas under the Lecompton Constitution. Delivered in the Senate of the United States, Mar. 23, 1858.* Washington, D.C.: Lemuel Towers, 1858.

————. *Speech of Hon. J. S. Green, of Missouri, on the Constitution of Kansas; Delivered in the Senate of the United States, Dec. 16, 1857.* Washington, D.C.: Congressional Globe Office, 1857.

————. *Territorial Policy. Speech of Hon. James S. Green, of Missouri, in the Senate of the United States, Jan. 10 & 11, 1860.* Washington, D.C.: Congressional Globe Office, 1860.

————. *The War with Mexico. Speech of Hon. James S. Green, of Missouri, in the House of Representatives, Jan. 25, 1848. In Committee of the Whole on the State of the Union, on the Resolutions Referring the President's Message to the Various Standing Committees.* Washington, D.C.: Congressional Globe Office, 1848.

HOWARD, BENJAMIN (Md.; 24, 25)

————. *Address of the Hon. Benjamin C. Howard, Past Grand Master, Delivered before the Grand Lodge of F & A Masons of Maryland, May 15, 1860.* Baltimore: Joseph Robinson, Printer, 1860.

HUBARD, EDMUND W. (Va.; 27, 28, 29)

————. *Speech of Edmund W. Hubard, of Virginia, on the United States Fiscal Bank Bill: Delivered in the House of Representatives, Aug. 4, 1841.* Washington, D.C.: Blair & Rives, Printers, 1841.

————. *Speech of Mr. Hubard, of Virginia, against the Tariff. Delivered in the House of Representatives, Wednesday, June 23, 1842.* n.p., [1842].

HUBBARD, DAVID (Ala.; 26, 31)

————. *Letter of Hon. David Hubbard, to the Voters of the Second Congressional District of the State of Alabama.* Washington, D.C.: Congressional Globe Office, 1840.

————. *Speech of Mr. David Hubbard, of Alabama, upon the Bill Granting the Right of Way through the Public Lands, and Granting Alternate Sections to the State of Alabama along the Line of the Chattanooga Railroad. Delivered in the House of Representatives, Feb. 27, 1851.* Washington, D.C.: Jus. T. Towers, Printers, 1851.

HUNTER, R. M. T. (Va.; 25, 27, 29)

————. *Correspondence of Robert M. T. Hunter, 1826–1876.* Edited by Charles Henry Ambler. Vol. II, *Annual Report of the American Historical Association for the Year 1916.* Washington, D.C.: American Historical Association, 1918.

————. *The Democratic Demonstration at Poughkeepsie. Speech of Hon. R. M. T. Hunter, of Virginia.* n.p., n.d.

————. *Diplomatic Relations with Austria. Speech of Hon. R. M. T. Hunter, of Virginia, in the Senate of the United States, Jan. 31, 1850.* Washington, D.C.: Congressional Globe Office, [1850].

————. *The Massachusetts Resolutions on the Sumner Assault, and the Slavery Issue. Speeches of Senators Butler, Evans, and Hunter, Delivered in the Senate of the United States.* Washington, D.C.: Congressional Globe Office, 1856.

————. "Observations on the History of Virginia: A Discourse Delivered before the Virginia Historical Society, at Their Eighth Annual Meeting, Dec. 14, 1854." *Virginia Historical Reporter* I (1854–1860):1–48. Richmond, Va.: Clemitt & Fore, Printers, 1855.

————. *Speeches of Hon. Francis Kernan, of New York, and Hon. R. M. T. Hunter, of Virginia, at the Mass Meeting in New York, on Thursday Evening, Sept. 12, 1872.* New York: John Polthemus, Printer, 1872.

————. *Speech of Hon. R. M. T. Hunter, of Virginia, on Invasion of States. Delivered in the Senate of the United States, Jan. 30, 1860.* Washington, D.C.: Lemuel Towers, Printer, 1860.

————. *Speech of Mr. R. M. T. Hunter, of Virginia, on the Ten Regiment Bill. Delivered in the Senate of the United States, Feb. 7, 1848.* Washington, D.C.: Towers, Printer, [1848].

————. *The Territorial Question. Speech of Hon. R. M. T. Hunter, of Virginia, in the Senate of the United States, Mar. 25, 1850.* Washington, D.C.: Congressional Globe Office, [1850].

Hunter, Martha. *A Memoir of Robert M. T. Hunter*. Washington, D.C.: Neale Pub. Co., 1903.

Simms, Henry Harrison. *Life of Robert M. T. Hunter: A Study in Sectionalism and Secession*. Richmond, Va.: William Byrd Press, 1935.

INGE, SAMUEL W. (Ala.; 30, 31)

———. *Speech of the Hon. S. W. Inge, of Alabama, on the Relation of Parties to the Mexican War. Delivered in the House of Representatives, Mar. 22, 1848.* Washington, D.C.: Lemuel Towers, [1848].

KAUFMAN, DAVID S. (Tex.; 29, 30, 31)

———. *Speech of Hon. David S. Kaufman, of Texas, on the Slavery Question. Delivered in the House of Representatives, Feb. 10, 1847.* Washington, D.C.: Blair & Rives, 1847.

———. *Speech of Mr. David S. Kaufman, of Texas, on the Subject of the Mexican War. Delivered in the House of Representatives, U.S., June 20, 1846.* Washington, D.C.: J. & G. S. Gideon, 1846.

———. *The Texas Boundary. Speech of Hon. David S. Kaufman, of Texas, Showing That Mexico Commenced the Late War with the United States, by Invading Territory That Belonged to Texas at the Period of her Annexation. Delivered in the House of Representatives, June 5, 1848.* Washington, D.C.: Congressional Globe Office, 1848.

KEITT, LAWRENCE M. (S. C.; 33, 34, 35, 36)

———. *American Politics. Speech of Hon. L. M. Keitt, of South Carolina, Delivered in the House of Representatives, Jan. 3, 1855.* Washington, D.C.: Congressional Globe Office, 1855.

———. *Speech of Hon. Lawrence M. Keitt, of South Carolina, on the Origin of Slavery; Delivered in the House of Representatives, May 24, 1858.* Washington, D.C.: Congressional Globe Office, 1858.

LAMAR, LUCIUS, Q. C. (Miss.; 35, 36)

———. *Letter of Lucius Q. C. Lamar, in Reply to Hon. P. F. Liddell, of Carrollton, Mississippi.* Washington, D.C.: n.p., 1860.

Cate, Wirt Armistead. *Lucius Q. C. Lamar*. Chapel Hill: University of North Carolina Press, 1935; New York: Russell & Russell, 1969.

Mayes, Edward. *Lucius Q. C. Lamar: His Life, Times, and Speeches, 1825–1893*. Nashville, Tenn.: Publishing House of the Methodist Episcopal Church, South, 1896.

Murphy, James B. *L. Q. C. Lamar, Pragmatic Patriot*. Baton Rouge: Louisiana State University Press, 1973.

LETCHER, JOHN (Va.; 32, 33, 34, 35)

———. *Address on the Re-Inauguration of the Bronze Statue of George Washington, at the Virginia Military Institute, Sept. 10, 1866.* Richmond, Va.: Whig Printers, [1866].

———. *Speech of Hon. J. Letcher, of Virginia, on the Public Expenditures. Delivered in the House of Representatives, June 12, 1858.* Washington, D.C.: Lemuel Towers, 1858.

———. *Speech of Hon. John Letcher, of Virginia, in the House of Representatives, Feb. 27, 1855, on Territorial Policy.* Washington, D.C.: Congressional Globe Office, 1855.

———. *Speech of Hon. John Letcher, of Virginia, on the Political Issues Now before the Country. Delivered in the House of Representatives, Aug. 2, 1856.* Washington, D.C.: Union Office, 1856.

———. *Speech of Hon. John Letcher, of Virginia, on the Printing Deficiency Bill; Delivered in the House of Representatives, Jan. 29, 1858.* Washington, D.C.: Congressional Globe Office, 1858.

———. *Speech of Hon. John Letcher, of Virginia, on the Resolution Reported by the Committee of Elections in the Contested-Election Case from Kansas Territory. Delivered in the House of Representatives, Mar. 13, 1856.* Washington, D.C.: Congressional Globe Office, 1856.

LEWIS, DIXON H. (Ala.; 24, 25, 26, 27, 28, 30)

———. *Remarks of the Hon. Dixon H. Lewis, and Hon. Seaborn Jones, on the Alabama Controversy. Delivered in the House of Representatives, Jan. 6, 1834.* Washington, D.C.: n.p., 1834.

McQUEEN, JOHN (S. C.; 31, 32, 33, 34, 35, 36)

———. *Speech of Hon. John McQueen, of South Carolina, on the Admission of California. Delivered in the House of Representatives, Thursday, June 3, 1850.* Washington, D.C.: Congressional Globe Office, 1850.

MORSE, ISAAC E. (La.; 29, 30, 31)

———. *Speech of Isaac E. Morse, of Louisiana, on the President's Message in Relation to California. Delivered in the House of Representatives, Mar. 14, 1850.* Washington, D.C.: Congressional Globe Office, 1850.

RENCHER, ABRAHAM (N. C.; 24, 25, 27)

———. *Circular Address of Abraham Rencher, of North Carolina, to His Constituents.* Washington, D.C.: n.p., Mar. 13, 1843.

SAUNDERS, ROMULUS M. (N. C.; 27, 28)

———. *Address Delivered before the Two Literary Societies of Wake Forest College, June 9, 1852.* Published by order of the Philomathesian Society. Raleigh, N. C.: Wm. W. Holden, Printer, 1852.

———. *An Address of R. M. Saunders to the People of North Carolina.* Washington, D.C.: n.p., 1843.

———. *Speech of Mr. Saunders, on the Proposition to Amend the Constitution of the United States, Respecting the Election of President and Vice President. Delivered in the House of Representatives, Feb. 24, 1866.* Washington, D.C.: n.p., 1866.

SEDDON, JAMES A. (Va.; 29, 31)

———. *Speech of Hon. Jas. A. Seddon, of Virginia, on the President's Message of Aug. 6, 1850, Concerning Texas and New Mexico. Delivered in the House of Representatives, Tuesday, Aug. 13, 1850.* Washington, D.C.: Congressional Globe Office, 1850.

———. *Speech of Hon. J. A. Seddon, of Virginia, on the Action of the Executive in Relation to California. Delivered in the House of Representatives, Jan. 23, 1850.* Washington, D.C.: Congressional Globe Office, 1850.

SHAW, HENRY M. (N. C.; 33, 35)

———. *The Kansas Question. Speech of Hon. Henry M. Shaw, of North Carolina, in the House of Representatives, Apr. 20, 1858.* Washington, D.C.: Congressional Globe Office, 1858.

SMITH, SAMUEL AXLEY (Tenn.; 34, 35)

———. *The President's Message. Speech of Hon. Samuel A. Smith, of Tennessee, Delivered in the House of Representatives, Dec. 9, 1856*. Washington, D.C.: Congressional Globe Office, 1856.

———. *Speech of Hon. S. A. Smith, of Tennessee, on the State of Affairs in Kansas. Delivered in the House of Representatives, June 25, 1856*. Washington, D.C.: n.p., 1856.

STEVENSON, JOHN W. (Ky.; 35, 36)

———. *Speech of Hon. J. W. Stevenson, of Kentucky, on the State of the Union. Delivered in the House of Representatives, Jan. 30, 1861*. Washington, D.C.: Lemuel Towers, 1861.

TALBOTT, ALBERT G. (Ky.; 34, 35)

———. *National Politics. Speech of Hon. Albert G. Talbott, of Kentucky, Delivered in the House of Representatives, July 28, 1856, Defining His Position on Know-Nothingism, Black-Republicanism, and Democracy*. Washington, D.C.: Congressional Globe Office, 1856.

THOMAS, JAMES H. (Tenn.; 30, 31, 36)

———. *Admission of California. Speech of Hon. J. H. Thomas, of Tennessee, in the House of Representatives, May 27, 1850, in Committee of the Whole on the State of the Union, on the President's Message Transmitting the Constitution of California*. Washington, D.C.: n.p., 1850.

———. *State of the Union. Speech of Hon. James H. Thomas, of Tennessee, in the House of Representatives, Jan. 17, 1861*. Washington, D.C.: Congressional Globe Office, 1861.

THOMPSON, JACOB (Miss.; 26, 27, 28, 29, 30, 31)

———. *Address, Delivered on Occasion of the Opening of the University of the State of Mississippi, in Behalf of the Board of Trustees, Nov. 6, 1848*. Memphis, Tenn.: Franklin Book & Job Office, 1849.

———. *Address of Hon. Jacob Thompson, of Mississippi, to His Constituents*. Washington, D.C.: Jus. T. Towers, Printer, 1851.

VENABLE, ABRAHAM W. (N. C.; 30, 31, 32)

———. *Slavery in the Territories. Speech of Hon. A. W. Venable, of N. Carolina, in the House of Representatives, June 1, 1848, in Committee of the Whole, upon the Power of Congress to Legislate upon the Subject of Slavery in the Territories*. Washington, D.C.: Congressional Globe Office, 1848.

———. *Speech of Hon. A. W. Venable of N. Carolina, on the Texas and New Mexico Question. Delivered in the House of Representatives, Thursday, Aug. 15, 1850*. Washington, D.C.: Congressional Globe Office, 1850.

———. *Speech of Hon A. W. Venable of N. C., on Printing the Seventh Census, Delivered in the House of Representatives, Jan. 26, 1852*. Washington, D.C.: Congressional Globe Office, 1852.

WATTERSON, HARVEY M. (Tenn.; 26, 27)

———. *Remarks of Hon. H. M. Watterson, of Tennessee, on the Loan Bill*. [Washington, D.C.: n.p., 1841].

WINSLOW, WARREN (N. C.; 34, 35, 36)

———. *Assault on Senator Sumner. Speech of Hon. Warren Winslow, of North Carolina, Delivered in the House of Representatives, July 11, 1856*. Washington, D.C.: n.p., 1856.

Northern Democratic Mavericks

BORDEN, NATHANIEL B. (Mass.; 24, 25, 27)

————. *Address of Hon. Nathaniel B. Borden, Mayor of the City of Fall River, at the Last Regular Meeting of the Board of Aldermen, for Municipal Year, Ending with April, 1858.* Fall River, Mass.: William S. Robertson, Printer, 1858.

BRODHEAD, RICHARD (Pa.; 28, 29, 30)

————. *Insane and Homestead Bills—Clayton Amendment. Views of Richard Brodhead, Expressed in the Senate of the United States.* Washington, D.C.: Congressional Globe Office, 1854.

————. *Speech of Hon. Richard Brodhead, of Pennsylvania, in the Senate of the United States, Mar. 15, 1852, on the Public Lands—Graduation and Reduction of the Price Thereof, Preferable to Grants of Alternate Sections to aid in the Construction of Railroads—Grants to Actual Settlers, Cession to the States, Etc., Briefly Considered.* Washington, D.C.: n.p., 1852.

BROWN, CHARLES (Pa.; 27, 30)

————. *Remarks of Mr. Charles Brown, of Pennsylvania, on the Navy Appropriation Bill. Delivered in the House of Representatives, May 20, 1842.* Washington, D.C.: n.p., 1842.

————. *Speech of Charles Brown, of Pennsylvania, on Abolition and Slavery: Delivered in the House of Representatives, Feb. 3 & 7, 1849.* Washington, D.C.: Congressional Globe Office, 1849.

BURKE, EDMOND (N. H.; 26, 27, 28)

————. *An Address Delivered before the Democratic Republican Citizens of Lempster, New Hampshire, on the Eighth of January, 1839.* n.p.: H. E. & S. C. Baldwin, Printers, 1839.

————. *An Important Appeal to the People of the United States. Slavery and Abolitionism. Union and Disunion.* n.p., [1856].

Ray, P. O., ed. "Some Papers of Franklin Pierce, 1852–1862." Reprinted from *American Historical Review* X, nos. 1–2 (Oct. 1904–Jan. 1905).

Sullivan Bros. & Libbie, Auctioneers, comp. *Catalogue of the Private Library of the Late Edmund Burke, of Newport, New Hampshire.* Boston: W. F. Brown & Co., Printers, 1883.

CARTTER, DAVID K. (Ohio; 31, 32)

Barnard, Job. "Early Days of the Supreme Court of the District of Columbia." *Records of the Columbia Historical Society* 22 (1919):1–35.

Curran, Ruth Gertrude. "David Kellogg Cartter." *Ohio Archaeological and Historical Quarterly* 42 (Jan. 1933):105–115.

CLARK, HORACE F. (N. Y.; 35, 36)

————. *Speech of Hon. H. F. Clark, of New York, upon the Subject of the Admission of Kansas as a State under the LeCompton Constitution. Delivered in the House of Representatives, Mar. 24, 1858.* Washington, D.C.: n.p., 1858.

DAVIS, RICHARD DAVID (N. Y.; 27, 28)

————. *An Address delivered before the Literary Societies of Geneva College, on the First of August, 1843.* Geneva, N. Y.: Scotten & Stow, 1843.

DISNEY, DAVID T. (Ohio; 31, 32, 33)

————. *Eulogy on the Death of General Thomas L. Hamer.* Cincinnati: John Hitchler, Printer, 1847.

DOTY, JAMES D. (Wis.; 31, 32)

Ellis, Gen. Albert G. "Life and Public Services of J. D. Doty." Vol. V, *Report and Collections of the State Historical Society of Wisconsin for the Years 1867, 1868, & 1869*. Madison, Wis.: Atwood & Rublee, State Printers, Journal Office, 1869.

Smith, Alice Elizabeth. *James Duane Doty, Frontier Promoter*. Madison: State Historical Society of Wisconsin, 1954.

Thwaites, Reuben Gold, ed. "Papers of James Duane Doty." Vol. XIII, *Collections of the State Historical Society of Wisconsin*. Madison, Wis.: Democrat Printing Co., State Printer, 1895.

DUNCAN, ALEXANDER (Ohio; 25, 26, 28)

————. *Speech of Mr. Duncan, of Ohio. Delivered in the House of Representatives, Mar. 6, 1844*. n.p., n.d.

————. *Speech of Mr. Duncan, of Ohio, in the House of Representatives, Feb. 19, in Committee on the Army Appropriations Bill*. Washington, D.C.: n.p., 1845.

————. *Speech of Mr. Duncan, of Ohio, on the Bill Making Appropriations for Harbors, and in Reply to Mr. Bond, of Ohio*. Washington, D.C.: Congressional Globe Office, 1838.

————. *Speech of Mr. Duncan, of Ohio, on the General Appropriation Bill for 1840*. New York: Evening Post Office, 1840.

FLORENCE, THOMAS B. (Pa.; 32, 33, 34, 35, 36)

————. *Speech of Hon. Thomas B. Florence, of Pennsylvania, in the House of Representatives, Apr. 14, 1852, on the Subject of the Public Printing, the Contract System, and in favor of the Immediate Establishment of a National Printing Office*. Washington, D.C.: Congressional Globe Office, [1852].

FRIES, GEORGE (Ohio; 29, 30)

————. *Speech in U. S. Congress. Speeches on the Oregon Question and on the Mexican War*. 29th Cong., 1st Sess., 1845–1846.

FULLER, THOMAS J. D. (Maine; 31, 32, 33, 34)

————. *Democracy National and Not Sectional. Speech of Hon. Thomas J. D. Fuller, of Maine, Delivered in the House of Representatives, Aug. 28, 1856*. Washington, D.C.: Congressional Globe Office, 1856.

HASKIN, JOHN B. (N. Y.; 35, 36)

————. *The Course of Hon. John B. Haskin, in the XXVth Congress, Its Own Vindication*. New York: Sackett & Cobb, Steam Book & Job Printers, 1858.

————. *Remarks of the Hon. John B. Haskin, of Westchester County, New York, in Reply to an Attack Made by the President's Home Organ, "The Constitution," upon Anti-Lecompton Democrats, and Colloquy between Mr. Logan, of Illinois, and Mr. Haskin. Delivered in the House of Representatives, Dec., 1859*. Washington, D.C.: Thomas McGill, Printer, 1859.

HENDRICKS, THOMAS A. R. (Ind.; 32, 33)

————. *Reconciliation and Union. Speech of Hon. Thomas A. Hendricks, of Indiana, in the United States Senate, June 4, 1866*. n.p., n.d.

————. *Speech of Hon. T. A. Hendricks, of Indiana. In the Senate of the United States, Feb. 16, 1866*. Washington, D.C.: H. Polkinhorn & Son, 1866.

HENLEY, THOMAS J. (Ind.; 28, 29, 30)

————. *The War with Mexico. Speech of Hon. Thomas J. Henley, of Indiana, in the House of Representatives, Jan. 26, 1848*. Washington, D.C.: Congressional Globe Office, 1848.

HICKMAN, JOHN (Pa.; 34, 35, 36)
————. *Democracy—The Old and the New. Speech of Hon. John Hickman, of Pennsylvania, on the Battle Ground of Brandywine, Sept. 11, 1860.* Washington, D.C.: [Buell & Blanchard, 1860].
————. *Kansas Contested Election. Speech of Hon. John Hickman, of Pennsylvania, Delivered in the House of Representatives, Mar. 19, 1856.* Washington, D.C.: Congressional Globe Office, [1856].
————. *Popular Sovereignty—The Will of the Majority against the Rule of a Minority. Speech of Hon. J. Hickman, of Pennsylvania, in the House of Representatives, Jan. 18, 1858.* Washington, D.C.: Congressional Globe Office, 1858.
————. *Southern Sectionalism. Speech of Hon. John Hickman, of Pennsylvania. Delivered in the U.S. House of Representatives, May 1, 1860.* [Washington, D.C.: Buell & Blanchard, 1860].
————. *Who Have Violated Compromises. Speech of Hon. John Hickman, of Pennsylvania. Delivered in the House of Representatives, Dec. 12, 1859.* Washington, D.C.: Buell & Blanchard, 1859.
HOGE, JOSEPH P. (Ill.; 28, 29)
————. *Speech* in U.S. Congress. *Speeches on the Oregon Question and on the Mexican War.* 29th Cong., 1st Sess., 1845–1846.
INGERSOLL, CHARLES J. (Pa.; 27, 28, 29, 30)
————. *African Slavery in America.* Philadelphia: T. K. & P. G. Collins, Printers, 1856.
————. *A Communication on the Improvement of Government: Read before the American Philosophical Society, at a Meeting Attended by General LaFayette, Oct. 1st, 1824.* Philadelphia: Abraham Small, Printer, 1824.
————. *A Discourse Concerning the Influence of America on the Mind; Being the Annual Oration Delivered before the American Philosophical Society, at the University in Philadelphia, on the 18th Oct., 1823.* Philadelphia: Abraham Small, 1823.
————. *A Discourse Delivered before the Society for the Commemoration of the Landing of William Penn, on the 24th of Oct., 1825.* Philadelphia: R. H. Small, 1825.
————. *Historical Sketch of the Second War between the United States of America, and Great Britain.* Philadelphia: Lea & Blanchard, 1845.
————. *Recollections, Historical, Political, Biographical, and Social, of Charles J. Ingersoll.* Philadelphia: J. B. Lippincott & Co., 1861.
————. *Speech of Hon. C. J. Ingersoll, of Pennsylvania, on the Mexican War. Delivered in the House of Representatives, Tuesday, Jan. 19, 1847.* Washington, D.C.: Blair & Rives, 1847.
————. *A View of the Rights and Wrongs, Power and Policy, of the United States of America.* Philadelphia: O. & A. Conrad & Co., 1808.
Meigs, William M. *The Life of Charles Jared Ingersoll.* Philadelphia: J. B. Lippincott Co., 1897.
KING, PRESTON (N. Y.; 28, 29, 31, 32)
————. *The Rights of the People of Kansas. Speech of Preston King, of New York, in the Senate of the United States, Mar. 16th, 1858, on the Frauds, Usurpation and Purpose, in Which the Slave Constitution of the Lecompton Convention Had Its Origin.* Washington, D.C.: Buell & Blanchard, 1858.
McCLERNAND, JOHN A. (Ill.; 28, 29, 30, 31, 36)
————. *Address of John A. McClernand, of Illinois, to His Constituents.* Washington, D.C.: Congressional Globe Office, 1848.

————. *Speech of Hon. J. A. McClernand, of Illinois, in Review of the Internal or Domestic Policy of the Present Administration of the Government. Delivered in the House of Representatives, Jan. 10, 1848.* Washington, D.C.: Blair & Rives, 1848.

————. *Speech of Hon. John A. McClernand, of Illinois, on the State of the Union: Delivered in the House of Representatives, Jan. 14, 1861.* Washington, D.C.: Congressional Globe Office, 1861.

McKEON, JOHN (N. Y.; 24, 27)

————. *The Administration Reviewed. Speech of Hon. John McKeon before the Democratic Union Association, Wed., Oct. 29, 1862.* New York: Van Evrie, Horton & Co., 1862.

————. *Peace and Union—War and Disunion. Speech of Hon. John McKeon, Delivered before the Democratic Union Association.* New York: Van Evrie, Horton & Co., 1863.

MORRIS, ISAAC N. (Ill.; 35, 36)

————. *Speech of Hon. I. N. Morris, on the Status of the States and Questions Incidentally Connected Therewith. Delivered at the House of Representatives, Springfield, Ill., Jan. 11, 1867.* n.p., n.d.

MURPHY, HENRY C. (N. Y.; 28, 30)

————. *Anthology of New Netherland or Translations from the Early Dutch Poets of New York with Memoirs of Their Lives.* New York, 1865; Amsterdam: N. Israel, 1966.

[————]. *A Catalogue of an American Library, Chronologically Arranged.* Brooklyn, N. Y.: I. Van Anden, Printer, [1875].

————. *Henry Hudson in Holland. An Inquiry into the Origins and Objects of the Voyage Which Led to the Discovery of the Hudson River. With Bibliographical Notes.* The Hague: The Brothers Giunta D'Albani, 1859.

————. *Remarks of Mr. Murphy, of New York, Delivered in the House of Representatives, on the 24th of Feb., 1849.* n.p., [1849].

————. *Speech of Hon. H. C. Murphy, of New York, on Slavery in the Territories. Delivered in the House of Representatives, May 17, 1848.* Washington, D.C.: Congressional Globe Office, 1848.

PARMENTER, WILLIAM (Mass.; 25, 26, 27, 28)

————. U.S. Congress. House. Committee on Naval Affairs. *Accident on Steam-Ship "Princeton." Report No. 479.* Washington, D.C.: Blair & Rives, Printer, 1844.

PENDLETON, GEORGE H. (Ohio; 35, 36)

————. *But, Sir, Armies, Money, Blood Cannot Maintain This Union—Justice, Reason, Peace May. Speech of Hon. George H. Pendleton, of Ohio, on the State of the Union. Delivered in the House of Representatives, Jan. 18, 1861.* Washington, D.C.: Lemuel Towers, 1861.

————. *Payment of the Public Debt in Legal Tender Notes. Speech of Hon. George H. Pendleton, Milwaukee, Nov. 2, 1867.* n.p., n.d.

SCOTT, CHARLES L. (Calif.; 34, 35, 36)

————. *Speech of Hon. Charles L. Scott, of California, on the Steamboat Passenger Bill; Delivered in the House of Representatives, Feb. 10, 1858.* Washington, D.C.: Congressional Globe Office, 1858.

SMART, EPHRAIM K. (Maine; 30, 32)

————. *Speech of Hon. E. K. Smart, of Maine, in Defence [sic] of the North against*

the Charge of Aggression upon the South. Delivered in the House of Represen-
tatives, Apr. 23, 1852. Washington, D.C.: Congressional Globe Office, 1852.
WARD, AARON (N. Y.; 24, 27)
———. *Around the Pyramids: Being a Tour in the Holy Land, and Incidentally, through*
Several European Countries and Portions of Africa, During the Years 1859–60.
4th ed. New York: Carleton, Publisher, 1865.
———. *Speech of General Aaron Ward, of Westchester County, New York, at a Dem-*
ocratic Meeting Held at New Rochelle, Mar. 27, 1858, at which Richard Lathers,
Esq., Presided. New York: J. W. Bell, Printer, 1858.
———. *Speech of Mr. Ward, of New York, on the Bill Making Appropriations for the*
Military Academy at West Point. [Washington, D.C. n.p., 1834].
WENTWORTH, JOHN (Ill.; 28, 29, 30, 31)
———. *Congressional Reminiscences. Adams, Benton, Calhoun, Clay, and Webster.*
An Address Delivered at Central Music Hall, Thursday Eve, Mar. 16, 1882,
before the Chicago Historical Society. Fergus Historical Series, no. 24. Chicago:
Fergus Printing Co., 1882.
———. *Early Chicago: A Lecture. Delivered before the Sunday Lecture Society. Apr.*
11, 1875, with Supplemental Notes. Chicago: Fergus Printing Co., 1876.
———. *Early Chicago: A Lecture, Delivered before the Sunday Lecture Society, May*
7, 1876. Chicago: Fergus Printing Co., 1876.
———. *Loan Bill. Speech of Hon. John Wentworth, of Illinois, in the House of Rep-*
resentatives, Mar. 15, 1866. Washington, D.C.: Congressional Globe Office,
1866.
———. *The Wentworth Genealogy: English and American.* Boston: Little, Brown, &
Co., 1878.
Fehrenbacher, Don Edward. *Chicago Giant: A Biography of "Long John" Wentworth.*
Madison, Wis.: American History Research Center, 1957.
WILMOT, DAVID (Pa.; 29, 30, 31)
———. *Slavery in the Territories. Speech of Hon. D. Wilmot, of Pennsylvania, in the*
House of Representatives, May 3, 1850, in Committee of the Whole on the State
of the Union, on the President's Message Transmitting the Constitution of Cali-
fornia. Washington, D.C.: Congressional Globe Office, 1850.
Going, Charles Buxton. *David Wilmot, Free Soiler: A Biography of the Great Advocate*
of the Wilmot Proviso. n.p.: D. Appleton & Co., c. 1924; Gloucester, Mass.:
Peter Smith, 1966.

Southern Democratic Mavericks

BOWIE, THOMAS FIELDER (Md.; 34, 35)
———. *Speech of Hon. T. F. Bowie, of Maryland, on the Organization of the House.*
Delivered in the House of Representatives, Jan. 9, 1856. Washington, D.C.:
Congressional Globe Office, 1856.
———. *Speech of Hon. T. F. Bowie, of Maryland, on the Resolution Reported by the*
Committee of Elections in the Contested-Election Case from Kansas Territory.
Delivered in the House of Representatives, Mar. 19, 1856. Washington, D.C.:
Congressional Globe Office, 1856. In *Buchanan and Breckinridge. The Demo-*
cratic Handbook, compiled by Mich. W. Cluskey. Washington, D.C.: R. A.
Waters, Printer, 1856.

Bowie, Effie Gwynn. *Across the Years in Prince George's County.* Richmond, Va.: Garrett & Drossie, 1947.

BOWLIN, JAMES BUTLER (Mo.; 28, 29, 30, 31)

————. *Speech* in U.S. Congress. *Speeches on the Oregon Question and on the Mexican War.* 29th Cong., 1st Sess., 1845–1846.

CHAPMAN, REUBEN (Ala.; 24, 25, 26, 27, 28, 29)

————. *Speech of Hon. R. Chapman, of Alabama, on the Bill to Protect the Rights of American Settlers in Oregon. Delivered in the House of Representatives, Apr. 17, 1846.* n.p., n.d.

CLEMENS, SHERRARD (Va.; 35, 36)

————. *Speech of Hon. Sherrard Clemens, of Virginia, on the President's Kansas Message; Delivered in the House of Representatives, Feb. 18, 1858.* Washington, D.C.: Congressional Globe Office, 1858.

————. *State of the Union. Speech of Hon. Sherrard Clemens, of Virginia, in the House of Representatives, Jan. 22, 1861.* Washington, D.C.: Congressional Globe Office, 1861.

CLINGMAN, THOMAS L. (N. C.; 28, 30, 31, W; 32, 33, 34, 35, D)

————. *The Geneva Award.* Washington, D.C.: McGill & Witherow, Printers, 1876.

————. *Letter of T. L. Clingman to the Editors of the "Republic."* Washington, D.C.: Gideon & Co., Printers, 1850.

————. *Nebraska and Kansas. Speech of Mr. Clingman, of North Carolina, in the House of Representatives, Apr. 4, 1854.* n.p., n.d.

————. *Selections from the Speeches and Writings of Hon. Thomas L. Clingman of North Carolina.* Raleigh, N. C.: J. Nichols, Printer, 1877.

————. *Speech of Hon. Thomas L. Clingman, of North Carolina, aginst the Revolutionary Movement of the Anti-Slavery Party: Delivered in the Senate of the United States, Jan. 16, 1860.* Washington, D.C.: Congressional Globe Office, 1860.

————. *Speech of Hon. Thomas L. Clingman, of North Carolina, on British Policy in Central America and Cuba. House of Representatives, Feb. 5, 1857.* Washington, D.C.: Congressional Globe Office, 1857.

————. *Speech of Hon. Thomas L. Clingman, of North Carolina, on the Resolutions Reported by the Select Committee to Investigate the Alleged Assault upon Senator Sumner by Mr. Brooks; Delivered in the House of Representatives, July 9, 1856.* n.p., n.d.

————. *Speech of Hon. Thomas L. Clingman, of North Carolina, on the Subject of Congressional Legislation, as to the Rights of Property in the Territories, Delivered in the Senate of the United States, May 7 & 8, 1860.* Baltimore: John Murphy & Co., Printers, 1860.

————. *Speech of Hon. T. L. Clingman, of N. C., in Favor of His Proposition for a Mediation in the Eastern War. Delivered in the House of Representatives, Jan. 3, 1855.* Washington, D.C.: Congressional Globe Office, 1855.

————. *Speech of T. L. Clingman, of North Carolina, on the Late Presidential Election. Delivered in the House of Representatives, U.S., Jan. 6, 1845.* n.p., n.d.

————. *The Tobacco Remedy.* New York: Orange Judd Co., 1885.

Huger, John M. *Memoranda of the Late Affair of Honor between Hon. T. L. Clingman, of North Carolina, and Hon. William L. Yancey, of Alabama.* Washington, D.C.: n.p., 1845.

COBB, WILLIAMSON R. W. (Ala.; 30, 31, 32, 33, 34, 35, 36)

————. *Railroad in Alabama, and the Public Lands. Speech of Hon. W. R. W. Cobb, of Alabama, in House of Representatives, in Committee of the Whole, upon the Contemplated Railroad in Alabama, and the Condition of the Public Lands Generally.* Washington, D.C.: Congressional Globe Office, 1851.

GARLAND, JAMES (Va.; 24, 25, 26)

————. *Letter of James Garland to His Constituents.* 2d ed. Washington, D.C.: n.p., Apr. 18, 1840.

————. *Speech of James Garland, of Virginia, against the Financial Policy of the Administration and in Vindication of the Conservative Republicans; Delivered in the House of Representatives, Feb. 23, 1839.* Washington, D.C.: Madisonian Office, 1839.

GARNETT, MUSCOE R. H. (Va.; 35, 36)

————. *An Address Delivered before the Society of Alumni of the University of Virginia, at Its Annual Meeting. Held in the Rotunda, on the 29th of June, 1850. Published by order of the Society.* Charlottesville, Va.: G. S. Allen & Co., Printer, 1850.

————. *Speech of Hon. M. R. H. Garnett, of Virginia, on the State of the Union, Delivered in the House of Representatives, Jan. 16, 1861.* Washington, D.C.: McGill & Witherow, Printers, 1861.

[————]. *The Union, Past and Future: How It Works, and How to Save It. By A Citizen of Virginia.* Washington, D.C.: Jus. T. Towers, Printer, 1850.

Garnett, James Mercer. *Biographical Sketch of Hon. Muscoe Russell Hunter Garnett.* Reprint. *William and Mary College Quarterly Magazine,* July and Oct. Numbers (1909).

GREENWOOD, ALFRED B. (Ark.; 33, 34, 35)

————. *Letter of Hon. Alfred B. Greenwood, of Arkansas, to His Constituents.* Washington, D.C.: Congressional Globe Office, 1856.

HOLMES, ISAAC E. (S. C.; 26, 27, 28, 29, 30, 31)

————. *Speech of the Hon. Isaac Holmes, of South Carolina, on the Annexation of Texas to the United States. Delivered in the House of Representatives, Jan. 14, 1845.* [Washington, D.C.: n.p., 1845.]

HOPKINS, GEORGE W. (Va.; 24, 25, 26, 27, 28, 29, 35)

————. *Letter of George W. Hopkins, of Russell, to Col. James H. Piper, of Wythe.* Washington, D.C.: n.p., 1840.

HOUSTON, GEORGE S. (Ala.; 27, 28, 29, 30, 32, 33, 34, 35, 36)

————. *Speech of Hon. George S. Houston, of Alabama, on the Bill Reducing and Graduating the Price of the Public Lands of the United States. Delivered in the House of Representative, Feb. 5, 1845.* [Washington, D.C.: n.p., 1845].

Memorial Addresses on the Life & Character of George S. Houston, Delivered in the Senate and House of Representatives, Forty-Sixth Congress, Second Session, Feb. 26 and Mar. 3, 1880, with the Proceedings Connected with the Funeral of the Deceased. Washington, D.C.: Government Printing Office, 1880.

JONES, GEORGE W. (Tenn.; 28, 29, 30, 31, 32, 33, 34, 35)

————. *Letter of Hon. G. W. Jones, of Tennessee, to His Constituents.* [n.p., 1856].

————. *Oration of Hon. George W. Jones, with Other Proceedings, at the Unveiling of the Monument to the Memory of Ex-President Andrew Johnson, at Greeneville, Tennessee, June 5, 1878.* Nashville, Tenn.: The American, Printer, 1878.

McMULLEN, FAYETTE (Va.; 31, 32, 33, 34)

————. *Letter of Hon. Fayette McMullen to the People of the Thirteenth Congressional District of Virginia*. n.p., 1856.

ORR, JAMES L. (S. C.; 31, 32, 33, 34, 35)

————. *An Address Delivered before the Philosophian & Adelphian Societies of the Furman University, at Their Annual Meeting, Greenville, South Carolina, July 18, 1855*. Greenville, S. C.: G. E. Elford & Co., Printer, 1855.

————. *The Cincinnati Convention. Letter from James L. Orr, of South Carolina, to Hon. C. W. Dudley, on the Propriety of Having the State of South Carolina Represented in the Democratic National Convention, to be Held in Cincinnati.* [Washington, D.C.: n.p., 1855].

Leemhuis, Roger P. *James L. Orr and the Sectional Conflict*. Washington, D.C.: University Press of America, 1979.

PHELPS, JOHN S. (Mo.; 29, 30, 31, 32, 33, 34, 35, 36)

————. *Letter of Hon. John S. Phelps, of Missouri, to His Constituents*. Washington, D.C.: n.p., 1856.

RHETT, ROBERT BARNWELL (S. C.; 25, 26, 27, 28, 29, 30)

————. *Address to the People of Beaufort and Colleton Districts, upon the Subject of Abolition, by Robert Barnwell Rhett. Jan. 15, 1838*. [Washington, D.C.: n.p., 1838].

————. *Letter of the Hon. R. B. Rhett, to the Editors of the National Intelligencer on the Right of Debate in Congress*. Washington, D.C.: Congressional Globe Office, 1841.

————. *Speech of Mr. R. Barnwell Rhett, of South Carolina, on the Veto Power: Delivered in the House of Representatives, July 1, 1842*. Washington, D.C.: Congressional Globe Office, 1842.

————. *Speech of Mr. Rhett, of South Carolina, on the Oregon Question. Delivered in the House of Representatives, U.S., Jan. 5, 1846*. Washington, D.C.: J. & G. S. Gideon, 1846.

————. *Speech of Mr. Rhett, of South Carolina, on the Subject of Taxation, Delivered on the General Appropriation Bill in the House of Representatives of the United States on Friday, Feb. 19, 1841*. Washington, D.C.: Blair & Rives, 1841.

————. *Speech of Robert Barnwell Rhett, on the Treasury Note Bill, Delivered in the House of Representatives, Jan. 21, 1841*. Washington, D.C.: Blair & Rives, 1841.

White, Laura. *Robert Barnwell Rhett: the Father of Secession*. New York: Century Company, 1931.

SAVAGE, JOHN H. (Tenn.; 32, 34, 35)

————. *Speech of Hon. John H. Savage, of Tennessee, on the Kansas Contested Election. Delivered in the House of Representatives, July 31, 1856*. Washington, D.C.: Congressional Globe Office, 1856.

SMITH, WILLIAM (Va.; 33, 34, 35, 36)

————. *Speech of Hon. William Smith, of Virginia, on the Bill for the Admission of Minnesota; Delivered in the House of Representatives, May 6, 1858*. Washington, D.C.: Congressional Globe Office, 1858.

————. *Speech of Mr. William Smith, of Virginia: on the Tariff Bill, Delivered in the House of Representatives, July 9, 1842*. Washington, D.C.: Congressional Globe Office, 1842.

Bell, John W. *Memoirs of Governor William Smith, of Virginia. His Political, Military, and Personal History.* New York: Moss Engraving Co., 1891.

STANTON, FREDERICK P. (Tenn.; 29, 30, 31, 32, 33)

————. *Address Delivered by Mr. Fred P. Stanton, of Tennessee, before the Metropolitan Mechanics Institute, at the Opening of Its Annual Exhibition in Washington, D.C., Mar. 2, 1857.* Washington, D.C.: n.p., 1857.

————. *The Character of Modern Science, or, the Mission of the Educated Man. An Address Delivered before the Alumni Association of Columbian College, July 21, 1852.* Washington, D.C.: Robert A. Waters, Printer, 1852.

————. *Great Meeting at Philadelphia. The Democracy at National Hall, Feb. 8, 1858. Speech of Hon. F. P. Stanton & Letter of Governor Walker.* Philadelphia: Forney's Philadelphia Press, 1858.

————. *A Lecture Delivered by the Hon. F. P. Stanton, on the Navy of the United States, before the Mercantile Library Association, Feb. 3, 1854.* New York: Samuel T. Callahan, 1854.

————. *Letter of F. P. Stanton to the Secretary of the Navy, in Relation to Pirsson's Condenser.* Washington, D.C.: n.p., May 31, 1855.

STANTON, RICHARD H. (Ky.; 31, 32, 33)

————. *Speech of Richard H. Stanton, Esq., in Defence of the Mexican War; Delivered at the War Meeting, Maysville, Saturday, Dec. 18, 1847.* Maysville, Ky.: Kentucky Flag Office, Printer, 1848.

WATKINS, ALBERT G. (Tenn.; 31, 32, W; 34, 35, D)

————. *Circular of Albert G. Watkins, of Tennessee, to His Constituents of the First Congressional District.* Washington, D.C.: Congressional Globe Office, 1856.

Northern Whig and Republican Conformists

BAKER, EDWARD D. (Ill.; 29, 31, W)

————. *Masterpieces of E. D. Baker.* In *Eloquence of the Far West*, edited by Oscar T. Shuck, no. 1. San Francisco: Published by the Editor, 1899.

Blair, Harry C., and Rebecca Tarshis. *Lincoln's Constant Ally: The Life of Colonel Edward D. Baker.* Portland: Oregon Historical Society, 1960.

Kennedy, Elijah R. *The Contest for California in 1861: How Colonel E. D. Baker Saved the Pacific States to the Union.* Boston & New York: Houghton, Mifflin & Co., 1912.

Wallace, Joseph. *Sketch of the Life and Public Services of Edward D. Baker, United States Senator from Oregon.* Springfield, Ill.: Journal Co., Printers & Binders, 1870.

BENNETT, HENRY (N. Y.; 31, 32, 33, W; 34, 35, R)

————. *Kansas and Slavery. Speech of Hon. Henry Bennett, of New York. Delivered in the U. S. House of Representatives, Mar. 29, 1858.* Washington, D.C.: Buell & Blanchard, 1858.

————. *Kansas Must be Free. The Political Effects of Slavery. Speech of Hon. Henry Bennett, of New York, on the Bill for the Admission of Kansas as a Free State, Delivered in the House of Representatives, June 30, 1856.* n.p., n.d.

BIDDLE, RICHARD (Pa.; 25, 26, W)

————. *Captain Hall in America. By an American.* Philadelphia: Carey & Lea, 1830.

————. *A Memoir of Sebastian Cabot; with a Review of the History of Maritime Discovery.* London: Hurst, Chance, & Co., 1831.

————. *Remarks of Mr. Biddle of Pennsylvania, on the Bill to Postpone the Fourth Instalment [sic] Payable under the Deposit Act. Delivered in the House of Representatives, Sept., 1837.* Washington, D.C.: Gales & Seaton, Printers, 1837.

————. *Speech of Mr. Biddle, on the Bill to Authorize the Issue of Treasury Notes. Delivered in the House of Representatives, May 15, 1838.* Washington, D.C.: n.p., 1838.

BLISS, PHILEMON (Ohio; 34, 35, R)

————. *Complaints of the Extensionists—Their Falsity. Speech of Hon. Philemon Bliss, of Ohio, in the House of Representatives, May 21, 1856.* n.p., n.d.

————. *Letter to the People of the Fourteenth Congressional District. Appended to Free Sugar Speech of Hon. Schuyler Colfax, of Indiana.* Washington, D.C.: Buell & Blanchard, 1857.

————. *Success of the Abolitionists. Their Idealism; What and Whence Is It? Speech of Hon. Philemon Bliss, of Ohio, in the House of Representatives, May 24, 1858.* Washington, D.C.: Buell & Blanchard, 1858.

BOND, WILLIAM KEY (Ohio; 24, 25, 26, W)

————. *Speech of Mr. Bond, of Ohio, on the Treasury Note Bill. Delivered in the House of Representatives, Mar. 18, 1840.* Washington, D.C.: n.p., 1840.

————. *Speech of Mr. Bond, of Ohio, upon the Resolution to Correct Abuses in the Public Expenditures, and to Separate the Government from the Press. Delivered in the House of Representatives, Apr., 1838.* Washington, D.C.: n.p., 1838.

BRIGGS, GEORGE NIXON (Mass.; 24, 25, 26, 27, W)

Richards, William C. *Great in Goodness: A Memoir of George N. Briggs.* Boston: Gould & Lincoln, 1866.

BUFFINTON, JAMES (Mass.; 34, 35, 36, R)

————. *Kansas—The Lecompton Constitution. Speech of Hon. James Buffinton, of Massachusetts. Delivered in the House of Representatives, Mar. 24, 1858.* Washington, D.C.: Buell & Blanchard, 1858.

————. *Position of Massachusetts on the Slavery Question. Speech of Hon. James Buffinton, of Massachusetts, in the House of Representatives, Apr. 30, 1856.* Washington, D.C.: Buell & Blanchard, 1856.

BURLINGAME, ANSON (Mass.; 34, 35, 36, R)

————. *An Appeal to Patriots against Fraud and Disunion. Speech of Hon. Anson Burlingame, of Massachusetts. Delivered in the U. S. House of Representatives, Mar. 31, 1858.* Washington, D.C.: Buell & Blanchard, 1858.

————. *Defence [sic] of Massachusetts. Speech of Hon. Anson Burlingame, of Massachusetts, in the United States House of Representatives, June 21, 1856.* Cambridge, Mass.: Printed for private distribution, 1856.

Williams, Frederick Wells. *Anson Burlingame and the First Chinese Mission to Foreign Powers.* New York: Charles Scribner's Sons, 1912.

Yeager, Carl Francis, Jr. "Anson Burlingame: His Mission to China and the First Chinese Mission to Western Nations." Diss., Georgetown University, May 25, 1950.

CALHOUN, WILLIAM B. (Mass.; 24, 25, 26, 27, W)

————. *Addresses at the Dedication of the New Cabinet and Observatory of Amherst College, June 28, 1848.* Amherst, Mass.: J. S. & C. Adams, Printers, 1848.

COCHRANE, CLARK B. (N. Y.; 35, 36, R)

————. *The Lecompton Constitution. Speech of Hon. Clark B. Cochrane, of New York.*

Delivered in the U. S. House of Representatives, Jan. 26, 1858. Washington, D.C.: Buell & Blanchard, 1858.

————. *Memorial of Clark B. Cochrane.* Albany, N. Y.: Joel Munsell, 1867.

COLFAX, SCHUYLER (Ind.; 34, 35, 36, R)

————. *Example and Effort. An Address, Delivered before the Congressional Temperance Society, at Washington, D. C.* New York: National Temperance Society & Publication House, 1872.

————. *Kansas—The Lecompton Constitution. Speech of Hon. Schuyler Colfax, of Indiana, in the House of Representatives, Mar. 20, 1858.* Washington, D.C.: Buell & Blanchard, Printers, 1858.

————. *The "Laws" of Kansas. Speech of Hon. Schuyler Colfax, of Indiana. In the House of Representatives, June 21, 1856.* New York: Tribune Office, 1856.

————. *Life and Principles of Abraham Lincoln. Delivered in the Court House Square at South Bend, Apr. 24, 1865.* Philadelphia: Jas. B. Rodgers, Printer, 1865.

Hollister, O. J. *Life of Schuyler Colfax.* New York: Funk & Wagnalls, 1886.

Smith, Willard H. *Schuyler Colfax, The Changing Fortunes of a Political Idol.* Indiana Historical Collection, vol. XXXIII. Indianapolis: Indiana Historical Bureau, 1952.

CORWIN, THOMAS (Ohio; 24, 25, 26, W; 36, R)

————. *Life and Speeches of Thomas Corwin, Orator, Lawyer and Statesman.* Edited by Josiah Marrow. Cincinnati: W. H. Anderson & Co., 1896.

COVODE, JOHN (Pa.; 34, 35, 36, R)

————. *Kansas—The Lecompton Constitution. Popular Sovereignty, Theoretical and Practical. Speech of Hon. Jno. Covode, of Pennsylvania. Delivered in the House of Representatives, Mar. 25, 1858.* Washington, D.C.: Buell & Blanchard, 1858.

CURTIS, SAMUEL R. (Iowa; 35, 36, R)

————. *The Central American Question. Speech of Hon. Samuel R. Curtis, of Iowa, Delivered in the House of Representatives, Jan. 15, 1858.* Washington, D.C.: Buell & Blanchard, 1858.

————. *The Mormon Rebellion and the Bill to Raise Volunteers. Speech of Hon. Samuel R. Curtis, of Iowa. Delivered in the U. S. House of Representatives, Mar. 10, 1858.* Washington, D.C.: n.p., 1858.

————. *Remarks of Hon. Samuel R. Curtis, of Iowa, on the Bill Granting Pensions to Soldiers Who Served in the Last War with Great Britain and the Indian Wars Preceding. Delivered in the U. S. House of Representatives, Apr. 27, 1858.* Washington, D.C.: Buell & Blanchard, 1858.

DAWES, HENRY L. (Mass.; 35, 36, R)

————. *The Admission of Oregon. Speech of Hon. Henry L. Dawes, of Massachusetts. Delivered in the U. S. House of Representatives, Feb. 11, 1859.* Washington, D.C.: Buell & Blanchard, 1859.

————. *Defence [sic] of the Committee on Government Contracts. Speech of Hon. Henry L. Dawes, of Massachusetts, Delivered in the U. S. House of Representatives, Apr. 25, 1862.* Washington, D.C.: Scammell & Co., Printers, 1862.

————. *Government Contracts. Speech of Hon. Henry L. Dawes of Massachusetts. Delivered in the House of Representatives, Jan. 13, 1862.* Washington, D.C.: Scammell & Co., Printers, 1862.

————. *The Lecompton Constitution Founded Neither in Law nor the Will of the People. Speech of Hon. Henry L. Dawes, of Massachusetts. Delivered in the U. S. House of Representatives, Mar. 8, 1858*. Washington, D.C.: Buell & Blanchard, Printers, 1858.

————. *The Mission to Rome. Remarks of Hons. John A. Bingham, H. L. Dawes, G. S. Orth, and George T. Hoar. In the House of Representatives, May 19, 1870*. Washington, D.C.: Cunningham & McIntosh, Printers, 1870.

————. *The New Dogma of the South—"Slavery a Blessing." Speech of Hon. Henry L. Dawes, of Massachusetts. Delivered in the House of Representatives, Apr. 12, 1860*. n.p., n.d.

————. *Speech of Hon. Henry L. Dawes, of Massachusetts, in the House of Representatives of the U. S. Mar. 2nd, 1865. Printed Feb. 6, 1903, the Day of the Announcement of His Death. Issued the Day of His Funeral in Honor of His Memory, by Franklin Webster Smith, in Grateful Remembrance*. n.p., 1903.

DIXON, JAMES (Conn.; 29, 30, W)

————. *American Labor: Its Necessities and Prospects. Delivered before the American Institute, Thursday Evening, Oct. 2, 1852*. New York: Mann & Spear, Printers, 1852.

————. *Peace and ReUnion. Speech of Hon. James Dixon, (of Connecticut,) Delivered in the Senate of the United States, Feb. 27, 1866*. Washington, D.C.: Henry Polkinhorn & Son, Book & Job Printers, 1866.

————. *Speech of Hon. James Dixon, of Connecticut, on the National Finances, in Reply to Mr. Morton and Mr. Terry. Delivered in the Senate of the United States, Dec. 17, 1868*. Washington, D.C.: F. & J. Rives & Geo. A. Bailey, 1868.

————. *Speech of Hon. James Dixon, of Connecticut, on the Thirty Million Bill, for the Acquisition of Cuba. Delivered in the Senate of the United States, Feb. 25, 1859*. Washington, D.C.: Lemuel Towers, Printer, 1859.

————. *Speech of James Dixon, of Connecticut. Delivered in the Senate of the United States, Feb. 9, 1858*. Washington, D.C.: Buell & Blanchard, 1858.

————. *Speech of Mr. Dixon, of Connecticut, on the Reference of the President's Message. Delivered in the House of Representatives of the United States, Jan. 24, 1848*. Washington, D.C.: J. & G. S. Gideon, 1848.

DUER, WILLIAM (N. Y.; 30, 31, W)

————. *Speech of Mr. William Duer, of New York, on the Origin of the War with Mexico, and the Objects of the Administration in Its Prosecution. Delivered in the House of Representatives of the U. States, Feb. 14, 1848*. Washington, D.C.: J. & G. S. Gideon, Printers, 1848.

DUNCAN, JAMES HENRY (Mass.; 31, 32, W)

————. *Address of James H. Duncan, Esq. Transactions*, Essex Agricultural Society, vol. I, no. 10. Salem, Mass.: W. & S. B. Ives, Printers, Observer Office, 1831.

Munger, Theodore Thornton. *In Memoriam. James Henry Duncan*. Cambridge, Mass.: Press of John Wilson & Sons, n.d.

ELIOT, THOMAS D. (Mass.; 33, W; 36, R)

————. *Address of Thomas D. Eliot, of the 1st Congressional District of Massachusetts, to His Constituents*. Washington, D.C.: H. Polkinhorn, 1861.

————. *Freedmen's Bureau. Speech of Hon. Thomas D. Eliot, of Massachusetts, in the House of Representatives, May 23, 1866*. Washington, D.C.: Congressional Globe Office, [1866].

————. *Independence of Hayti. Speech of Hon. Thomas D. Eliot, of Massachusetts, in the House of Representatives, June 3, 1862*. Washington, D.C.: Scammell & Co., Printers, 1862.

———. *Nebraska and Kansas. Speech of Hon. T. D. Eliot, of Massachusetts, in the House of Representatives, May 10, 1854*. n.p., n.d.

———. *Objects of the War. Speech of Hon. Thomas D. Eliot, of Massachusetts, in the House of Representatives, Dec. 12, 1861*. Washington, D.C.: H. Polkinhorn, Printer, 1861.

———. *Speech of Thomas D. Eliot, of Massachusetts. Delivered in the House of Representatives Feb. 10, 1864, on the Bill for the Establishment of a Bureau of Freedman's Affairs*. Washington, D.C.: H. Polkinhorn, Printer, [1864].

———. *The Territorial Slave Policy; The Republican Party; What the North Has to Do with Slavery. Speech of Hon. Thomas D. Eliot, of Massachusetts. Delivered in the House of Representatives, Apr. 25, 1860*. n.p., n.d.

EVANS, GEORGE (Maine; 24, 25, 26, W)

———. *Discussion on the Tariff. Reply to Mr. Evans, of Maine, to Mr. McDuffie's Second Speech on the Tariff. Delivered in the Senate of the United States, Feb. 6 & 7, 1844*. Washington, D.C.: Gales & Seaton, 1844.

———. *The Tariff of 1842 Vindicated. Speech of George Evans, of Maine, in Reply to the Hon. Mr. McDuffie, of South Carolina, on the Tariff. Delivered in the Senate of the United States, Jan. 22 & 23rd, 1844*. Washington, D.C.: Gales & Seaton, Printers, 1844.

EVERETT, HORACE (Vt.; 24, 25, 26, 27, W)

———. *Mr. Everett's Address to the Whigs of Vermont. July, 1848*. Windsor, Vt.: Bishop & Tracy's Steam Press, 1848.

———. *Speech of Horace Everett, of Vermont: Delivered in the House of Representatives, in Committee of the Whole, on the Indian Annuity Bill, Friday, June 3, 1836*. Washington, D.C.: National Intelligencer Office, 1836.

———. *Speech of Mr. H. Everett of Vermont, on the Case of Alexander McLeod. Delivered in the House of Representatives of the United States, Sept. 3, 1841*. Washington, D.C.: National Intelligencer Office, 1841.

FARNSWORTH, JOHN F. (Ill.; 35, 36, R)

———. *Inter-state Railroad Commerce. Address of J. F. Farnsworth, before the Committee on Commerce of the House of Representatives, Jan. 21st, 1880, on the "Reagan Bill."* n.p., n.d.

———. *Speech of Hon. J. F. Farnsworth, of Illinois. Delivered in the House of Representatives, Dec. 23, 1859*. Washington, D.C.: Buell & Blanchard, 1859.

FENTON, REUBEN E. (N. Y.; 33, 35, 36, R)

———. *Designs of the Slave Power. Speech of Hon. Reuben E. Fenton, of New York. Delivered in the U. S. House of Representatives, Feb. 24, 1858*. Washington, D.C.: Buell & Blanchard, 1858.

———. *Position of Parties and Abuses of Power. Speech of Hon. Reuben E. Fenton, of New York. Delivered in the House of Representatives, Feb. 16, 1860*. Washington, D.C.: n.p., 1860.

———. *Revolutionary Claims. Speech of Hon. R. E. Fenton, of New York. In the House of Representatives, June 11, 1858*. Washington, D.C.: Buell & Blanchard, Printers, 1858.

FILLMORE, MILLARD (N. Y.; 25, 26, 27, W)

————. *Millard Fillmore Papers*. In *Publications of the Buffalo Historical Society*. Edited by Frank H. Severance. Vol. I. Buffalo: Buffalo Historical Society, 1907.

Rayback, Robert J. *Millard Fillmore*. Buffalo: Henry Stewart, 1959.

Richardson, James D., ed. *A Compilation of the Messages and Papers of the Presidents*. Vol. VI. New York: Bureau of National Literature Inc., 1897.

FOSTER, STEPHEN C. (Maine; 35, 36, R)

————. *The Rights of White Men Vindicated. Speech of Hon. Stephen C. Foster, of Maine. Delivered in the U. S. House of Representatives, Mar. 10th, 1858*. Washington, D.C.: Buell & Blanchard, 1858.

FULLER, HENRY M. (Pa.; 32, 34, W)

————. *Speech of Mr. Henry M. Fuller, of Pennsylvania, Delivered in the House of Representatives of the United States, May 10, 1856*. [Washington, D.C.]: American Organ, [1856].

GOOCH, DANIEL W. (Mass.; 35, 36, R)

————. *Any Compromise a Surrender. Speech of Hon. D. W. Gooch, of Massachusetts, in the House of Representatives, Feb. 23, 1861*. Washington, D.C.: National Republican Office, 1861.

————. *Organization of the Territories. Speech of Hon. Daniel W. Gooch, of Massachusetts. Delivered in the House of Representatives, May 11, 1860*. Washington, D.C.: Buell & Blanchard, 1860.

————. *Polygamy in Utah. Speech of Hon. Daniel W. Gooch, of Massachusetts. Delivered in the House of Representatives, Apr. 4, 1860*. n.p., n.d.

————. *Recognition of Hayti and Liberia. Speech of Hon. D. W. Gooch, of Massachusetts, Delivered in the House of Representatives, June 2, 1862*. Washington, D.C.: McGill, Witherow & Co., [1862].

GOODRICH, JOHN Z. (Mass.; 32, 33, W)

————. *Speech of Hon. J. Z. Goodrich, of Massachusetts. Delivered in the Peace Convention in Washington, Feb., 1861*. Boston; J. E. Farwell & Co., Printers, 1864.

GRINNELL, JOSEPH (Mass.; 28, 29, 30, 31, W)

[Rodman, Benjamin]. *Memoir of Joseph Grinnell. Read at a Dinner at William T. Russell's, on the 7th Day of Mar., 1862*. Boston: D. Clapp, Printer, 1863.

HALL, HILAND (Vt.; 24, 25, 26, 27, W)

————. "The Capture of Fort Ticonderoga in 1775." Vermont Historical Society. *Proceedings*, pp. 3–32 (Oct. 19 & 20, 1869). Montpelier: Journal Printing Establishment, 1869.

————. *The History of Vermont, from Its Discovery to Its Admission into the Union in 1791*. Albany, N. Y.: Joel Munsell, 1868.

————. *The Local History of Bennington, 1860–1883. The Military History of the County*. Edited by Abby Maria Hemenway. Chicago: n.p., n.d.

————. *Remarks of the Hon. Hiland Hall, made in the House of Representatives, May 5, 1834, on Presenting a Memorial from Windham County, Vermont, on the Subject of the Removal of the Public Deposites* [sic]. Washington, D.C.: Gales & Seaton, 1834.

————. *Vindication of Volume First of the Collections of the Vermont Historical Society from the Attacks of the New York Historical Magazine*. Montpelier: J. & J. M. Poland's Steam Press, 1871.

————. *Why the Early Inhabitants of Vermont Disclaimed the Jurisdiction of New York, and Established an Independent Government. An Address Delivered before the New York Historical Society, Dec. 4, 1860*. Bennington, Vt.: C. A. Pierce & Co., Printers, 1872.

Hall, Henry Davis. *Memoir of Hon. Hiland Hall, LL. D*. Boston: David Clapp & Son, 1885.

HALL, ROBERT B. (Mass.; 34, 35, R)

————. *Admission of Kansas. Speech of Hon. Robert B. Hall, of Massachusetts. Delivered in the House of Representatives, Mar. 27, 1858*. n.p., n.d.

————. *Speech of Hon. Robert B. Hall, of Massachusetts, on the Assault on Senator Sumner. Delivered in the House of Representatives, July 12, 1856*. Washington, D.C.: Congressional Globe Office, 1856.

HALSTEAD, WILLIAM (N. J.: 25, 26, 27, W)

————. *A Vindication of the Four Laymen, Who Requested the Three Bishops to Present Charges against Bishop Doane*. Trenton, N. J.: Brown & Borden, Printers, 1853.

HAMPTON, MOSES (Pa.; 30, 31, W)

————. *Speech of Mr. Hampton, of Pennsylvania, on Rivers & Harbors, and the Policy of Protection and Free Trade. Delivered in the House of Representatives, Mar. 9, 1848*. Washington, D.C.: John T. Towers, Printer, 1848.

HEBARD, WILLIAM (Vt.; 31, 32, W)

————. *Speech of Mr. Hebard, of Vermont, on the President's Message, Communicating the Constitution of California. Delivered in the House of Representatives, U. S., in Committee of the Whole on the State of the Union, Mar. 14, 1850*. Washington, D.C.: Gideon & Co., Printers, 1850.

————. *Trial of Mrs. Rebecca Peake, Indicted for the Murder of Ephraim Peake, Tried at Orange County Court, Dec. Term, 1835. Embracing the Evidence, Arguments of Counsel, Charge, and Sentence*. Montpelier: E. P. Walton & Son, Publishers, 1836.

HENRY, THOMAS (Pa.; 25, 26, 27, W)

————. "Early Struggles of the Ohio and Big Beaver Regions." Ch. II in *History of Beaver County, Pennsylvania*. Philadelphia & Chicago: A. Warner & Co., Publishers, 1888.

HUBBARD, SAMUEL D. (Conn.; 29, 30, W)

————. *Letter of S. D. Hubbard, of Connecticut, to His Constituents, on the Alarming Crisis in the Affairs of the Country*. Washington, D.C.: J. & G. S. Gideon, Printers, 1846.

HUDSON, CHARLES (Mass.; 27, 28, 29, 30, W)

————. *Doubts Concerning the Battle of Bunker Hill. Addressed to the Christian Public*. Printed from the *Christian Examiner* of Mar. 1846. Boston & Cambridge, Mass.: James Munroe & Co., 1857.

————. *History of the Town of Marlborough, Middlesex County, Massachusetts, from Its First Settlement in 1657 to 1861; with a Brief Sketch of the Town of Northborough, a Genealogy of the Families in Marlborough to 1800, and an Account of the Celebration of the Two Hundredth Anniversary of the Incorporation of the Town*. Boston: Press of T. R. Marvin & Son, 1862.

————. *Speech of Mr. Charles Hudson, of Massachusetts, on the Constitutional Power of Congress over the Territories, and the Right of Excluding Slavery Therefrom. Delivered in the House of Representatives of the U. S., June 20, 1848*. Washington, D.C.: J. & G. S. Gideon, Printers, 1848.

————. *Speech of Mr. Charles Hudson, of Massachusetts, on the Portion of the President's Message Relating to the Mexican War. Delivered in the House of Representatives, Dec. 16, 1846.* Washington, D.C.: J. & G. S. Gideon, Printers, 1846.

————. *Speech in U. S. Congress. Speeches on the Oregon Question and on the Mexican War.* 29th Cong., 1st Sess., 1845–1846.

————. *Speech of Mr. Hudson, of Massachusetts, on the Cost of the War and Finances of the Country. Delivered in the House of Representatives of the U. States, Feb. 15, 1848.* Washington, D.C.: J. & G. S. Gideon, Printers, 1848.

HUNT, HIRAM P. (N. J.; 24, W; N. Y.; 26, 27 W)

————. *Speech of Mr. Hunt, of New York, on the Subtreasury Bill. Delivered in the House of Representatives, June 3, 1840.* Washington, D.C.: Gales & Seaton, 1840.

HUNT, WASHINGTON (N. Y.; 28, 29, 30, W)

————. "Eulogy on the Hon. Charles E. Dudley." In *Annals of the Dudley Observatory.* Vol. I. Albany: Weld, Parsons & Co., Printers, 1866.

————. *Speech in U. S. Congress. Speeches on the Oregon Question and on the Mexican War.* 29th Cong., 1st Sess., 1845–1846.

————. *Speech of Washington Hunt, at the Union Meeting in New York, Dec. 19th, 1859.* New York: Hall, Clayton & Co., Printers, 1859.

KELLOGG, WILLIAM (Ill.; 35, 36, R)

————. *Confiscation of Rebel Property. Speech of Hon. William Kellogg, of Illinois, Delivered in the House of Representatives, May 24, 1862.* Washington, D.C.: Scammell & Co., Printers, 1862.

————. *The Incidents of the Lecompton Struggle in Congress and the Campaign of 1858 in Illinois. Speech of Hon. William Kellogg, of Illinois. Delivered in the House of Representatives, Mar. 13, 1860.* Washington, D.C.: Buell & Blanchard, 1860.

————. *Speech of Hon. Wm. Kellogg, of Illinois, in Favor of the Union. Delivered in the House of Representatives, Feb. 8, 1861.* Washington, D.C.: Lemuel Towers, Printer, [1861].

KELSEY, WILLIAM H. (N. Y.; 34, 35, R)

————. *Speech of Hon. William H. Kelsey, of New York, on the Slavery Question; Delivered in the House of Representatives, July 29, 1856.* Washington, D.C.: Congressional Globe Office, 1856.

KILGORE, DAVID (Ind.; 35, 36, R)

————. *Kansas—The Lecompton Constitution. Speech of Hon. David Kilgore, of Indiana. Delivered in the U. S. House of Representatives, Mar. 24, 1858.* Washington, D.C.: Buell & Blanchard, Printers, 1858.

KING, DANIEL P. (Mass.; 28, 29, 30, 31, W)

————. *The California Question and the Ordinance of '87. Speech of Hon. D. P. King, of Massachusetts, in the House of Representatives, May 21, 1850.* Washington, D.C.: Congressional Globe Office, [1850].

KNOX, JAMES (Ill.; 33, W; 34, R)

————. *Nebraska and Kansas. Speech of Hon. James Knox, of Illinois, in the House of Representatives, May 19, 1854.* Washington, D.C.: Congressional Globe Office, [1854].

LAWRENCE, ABBOTT (Mass.; 24, 26, W)

————. *Remarks of Hon. Abbott Lawrence before the Convention of Manufacturers,*

Dealers, and Operatives, in the Shoe and Leather Trade, Held in the Marlboro Chapel, Boston, Mar. 2, 1842. n.p., n.d.

Appleton, Nathan. *Memoir of Hon. Abbott Lawrence.* Prepared for the Massachusetts Historical Society. Boston: J. H. Eastburn's Press, 1856.

Hill, Hamilton A. *Memoir of Abbott Lawrence.* 2d ed. Boston: Little, Brown & Co., 1884.

LEACH, DEWITT CLINTON (Mich.; 35, 36, R)

————. *The Amistad Case. Men Not Recognized as Property by the Constitution. Speech of Hon. DeWitt C. Leach, of Michigan. Delivered in the House of Representatives, Jan. 27, 1858.* Washington, D.C.: Buell & Blanchard, 1858.

LEITER, BENJAMIN FRANKLIN (Ohio; 34, 35, R)

————. *National Politics. Speech of Hon. Benjamin F. Leiter, of Ohio, Delivered in the House of Representatives, Aug. 12, 1856.* Washington, D.C.: Congressional Globe Office, [1856].

LINCOLN, LEVI (Mass.; 24, 25, 26, W)

————. *An Address Delivered on the Consecration of the Worcester Rural Cemetary [sic], Sept. 8, 1838.* Boston: Dutton & Wentworth, Printers, 1838.

————. *Speech of Mr. Lincoln, a Whig Representative in Congress from Massachusetts, in Reply to Mr. Ogle, upon the Proposition of the Latter to Strike Out of the General Appropriation Bill, a Small Item for Alterations and Repairs of the President's House, etc.* Washington, D.C.: n.p., Apr. 16, 1840.

————. *Speech of Mr. Lincoln, of Massachusetts: Delivered in the House of Representatives of the U. S. Feb. 7, 1837, on the Resolution to Censure the Hon. John Q. Adams, for Inquiring of the Speaker, whether a Paper, Purporting to Come from Slaves, Came within the Resolution Laying on the Table All Petitions Relating to Slavery.* [Reported by the Editor of the *Boston Daily Advocate.*] Washington, D.C.: Gales & Seaton, Printers, 1837.

MARSH, GEORGE PERKINS (Vt.; 28, 29, 30, W)

————. *Address Delivered before the Agricultural Society of Rutland County, Sept. 30, 1847.* Rutland, Vt.: Herald Office, Printers, 1848.

————. *The American Historical School: A Discourse Delivered before the Literary Societies of Union College.* Troy, N. Y.: Steam Press of Kneeland & Co., 1847.

————. *The Goths in New England. A Discourse Delivered at the Anniversary of the Philomathesian Society of Middlebury College, Aug. 15, 1843.* Middlebury, Vt.: J. Cobb, Jr., Printer, 1843.

————. *Remarks of George Perkins Marsh, of Vermont, on Slavery in the Territories of New Mexico, California and Oregon; Delivered in the House of Representatives, Aug. 3d, 1848.* Burlington, Vt.: Free Press Office, Printers, [1848].

————. *Speech of Mr. George P. Marsh, of Vermont, on the Tariff Bill. Delivered in the House of Representatives of the United States, on the 30th of Apr., 1844.* St. Albans, Vt.: E. B. Whiting, Printer, 1844.

Feuer, Lewis S. "James Marsh and the Conservative Transcendentalist Philosophy." *New England Quarterly* 31 (Mar. 1958):3–31.

Lowenthal, David. *George Perkins Marsh, Versatile Vermonter.* New York: Columbia University Press, 1958.

Marsh, Caroline Crane. *Life and Letters of George Perkins Marsh.* 2 vols. New York: Charles Scribner's Sons, 1888.

MARVIN, RICHARD P. (N. Y.; 25, 26, W)

———. *Speech of Mr. Marvin, of New York, on the Report of the Committee of Ways and Means Relating to the State of the National Treasury, and the Expenditures of the General Government. Delivered in the House of Representatives, Feb. 5, 1839.* Washington, D.C.: Gales & Seaton, Printers, 1839.

MASON, SAMSON (Ohio; 24, 25, 26, 27, W)

———. *Charges against General Harrison for Voting to Sell White Men for Debt. Speech of Mr. Mason, of Ohio, on the General Appropriation Bill. Delivered in Committee of the Whole in the House of Representatives, Apr. 24, 1849.* n.p., n.d.

———. *Speech of Mr. Mason, of Ohio, on the Obligation of the United States, Founded on Compacts with the States of Ohio, Indiana, Illinois, & Missouri, to Construct the Cumberland Road. Delivered in the House of Representatives, Feb. 11, 1840.* Washington, D.C.: Gales & Seaton, Printers, 1840.

———. *Speech of Mr. S. Mason, of Ohio, on the Objections of the President to the Bill to Establish a Fiscal Corporation. Delivered in the House of Representatives, Sept. 10, 1841.* Washington, D.C.: National Intelligencer Office, 1841.

MATTESON, ORASMUS (N. Y.; 31, 33, W; 34, 35, R)

———. *Speech of Hon. O. B. Matteson, of New York, on the Cheap Postage Bill. Delivered in the House of Representatives, Jan. 11, 1851.* Washington, D.C.: Buell & Blanchard, 1851.

NEWELL, WILLIAM A. (N. J.; 30, 31, W)

———. *Reconstruction. Speech of Hon. William A. Newell, of New Jersey, in the House of Representatives, Feb. 15, 1866.* Washington, D.C.: Congressional Globe Office, [1866].

———. *Remarks of William A. Newell, of New Jersey, on a Proposition to Devise Means for the Preservation of Life and Property from Wrecks on the New Jersey Coast. Delivered in the House of Representatives, Aug. 3, 1848.* Washington, D.C.: John T. Towers, 1848.

———. *Restoration of the Rebellious States. Speech of Hon. William A. Newell, of New Jersey, in the House of Representatives, Jan. 4, 1867.* Washington, D.C.: Congressional Globe Office, [1867].

NORTON, JESSE O. (Ill.; 33, W; 34, R)

———. *Speech of Hon. Jesse O. Norton, of Illinois, on the Illinois Contested Election. Delivered in the House of Representatives, July 17, 1856.* Washington, D.C.: Congressional Globe Office, 1856.

OGLE, CHARLES (Pa.; 25, 26, W)

———. *Speech of Mr. Ogle, of Pennsylvania, on the Regal Splendor of the President's Palace. Delivered in the House of Representatives, Apr. 14, 1840.* Boston: Weeks Jordan & Co., [1840].

OLIN, ABRAM B. (N. Y.; 35, 36, R)

———. *Admission of Kansas. Speech of Hon. Abram B. Olin, of New York, Delivered in the House of Representatives, Mar. 29, 1858.* Washington, D.C.: Buell & Blanchard, 1858.

PERRY, JOHN J. (Maine; 34, 36, R)

———. *The Filibustering Policy of the Sham Democracy. Speech of Hon. John J. Perry, of Maine. Delivered in the House of Representatives, May 29, 1860.* [Washington, D.C.]: Published by the Republican Congressional Committee, [1860].

———. *Freedom National—Slavery Sectional. Speech of Hon. John J. Perry, of Maine, on the Comparative Nationality and Sectionalism of the Republican and Demo-*

cratic Parties; Delivered in the House of Representatives, May 1, 1856. Washington, D.C.: Congressional Globe Office, 1856.

──────. *Platforms and Candidates of 1856. Speech of Hon. John J. Perry, of Maine, Delivered in the House of Representatives, Aug. 7, 1856.* Washington, D.C.: Congressional Globe Office, 1856.

──────. *Posting the Books between the North and the South. Speech of Hon. John J. Perry, of Maine. Delivered in the U. S. House of Representatives, Mar. 7, 1860.* Washington, D.C.: Buell & Blanchard, Printers, 1860.

PETTIT, JOHN UPFOLD (Ind.; 34, 35, 36, R)

──────. *Speech of Hon. John U. Pettit, of Indiana, on the Restoration of the Missouri Compromise. Delivered in the House of Representatives, Aug. 2, 1856.* Washington, D.C.: Congressional Globe Office, 1856.

PHILLIPS, STEPHEN C. (Mass.; 24, 25, W)

──────. *An Address on the Annexation of Texas, and the Aspect of Slavery in the United States, in Connection therewith: Delivered in Boston, Nov. 14 & 18, 1845.* Boston: Wm. Crosby & H. P. Nichols, 1845.

──────. *Speech of Mr. Phillips, of Massachusetts, upon the Bill for the Relief of the Sufferers by the Fire at New York. Delivered in the House of Representatives, Feb. 16, 1836.* Washington, D.C.: National Intelligencer Office, 1836.

POTTLE, EMORY B. (N. Y.; 35, 36, R)

──────. *Kansas—The Lecompton Constitution. Speech of Hon. Emory B. Pottle, of New York. Delivered in the House of Representatives, Mar. 22, 1858.* Washington, D.C.: Buell & Blanchard, 1858.

──────. *The Republican Party—The Message. Speech of Hon. Emory B. Pottle, of New York. Delivered in the House of Representatives, Jan. 31, 1859.* Washington, D.C.: Buell & Blanchard, 1859.

──────. *Speech of Hon. Emory B. Pottle, of New York, upon the Report of the Committee of Thirty-three upon the State of the Union. Delivered in the House of Representatives, Jan. 25, 1861.* n.p., n.d.

PRINGLE, BENJAMIN (N. Y.; 33, W; 34, R)

──────. *Speech of Hon. Benjamin Pringle, of New York, on the Nebraska and Kansas Bill, Delivered in the House of Representatives, May 19, 1854.* Washington, D.C.: Congressional Globe Office, 1854.

RAMSEY, ALEXANDER (Pa.; 28, 29, W)

──────. "Address of Gov. A. Ramsey, President of the Society." In *Annals of the Minnesota Historical Society, for the Year A.D. 1850-1.* St. Paul: D. A. Robertson, Printer, 1851.

──────. *Annual Message of Governor Ramsey to the Legislature of Minnesota, Delivered Jan. 7th, 1863.* St. Paul: Wm. R. Marshall, State Printer, 1863.

Ryland, William James. *Alexander Ramsey: A Study of a Frontier Politician and the Transition of Minnesota from a Territory to a State.* Philadelphia: Harris & Partridge Co., 1941.

REED, JOHN (Mass.; 24, 25, 26, W)

──────. *Speech of Mr. Reed, of Massachusetts, in Relation to the Failure of the Bill Making Appropriations for Fortifications at the Last Session of Congress. Delivered in the House of Representatives, Jan. 27, 1836.* Washington, D.C.: National Intelligencer Office, 1836.

ROCKWELL, JOHN ARNOLD (Conn.; 29, 30, W)

————. "Address on the Life and Times of Major John Mason." In *The Norwich Jubilee*. Norwich, Conn.: John W. Stedman, 1859.

————. *Remarks of Mr. Rockwell, of Connecticut, in the House of Representatives, U. S., Dec. 15, 1845.* Washington, D.C.: J. & G. S. Gideon, Printers, [1845].

[————]. *States vs. Territories. A True Solution of the Territorial Question. By an Old Line Whig.* n.p., Aug. 15, 1860.

ROCKWELL, JULIUS (Mass.; 28, 29, 30, 31, W)

————. *Speech of Mr. Julius Rockwell, of Massachusetts, on the Government of the Territories, the Ordinance of 1787, and the Presidential Election. Delivered in the House of Representatives of the United States, June 27th, 1848.* Washington, D.C.: J. & G. S. Gideon, Printers, 1848.

ROOT, JOSEPH MOSLEY (Ohio; 29, 30, 31, W)

————. *California and New Mexico. Speech of Hon. Joseph M. Root, of Ohio, in the House of Representatives, Feb. 15, 1850, in Committee of the Whole on the State of the Union, on the Resolution Referring the President's Message to the Appropriate Standing Committees.* Washington, D.C.: Congressional Globe Office, [1850].

————. *Speech of Mr. Joseph M. Root, of Ohio, on the Tariff. Delivered in the House of Representatives of the U. S., July 1, 1846.* Washington, D.C.: J. & G. S. Gideon, [1846].

SABIN, ALVAH (Vt.; 33, W; 34, R)

Hobart, Alvah S. *Eighty-Three Years a Servant, or the Life of Rev. Alvah Sabin.* Cincinnati: Review Printing Co., 1855.

SACKETT, WILLIAM A. (N. Y.; 31, 32, W)

————. *Shall Slavery Be Extended? Speech of Hon. W. A. Sackett, of New York, in the House of Representatives, Mar. 4, 1850.* Washington, D.C.: Congressional Globe Office, [1850].

SALTONSTALL, LEVERETT (Mass.; 26, 27, W)

[————]. "An Historical Sketch of Haverhill, in the County of Essex, and Commonwealth of Massachusetts; with Biographical Notice." In *Collections of the Massachusetts Historical Society*, Vol. IV, 2d Series. Boston: Charles C. Little & James Brown, 1816; reprinted 1846.

SAPP, WILLIAM R. (Ohio; 33, W; 34, R)

————. *Speech of Hon. William R. Sapp, of Ohio, against the Outrages in Kansas, and in favor of Freedom and Frémont. Delivered in the House of Representatives, July 23, 1856.* Washington, D.C.: Congressional Globe Office, 1856.

————. *Speech of Hon. William R. Sapp, of Ohio, on the Bill to Organize Territorial Governments in Nebraska and Kansas, Opposing the Repeal of the Missouri Compromise. House of Representatives, Apr. 28, 1854.* Washington, D.C.: Congressional Globe Office, 1854.

SCHENCK, ROBERT C. (Ohio; 28, 29, 30, 31, W)

————. *Mr. Schenck—In Reply to Mr. Giddings. Speech of Mr. Robert C. Schenck, of Ohio, in the House of Representatives, Dec. 27, 1849.* Washington, D.C.: Congressional Globe Office, [1849].

————. *No Compromise with Treason. Remarks of Mr. Schenck, of Ohio, in Reply to Mr. Fernando Wood, of New York, in the Debate on the Resolution to Expel Mr. Long. Delivered in the House of Representatives, Apr. 11, 1864.* Washington, D.C.: L. Towers, Printer, for the Union Congressional Committee, n.d.

————. *Speech of Mr. Schenck, of Ohio, on the Bill to Refund General Jackson's Fine, in the House of Representatives, Jan. 8, 1844*. n.p., n.d.

In Memoriam: General Robert C. Schenck. Record of Proceedings of Memorial Service, Dayton, Ohio, Apr. 25, 1890. Dayton, Ohio: Garfield Club, n.d.

SERGEANT, JOHN (Pa.; 25, 26, 27, W)

————. *An Address Delivered at the Request of the Managers of the Apprentices' Library Company of Philadelphia, 23 Nov., 1832*. Philadelphia: James Kay, Jr. & Co., Printers, n.d.

————. *An Address Delivered before the Alumni Association of Nassau Hall, on the Day of the Annual Commencement of the College Sept. 25, 1833*. Princeton, N. J.: Baker & Connolly, Printers, 1833.

————. *Eulogy on Charles Carroll of Carrollton. Delivered at the Request of the Select and Common Councils of the City of Philadelphia, Dec. 31, 1832*. Philadelphia: Lydia R. Bailey, Printer, 1833.

————. *A Lecture Delivered before the Mercantile Library Company of Philadelphia, Nov. 1, 1839*. Philadelphia: Henry Perkins, 1839.

————. *Speech of Mr. John Sergeant, on the Missouri Question. In the House of Representatives of the U. States*. n.p., n.d.

————. *Speech of Mr. Sergeant of Pennsylvania, on the Sub-Treasury Bill. Delivered in the House of Representatives, June 24, 1840*. Washington, D.C.: Gales & Seaton, Printers, 1840.

SEVERANCE, LUTHER (Maine; 28, 29, W)

————. *Speech, of Mr. Severance, of Maine, on the Right of Petition. Delivered in the House of Representatives, Feb. 16, 1844*. Washington, D.C.: J. & G. S. Gideon, 1844.

SHERMAN, JOHN (Ohio; 31, W; 34, 35, 36 R)

————. *Selected Speeches and Reports on Finance and Taxation, from 1859 to 1878*. New York: D. Appleton & Co., 1879.

————. *Slaves and Slavery: How Affected by the War. Remarks of Hon. John Sherman, of Ohio, in the Senate of the United States, Apr. 2, 1862*. Washington, D.C.: Schammel & Co., 1862.

————. *Speech of Hon. John Sherman, of Ohio, in Reply to Mr. Stephens, of Georgia, and Review of Mr. Oliver's Minority Report. Delivered in the House of Representatives, July 30, 1850*. Washington, D.C.: Buell & Blanchard, n.d.

Burton, Theodore. *John Sherman*. American Statesmen, 2d Series. Boston & New York: Houghton, Mifflin & Co., 1906.

Kerr, Winfield S. *John Sherman, His Life and Public Services*. 2 vols. Boston: Sherman, French & Co., 1908.

Thorndike, Rachel Sherman, ed. *The Sherman Letters, Correspondence between General Sherman and Senator Sherman from 1837 to 1891*. Da Capo Press Reprint Series, The American Scene: Comments and Commentators, edited by Wallace D. Farnham. New York: Da Capo Press, 1969.

SMITH, ALBERT (N. Y.; 28, 29, W)

————. *Speech of Albert Smith, of New York, on the Tariff and in Reply to the Speech of Mr. Collins, of New York. Delivered in the House of Representatives of the U. S., July 1, 1846*. Washington, D.C.: J. & G. S. Gideon, 1846.

SMITH, CALEB B. (Ind.; 28, 29, 30, W)

————. *Executive Vetoes. Speech of Caleb B. Smith, of Indiana, on the Veto Power;*

Delivered in the House of Representatives, July 21, 1848. Washington, D.C.: J. & G. S. Gideon, 1848.

SMITH, TRUMAN (Conn.; 26, 27, 28, 29, 30, W)

———. *Considerations of the Slavery Question, Addressed to the President of the United States*. New York: n.p., Dec. 24, 1862.

———. *Speech of Hon. Truman Smith, of Connecticut, on Printing the Returns of the Seventh Census, and on Congressional and Departmental Printing Generally; Delivered in the Senate of the United States, Jan. 12, 1852*. Washington, D.C.: John T. Towers, 1852.

———. *Speech of Mr. Truman Smith, of Connecticut, on Removals and Appointments to Office. Delivered in the Senate of the United States, Mar. 21 & 23, 1830*. Washington, D.C.: Towers, Printer, 1850.

———. *Speech of Truman Smith, of Connecticut, on the Nebraska Question. Delivered in the Senate of the United States, Feb. 10 & 11, 1854*. Washington, D.C.: John T. & Lemuel Towers, 1854.

———. *Speech of Truman Smith, of Connecticut, on the Physical Character of the Northern States of Mexico, Delivered in the House of Representatives of the U. States, Mar. 2, 1848*. Washington, D.C.: J. & G. S. Gideon, Printers [1848].

———. *To the Public: Letter to Zachary Taylor*. Washington, D.C.: J. S. Gideon, [1849].

SPAULDING, ELBRIDGE GERRY (N. Y.; 31, W; 36, R)

———. *Address at the Formal Opening of the Bank Officer's and Bankers' Building, Centennial Grounds, Fairmont Park, Philadelphia, May 30th, 1876*. Philadelphia: Richard Magee & Son, Printers, 1876.

———. *National Finances. Confiscation and Emancipation. Speech of Hon. E. G. Spaulding, of New York, Delivered in the House of Representatives, Tuesday, June 17, 1862*. Washington, D.C.: Scammell & Co., 1862.

———. *The Republican Platform. Revised Speech of Hon. E. G. Spaulding, of New York, Delivered at Buffalo and Washington, at Meetings Held to Ratify the Nomination of Abraham Lincoln and Hannibal Hamlin, for President and Vice-President*. [Washington, D.C.: n.p., 1860].

———. *Speech of Hon. E. G. Spaulding, of New York, Delivered in the House of Representatives, Jan. 28, 1862, on the Finances, and the Power of Congress to Issue demand Treasury Notes and Make Them a Legal Tender in Payment of Debts: to Which is Appended Tables Showing the Value of the Real and Personal Property in the United States, and a Letter of the Secretary of the Treasury*. Washington, D.C.: Scammell & Co., Printers, 1862.

STEWART, ANDREW C. (Pa.; 28, 29, 30, 31, W)

———. *The American System. Speeches on the Tariff Question and on Internal Improvements, Principally Delivered in the House of Representatives of the United States*. Philadelphia: Henry Carey Baird, 1872.

———. *Speech of Andrew Stewart, of Pennsylvania, on the Presidential Question; Delivered in the House of Representatives of the United States, June 26, 1848*. Washington, D.C.: J. & G. S. Gideon, 1848.

TAYLOR, JOHN L. (Ohio; 30, 31, 32, 33, W)

———. *Speech of Hon. John L. Taylor of Ohio, on the Army Bill, the Veto Power, and the Ordinance of 1787; Delivered in the House of Representatives of the United States, Aug. 3, 1848*. Washington, D.C.: J. & G. S. Gideon, 1848.

———. *Speech of Hon. John L. Taylor, of Ohio, on the Nebraska and Kansas Territorial*

Bill. Delivered in the House of Representatives, Apr. 26, 1854. Washington, D.C.: Congressional Globe Office, 1854.

THOMPSON, BENJAMIN (Mass.; 29, 32, W)

————. *A Funeral Oration on the Death of Zachary Taylor, (Late President of the United States,) Delivered by Request of the City Council, Charlestown, July 31st, 1850.* Charlestown, [Mass.]: Caleb Rand, 1850.

THOMPSON, RICHARD W. (Ind.; 27, 30, W)

————. *The Footprints of the Jesuits.* Cincinnati: Cranston & Curts, 1894.

————. *Recollections of Sixteen Presidents from Washington to Lincoln.* Indianapolis: Bowen-Merrill Co., 1894.

————. *Remarks of Mr. Thompson, of Indiana, on the Bill to Incorporate the Subscribers to a Fiscal Bank of the United States. Delivered in the House of Representatives, Aug., 1841.* Washington, D.C.: n.p., 1841.

————. *Speech of Mr. R. W. Thompson, of Indiana, on the Reference of the President's Annual Message. Delivered in the House of Representatives of the United States, Jan. 27, 1848.* Washington, D.C.: J. & G. S. Gideon, 1848.

Roll, Charles. *Colonel Dick Thompson, The Persistent Whig.* Indiana Historical Collections, vol. XXX. Indianapolis: Indiana Historical Bureau, 1948.

TILDEN, DANIEL R. (Ohio; 28, 29, W)

————. *Letter to Mr. Giddings, Giving His Reasons for Supporting General Scott.* n.p., n.d.

TILLINGHAST, JOSEPH L. (R. I.; 25, 26, 27, W)

————. *Eulogy Pronounced in Providence, July 17, 1826, upon the Characters of John Adams and Thos. Jefferson, Late Presidents of the United States.* Providence: Miller & Grattan, Printers, 1826.

TUCK, AMOS (N. H.; 30, 31, 32, W)

————. *Speech of Hon. Amos Tuck on the New England Fisheries, Reciprocal Trade with British North American Provinces, and the Free Navigation of the St. Lawrence, Delivered in the House of Representatives, Aug. 27, 1852.* Washington, D.C.: Lemuel Towers, 1852.

Corning, Charles R. *Amos Tuck.* Exeter, N. H.: News Letter Press, 1902.

VANCE, JOSEPH (Ohio; 28, 29, W)

Prince, Benjamin F. "Joseph Vance and His Times." *Ohio Archaeological and Historical Quarterly* 19 (July 1910):229–249.

WALDRON, HENRY (Mich.; 34, 35, 36, R)

————. *Kansas Affairs. Speech of Hon. Henry Waldron, of Michigan, in the House of Representatives, Apr. 8, 1856, in Committee of the Whole on the State of the Union.* Washington, D.C.: Buell & Blanchard, [1856].

————. *Modern Democracy against the Union, the Constitution, the Policy of Our Fathers, and the Rights of Free Labor. Speech of Hon. Henry Waldron, of Michigan. Delivered in the House of Representatives, Apr. 26, 1860.* Published by the Republican Executive Congressional Committee, n.p., n.d.

WALTON, ELIAKIM P. (Vt.; 35, 36, R)

————. "The First Legislature of Vermont." In *Proceedings of the Vermont Historical Society,* Oct. 15, 1878. Montpelier: J. & J. M. Poland, 1878.

————. *State of the Union. Speech of Hon. E. P. Walton, of Vermont, upon the Report of the Committee of Thirty-three upon the State of the Union. Delivered in the*

House of Representatives, Feb. 16, 1861. Washington, D.C.: W. H. Moore, Printer, [1861].

Hemenway, Abby Maria, ed. "The History of the Town of Montpelier." In *Vermont Historical Gazeteer*, IV. Montpelier: Published by Miss A. M. Hemenway, 1882.

WASHBURNE, ELIHU B. (Ill.; 33, W; 34, 35, 36, R)

———. *Sketch of Edward Coles, Second Governor of Illinois, and of the Slavery Struggle of 1823–4.* Prepared for the Chicago Historical Society. n.p.: Jansen, McClung, & Co., 1882; New York: Negro Universities Press, 1969.

Hunt, Gaillard. *Israel, Elihu and Cadwallader Washburn, A Chapter in American Biography.* New York: MacMillan Co., 1925.

WHITTLESEY, ELISHA (Ohio; 24, 25, W)

———. *An Address Delivered before the Tallmadge Colonization Society on the Fourth of July, 1833.* Ravenna, Ohio: Office of the Ohio Star, July 1833.

———. *Address of Elisha Whittlesey, Delivered at a Meeting of the Whittlesey family, Which Convened at Saybrook, Connecticut, Sept. 20, 1855.* Washington, D.C.: n.p., 1855.

———. *Address, Prepared for the 45th Anniversary of the Defence [sic] of Ft. Stephenson at Lower Sandersky, (now Fremont,) Ohio.* Toledo: Blade Job Office, Printer, 1858.

———. *Twelfth Annual Address Delivered before the Mahoning County Agricultural Society, By Hon. Elisha Whittlesey, at Canfield, Ohio, Oct., 1858.* Canfield: John M. Webb, Printer, 1858.

WILSON, JAMES (N. H.; 30, 31, W)

———. *Speech of Mr. Jas. Wilson, of N. Hampshire, on the Political Influence of Slavery, and the Expediency of Permitting Slavery in the Territories Recently Acquired from Mexico. Delivered in the House of Representatives of the United States, Feb. 16, 1849.* Washington, D.C.: J. & G. S. Gideon, Printers, 1849.

Briggs, James F. *Sketch of General James Wilson of New Hampshire.* Manchester, N.H.: Manchester Historical Association, 1902.

YATES, RICHARD (Ill.; 32, 33, W)

Yates, Richard, and Yates Pickering, Catharine. *Richard Yates: Civil War Governor.* Edited by John H. Krenkel. Danville, Ill.: Interstate Printers & Publishers, 1966.

Southern Whig and Republican Conformists

ADAMS, GREEN (Ky.; 30, 36, W)

———. *Speech of Green Adams, of Kentucky, on the Oregon Bill.* Washington, D.C.: John T. Towers, Printer, 1848.

ALFORD, JULIUS CAESAR (Ga.; 26, 27, W)

———. *Address of J. C. Alford, William C. Dawson, Richard W. Habersham, Thos. Butler King, E. A. Nesbit and Lott Warren, Representatives from the State of Georgia, in the Twenty-Sixth Congress of the United States, to Their Constituents.* n.p., May 27, 1840.

———. *Speech of Mr. J. C. Alford, of Georgia, on Abolition Petitions. Delivered in the House of Representatives, Jan. 22, 1840.* Washington, D.C.: Gales & Seaton, Printers, 1840.

ANDERSON, THOMAS L. (Mo.; 35, 36, W)

———. *Speech of Hon. T. L. Anderson of Missouri, on the Principles and Policy of the Black Republican Party, and the Duty of Whigs and Americans in the Approaching*

State and Presidential Elections. Washington, D.C.: Lemuel Towers, Printer, 1860.

BARRINGER, DANIEL MOREAU (N. C.; 28, 29, 30, 31, W)

―――. *Speech of Mr. Daniel Moreau Barringer, of North Carolina, on the Tariff. Delivered in the House of Representatives of the U. S., July 1, 1846*. n.p., n.d.

CABELL, EDWARD CARRINGTON (Fla.; 29, 30, 31, 32, W)

―――. *Address of E. C. Cabell, of Florida, to His Constituents*. Washington, D.C.: n.p., 1850.

―――. *Letter to Dr. G. D. Fisher*. Washington, D.C.: n.p., Sept. 8, 1850.

―――. *The Slave Question. Speech of Hon. E. C. Cabell, of Florida, in the House of Representatives, Mar. 5, 1850*. Washington, D.C.: Congressional Globe Office, 1850.

CAMPBELL, WILLIAM BOWEN (Tenn.; 25, 26, 27, W)

―――. *Mexican War Letters of Col. William Bowen Campbell of Tennessee, Written to Governor David Campbell of Virginia, 1846–1847*. Reprinted from *Tennessee Historical Magazine*, June 1915.

―――. *Speech of William B. Campbell, of Tennessee, on the Sub-Treasury Bill. Delivered in the House of Representatives, June 27, 1840*. Washington, D.C.: Gales & Seaton, 1840.

GILMER, JOHN A. (N. C.; 35, 36, W)

―――. *The Kansas Question. Speech of Hon. John A. Gilmer, of North Carolina. Delivered in the House of Representatives, on the 30th of Mar., 1858*. Washington, D.C.: C. W. Fenton, Printer, 1858.

GOGGIN, WILLIAM L. (Va.; 26, 27, 28, 30, W)

―――. *Speech of William L. Goggin, of Bedford, on Federal Relations, in the Convention of Virginia, on the 26th and 27th Feb., 1861*. Richmond: Whig Book & Job Office, Printers, 1861.

HILL, JOSHUA (Ga.; 35, 36, W)

―――. *Letter of Hon. Joshua Hill, of Georgia, on the Election of U. S. Senators*. n.p., 1866.

―――. *Speech of Hon. Joshua Hill, of Georgia, on the Admission of Kansas; Delivered in the House of Representatives, Mar. 29, 1858*. Washington, D.C.: Congressional Globe Office, 1858.

MAURY, ABRAM P. (Tenn.; 24, 25, W)

―――. *Address of the Honorable Abram P. Maury, on the Life and Character of Hugh Lawson White, Delivered at Franklin, May 9, 1840*. Franklin, Tenn.: Review Office, 1840.

―――. *Address on the Peculiar Advantages of the United States in Comparison with Other Nations. Delivered before the Franklin Library Association, on the 28th of Jan., 1847*. Nashville: W. F. Bang & Co., Printers, Republican Banner Office, 1847.

MAYNARD, HORACE (Tenn.; 35, 36, W)

―――. *Political Education. An Address, Delivered before the Social Union of Amherst College at the Annual Commencement, Wednesday, Aug. 8, 1860*. Boston: Geo. C. Rand & Avery Press, 1861.

MERCER, CHARLES (Va.; 24, 25, 26, W)

―――. *The Weakness and Inefficiency of the Government of the United States of North America, by a Late American Statesman*. London: Goulston & Wright, 1863.

PEARCE, JAMES A. (Md.; 24, 25, 27, W)
———. *Letter from Senator Pearce, of Maryland, on the Politics of the Day*. Washington, D.C.: n.p., 1856.
———. *Report of the Special Committee of the Board of Regents of the Smithsonian Institution, on the Distribution of the Income of the Smithsonian Fund, etc., from the Eighth Annual Report of the Regents to Congress*. Washington, D.C.: n.p., 1854.
———. *Speech of Hon. J. A. Pearce, of Maryland, on the Governmental Administration of Affairs in California, and on the Governmental Expenditures Generally. Delivered in the Senate of the United States, Apr. 29, 1852*. Washington, D.C.: Congressional Globe Office, 1852.
———. *Writ of Habeas Corpus. Speech of Hon. James A. Pearce, of Maryland, in the Senate of the U. S. July 30, 1861*. Washington, D.C.: n.p., 1861.
RAYNER, KENNETH (N. C.; 26, 27, 28, W)
[———]. *Life and Times of Andrew Johnson, Seventeenth President of the United States. Written from a National Stand-Point. By a National Man*. New York: D. Appleton & Co., 1866.
———. *Speech of Mr. Kenneth Rayner, of N. Carolina, on the Bill Proposing to Distribute Annually, among the Several States, the Proceeds of the Sales of the Public Lands. Delivered in the House of Representatives of the U. States, July 6, 1841*. n.p., n.d.
———. *Speech of Mr. Rayner, of North Carolina, on the Question of the Reception of Abolition Petitions. Delivered in the House of Representatives of the U. States, on Tuesday, June 15, 1851*. n.p., n.d.
ROBERTSON, JOHN (Va.; 24, 25, W)
———. *Opuscula. Seria ac Jocasa. Found in the Scrutoir of an Ultra Octogenarian. Written during Intervals of Relaxation from the Duties of a Busy Life*. n.p., 1870.
———. *Riego, or The Spanish Martyr. A Tragedy: in Five Acts*. Richmond, Va.: P. D. Bernard, Printer & Publisher, 1850.
———. *Speech of Mr. Robertson, of Virginia, on His Motion to Recommit the Report and Resolutions of the Select Committee on the Subject of Abolition. Delivered in the House of Representatives, May 1836*. Washington, D.C.: Duff Green, Printer, 1836.
THOMPSON, WADDY (S. C.; 24, 25, 26, W)
———. *Speech of Waddy Thompson, of South-Carolina, in the House of Representatives of the United States, Being in Committee of the Whole on the State of the Union. Delivered Feb. 5, 1839*. Washington, D.C.: Madisonian Office, 1839.
———. *Speech of Waddy Thompson, of South Carolina, on the President's Annual Message to Congress. Delivered in the House of Representatives, Dec. 30, 1839*. Washington, D.C.: n.p., 1840.
———. *To the Honorable the Senate of the United States* [*sic*]. Washington, D.C.: J. & G. S. Gideon, Printers, n.d.

Northern Whig and Republican Mavericks

ADAMS, JOHN QUINCY (Mass.; 24, 25, 26, 27, 28, 29, 30, W)
———. *An Answer to Pain's Rights of Man. By John Adams, Esq*. London: Printed for J. Stockdale, 1793.

————. *Dermot MacMorrogh, or the Conquest of Ireland; An Historical Tale of the Twelfth Century. In Four Cantos.* Boston: Carter, Hendee & Co., 1832.

————. *The Diary of John Quincy Adams, 1794–1845; American Diplomacy, and Political, Social, and Intellectual Life, from Washington to Polk.* Edited by Allan Nevins. New York: F. Ungar Pub. Co., [1969, c. 1951].

————. *Lectures on Rhetoric and Oratory, Delivered to the Classes of Senior and Junior Sophisters in Harvard University.* 2 vols. Cambridge, Mass.: Hilliard & Metcalf, Printers, 1810.

————. *Memoirs of John Quincy Adams, Comprising Portions of His Diary from 1785 to 1848.* Edited by Charles Francis Adams. 12 vols. Philadelphia: J. B. Lippincott & Co., 1874–1877.

————. *Poems of Religion and Society.* Auburn & Buffalo, N. Y.: Miller, Orton & Mulligan, 1854.

————. *Writings of John Quincy Adams.* Edited by Worthington Chauncey Ford. 7 vols. New York: Greenwood Press, 1968.

Adams, Henry. *A Catalogue of the Books of John Quincy Adams Deposited in the Boston Athenaeum.* Introduction by Worthington Chauncey Ford. Boston: Printed for the Athenaeum, 1938.

Bemis, Samuel Flagg. *John Quincy Adams and the Union.* New York: Alfred A. Knopf, 1956.

Lipsky, George A. *John Quincy Adams, His Theory and Ideas.* New York: Thomas Y. Crowell Co., 1950.

BINGHAM, JOHN ARMOUR (Ohio; 34, 35, 36, R)

————. *The Assault upon Senator Sumner, a Crime against the People. Speech of Hon. John A. Bingham, of Ohio, in the House of Representatives, July 9, 1856.* Washington, D.C.: Buell & Blanchard, Printers, [1856].

————. *The Conference Bill for the Admission of Kansas. Speech of Hon. John A. Bingham, of Ohio. Delivered in the U. S. House of Representatives, Apr. 28, 1858.* Washington, D.C.: Buell & Blanchard, 1858.

————. *The Equality of All, the Basis of the Constitution. Speech of Hon. John A. Bingham, of Ohio, on the President's Message. Delivered in the House of Representatives, Jan. 13, 1857.* Washington, D.C.: Buell & Blanchard, 1857.

————. *The Lecompton Conspiracy. Speech of Hon. John A. Bingham, of Ohio. Delivered in the House of Representatives, Jan. 25, 1858.* Washington, D.C.: Buell & Blanchard, 1858.

————. *The Power and Duty of Congress to Provide for the Common Defence [sic] and the Suppression of the Rebellion. Speech of Hon. Jno. A. Bingham, of Ohio, in the House of Representatives, Jan. 15, 1862.* Washington, D.C.: Scammell & Co., Printers, [1862].

————. *State of the Union. Speech of the Hon. John A. Bingham, of Ohio, in the House of Representatives, Jan. 22, 1861.* Washington, D.C.: Congressional Globe Office, 1861.

————. *The Treasury Note Bill. Speech of Hon. Jno. A. Bingham, of Ohio, in the House of Representatives, Feb. 4, 1862.* Washington, D.C.: Scammell & Co., [1862].

Foraker, John B. "John A. Bingham." *Ohio Archaelogical and Historical Quarterly* 10 (Jan. 1902):331–351.

Pittenger, William. *Oratory Sacred and Secular: or, the Extemporaneous Speaker, with*

Sketches of the Most Eminent Speakers of All Ages. Introduction by Hon. John A. Bingham. New York: Samuel R. Wells, Publisher, 1868.

CAMPBELL, LEWIS DAVIS (Ohio; 31, 32, W; 33, 34, R)

————. *Kansas and Nebraska—Georgia and Ohio—Free Labor and Slave Labor. Speech of Hon. Lewis D. Campbell, of Ohio, in the House of Representatives, Dec. 14, 1854.* Washington, D.C.: Congressional Globe Office, [1854].

————. *Railroads for the West—"Lands for the Landless"—and "Virginia Abstractions." Speech of Hon. L. D. Campbell, of Ohio, in the House of Representatives, Mar. 7, 1854.* Washington, D.C.: Congressional Globe Office, [1854].

————. *Speech of Hon. L. D. Campbell, of Ohio, on Southern Aggression, the Purposes of the Union, and the Comparative Effects of Slavery and Freedom. Delivered in the House of Representatives, Feb. 19, 1850.* Washington, D.C.: Buell & Blanchard, 1850.

————. *Speech of Hon. Lewis Davis Campbell, of Ohio, in Reply to Mr. Stephens, of Georgia, Delivered in the House of Representatives, Feb. 28, 1855.* Washington, D.C.: Congressional Globe Office, 1855.

————. *Supremacy of the Constitution and Laws. Speech of Hon. Lewis D. Campbell, of Ohio, in the House of Representatives, in Reply to His Colleague, Mr. J. R. Giddings. The Senate's Amendment to the Deficiency Bill Being under Consideration.* Washington, D.C.: Buell & Blanchard, 1856.

————. *The Tariff on Agricultural Products. Speech of Hon. Lewis D. Campbell, of Butler County, Delivered in the Senate of Ohio, Wednesday, Mar. 9th, 1870.* n.p., n.d.

Barnes, William H. *Lewis D. Campbell.* Washington, D.C.: n.p., 1879.

CUSHING, CALEB (Mass.; 24, 25, 26, 27, W)

————. *Address. Delivered Sept. 26, 1850, at Salem, before the Essex Agricultural Society.* Salem, Mass.: Salem Gazette and Essex County Mercury, printers, Dec., 1850.

————. *Discourse on the Social Influence of Christianity, Delivered at Providence, Rhode Island, Sept. 1838, at the Instance of the Phi Beta Kappa Society of Brown University.* Andover, Mass.: Gould & Newman, Printers, 1839.

————. *"Eulogy, Pronounced at Newburyport, Massachusetts, July 15, 1826." In A Selection of Eulogies, Pronounced in the Several States, in Honor of Those Illustrious Patriots and Statesmen, John Adams and Thomas Jefferson,* 19–57. Hartford, Conn.: D. F. Robinson & Co. and Norton & Russell, 1826.

————. *An Oration on the Material Growth and Territorial Progress of the United States, Delivered at Springfield, Massachusetts on the Fourth of July, 1839.* Springfield, Mass.: Merriam, Wood & Co., Printers, 1839.

————. *Reminiscences of Spain, the Country, Its People, History, and Monuments.* 2 vols. Boston: Carter, Hendee & Co., and Allen & Ticknor, 1833.

————. *A Reply to the Letter of J. Fenimore Cooper. By One of His Countrymen.* Boston: J. T. Buckingham, 1834.

————. *Review, Historical and Political, of the Late Revolution in France, and of the Consequent Events in Belgium, Poland, Great Britain, and Other Parts of Europe.* 2 vols. Boston: Carter, Hendee & Co.; Newburyport: Thomas B. White, 1833.

————. *Speech of Mr. Cushing, of Massachusetts, on the Right of Petition, as Connected with Petitions for the Abolition of Slavery and the Slave Trade in the District of*

Columbia: Delivered in the House of Representatives, Jan. 25, 1836. Washington, D.C.: Gales & Seaton, Printers, 1836.

Catalogue of the Law Library of the Late Hon. Caleb Cushing, of Newburyport, Massachusetts. Boston: W. F. Brown & Co., Printers, 1879.

Catalogue of the Private Library of the Late Hon. Caleb Cushing, of Newburyport, Massachusetts. Boston: W. F. Brown & Co., Printers, 1879.

Fuess, Claude M. *The Life of Caleb Cushing.* New York: Harcourt, Brace & World, 1923.

FOWLER, ORIN (Mass.; 31, 32, W)

————. *History of Fall River.* Fall River, Mass.: Almy & Milne, Printers, 1862.

————. *Remarks of Mr. Orin Fowler, of Massachusetts, on a Motion to Reduce Postage on All Letters to Two Cents. Made in the House of Representatives of the United States, Dec. 31, 1850.* Washington, D.C.: Buell & Blanchard, Printers, 1851.

————. *Slavery in California and New Mexico. Speech of Mr. Orin Fowler, of Massachusetts, in the House of Representatives, Mar. 11, 1850.* Washington, D.C.: Buell & Blanchard, [1850].

————. *Speech of the Hon. Orin Fowler, of Massachusetts, on the Legislation of Massachusetts—Our Government—the Disposal of the Public Lands—the Tariff—Constitutional Law—and Our Foreign Relations.* Washington, D.C.: Buell & Blanchard, 1852.

GIDDINGS, JOSHUA REED (Ohio; 26, 27, 28, 29, 30, 31, 32, 33, W; 34, 35, R)

————. *The Exiles of Florida: or, the Crimes Committed by Our Government against the Maroons, Who Fled from South Carolina and Other Spanish Slave States, Seeking Protection under Spanish Laws.* 1858. Reprint. Gainesville: University of Florida Press, 1964.

————. *History of the Rebellion: Its Authors and Causes.* New York: Follett, Foster & Co., 1864.

————. *Speeches in Congress.* Boston: John P. Jewett & Co., 1853.

Julian, George W. *The Life of Joshua R. Giddings.* Chicago: A. C. McClung & Co., 1892.

Stewart, James B. *Joshua R. Giddings and the Tactics of Radical Politics.* Cleveland: Press of Case Western Reserve University, 1970.

KING, GEORGE G. (R. I.; 31, 32, W)

————. *The Library of George Gordon King. In Two Parts. Part I—the Books. Part II—Prints.* Newport, R. I.: n.p., 1885.

LEVIN, LEWIS CHARLES (Pa.; 28, 29, 30, 31, W)

————. *Speech in U. S. Congress. Speeches on the Oregon Question and on the Mexican War.* 29th Cong., 1st Sess., 1845–1846.

————. *Speech of Mr. L. C. Levin, of Pennsylvania, on the Bill to Raise a Regiment of Mounted Riflemen. Delivered in the House of Representatives of the United States, Apr. 7, 1846.* Washington, D.C.: J. & G. S. Gideon, Printers, 1846.

————. *Speech of Mr. L. C. Levin, of Pennsylvania, on the Emigration of Paupers and Criminals. Delivered in the House of Representatives, Feb. 1, 1847.* n.p., n.d.

————. *Speech of Mr. L. C. Levin, of Pennsylvania, on the Proposed Mission to Rome, Delivered in the House of Representatives of the United States, Mar. 2, 1848.* Washington, D.C.: J. & G. S. Gideon, Printers, [1848].

————. *Speech of Mr. L. C. Levin, of Pennsylvania, on the Subject of Altering the*

Naturalization Laws. Delivered in the House of Representatives of the United States, Dec. 18, 1845. Washington, D.C.: J. & G. S. Gideon, 1846.

MEACHAM, JAMES (Vt.; 31, 32, 33, 34, W)

———. *Defense of the Clergy. Speech of Hon. J. Meacham, of Vermont, in the House of Representative, May 17, 1854.* [Washington, D.C.: n.p., 1854].

———. *Report of Hon. James Meacham, of the Special Committee of the Board of Regents of the Smithsonian Institution, on the Distribution of the Income of the Smithsonian Fund, etc.* Washington, D.C.: For the Smithsonian Institution, 1854.

———. *Speech of Hon. James Meacham, of Vermont, on Kansas Affairs, Delivered in the House of Representatives, Apr. 30, 1856.* Washington, D.C.: Congressional Globe Office, 1856.

NICHOLS, MATTHIAS H. (Ohio; 33, D; 34, 35, R)

———. *Nebraska and Kansas. Speech of Hon. M..A.* [i.e., H.] *Nichols, of Ohio, in the House of Representatives, Apr. 5, 1854, Delivered in the Committee of the Whole on the State of the Union.* Washington, D.C.: Congressional Globe Office, 1854.

OLIVER, ANDREW (N. Y.; 33, D; 34, R)

———. *Assault on Mr. Sumner. Speech of Hon. Andrew Oliver, of New York, Delivered in the House of Representatives, July 12, 1856.* Washington, D.C.: Congressional Globe Office, 1856.

VAN DYKE, JOHN (N. J.; 30, 31, W)

———. *Slaveholding Not Sinful: A Reply to the Argument of Rev. Dr. How.* New Brunswick, N. J.: Fredonian & Daily New-Brunswicker Office, Printers, 1856.

———. *Speech of Mr. John Van Dyke, of New Jersey, Delivered in the House of Representatives of the U. States, Mar. 4, 1850, on the Subject of Slavery and in Vindication of the North from the Charges Brought against It by the South.* Washington, D.C.: Gideon & Co., Printers, 1850.

Southern Whig and Republican Mavericks

BLAIR, FRANCIS PRESTON, JR. (Mo.; 34, 35, 36, R)

———. *The Destiny of the Races of This Continent. An Address Delivered before the Mercantile Library Association of Boston, Massachusetts, on the 26th of Jan., 1859.* Washington, D.C.: Buell & Blanchard, Printers, 1859.

———. *Pacific Railroad. Speech of Hon. F. P. Blair, Jr., of Missouri, in the House of Representatives, May 26, 1858.* Washington, D.C.: Congressional Globe Office, 1858.

———. *Speech of Hon. F. P. Blair, Jr., of Missouri, at the Cooper Institute, New York City, Wednesday, Jan. 25, 1860.* Washington, D.C.: Buell & Blanchard, 1860.

———. *Speech of Hon. Francis P. Blair, Jr., of Missouri, on the Kansas Question; Delivered in the House of Representatives, Mar. 23, 1858.* Washington, D.C.: Congressional Globe Office, 1858.

Smith, William Ernest. *The Francis Preston Blair Family in Politics.* 2 vols. New York: Macmillan Co., 1933.

BOTTS, JOHN MINOR (Va.; 26, 27, 30, W)

———. *The Great Rebellion: Its Secret History, Rise, Progress and Disastrous Failure.* New York: Harper & Bros., Publishers, 1866.

———. *Letter to the Editors of The Whig. Jan. 29, 1848.* [Washington, D.C.]: J. & G. S. Gideon, Printers, n.d.

———. *The Past, the Present, and the Future of Our Country. Interesting and Important*

Correspondence between Opposition Members of the Legislature of Virginia and Hon. John Minor Botts, Jan. 17, 1860. Washington, D.C.: Lemuel Towers, Printers, 1860.

————. *Speech of Hon. John M. Botts, of Henrico County, in Committee of the Whole, on the Basis Question, Delivered in the Virginia Reform Convention, on Monday, Apr. 21, 1851.* Richmond: R. H. Gallaher—Republican Office, Printer, 1851.

————. *Speech of the Hon. John Minor Botts, of Virginia, Delivered at the Academy of Music, New York, on the 22nd Feb., 1859, Being the 127th Anniversary of Washington's Birthday.* New York: McKee & Co., 1859.

————. *Speech of John Minor Botts, at a Dinner at Powhatan Courthouse, Virginia, June 15, 1850.* [Richmond]: n.p., 1850.

————. *Union or Disunion. The Union Cannot and Shall Not Be Dissolved. Mr. Lincoln Not an Abolitionist. Speech of the Hon. John M. Botts, at Holcombe Hall, in Lynchburg, Virginia, on Thursday Evening, Oct. 18.* n.p., [1860].

CAMPBELL, JOHN (S. C.; 24, 25, 26, W; 27, 28, D)

————. *Speech of John Campbell, of South Carolina, on the Bill Relating to Duties and Drawbacks. Delivered in the House of Representatives of the United States, July 26, 1841.* Washington, D.C.: National Intelligencer Office, 1841.

————. *Speech of Mr. Campbell, of South Carolina, on the Reasons Filed by the President for Approving the Apportionment Bill: Delivered in the House of Representatives, July 6, 1842.* Washington, D.C.: Globe Office, 1842.

CULLOM, WILLIAM (Tenn.; 32, 33, W)

————. *To the Public.* n.p., n.d.

————. *Speech of Hon. Wm. Cullom, of Tennessee, on the Nebraska and Kansas Bill, in the House of Representatives, Apr. 11, 1854.* Washington, D.C.: Congressional Globe Office, 1854.

DAVIS, HENRY WINTER (Md.; 34, 35, W; 36, R[?])

————. [pseud. Ulric von Hutter]. *An Epistle Congratulatory to the Right Reverend the Bishops of the Episcopal Court at Camden.* New York: n.p., 1853.

————. *The Origin, Principles and Purposes of the American Party.* Baltimore: [In exchange] Peabody Institute, 1928.

————. *Speeches and Addresses Delivered in the Congress of the United States and on Several Public Occasions, by Henry Winter Davis, of Maryland.* New York: Harper & Bros., Publishers, 1867.

————. *The War of Ormuzd and Ahriman in the Nineteenth Century.* Baltimore: James S. Waters, 1852.

Henig, Gerald. *Henry Winter Davis: Antebellum and Civil War Congressman from Maryland.* New York: Twayne, 1973.

Steiner, Bernard C. *Life of Henry Winter Davis.* Baltimore: John Murphy Co., 1916.

ETHERIDGE, EMERSON (Tenn.; 33, 34, 36, W)

————. *The Assault by Mr. Brooks on Mr. Sumner. Speech of Hon. E. Etheridge, of Tennessee, Delivered in the House of Representatives, July 12, 1856.* Washington, D.C.: Congressional Globe Office, 1856.

————. *Speech of Emerson Etheridge, of Tennessee, Delivered in the House of Representatives, Apr. 2, 1860.* Washington, D.C.: Lemuel Towers, Printer, 1860.

————. *State of the Union. Speech of Hon. Emerson Etheridge, of Tennessee, Delivered in the House of Representatives, Jan. 23, 1861.* Washington, D.C.: Henry Polkinhorn, Printer, 1861.

GILMER, THOMAS W. (Va.; 27, W; 28, D)

————. *To the People of the Twelfth Congressional District of Virginia.* Charlottesville: Jeffersonian Republican Office, 1841.

Tyler, L. G. *Life & Times of the Tylers.* 3 vols. Richmond, Va.: Whittel & Shepperson, 1884–1896.

HABERSHAM, RICHARD W. (Ga.; 26, D; 27, W)

————. *Speech of Mr. Habersham, of Georgia, on the Treasury Note Bill. Delivered in the House of Representatives, Mar. 24, 1840.* Washington, D.C.: Gales & Seaton, Printers, 1840.

HILLIARD, HENRY WASHINGTON (Ala.; 29, 30, 31, W)

————. *DeVane: A Story of Plebeians and Patricians.* New York: Blelock & Co., 1865.

————. *Politics and Pen Pictures at Home and Abroad.* New York: G. P. Putnam's Sons, 1892.

————. *Speeches and Addresses.* New York: Harper & Bros., 1855.

Cozart, Miss Toccoa. "Henry W. Hilliard." Vol. IV (1899–1903). Reprint. *Transactions of the Alabama Historical Society,* 277–299. Montgomery, Ala.: 1904.

JOHNSON, WILLIAM COST (Md.; 25, 26, 27, W)

————. *Speech of William Cost Johnson, of Maryland, on Resolutions Which He Had Offered Proposing to Appropriate Public Land for Educational Purposes, to All the States and Territories. Delivered in the House of Representatives, Feb., 1838.* Washington, D.C.: Gales & Seaton, 1838.

————. *Speech of William Cost Johnson, of Maryland, on the Subject of the Rejection of Petitions for the Abolition of Slavery; with Supplemental Remarks, in Reply to Certain Charges against General Harrison. Delivered in the House of Representatives, Jan. 25, 27, & 28, 1840.* Washington, D.C.: Gales & Seaton, Printers, 1840.

————. *Speech of William Cost Johnson, of Maryland, on the Sub-Treasury Bill. Delivered in the House of Representatives, June 25, 1840.* Washington, D.C.: Gales & Seaton, Printers, 1840.

————. *Speech of William Cost Johnson, of Maryland, on the Sub-Treasury Bill, Entitled a Bill Imposing Additional Duties, as Repositories, in Certain Cases, on Public Officers. Delivered in the House of Representatives, Oct. 12, 1837.* Washington, D.C.: National Register Office, [1837].

KENNEDY, JOHN PENDLETON (Md.; 25, 27, 28, W)

————. *Horse-shoe Robinson.* Edited by Ernest E. Leisy. Hafner Library of Classics, no. 23. New York: Hafner Pub. Co., 1962.

————. *Occasional Addresses; and the Letters of Mr. Ambrose on the Rebellion.* New York: G. P. Putnam & Sons, 1872.

————. *Quodlibet: Containing Some Annals Thereof.* Edited by Solomon Secondthoughts. Philadelphia: Lea & Blanchard, 1840.

————. *Rob of the Bowl.* Edited by William S. Osborne. The Masterworks of Literature Series. New Haven, Conn.: College & University Press, 1965.

————. *Swallow Barn, or—A Sojourn in the Old Dominion.* Introduction and notes by William S. Osborne. Hafner Library of Classics, no. 22. New York: Hafner Pub. Co., 1962.

Bohner, Charles H. *John Pendleton Kennedy, Gentleman from Baltimore.* Baltimore: Johns Hopkins Press, 1961.

Tuckerman, Henry T. *The Life of John Pendleton Kennedy.* New York: G. P. Putnam & Sons, 1871.

MARSHALL, HUMPHREY (Ky.; 34, 35, W)

————. "Address of Col. Marshall upon the Life & Character of Capt. Ballard." In *Obituary Addresses Delivered upon the Occasion of the Re-interment of the Remains of Gen. Chas. Scott, Maj. W. T. Barry, and Capt. Bland Ballard and Wife, in the Cemetary, at Frankfort, Nov. 8, 1854.* Frankfort, Ky.: A. G. Hodges, State Printer, 1855.

————. *California and New Mexico. Speech of Hon. H. Marshall, of Kentucky, in the House of Representatives, Apr. 3, 1850.* Washington, D.C.: Congressional Globe Office, [1850].

————, and Davis, Henry Winter. *Speeches of Hon. H. Marshall, of Kentucky, and Hon. H. Winter Davis, of Maryland, on the Bill Regulating Municipal Elections in the City of Washington. Delivered in the House of Representatives, May 23, 1858.* n.p., n.d.

PICKENS, FRANCIS W. (S. C.; 24, 25, 26, 27, W)

————. *Oration delivered before the Euphradian and Clarisophic Societies, on the Influences of Government upon the Nature and Destiny of Man, by F. W. Pickens.* Columbia, S. C.: Steam-Power Press of Gibbes & Johnston, 1855.

————. *Speech of Hon. F. W. Pickens, Delivered before a Public Meeting of the People of the District, Held at Edgefield C[ourt] H[ouse], South Carolina, July 7, 1851.* Edgefield, S. C.: Advertiser Office, 1851.

————. *Speech of Mr. F. W. Pickens, of South Carolina, in the House of Representatives, Jan. 21, 1836, on the Abolition Question.* Washington, D.C.: Gales & Seaton, Printers, 1836.

————. *Speech of Mr. F. W. Pickens, of South Carolina, on the Two Per Cent Fund, the Cumberland Road, and the Power of the Government to Make Internal Improvements. House of Representatives, Feb. 13, 1840.* Washington, D.C.: Blair & Rives, Printers, 1840.

————. *Speech of Mr. Pickens, of South Carolina; Delivered in the House of Representatives, May 23, 1836, the House Being in Committee of the Whole on the Fortification Bill.* Washington, D.C.: Duff Green, Printer, 1836.

STANLY, EDWARD (N. C.; 25, 26, 27, 31, 32, W)

————. *Letter of Edward Stanly, of North Carolina, to Col. Henry A. Gilliam, Refuting Certain Charges and Insinuations Made by Hon. George E. Badger, in Behalf of the Southern Confederacy.* [New Bern, N. C.: n.p., 1862].

————. *Letter of Edward Stanly, of North Carolina, to Mr. Botts, of Virginia.* Washington, D.C.: n.p., 1840.

————. *Speech of Hon. Edward Stanly, of North Carolina, Establishing Proofs That the Abolitionists Are Opposed to Gen. Harrison and That General Harrison Is Opposed to Their "Unconstitutional Efforts." Delivered in the House of Representatives of the United States, Apr. 13, 1840.* Washington, D.C.: n.p., 1840.

Brown, Norman D. *Edward Stanly: Whiggery's Tarheel "Conqueror."* Southern Historical Publication no. 18. University: University of Alabama Press, 1974.

STEPHENS, ALEXANDER H. (Ga.; 28, 29, 30, 31, 32, 33, W; 34, 35, D)

————. *A Compendium of the History of the United States, from the Earliest Settlements to 1883.* New ed., rev. & enl. by Mr. Stephens. Columbia, S. C.: W. J. Duffie, 1885.

————. *A Constitutional View of the Late War between the States; Its Causes, Character, Conduct, and Results. Presented in a Series of Colloquies at Liberty Hall.* Philadelphia: National Publishing Co., 1868–70.

————. *Recollections of Alexander H. Stephens, His Diary Kept When a Prisoner at Fort Warren, Boston Harbour, 1865; Giving Incidents and Reflections of His Prison Life and Some Letters and Remininiscences.* Edited with a biographical study, by Myrta Lockett Avary. New York: Doubleday, Page & Co., 1910.

Cleveland, Henry. *Alexander H. Stephens in Public and Private. With Letters and Speeches before, during, and since the War.* Philadelphia: National Publishing Co., 1866.

Johnston, Richard Malcolm and William Hand Browne. *Life of Alexander H. Stephens.* Philadelphia: J. B. Lippincott & Co., 1878.

Phillips, U. B., ed. *The Correspondence of Robert Toombs, Alexander H. Stephens, and Howell Cobb.* In *Annual Report of the American Historical Association for the Year 1911.* Vol. II. Washington, D.C.: American Historical Association, 1913.

Rabun, James Z., ed. *A Letter for Posterity: Alex Stephens to His Brother Linton on June 3, 1864.* Atlanta: Library, Emory University, 1954.

von Abele, Rudolph. *Alexander H. Stephens.* New York: Alfred A. Knopf, 1946.

TOOMBS, ROBERT (Ga.; 29, 30, 31, W; 32, D)

————. *A Lecture Delivered in the Tremont Temple, Boston, Massachusetts, on Jan. 26, 1856. Slavery in the United States—Its Relation to the Federal Constitution, and Its Influence on the Well-Being of the Slave and Society.* Washington, D.C.: Jno. T. & Lem. Towers, Printers, 1856.

————. *Speech of Hon. Robert Toombs, on the Crisis. Delivered before the Georgia Legislature, Dec. 7, 1860.* Washington, D.C.: Lemuel Towers, Printer, 1860.

Phillips, U. B., ed. *The Correspondence of Robert Toombs, Alexander H. Stephens, and Howell Cobb.* In *Annual Report of the American Historical Association for the Year 1911.* Vol. II. Washington, D.C.: American Historical Association, 1913.

Phillips, U. B. *The Life of Robert Toombs.* New York: Macmillan Co., 1913.

Thompson, William Y. *Robert Toombs of Georgia.* Southern Biography Series, edited by T. Harry Williams. Baton Rouge: Louisiana State University Press, 1966.

UNDERWOOD, JOSEPH R. (Ky.; 24, 25, 26, 27, W)

————. *An Address Delivered to the Colonization Society of Kentucky, at Frankfort, Jan. 15, 1835.* Frankfort: Albert G. Hodges, Printer, 1835.

————. *Oration Delivered in "Parrott's Woods," Heights of Georgetown, D. C., by the Hon. Joseph R. Underwood, on the Fourth of July, 1842.* n.p., n.d.

————. *Speech of Mr. J. R. Underwood, upon the Resolution Proposing to Censure John Quincy Adams for Presenting to the House of Representatives a Petition Praying for the Dissolution of the Union. Delivered in the House of Representatives, on the 27th of Jan., 1842.* Washington, D.C.: National Intelligencer Office, 1842.

————. *Stipulated Arbitration. A Report Made to the Senate of the United States, Feb. 23, 1853.* [Boston]: *Advocate of Peace Extra,* Apr. 1853.

WHITE, JOHN (Ky.; 24, 25, 26, 28, W)

————. *Speech of Mr. John White, of Kentucky, Delivered in the House of Representatives, on Friday, June 5, 1840, in Committee of the Whole on the State of the Union, in Opposition to the Sub-Treasury Bill.* Washington, D.C.: Gideon, [1840].

WISE, HENRY A. (Va.; 24, 25, 26, 27, W; 28, D)

————. *Seven Decades of the Union. The Humanities and Materialism, Illustrated by a*

Memoir of John Tyler, with Reminiscences of Some of His Great Contemporaries.
Philadelphia: J. B. Lippincott & Co., 1872.
Wise, Barton H. *The Life of Henry A. Wise of Virginia, 1806–1876*. New York: Macmillan
Co., 1899.

Other Contemporary Literature and Debate

Emerson, Ralph Waldo. *The Selected Writings of Ralph Waldo Emerson*. Edited, with a
biographical introduction, by Brooks Atkinson. Modern Library College Editions.
New York: Random House, 1940.
Kent, James. "From *Reports on the Proceedings and Debates of the Convention of 1821.*"
In *American Issues: The Social Record.* Vol. I. Edited by Merle Curti, Willard
Thorp, and Carlos Baker. 2 vols. 4th ed. Philadelphia: J. B. Lippincott, 1960.
Lowell, James Russell. *Biglow Papers, First Series.* In *The American Tradition in Lit-
erature*, Vol. I. Edited by Sculley Bradley, Richard C. Beatty, and E. Hudson
Long. 2 vols. New York: W. W. Norton & Co., 1967.
Melville, Herman. *Moby Dick or The Whale.* Introduction by Newton Arvin. New York:
Holt, Rinehart, & Winston, 1961 [c. 1948].
Thoreau, Henry David. *Walden and Other Writings.* Edited by Brooks Atkinson. Modern
Library Editions. New York: Random House, 1937.
Tocqueville, Alexis de. *Democracy in America.* Edited by Phillips Bradley. 2 vols. New
York: Vintage Books, 1961.
Whitman, Walt. *Leaves of Grass, and Selected Prose.* Edited with an introduction by
Sculley Bradley. New York: Holt, Rinehart & Winston, 1962.

Government Documents

U. S. Congress. *Biographical Directory of the American Congresses, 1774–1961.* Washington, D. C.: U. S. Government Printing Office, 1961.
U. S. Congress. *Congressional Globe.* 24th–36th Congresses.
U. S. Congress. *Speeches on the Oregon Question and on the Mexican War.* 29th Cong.,
1st Sess., 1845–1846.

SECONDARY MATERIALS

Books

Abzug, Robert H. *Passionate Liberator: Theodore Dwight Weld and the Dilemma of
Reform.* New York: Oxford University Press, 1980.
Alexander, DeAlva Stanwood. *History and Procedure of the House of Representatives.*
Boston: Houghton Mifflin Co., 1916.
Alexander, Thomas B. *Sectional Stress and Party Strength: A Study of Roll-Call Voting
Patterns in the United States House of Representatives, 1836–1860.* Nashville:
Vanderbilt University Press, 1967.
Alexander, Thomas B., and Beringer, Richard E. *The Anatomy of the Confederate Con-
gress: A Study of the Influences of Member Characteristics on Legislative Voting
Behavior, 1861–1865.* Nashville: Vanderbilt University Press, 1972.

Allen, Gay Wilson. *The Solitary Singer: A Critical Biography of Walt Whitman*. New York: New York University Press, 1967.

Anderson, Lee F.; Watts, Meredith W., Jr.; and Wilcox, Allen R. *Legislative Roll-Call Analysis*. Evanston, Ill.: Northwestern University Press, 1966.

Apter, David E., ed. *Ideology and Discontent*. International Yearbook of Political Behavior Research, vol. 5. New York: The Free Press, 1964.

Arieli, Yehoshua. *Individualism and Nationalism in American Ideology*. Baltimore: Penguin Books, 1966.

Baker, Jean H. *Affairs of Party: The Political Culture of Northern Democrats in the Mid–Nineteenth Century*. Ithaca: Cornell University Press, 1983.

Barker, Charles A. *American Conviction: Cycles of Public Thought, 1600–1850*. Philadelphia: J. B. Lippincott Co., 1970.

Bell, Rudolph M. *Party and Faction in American Politics: The House of Representatives, 1789–1801*. Westport, Conn.: Greenwood Press, 1973.

Benedict, Michael Les. *A Compromise of Principles: Congressional Republicans and Reconstruction, 1863–1869*. New York: W. W. Norton & Co., 1974.

Benson, Lee. *The Concept of Jacksonian Democracy: New York as a Test Case*. Princeton: Princeton University Press, 1961.

―――. *Toward the Scientific Study of History: Selected Essays*. Philadelphia: J. B. Lippincott Co., 1972.

Berkhofer, Robert, Jr. *A Behavioral Approach to Historical Analysis*. New York: The Free Press of Macmillan, 1969.

Bertelson, David. *The Lazy South*. New York: Oxford University Press, 1967.

Bidwell, Percy Wells, and Falconer, John I. *History of Agriculture in the Northern United States*. Washington, D.C.: The Carnegie Institution of Washington, 1925.

Binkley, Wilfred E. *American Political Parties: Their Natural History*. 4th ed. enl. New York: Alfred A. Knopf, 1964.

Blue, Frederick J. *The Free Soilers: Third Party Politics, 1848–1854*. Urbana: University of Illinois Press, 1973.

Bogue, Allan G. *The Earnest Men: Republicans of the Civil War Senate*. Ithaca, N. Y.: Cornell University Press, 1981.

Braden, Waldo W., ed. *Oratory in the Old South, 1820–1860*. Baton Rouge: Louisiana State University Press, 1970.

Brim, Orville G. "Adult Socialization," in *Socialization and Society*. Edited by John A. Clausen. Boston: Little, Brown & Co., 1968.

Brock, William R. *Parties and Political Conscience. American Dilemmas, 1840–1850*. KTO Studies in American History. Edited by Harold M. Hyman. Millwood, N. Y.: KTO Press, 1979.

Brown, Richard D. *Modernization: The Transformation of American Life, 1600–1865*. The American Century Series. Edited by Eric Foner. New York: Hill and Wang, 1976.

Bruchey, Stuart Weems. *The Roots of American Economic Growth, 1607–1861: An Essay in Social Causation*. New York: Harper & Row, 1965.

Carroll, E. Malcolm. *Origins of the Whig Party*. Durham, N. C.: Duke University Press, 1925.

Cash, Wilbur J. *The Mind of the South*. Vintage Books. New York: Random House, 1941.

Cave, Alfred A. *Jacksonian Democracy and the Historians*. Gainesville: University of
    Florida Press, 1964.
Chambers, William Nisbet. *Political Parties in a New Nation: The American Experience,
    1776–1809*. New York: Oxford University Press, 1963.
Cole, Arthur Charles. *The Whig Party in the South*. Washington, D.C.: American His-
    torical Association, 1914.
Cooper, Joseph. *The Origin of the Standing Committees and the Development of the
    Modern House*, LVI, *Studies*. Rice University, no. 3, 1970.
Cooper, William F. *The South and the Politics of Slavery, 1828–1853*. Baton Rouge:
    Louisiana State University Press, 1978.
Cunningham, Noble. *The Jeffersonian Republicans in Power: Party Operations, 1801–
    1809*. Chapel Hill: University of North Carolina Press, 1963.
———. *The Process of Government under Jefferson*. Princeton: Princeton University
    Press, 1978.
Dangerfield, George. *The Awakening of American Nationalism, 1815–1828*. The New
    American Nation Series, edited by Henry Steele Commager and Richard B. Morris.
    Harper Torchbooks. New York: Harper & Row, 1965.
Daniels, George H. *American Science in the Age of Jackson*. New York: Columbia
    University Press, 1968.
Davis, David Brion, ed. *Ante-bellum Reform*. New York: Harper & Row, 1967.
Degler, Carl. *The Other South: Southern Dissenters in the Nineteenth Century*. New
    York: Harper & Row, 1974.
DeGrazia, Alfred. *Public and Republic: Political Representation in America*. New York:
    Harper & Row, 1974.
Duberman, Martin, ed. *The Antislavery Vanguard: New Essays on the Abolitionists*.
    Princeton: Princeton University Press, 1965.
Easton, David, and Dennis, Jack. *Children in the Political System: Origins of Political
    Legitimacy*. New York: McGraw & Hill, 1979.
Eaton, Clement M. *The Mind of the Old South*. Rev. ed. Baton Rouge: Louisiana State
    University, 1967.
Erikson, Erik H. *Childhood and Society*. New York: W. W. Norton, 1950.
———. *Life History and the Historical Moment*. New York: W. W. Norton, 1975.
Foner, Eric. *Free Soil, Free Labor, Free Men: The Ideology of the Republican Party
    before the Civil War*. New York: Oxford University Press, 1970.
Formisano, Ronald P. *The Birth of Mass Political Parties: Michigan, 1827–1861*. Prince-
    ton: Princeton University Press, 1961.
———. *The Transformation of Political Culture: Massachusetts Parties, 1790s-1840s*.
    New York: Oxford University Press, 1983.
Franklin, John Hope. *The Militant South, 1800–1861*. Cambridge: The Belknap Press of
    Harvard University Press, 1956.
Frederickson, George M. *The Inner Civil War: Northern Intellectuals and the Crisis of
    the Union*. Harper Torchbooks. New York: Harper & Row, 1965.
Freeman, Douglas Southall. *R. E. Lee*. 4 vols. New York: Charles Scribner's Sons,
    1934–1935.
Friedman, Lawrence J. *Gregarious Saints: Self and Society in American Abolitionism,
    1830–1870*. Cambridge: Cambridge University Press, 1982.
———. *Inventors of the Promised Land*. New York: Alfred A. Knopf, 1975.
Gabriel, Ralph H. *The Course of American Democratic Thought: An Intellectual History*

Since 1815. Ronald Series in History, edited by R. C. Binkley and Ralph H. Gabriel. New York: Ronald Press Co., 1940.

Galloway, George. *History of the House of Representatives*. New York: Crowell, 1953.

Goffman, Erving. *The Presentation of Self in Everyday Life*. New York: Doubleday Anchor Books, 1959.

Gray, Lewis C. *History of Agriculture in the Southern United States to 1860*. 2 vols. Washington, D.C.: The Carnegie Institution of Washington, 1933.

Greenstein, Fred A. *Personality and Politics*. Chicago: Markham Publishing Co., 1969.

Grob, Gerald N., and Beck, Robert N., eds. *American Ideas: Source Readings in the Intellectual History of the United States*. 2 vols. New York: The Free Press, 1963.

Hamilton, Holman. *Prologue to Conflict: The Crisis and Compromise of 1850*. New York: W. W. Norton & Co., 1966.

Hammond, Bray. *Banks and Politics in America from the Revolution to the Civil War*. Princeton: Princeton University Press, 1957.

Hartz, Louis. *The Liberal Tradition in America: An Interpretation of American Political Thought Since the Revolution*. New York: Harcourt, Brace & World, 1955.

Henretta, James A. *The Evolution of American Society, 1700–1815: An Interdisciplinary Analysis*. Lexington, Mass.: D. C. Heath & Co., 1973.

Hofstadter, Richard. *Anti-Intellectualism in American Life*. Vintage Books. New York: Random House, 1963.

————. *The Idea of a Party System: The Rise of Legitimate Opposition in the United States, 1780–1840*. Berkeley: University of California Press, 1969.

Holt, Michael Fitzgibbon. *Forging a Majority: The Formation of the Republican Party in Pittsburgh, 1848–1860*. New Haven, Conn.: Yale University Press, 1969.

————. *The Political Crisis of the 1850s*. Critical Episodes in American Politics Series, edited by Robert A. Divine. New York: John Wiley and Sons, 1978.

Howe, Daniel Walker. *The Political Culture of the American Whigs*. Chicago: University of Chicago Press, 1979.

Huitt, Ralph K., and Peabody, Robert L., eds. *Congress: Two Decades of Analysis*. Harper's American Political Behavior Series, edited by David J. Danelski. New York: Harper & Row, 1969.

Kammen, Michael. *People of Paradox: An Inquiry Concerning the Origins of American Civilization*. New York: Random House, 1973.

Kelley, Robert. *The Cultural Pattern in American Politics: The First Century*. New York: Alfred A. Knopf, Borzoi Books, 1979.

Kennedy, John F. *Profiles in Courage*. New York: Harper & Bros., 1965.

Kiesler, Charles A., and Kiesler, Sara B. *Conformity*. New York: Addison-Wesley, 1969.

Kraditor, Aileen L. *Means and Ends in American Abolitionism: Garrison and His Critics on Strategy and Tactics, 1834–1850*. Vintage Books. New York: Random House, 1970.

Lewis, R. W. B. *The American Adam: Innocence, Tragedy and Tradition in the Nineteenth Century*. Phoenix Books. Chicago: University of Chicago Press, 1958.

Lipset, Seymour Martin, and Lowenthal, Leo. *Culture and Social Character: The Work of David Riesman*. Glencoe, Ill.: The Free Press, 1961.

Livermore, Shaw, Jr. *The Twilight of Federalism: The Disintegration of the Federalist Party, 1815–1830*. Princeton: Princeton University Press, 1962.

McCormick, Richard P. *The Presidential Game: The Origins of American Presidential Politics*. New York: Oxford University Press, 1982.

————. *The Second American Party System: Party Formation in the Jacksonian Period.* Chapel Hill: University of North Carolina Press, 1966.

McCoy, Drew R. *The Elusive Republic: Political Economy in Jeffersonian America.* New York: W. W. Norton & Co., 1982.

MacRae, Duncan, Jr. *Issues and Parties in Legislative Voting: Methods of Statistical Analysis.* New York: Harper & Row, 1970.

Maizlish, Stephen E., and Kushma, John J., eds. *Essays on American Antebellum Politics, 1840–1860.* The Walter Prescott Webb Memorial Lectures. College Station: Texas A & M University Press, 1982.

Malone, Dumas. *Jefferson and His Times.* 6 vols. Boston: Little, Brown & Company, 1948–1977.

Marx, Leo. *The Machine in the Garden: Technology and the Pastoral Ideal in America.* New York: Oxford University Press, 1964.

Matthews, Donald R. *U. S. Senators and Their World.* New York: Vintage Books, 1960.

Merk, Frederick. *Manifest Destiny and Mission in American History: A Reinterpretation.* New York: Alfred A. Knopf, 1963.

Merton, Robert K. *Social Theory and Social Structure.* Rev. and enl. New York: The Free Press, 1957.

Meyers, Marvin. *The Jacksonian Persuasion: Politics and Belief.* Stanford, Calif.: Stanford University Press, 1957.

Miller, Perry. *The Life of the Mind in America from the Revolution to the Civil War.* New York: Harcourt, Brace & World, 1965.

————. *Nature's Nation.* Cambridge: Belknap Press, 1967.

Morgan, Robert J. *A Whig Embattled: The Presidency under John Tyler.* Lincoln: University of Nebraska Press, 1954.

Morrison, Chaplain W. *Democratic Politics and Sectionalism: The Wilmot Proviso Controversy.* Chapel Hill: University of North Carolina Press, 1967.

Murphey, Murray C. *Understanding Our Historical Past.* Indianapolis and New York: Bobbs-Merrill, 1973.

Nagel, Paul. *One Nation Indivisible: The Union in American Thought, 1776–1861.* New York: Oxford University Press, 1964.

————. *This Sacred Trust: American Nationality, 1798–1898.* New York: Oxford University Press, 1971.

Nevins, Alan. *The Emergence of Lincoln.* 2 vols. New York: Charles Scribner's Sons, 1950.

————. *Ordeal of the Union.* 2 vols. New York: Charles Scribner's Sons, 1947.

Nichols, Roy F. *The Disruption of American Democracy.* New York: Macmillan Co., 1948.

————. *The Invention of American Political Parties.* New York: Macmillan, 1967.

North, Douglass C. *The Economic Growth of the United States, 1790–1860.* New York: W. W. Norton & Co., Norton Library, 1966.

————. *Growth and Welfare in the American Past: A New Economic History.* Englewood Cliffs: Prentic-Hall, 1966.

Ornstein, Norman, ed. *Changing Congress: The Committee System.* In *The Annals of the American Academy of Political and Social Science.* Edited by Richard D. Lambert. Vol. 411 (January 1974).

Parrington, Vernon L. *The Romantic Revolution in America, 1800–1860.* Vol. II of *Main*

Currents in American Thought. 3 vols. New York: Harcourt, Brace & World, 1927.

Patterson, Samuel C., ed. *American Legislative Behavior, a Reader.* Princeton: D. Van Nostrand Co., 1968.

Peabody, Robert L., and Polsby, Nelson W., eds. *New Perspectives on the House of Representatives.* 2d ed. Chicago: Rand McNally & Co., 1969.

Perry, Lewis, and Fellman, Michael, eds. *Antislavery Reconsidered: New Perspectives on the Abolitionists.* Baton Rouge: Louisiana State University Press, 1979.

Pessen, Edward. *Jacksonian America: Society, Personality, and Politics.* Rev. ed. Homewood, Ill.: The Dorsey Press, 1978.

———. *Most Uncommon Jacksonians: The Radical Leaders of the Early Labor Movement.* Albany, New York: State University of New York, 1968.

Pocock, J. G. A. *The Machiavellian Moment: Florentine Political Thought and the Atlantic Republican Tradition.* Princeton: Princeton University Press, 1975.

Pole, J. R. *The Gift of Government: Political Responsibility from the English Restoration to American Independence.* Athens: University of Georgia Press, 1983.

———. *Political Representation in England and the Origins of the American Republic.* London: Macmillan; New York: St. Martin's Press, 1966.

Potter, David M. *History and American Society.* Edited by Don E. Fehrenbacher. New York: Oxford University Press, 1973.

———. *The Impending Crisis, 1848–1861.* Completed and edited by Don E. Fehrenbacher. The New American Nation Series, edited by Henry Steele Commager and Richard B. Morris. New York: Harper & Row, 1976.

———. *Lincoln and His Party in the Secession Crisis.* New Haven, Conn.: Yale University Press, 1942.

———. *The South and the Sectional Conflict.* Baton Rouge: Louisiana State University Press, 1968.

Putnam, Robert D. *The Beliefs of Politicians: Ideology, Conflict, and Democracy in Britain and Italy.* New Haven: Yale University Press, 1973.

Randall, James G., and Donald, David. *The Civil War and Reconstruction.* 2d ed. rev. with enlarged bibliography. Lexington, Mass.: D. C. Heath & Co., 1969.

Remini, Robert V. *Martin Van Buren and the Making of the Democratic Party.* New York: W. W. Norton & Co., 1959.

Renshon, Stanley. *Handbook of Political Socialization Theory and Research.* New York: The Free Press, 1977.

Riesman, David; Glazer, Nathan; and Denny, Reuel. *The Lonely Crowd, a Study of the Changing American Character.* New Haven: Yale University Press, 1950.

Ripley, Randall B. *Party Leaders in the House of Representatives.* Washington, D. C.: The Brookings Institution, 1967.

Rostow, W. W. *The Stages of Economic Growth: A Non-Communist Manifesto.* New York: Cambridge University Press, 1960.

Rothman, David. *The Discovery of the Asylum: Social Order and Disorder in the New Republic.* Boston: Little, Brown & Co., 1971.

Russo, David J. *The Major Political Issues of the Jacksonian Period and the Development of Party Loyalty in Congress, 1830–1840.* Transactions of the American Philosophical Society; New Series, vol. 62, pt. 5. Philadelphia: American Philosophical Society, 1972.

Saum, Lewis O. *The Popular Mood of Pre–Civil War America*. Contributions in American Studies, no. 46. Westport, Conn.: Greenwood Press, 1980.

Schlesinger, Arthur M., Jr. *The Age of Jackson*. Boston: Little, Brown, & Co., 1945.

————, gen. ed. *History of the United States Political Parties*. 4 vols. New York: Chelsea House Publishers in association with R. R. Bowker Co., 1973.

Sellers, Charles G. "The Travail of Bondage." In *The Southerner as American*. Edited by Charles G. Sellers. Chapel Hill: University of North Carolina Press, 1960.

Sewell, Richard H. *Ballots for Freedom:Antislavery Politics in the United States, 1837–1860*. New York: W. W. Norton & Co., 1976.

Silbey, Joel H. *A Respectable Minority: The Democratic Party in the Civil War*. New York: W. W. Norton & Co., 1977.

————. *The Shrine of Party: Congressional Voting Behavior, 1841–1852*. Pittsburgh: University of Pittsburgh Press, 1967.

Somkin, Fred. *Unquiet Eagle: Memory and Desire in the Idea of American Freedom, 1815–1860*. Ithaca, N. Y.: Cornell University Press, 1967.

Sorin, Gerald. *Abolitionism: A New Perspective*. New York: Praeger, 1972.

Spiller, Robert Ernest et al. *Literary History of the United States*. 3 vols. New York: Macmillan Co., 1948.

Sternsher, Bernard. *Consensus, Conflict, and American Historians*. Bloomington: Indiana University Press, 1975.

Takaki, Ronald T. *A Pro-Slavery Crusade: The Agitation to Reopen the African Slave Trade*. New York: The Free Press, 1971.

Taylor, George Rogers. *The Transportation Revolution, 1815–1860*. New York: Holt, Rinehart & Winston, 1957.

Taylor, William. *Cavalier and Yankee: The Old South and American National Character*. New York: Braziller, 1961.

Temin, Peter. *The Jacksonian Economy*. New York: W. W. Norton & Co., 1969.

Thomas, Emory M. *The Confederate Nation: 1861–1865*. The New American Nation Series, edited by Henry Steele Commager and Richard B. Morris. Harper Torchbooks. New York: Harper & Row, 1979.

Turner, Frederick Jackson. *The United States, 1830–1850: The Nation and Its Sections*. With an Introduction by Avery Craven. Gloucester, Mass.: Peter Smith, 1958.

Tuveson, Ernest Lee. *Redeemer Nation: The Idea of America's Millenial Role*. Chicago: University of Chicago Press, 1968.

Tyler, Alice Felt. *Freedom's Ferment: Phases of American Social History from the Colonial Period to the Outbreak of the Civil War*. Harper Torchbooks. New York: Harper & Row, 1962.

Tyler, L. G. *Life and Times of the Tylers*. 3 vols. Richmond, Va.: Whittel and Shepperson, 1884–1896.

Van Deusen, Glyndon C. *The Jacksonian Era, 1828–1848*. The New American Nation Series, edited by Henry Steele Commager and Richard B. Morris. Harper Torchbooks. New York: Harper & Row, 1963.

————. *The Life of Henry Clay*. Boston: Little, Brown and Co., 1937.

Ward, John William. *Andrew Jackson, Symbol for an Age*. New York: Oxford University Press, 1968 [c. 1953].

Weinberg, Albert K. *Manifest Destiny: A Study of Nationalist Expansionism in American History*. Baltimore: Johns Hopkins Press, 1935.

Welter, Rush. *The Mind of America, 1820–1860*. New York: Columbia University Press, 1975.

White, Leonard. *The Federalists: A Study in Administrative History, 1789–1801*. New York: Macmillan Co., 1948.

———. *The Jacksonians: A Study in Administrative History, 1829–1861*. New York: Macmillan Co., 1954.

———. *The Jeffersonians: A Study in Administrative History, 1801–1829*. New York: Macmillan Co., 1959.

White, Morton G. *Science and Sentiment in America: Philosophical Thought from Jonathan Edwards to John Dewey*. New York: Oxford University Press, 1972.

Williamson, Chilton. *American Suffrage: from Property to Democracy, 1760–1860*. Princeton: Princeton University Press, 1960.

Wills, Gary. *Inventing America: Jefferson's Declaration of Independence*. New York: Random House, Vintage Books, 1979.

Wilson, Major L. *Space, Time, And Freedom: The Quest for Nationality and the Irrepressible Conflict, 1815–1861*. Contributions in American History, no. 35. Westport, Conn.: Greenwood Press, 1974.

Wilson, Woodrow. *Congressional Government: A Study in American Politics*. Boston: Houghton Mifflin Co., 1885.

Wiltse, Charles. *John C. Calhoun, Nullifier, 1829–1839*. New York: The Bobbs-Merrill Co., 1949.

———. *John C. Calhoun: Sectionalist, 1840–1850*. New York: The Bobbs-Merrill Co., 1951.

Wood, Gordon C. *The Creation of the American Republic, 1776–1787*. Chapel Hill: University of North Carolina Press and the Institute of Early American Culture at Williamsburg, Virginia, 1969; W. W. Norton & Co., 1972.

Woodward, C. Vann. *American Counterpoint: Slavery and Racism in the North-South Dialogue*. Boston: Little, Brown & Co., 1971.

Wyatt-Brown, Bertram. *Southern Honor: Ethics and Behavior in the Old South*. New York: Oxford University Press, 1982.

Young, James S. *The Washington Community, 1800–1828*. New York: Columbia University Press, 1966.

Zemsky, Robert. "American Legislative Behavior." In *Emerging Theoretical Models in Social and Political History*. Edited by Allan G. Bogue, Sage Contemporary Social Science Issues, vol. 9. Beverly Hills and London: Sage Publications, 1973.

Articles

Asher, Herbert B. "Learning of Legislative Norms." *American Political Science Review* 67 (June 1973):499–513.

Bogue, Allan; Chubb, Jerome M.; McKibben, Carroll R.; and Traugott, Santa A. "Members of the House of Representatives and the Process of Modernization, 1789–1960." *Journal of American History* 63 (September 1976):275–302.

Brown, Thomas. "Southern Whigs and the Policy of Statesmanship, 1833–1841." *Journal of Southern History* 46 (August 1980):361–380.

Cochrane, Thomas C. "The Paradox of American Economic Growth." *Journal of American History* 61 (March 1975):925–942.

Curry, Richard O., and Goodheart, Lawrence B. " 'Knives in Their Heads': Passionate

Self-Analysis and the Search for Identity in American Abolitionism." *Canadian Journal of American Studies* 14 (Winter 1983):401–414.

Diggins, John P. "Consciousness and Ideology in American History: The Burden of Daniel J. Boorstin." *American Historical Review* 76 (February 1970):98–118.

Donald, David. "The Proslavery Argument Reconsidered." *Journal of Southern History* 37 (February 1969):262–279.

Faust, Drew. "The Rhetoric and Ritual of Agriculture in Antebellum South Carolina." *Journal of Southern History* 45 (November 1979):541–568.

Foner, Eric. "The Wilmot Proviso Revisited." *Journal of American History* 56 (September 1969):262–279.

Formisano, Ronald P. "Deferential-Participant Politics: The Early Republic's Political Culture, 1789–1840." *American Political Science Review* 68 (June 1974):473–487.

————. "Political Character, Antipartyism, and the Second Party System." *American Quarterly* 21 (Winter 1969):685–688.

————. "Toward a Reorientation of Jacksonian Politics: A Review of the Literature, 1959–1975." *Journal of American History* 63 (June 1976):42–65.

Gleason, Philip. "Identifying Identity: A Semantic History." *Journal of American History* 69 (March 1983):910–931.

Goldman, Perry M. "Political Virtue in the Age of Jackson." *Political Science Quarterly* 87 (March 1972):46–62.

Gross, Donald A. "Representative Styles and Legislative Behavior." *Western Political Quarterly* 31 (September 1978):359–371.

Henretta, James A. "Modernization; Toward a False Synthesis." *Reviews in American History* 5 (December 1977):445–452.

Hutchinson, William R. "Cultural Strain and Protestant Liberalism." *American Historical Review* 76 (April 1971):386–411.

Kerber, Linda. "The Republican Mother: Women and the Enlightenment—An American Perspective." *American Quarterly* 28 (Summer 1976):187–205.

Latner, Richard. "A New Look at Jacksonian Politics." *Journal of American History* 61 (March 1975):943–969.

Luthin, Reinhard H. "A Discordant Chapter in Lincoln's Administration: The Davis–Blair Controversy." *Maryland Historical Magazine* 39 (1944):24–48.

McCormick, Richard L. "Ethno-Cultural Explanations of Nineteenth-Century American Voting Behavior." *Political Science Quarterly* 89 (June 1974):351–377.

McCormick, Richard P. "New Perspectives on Jacksonian Politics." *American Historical Review* 65 (January 1960):288–301.

McFaul, John. "Expediency vs. Morality: Jacksonian Politics and Slavery." *Journal of American History* 62 (June 1975):24–39.

Pessen, Edward. "The Egalitarian Myth and American Social Reality: Wealth, Mobility, and Equality in the 'Era of the Common Man.' " *American Historical Review* 72 (October 1971):989–1034.

Polsby, Nelson W. "The Institutionalization of the U. S. House of Representatives." *American Political Science Review* 62 (March 1968):144–168.

Potter, David M. "Historians and Their Use of Nationalism, and Vice Versa." *American Historical Review* 67 (July 1962):924–950.

Rosovsky, Henry. "The Take-Off into Sustained Controversy." *Journal of Economic History* 25 (June 1965):271–275.

Sellers, Charles G., Jr. "Andrew Jackson Versus the Historians." *Mississippi Valley Historical Review* 44 (March 1958):615–634.

Silbey, Joel H. "Parties and Politics in Mid–Nineteenth Century America: A Quantitative and Behavioral Examination." *Capitol Studies* 1 (Fall 1972):9–27.

Skinner, Quentin. "Some Problems in the Analysis of Political Thought and Action." *Political Theory* 2 (August 1974):277–303.

Van Deusen, Glyndon. "Some Aspects of Whig Thought and Theory in the Jacksonian Period." *American Historical Review* 63 (January 1958):305–322.

Yarbrough, Jean. "Republicanism Reconsidered: Some Thoughts on the Foundation and Preservation of the American Republic." *The Review of Politics* 40 (January 1979):61–95.

Yarwood, Dean L. "Norm Observance and Legislative Integration: The U. S. Senate in 1850 and 1860." *Social Science Quarterly* 51 (June 1970):57–69.

Zemsky, Robert. "Power, Influence, and Status: Leadership Patterns in the Massachusetts Assembly, 1740–1755." *William and Mary Quarterly*, Third Series, 26 (October 1969):502–520.

Index

Adams, Henry, 189 n.2, 192 n.48
Adams, John Quincy: ambition, 180; disregard for committees, 38–39; disruptive conduct, 49; influence of high expectations upon, 202; as influential Whig ideologist, 114; legislative style, 48; moral absolutism, 120–121; *Poems of Religion and Society*, 120; poetry quoted, 120–121, 130–131; as political intellectual, 137 n.21; relations with Giddings, 130, 135 n.2, 196, 203; scientific interests, 162, 174 n.32; and Smithsonian, 156
Adams, Sam, 13
Alexander, De Alva S., 43 n.17, 55 nn.9, 10, 13
Alexander, Thomas B., *Sectional Stress and Party Strength*, 3–6, 10 n.5, 221–224, 225
Ambition of mavericks, 131, 181–182
American Party, 113, 121, 168, 183–184
American Renaissance, 13–14
"American System," 16
Antebellum reform, 14, 155, 167, 170–171
Anti-intellectualism, 64–65, 69, 153–154
Antiparty ideas, 76 n.41, 51, 79–80, 86, 94 n.6. *See also* Republicanism
Antislavery: northern Democratic mavericks and, 88, 183; northern Whig conformists and, 102–103, 106; northern Whig/Republican mavericks and, 47–48, 103–104, 120–121, 125, 137 n.18, 206–207; southern Democratic mavericks and, 86–87, 92, 123–124; southern Democratic conformists and, 71; southern fear of, 71–72; southern Whig mavericks and, 127, 167
Anti-Slavery Standard, 158

Baker, Edward D., 106, 111 n.36
Baker, Jean, *Affairs of Party*, 65
Bancroft, George, 14, 66
Bentham, Jeremy, 209
Billington, Ray, *The Protestant Crusade*, 206
Bingham, John A., 118, 120, 135 n.2, 155, 187
Blair, Frank P., Jr.: career, 122; conflict with Davis, 135 n.2; conflict orientation, 191 n.32; *The Destiny of the Races of This Continent*, 123; familial influences upon, 200; as influential Democratic/Republican ideologist, 114; paradoxical elements in ideology, 123–124
Bohner, Charles, 170–171, 203–204
Botts, John M., 132, 182, 190 n.17; *The Great Rebellion*, 182
Bowie, Thomas F., 97 n.44

Bowlin, James, 50–51, 165–166
Boyd, Linn, 37–38
Braden, Waldo W., 74–75 n.29
Briggs, George N., 40, 101
Brooks, Preston, 192 n.43
Brown, Charles, 40–42, 44 n.27, 84–85, 95 n.25, 186
Brown, Richard D., *Modernization*, 197
Buchanan, James, 16
Burke, Edmund, 88–89, 161–162, 191 n.32
Burlingame, Anson, 192 n.43

Calhoun, John C., 37, 68, 75–76 n.39, 91
Cambreleng, Churchill C., 37, 39, 64
Campbell, John, 52, 55 n.13
Campbell, Lewis D., 46–47
Cartter, David K., 50–51, 205
Cash, Wilbur J., *The Mind of the South*, 68
Cicero, as model, 81
Civil War, xvi; and mavericks, 211; and Republicans, 107–108
Claiborne, John F. H., 71
Clemons, Sherrard, 87
Clingman, Thomas L.: as committee chairman, 52; conflict orientation, 186; dueling, 190 n.29; legislative style, 44 n.26, 53; political ideology, 89–90; scientific interests, 96–97 n.41
Cobb, Howell, 37–38, 43 n.17; *Necessity for Party Organization*, 38, 70
Cobb, Williamson R. W., 50–51, 185
Colfax, Schuyler, 103, 106
Committee chairmen. *See* House leaders; House of Representatives
Conflict orientation of mavericks, 135 n.2, 138 n.31, 186, 190 n.17, 191 n.32
Conformists: geographical distribution of, 7–9; ideas about representation, 41; as ideologists, 62–63; and legislative norm integration, 197; as manipulators, 187; methods of selection for, 3–6, 222–224; party distribution of, 7–9
Conformists, Democratic: and anti-intellectualism, 64–65; ideology summa-

rized, 133; and Manifest Destiny, 66–67; party loyalty of, 67, 70–71; southerners and defense of South, 67–70. *See also* Democratic party
Conformists, Whig and Republican: ideological coherence of Whigs, 100–101, 133; northern Whigs and antislavery, 102–103; northern Whigs and rise of Republican party, 106–107; political economy of Whigs, 102, 105; practical moralism of Whigs, 101–102, 105; Republicans, 107–108; social views of Whigs, 101, 104–105; southern Whigs and Unionism, 105–106. *See also* Republican party; Whig party
Conformists as House leaders, 33, 37; and committee regularity, 38–39; compared with mavericks, 46–47, 54; legislative style, 39–40; and party responsibility, 37; and purposes of House, 40–41. *See also* House of Representatives
Congressional Globe, 6, 30, 31, 42 n.6
Constitution, United States, 12, 14–15
Cooper, William J., 25 n.43, 110 n.23
Cultural change, mavericks and, 12–14, 117–118, 157–163, 193–194
Cultural mission, 163–172
Cumulative scale analysis, 4–5, 221–224
Cushing, Caleb: ambition, 180–181; career, 122; familial influences upon, 200; as influential ideologist, 114; legislative style, 48–49; paradoxical elements in ideology, 124–126

Davis, Henry Winter: and America's cultural mission, 168–170; conflict with Blair family, 135 n.2; familial influences upon, 200–201; as influential Whig/Republican ideologist, 114; romantic nationalism of, 121; social influences upon, 204; views on education, 155; views on southern culture, 176 n.70; *The War of Ormuzd and Ahriman in the Nineteenth Century*, 169–170
Davis, Richard D., 88
Dawson, John, 66

Debate, importance of, 50, 52, 81–84
Democratic party: appeal of, 17, 19; as
  defender of South, 68–69; conformists'
  ideology summarized, 64; conformity
  in, 63–64, 73 n.11; mavericks and
  conformists in, 71–72, 77–78, 93;
  pragmatism of, 63. *See also* Conformists, Democratic; Mavericks,
  Democratic
Disney, David, 50–51
Douglas, Stephen A.: anti-intellectualism
  of, 64; Burkean ideas of, 65, 73–74
  n.16; as committee chairman, 37; and
  Kansas-Nebraska Act, 154, 183; legislative style, 40, 56 n.42; and Oregon,
  175 n.48; and political moralism, 67.
  See also McClernand, John
Dromgoole, George, 70–71
Dueling, 190 n.29
Duncan, Alexander, 88
Duty, 183, 210; and Democratic mavericks, 88–89, 92–93; "the line of,"
  130; and Whig/Republican mavericks,
  113, 130–132

Economic developments, nineteenth century, 13, 168, 207–208
Edgerton, Alfred, 44 n.26
Education, mavericks and, 155–157
Egocentrism, of mavericks, 45, 50–
  51,180, 184–186
Emerson, Ralph Waldo, 99, 213, 158–
  159. Works: "The American Scholar,"
  xviii; "Eloquence," 187; *Nature*, 174–
  175 n.43
Everett, Horace, 110n.16

Fairfield, John, 197
Faust, Drew, proslavery ideology, 90;
  "The Rhetoric and Ritual of Agricul-
  ture in Antebellum South Carolina,"
  68–69
Fillmore, Millard, 37, 39–40, 46, 106
Florence, Thomas, 186
Fowler, Orin, 113, 120, 167–168
Franklin, John Hope, 190 n.29
Free Soil, 78, 88, 113, 124, 166

Fuess, Claude, 181
Fuller, Thomas J. D., 54

Gag rule, 48, 135 n.2
Garland, James, 51
Geertz, Clifford, 78–79
Garnett, Muscoe Russell Hunter: ambition, 181; and America's cultural mission, 164–165; familial influences
  upon, 200; influence of high expectations, 202; political ideology, 90–92;
  relations with Botts, 190 n.17; relations with Hunter, 91, 202; views on
  public printing, 96 n.29; views on
  southern mission, 165
Giddings, Joshua R.: antislavery views,
  137 n.18, 103–104; on duty, 131–132;
  as committee chairman, 48; conservative Whig opposition to, 110 n.16;
  History of the Rebellion, 203; influence
  of high expectations, 203; as influential
  Whig/Republican ideologist, 114; legislative style, 48; moral absolutism of,
  120; New England background as influence upon, 201; social influences
  upon, 207–208; relations with Adams,
  135 n.2, 196, 203; relations with
  Bingham, 135 n.2; views on cultural
  change, 158–159, 163
Gilmer, Thomas, 114
Governmental institutions, growth of, 15
Greenwood, Alfred, 50–51

Hawthorne, Nathaniel, *The Scarlet Letter*, 14, 134–135
Henley, John, 54
Hickman, John, 183
Hilliard, Henry W.: antislavery views,
  127; career, 122; criticism of southern
  society, 160–161; debate with Yancey,
  190–191 n.29; *DeVane: A Story of
  Plebeians and Patricians*, 126–127,
  159–161, 173 nn. 21–25; paradoxical
  elements in ideology, 126–127; social
  ideals of, 205; views on cultural
  change, 117, 159–161, 163
Hofstadter, Richard, *Anti-intellectualism
  in American Life*, 153–154

Holmes, Isaac, 84, 95 nn.20, 22
House leaders: conformists as, 33, 37;
    distribution of mavericks and conform-
    ists as, 32–37; importance of legisla-
    tive responsibility for, 32; mavericks
    as, 47; method of assessing styles of,
    42 n.6; power of, 31; roles of, 31; sen-
    iority and, 33, 36
House of Representatives: influence of
    mavericks in, 212–213; institutionaliza-
    tion of, 29, 194–195; legislative styles
    in, 30; length of service of members,
    24 n.36; membership characteristics of,
    16–17; parties and voting patterns in,
    17; patterns of floor activity in, 29–30;
    powers of Speakers in, 31; sectional
    influences in, 19
Houston, George S., 46–47, 55 n.9
Howard, Benjamin, 37, 39
Howe, Daniel W., 100, 109 n.5
Huitt, Ralph K., 42–43 n.12
Hunt, Washington, 101, 111 n.30
Hunter, Robert M. T.: anti-intellectualism
    of, 69; antiparty views of, 76 n.41; on
    importance of parties, 43 n.15; rela-
    tions with Garnett, 91, 202; and party
    responsibility, 37; as Speaker, 37

Ingersoll, Charles J.: and America's cul-
    tural mission, 164; as committee chair-
    man, 175 n.50; *A Discourse
    Concerning the Influence of America
    on the Mind*, 164; as example of Dem-
    ocratic mavericks, 80–84; familial in-
    fluence upon, 200; legislative style,
    48–49; mixing of Republican and
    Democratic influences, 80–84; *Recol-
    lections*, 81–84
Ingersoll, Jared, 80
Ingersoll, Joseph, 80

Jackson, Andrew, 17, 81
Jefferson, Thomas, 13, 15, 199; *Manual
    of Parliamentary Practice*, 61; as
    model statesman, 80–81; as practical
    statesman, 61
Johnson, William Cost, 51, 205
Jones, George W., 52–53

Julian, George W., 207

Kansas-Nebraska Act, and Douglas, 154,
    183
Keitt, Lawrence, 43–44 n.26, 189 n.18
Kennedy, John Pendleton: and America's
    cultural mission, 170–171; as commit-
    tee chairman, 53–54; influence of high
    expectations upon, 203–204; as influ-
    ential Whig ideologist, 114; as moder-
    ate progressive, 118; as romantic, 159.
    Works: *Horse-Shoe Robinson*, 159;
    Rob of the Bowl, 159; *Quodlibet*, 171,
    176 n.78, 184; *Swallow Barn*, 159,
    170–171, 173 n.18
Know-Nothing party, 114

Laissez-faire theory, 70, 80, 85–86, 88–
    89
Lamar, L.Q.C., 75 n.36
Lawrence, Abbott, 102
Legislative decision-making, 214, n.5
Legislative norms, 197, 214 n.7. *See also*
    House of Representatives
Legislative style, 30, 54; of conformists,
    38–40, 43 n.17, 43–44 n.26, 44 n.27,
    56 n.42; of mavericks, 40–41, 44
    nn.26–27, 48–54, 55 n.9
Levin, Lewis, 114, 121, 183–184, 206,
    217 n.45
Lewis, R.W.B., 14
Liberty Party, 113
Lincoln, Levi, 40
Lowenthal, David, 156

McClernand, John, 50–51, 95 n.26, 165–
    166, 175 nn.48, 51
McKeon, John, 191 n.32
Madison, James, 15; #10 of *The Feder-
    alist Papers*, 12, 16
Manifest Destiny, 66–67, 88, 123–124,
    171
Marsh, George Perkins, 156
Marshall, Humphrey, 179
Masters, Nicholas, 32–33
Mavericks: as creative ideologists, 62–63;
    geographical distribution of, 7–9; influ-
    ence on political parties, 212; methods

of selection, 3–6, 222–224; party distribution of, 7–9; prominence in South of, 7; reputations of, xv; similarities among, 134

Mavericks, Democratic: antiparty ideas of, 79–80, 86; diversity among, 77, 80; ideological creativity of, 78–80; laissez-faire theory of, 80, 85–86; and models of independence, 92–93; northern, 87–88; republicanism of, 79–80, 83–85, 87; southern, 86–87, 89; as spokesman for plain people, 50–51; views of, summarized, 77–89. *See also* Democratic party

Mavericks, influences upon characters of: cultural change, 193–194, 198; families, 199–201; high expectations, 202–204; ideas, 209–210; New England backgrounds, 201; political institutions, 19–20, 194–195; republicanism, 198–201; social change, 204–209. *See also* House of Representatives, institutionalization of; Political socialization

Mavericks, political characters of: egotism, 180, 184–185; and legislative norm integration, 197; as political intellectuals, 153–154, 171–172, 178–179; and rhetoric of masculine integrity, 182–184; self-concepts summarized, 177–178; views of America's cultural mission, 163–172; views of cultural change, 157–163; views on education, 155–157

Mavericks, Whig and Republican: ideological creativity of, 114–117; northern Whigs, 120–121; political independence among, 129–132; relations among, 135–136 n.2; romantic nationalism of, 121; significance of, 133; southern Whigs, 118–119; Tyler Whigs, 40, 52, 113, 135 n.2; views of social flux, 117–118. *See also* Republican party; Whig party

Mavericks, as House leaders: compared with conformists, 46–47, 54; conflicts among, 52–53; emphasis upon debate of, 50, 52; influence in House, 212–213; intellectual orientation of, 48–49;

leadership concepts of, 178–179; nonconformity in styles of, 45, 47, 50–51, 53–54; shortcomings of leadership, 210–213; southern styles of, 51–53. *See also* House leaders; House of Representatives

Meacham, James, 54, 156–157, 172–173 n.12

Melville, Herman, *Moby Dick*, 14, 177

Mexican War, 104, 127

Modernization, 214 n.2

Moral absolutism, 88–89, 113, 119–121

Murphy, Henry, 191 n.32

Nativism, 183–184, 190 n.28

Natural aristocracy, 199

Natural law, 12, 64, 87–91, 119

Oratory, 187. *See also* Political ideologies; Political rhetoric

Orr, James L., 46, 55 n.6, 157

Owen, Robert Dale, 40, 65–66, 156

Owen, Robert, 65

Party responsibility, 37, 67, 70–71

Paternalism, 45, 80–84

Pessen, Edward, 100

Pickens, Francis W., 52, 76 n.40, 118–119, 183, 209

Political culture, American, 14–17, 78–79; and conformists, 41; and mavericks, 54–55, 115–116, 134–135, 194–196, 213; of Whigs, 100–101, 108–109

Political economy, Whig, 16, 100, 102

Political ideologies: conformists and, 62–63; creativity in, 78–79; different contributions of mavericks and conformists to, 62–63; innovation, 114–115; mavericks and, 134–135; and nineteenth-century moral absolutes, 119; purposes of, 61–62; Skinner and "untoward actions," 115; voter interests and, 72 n.3. *See also* Mavericks; Oratory; Political rhetoric; and *individual names of mavericks*

Political independence: mavericks' views

on, 77, 92, 97 n.46, 129–132, 179;
models for, 92–93; and parties, 15
Political intellectuals, mavericks as, 48–
49, 137 n.21, 153–154, 171–172, 172–
173 n.12, 178–179
Political parties: and democratization, 15–
16; development in 1790s of, 15; impact on political character of, 15–16;
influence of mavericks in, 212; machinery of, 16; professionalization of,
72–73 n.8; realignment in 1850s of,
18. *See also* Democratic party; Republican party; Whig party
Political rhetoric: as historical evidence,
xvii; in South, 67–69, 74–75 n.29; and
partisan political cultures, 115. *See
also* Oratory; Political ideologies
Political socialization, 213–214 n.1, 216
n.24
Polsby, Newson W., "The Institutionalization of the U.S. House of Representatives," 41, 95 n.22
Potter, David M., xviii–xix n.2, 112 n.41
Practical moralism, of Whigs, 101–102,
105, 133
Pragmatism: and conformists, 79; and
Democratic conformists, 55, 63–67,
69, 72, 116, 133; and Whig conformists, 100–101, 105
Proslavery, 90–92, 127–128, 137 n.16
Psychohistory, 216 n.25

Reform. *See* Antebellum reform
Representation, concept of, 15–16, 41,
65–66, 80, 94 n.7
Republicanism: and antiparty ideas, 51;
and Democratic mavericks, 78–80, 85–
87; and individualism, 12; influence
upon mavericks, 198–201; and mavericks' views of legislative responsibility,
54
Republican party: appeal of, 18–19; conformists in, 133; factionalism in, 108;
former Democrats among conformists
in, 108; former Whigs among conformists in, 106–108; influential mavericks in, 114–17. *See also*

Conformists, Whig and Republican;
Mavericks, Whig and Republican
"Respectability," of Whig, 99, 109 n.2
Reynolds, John, 3
Rhetoric of masculine integrity, and mavericks, 182–184, 189 n.18
Rhett, Robert Barnwell: changes name,
215 n.18; familial influences upon,
200; links slavery and laissez faire,
75–76 n.39; political ideology, 89–90;
political independence of, 97 n.46; social influences upon, 204, 206; views
of legislator as model, 45
Richmond Enquirer, 128
Riesman, David, *The Lonely Crowd*, 197
Romanticism, 12, 91, 116–117, 121,
158–161

Schenck, Robert, 37
Science, 96–97 n.41, 162–163, 174 n.32
Shakespeare, 92, 115–116
Sherman, John, 37–38
Silbey, Joel, *The Shrine of Party*, 4
Skinner, Quentin, 115, 215 n.9
Slavery, 127–128; and laissez-faire the-
ory, 70, 75–76 n.39, 104–105; and re-
alignment in 1850s, 18; southern Whig
conformists and, 104–106; and south-
ern Whig mavericks, 119; and voting
patterns in House, 4–5. *See also* South
Slavocracy theory, 123
Smith, William, 85–86, 95–96 n.28, 179
Smithsonian Institution, 156–157
South: Democratic conformists defense
of, 68–70; Democratic party in, 18;
and slavery 75–76 n.39. *See also*
Slavery
Speaker of the House, 31; conformists as,
31, 37–38, 46; mavericks as, 46. *See
also* House leaders; House of
Representatives
Stanly, Edward, 185–186, 190 n.29
Stanton, Frederick M., "The Character
of Modern Science, or, the Mission of
the Educated Man," 162–163; interest
in science, 162–163; legislative style,
48–49; political ideology, 90–91; political independence, 77, 92

States' rights, 69–70, 114. *See also* Democratic party; Slavery; South

Stephens, Alexander H.: ambition of, 131, 181–182; as committee chairman, 52; "Constitutional View of the Late War between the States," 119; Freudian interpretation of, 216 n.29; influence of high expectations upon, 202–203; as influential Whig ideologist, 114; legislative style, 53; party-switching, 76 n.40; political independence, 129–130; relations with Toombs, 196; slavery, 137 n.16, 119

Stewart, James B., 203

Texas, 38–39

Thomas, Emory, 76 n.46

Thompson, Richard W., 40–41, 44 n.27, 99, 102–103, 106

Thoreau, Henry David, 11–14, 19; *Civil Disobedience*, 14, 153; *Walden*, 11–12

Tilden, Daniel, 103–104

Tocqueville, Alexis de, *Democracy in America*, 12, 78, 193, 209, 214 n.3; views on House of Representatives, 3, 10 n.1

Toombs, Robert, 76 n.40, 196

Tucker, Henry St. George, 128

Tyler, John, 16

Tyler Whigs, 40, 52, 113, 135 n.2

Underwood, Joseph R., 55–56 n.16, 114, 117, 167

Unionism, 104, 132, 182

Vallandigham, Clement L., 61, 65

Washburne, Elihu, 37

Wentworth, John, 85, 156, 191 n.32, 201, 205

Whig party: appeal of, 17–18; factionalism in 27th Congress, 46; ideological cohesion of, 99–100, 104; Tyler Whigs, 40, 135 n.2, 52. *See also* Conformists, Whig and Republican; Mavericks, Whig and Republican

White, John, 46, 55 n.5

Whitman, Walt, 191 n.32; *Leaves of Grass*, 193

Whittlesey, Elisha, 37, 102

Wilmot, David, 85, 88, 188, 201

Wilson, Woodrow, *Congressional Government*, 29

Wise, Henry A.: career, 122; as Civil War general, 138 n.31; as committee chairman, 52; dueling, 190 n.29; egotism of 185–188; as influential ideologist, 114; legislative style, 40; paradoxical elements in ideology of, 127–129; *Seven Decades of the Union*, 129; social influences upon, 204–205. *See also* Tyler Whigs

Wylie, Andrew, 128

Yancey, William L., 190–191 n.29

Yarbrough, Jean, 78

Young, James S., *The Washington Community*, 31

About the Author

JOHANNA NICOL SHIELDS is Associate Professor of History at the University of Alabama in Huntsville. Her writings have appeared in the *Alabama Review* and the *Journal of the Early Republic*.